International Conference on Interfaces and Human Computer Interaction 2017

Held at the Multi-Conference on Computer Science and Information Systems (MCCSIS 2017)

Lisbon, Portugal
20 – 23 July 2017

Editors:

Katherine Blashki
Piet Kommers
Pedro Isaias
Luis Rodrigues

ISBN: 978-1-5108-6532-7

Printed from e-media with permission by:

Curran Associates, Inc.
57 Morehouse Lane
Red Hook, NY 12571

Some format issues inherent in the e-media version may also appear in this print version.

Printed by Curran Associates, Inc. (2018)

For permission requests, please contact International Association for Development of the Information Society (IADIS) at the address below.

International Association for Development of the Information Society (IADIS)
Rua Sao Sebastiao Da Pedreira
No. 100, 30, 1050-209
Lisbon, Portugal

Phone: 351 21 3151373
Fax: 351 21 3151244

secretariat@iadis.org

Additional copies of this publication are available from:

Curran Associates, Inc.
57 Morehouse Lane
Red Hook, NY 12571 USA
Phone: 845-758-0400
Fax: 845-758-2633
Email: curran@proceedings.com
Web: www.proceedings.com

INTERNATIONAL CONFERENCE

INTERFACES AND HUMAN COMPUTER INTERACTION 2017

part of the

MULTI CONFERENCE ON COMPUTER SCIENCE AND INFORMATION SYSTEMS 2017

PROCEEDINGS OF THE INTERNATIONAL CONFERENCE

INTERFACES AND HUMAN COMPUTER INTERACTION 2017

Lisbon, Portugal
JULY 21 - 23, 2017

Organised by
IADIS
International Association for Development of the Information Society

Volume Editor:
Katherine Blashki

Computer Science and Information Systems Series Editors:
Piet Kommers and Pedro Isaías

Associate Editor: Luís Rodrigues

TABLE OF CONTENTS

SHORT PAPERS

REFLECTION PAPERS

FOREWORD

These proceedings contain the papers of the 11th International Conference on Interfaces and Human Computer Interaction 2017, which was organised by the International Association for Development of the Information Society, from 21 - 23 July, 2017. This conference is part of the Multi Conference on Computer Science and Information Systems 2017, 20 - 23 July, which had a total of 652 submissions.

The Interfaces and Human Computer Interaction (IHCI) 2017 conference aims to address the main issues of concern within Interface Culture and Design with a particular emphasis on the affective aspects of design, development and implementation of interfaces and the generational implications for design of human and technology interaction. This conference aims to explore and discuss innovative studies of technology and its application in interfaces and welcomes research in progress, case studies, practical demonstrations and workshops in addition to the traditional submission categories.

This conference seeks to cover both technological as well as non-technological issues related to these developments.

Submissions were accepted under the following topics:
- Affective User-Centred Analysis, Design and Evaluation
- The Value of Affective Interfaces / Systems / Application / Interaction
- Generational differences and technology design
- Measurement of success of emotional technology / interfaces
- Supporting user populations from specific Generations
- Supporting user populations with Physical Disabilities
- Supporting user populations with Intellectual Disabilities
- Creativity Support Systems
- Emotional Design issues / methods / experiences for novel interfaces including tangible, Mobile and Ubiquitous computing, mixed reality interfaces and multi-modal interfaces
- Usability
- User studies and fieldwork
- Methodological implications of Emotional User Studies
- Participatory design and Cooperative design techniques
- Ethical issues in emotional design
- HCI and Design education
- Eliciting User Requirements

The IHCI 2017 conference received 127 submissions from more than 28 countries. This conference includes the submissions from the Game and Entertainment Technologies conference that has been integrated into IHCI 2017. Its committees are listed as part of this proceedings book. Each submission has been anonymously reviewed by an average of five independent reviewers, to ensure that accepted submissions were of a high standard. Consequently, only 25 full papers were approved which means an acceptance rate of 20%. A few more submissions were accepted as short papers and reflection papers. An extended version of the best papers will be published in the IADIS International Journal on WWW/Internet (ISSN: 1645-7641) and also in other selected journals, including journals from Inderscience.

Besides the presentation of full papers, short papers and reflection papers, the conferences also included a keynote presentation from an internationally distinguished researcher. We would therefore like to express our gratitude to Dr. Dr. Norbert Streitz, Scientific Director, Smart Future Initiative, Germany, for accepting our invitation to be the keynote speaker.
This volume has taken shape as a result of the contributions from a number of individuals. We are grateful to all authors who have submitted their papers to enrich these conferences proceedings. We wish to thank all members of the organizing committee, delegates, invitees and guests whose contribution and involvement are crucial for the success of the conference.

Last but not the least, we hope that everybody had a good time in Lisbon, and we invite all participants for the next edition of this conference.

Katherine Blashki, Noroff University College, Norway
Interfaces and Human Computer Interaction 2017 Program Chair

Piet Kommers, University of Twente, The Netherlands
Pedro Isaías, The University of Queensland, Australia
MCCSIS 2017 General Conference Co-Chairs

Lisbon, Portugal
July 2017

PROGRAM COMMITTEE

INTERFACES AND HUMAN COMPUTER INTERACTION CONFERENCE

PROGRAM CHAIR

Katherine Blashki, Noroff University College, Norway

MCCSIS GENERAL CONFERENCE CO-CHAIRS

Piet Kommers, University of Twente, The Netherlands
Pedro Isaías, The University of Queensland, Australia

INTERFACES AND HUMAN COMPUTER INTERACTION CONFERENCE

COMMITTEE MEMBERS

Alexander Kröner, Technische Hochschule Nürnberg Georg Simon Ohm, Germany
Ana Cristina Bicharra Garcia, Universidade Federal Flumninese, Brazil
Antonio Maria Rinaldi, University Napoli Federico II, Italy
Arcadio Reyes, Universidad de Malaga, Spain
Arianna D. Ulizia, IRPPS-CNR, Italy
Aris Alissandrakis, Linnaeus University, Sweden
Bruno Santana da Silva, Federal University of Rio Grande do Norte, Brazil
Caterina Senette, Istituto di Informatica e Telematica, CNR (Pisa), Italy
Celia Martinie, Universite Paul Sabatier, France
Connie Veugen, Vrije Universiteit Amsterdam, Netherlands
Daniela Trevisan, Universidade Federal Fluminense, Brazil
Eduardo Tanaka, Eldorado Research Institute, Brazil
Elaine Hayashi, University of Campinas, Brazil
Fazel Naghdy, University of Wollongong, Australia
Francisco Madera Ramirez, Universidad Autonoma de Yucatan, Mexico
Heiko Hornung, University of Campinas, Brazil
Hideki Aoyama, Keio University, Japan
Isabela Gasparini, Universidade do Estado de Santa Catarina (UDESC), Brazil
Jesuk Ko, Gwangju University, South Korea
Jon Preston, Southern Polytechnic State University, USA
José Antonio Macías Iglesias, Universidad Autónoma de Madrid, Spain
José Luis Tapia Fabela, Universidad Autónoma del Estado de México, Mexico
Kathia Oliveira, Université de Valenciennes et du Hainaut-Cambrésis, France
Keith Nesbitt, University of Newcastle, Australia
Khaled Khankan, Taibah University, Saudi Arabia
Larbi Esmahi, Athabasca University, Canada
Leonelo Almeida, Federal University of Technology, Paraná, Brazil
Lucia Vilela Leite Filgueiras, Escola Politécnica da Universidade de São Paulo, Brazil
Luciana Romani, Embrapa Agricultural Informatics, Brazil
Maki K. Habib, The American University in Cairo, Egypt
Marcelo Romero Huertas, Universidad Autonoma del Estado de Mexico, Mexico

Marco Antonio Ramos Corchado, Universidad Autonoma del Estado de Mexico, Mexico
Marina Buzzi, Istituto di Informatica e Telematica, CNR, Italy
Marja Kankaanranta, University of Jyvaskyla, Finland
Masahiro Takatsuka, The University of Sydney, Australia
Maxim Bakaev, Novosibirsk State Technical University, Russia
Melissa Lee Price, Staffordshire University, United Kingdom
Michael Hohl, HS Anhalt/FB Design, Germany
Monica Bordegoni, Politecnico di Milano, Italy
Nadine Vigouroux, IRIT, CNRS, Paul Sabtier University, France
Nayat Sanchez-Pi, Universidade do Estado do Rio de Janeiro, Brazil
Niki Lambropoulos, Intelligenesis, United Kingdom
Niklas Ravaja, University of Helsinki, Finland
Otniel Portillo Rodriguez, Universidad Autonóma del Estado de México, Mexico
Philip Breedon, Nottingham Trent University, United Kingdom
Rodrigo Bonacin, Dssd - CTI Renato Archer, Brazil
Rommert Casimir, Tilburg University, Netherlands
Sandro José Rigo, Unisinos, Brazil
Silvio Cazella, UFCSPA, Brazil
Sylvia Tzvetanova Yung, University of Bedfordshire, United Kingdom
Tom Garner, University of Portsmouth, UK
Toni Granollers, University of Lleida, Spain
Vagner Figueredo de Santana, IBM Research, Brazil
Xiaokun Zhang, Athabasca University, Canada

GAME AND ENTERTAINMENT TECHNOLOGIES

COMMITTEE MEMBERS

Abdennour El Rhalibi, Liverpool John Moores University, United Kingdom
Alf Inge Wang, Norwegian University of Science and Technology, Norway
Ali Arya, Carleton University, Canada
Anastasios Karakostas, Aristotle University of Thessaloniki, Greece
Anthony Whitehead, Carleton University, Canada
Armelle Prigent, Universite de La Rochelle/L3I, France
Arttu Perttula, Tampere University of Technology, Finland
Castulus Kolo, Macromedia University of Applied Sciences, Germany
Christos Bouras, University of Patras and Computer Technology Institute
and Press "Diophantus", Greece
Connie Veugen, Vrije Universiteit Amsterdam, Netherlands
Daniel Cermak-Sassenrath, IT University of Copenhagen, Denmark
Ellen Brox, Norut - Northen Research Institute, Norway
Emanuele Carlini, ISTI, CNR, Italy
Emmanuel Tsekleves, Lancaster University, United Kingdom
Eric Gressier, Cnam - Cedric, France
Eva Hudlicka, Psychometrix Associates, USA
Evi Sampanikou, University of The Aegean, Greece
Gabriele D`Angelo, University of Bologna, Italy
Harry Agius, Brunel University London, United Kingdom
Isabelle Astic, Cnam, France
Jerome Dupire, Cnam - Cedric, France

KEYNOTE LECTURE

RE-DEFINING THE "SMART EVERYTHING" PARADIGM TOWARDS RECONCILING HUMANS AND TECHNOLOGY

Dr. Dr. Norbert Streitz, Scientific Director, Smart Future Initiative, Germany

ABSTRACT

My keynote presentation will address multiple issues in the intersection of the following three conferences at MCCSIS 2017: 1) Connected Smart Cities 2) ICT, Society, and Human Beings 3) Interfaces and Human-Computer Interaction.

Starting out with the context of living in the Urban Age, I will discuss different notions of "smart cities", being propagated as the blueprint for our cities in the future, and complement them with the concept of "hybrid" cities, i.e., integrating the virtual, digital world with the real, physical world of our urban environments. One can currently observe a big hype about the opportunities of smart cities based on an Internet of Things (IoT) infrastructure monitoring states and dynamics of urban objects and their combination with data about citizens obtained in urban contexts for providing smart services.

With the increasing penetration of IoT and the proliferation of smart services, one can actually speak of a "smart everything" paradigm permeating very diverse spheres of our society and determining our personal and public life in many ways. Thus, it is necessary to investigate the implications for individuals as well as for society. Exploring the challenges, but also the venues towards a human-/citizen- centered design approach, I will take a critical look at smart services based on matching people's profiles and interests with service options available at specific locations. A major focus will be on the risks resulting from these smart city installations, especially the serious infringements of privacy rights, i.e., usage of personal data without consent of the people concerned.

Besides the issues of privacy, designing interfaces and human-computer interaction or more general human-technology, resp. citizen-urban environment interaction is of major importance. A prominent challenge is the property that "traditional" affordances are often hidden in these kinds of environments. (=> invisible or disappearing computer). How can people know how to interact, when they are not aware of the options? How can people protect their privacy, when they don't "see" the sensors, the hidden devices? Another aspect is the shift from information design to experience design.

A critical reflection of different manifestations of the "smart everything and everywhere" paradigm is needed in order to meet the overall goal of reconciling humans and technology. A central aspect of this goal is to keep the human in the loop and in control. Therefore, a citizen-centered design approach for future cities is needed for helping us to go "beyond smart cities" and transform them into Humane, Sociable and Cooperative Hybrid Cities.

Full Papers

POLYHINGE: SHAPE CHANGING TUI ON TABLETOP

Meng Wang[1, 2], Haipeng Mi[1], Yejun Liu[1] and Yingqing Xu[1, 2]
[1]*Academy of Arts and Design*
[2]*The lab for Lifelong Learning*
Tsinghua University, Beijing, China

ABSTRACT

This paper presents PolyHinge, a variable-form Tangible User Interface (TUI) that provides dynamic affordance and semantics and extends its malleability and mutability by enabling active shape-changing outputs. It is superior to traditional rigid TUIs in that it can provide multistate geometric transformations in the physical world. Highly diverse forms of transformations are allowed as PolyHinge is based upon extended structures of hinged dissections and connections. In addition, the concept of dynamic affordance and semantics is further developed within the context of shape-changing interfaces, as a functional and bidirectional interface applicable for both input and output. Meanwhile, a series of applications are developed, demonstrating how users can interact with PolyHinge on a tabletop, and how the dynamic affordance and semantics can aid users.

KEYWORDS

Shape changing interfaces; tabletop tangible interfaces; self-actuation; dynamic affordance and semantics

1. INTRODUCTION

The way we understand the physical world is inherently shaped by our interactions with and perceptions of interfaces, yet traditional forms of Tangible User Interfaces (TUIs) are not capable of allowing full understanding of digital content. Usually such interfaces allow a user to control digital content through physical manipulation (Hiroshi Ishii and Brygg Ullmer, 1997), but lack physical feedback for the user.

However, with improvements in actuation, haptics, and material qualities, self-actuated TUIs and Organic User Interfaces (OUIs) are increasingly able to provide physical feedback and present content in more diverse ways. As such they are becoming more common as research topics in the field of HCI.

Among research on self-actuated TUIs and OUIs, shape-changing interfaces are an especially challenging topic due to the complexity of performing physical transformations. Many kinds of soft materials are used to create shape changing interfaces, but the forms of transformation are still nonetheless restricted. In addition, the ability to change shape is often more regarded as an output method, rather than a characteristic of a functional and bidirectional interface.

In this paper we present PolyHinge, a series of novel shape-changing TUIs that use hinge connections to perform physical geometric transformations. PolyHinge can work together with multi-touch tabletop screens to allow the user to interact with digital content. In addition, the concept of dynamic affordance and semantics is further developed within the context of shape changing interfaces. We also developed a series of applications allowing PolyHinge interaction on a tabletop, demonstrating how this concept can assist users. Interaction with PolyHinge is very natural and thus is both accessible and attractive to users.

2. RELATED WORK

2.1 Adding Actuation to Passive TUIs

Previous research extensively explored methods of adding actuations to passive TUIs. With actuated TUIs, users can get feedback on changes in digital information that passive TUIs cannot.

Ivan Poupyrev et al.'s (2007) research discusses many details about TUIs and actuation. Esben Warming Pedersen & Kasper Hornbæk's (2011) Tangible Bots provide movement and haptic feedback for tangible tabletop interfaces by using active, motorized tangibles, as well as putting forward an interaction framework that can be applied to many actuated TUIs.

Recently, shape-changing interfaces have emerged as a popular research topic in the field of actuated TUIs. Notable and relevant examples of recently developed shape changing TUIs include: Height-Adjustable TUIs (Haipeng Mi and Masanori Sugimoto, 2011); Changibles (Anne Roudaut et al, 2014), which are interactive wireless tokens that can reshape themselves and attach together to create animated assemblies; GaussBricks (Rong-Hao Liang et al, 2014), which are magnetic building blocks connected by magnetic joints, enabling motion, force feedback and shape changes; PneUI (Lining Yao et al, 2013), which is a technology enabling the building of shape-changing interfaces through pneumatically-actuated soft composite materials.

The properties enabling physical feedback present in each of these systems served as inspiration to our approach, and we attempt to extend these approaches into our work.

2.2 Affordance

The term "affordance" originated from the field of Psychology, and is now widely used by HCI researchers. Orit Shaer and Eva Hornecker (2010) frequently discusses cuing interaction with affordances. Norman (1999) presents the idea that affordances reflect the possible relationships among actors and objects. Similarly, Dhaval Vyas et al.'s (2006) research emphasizes that affordance is an interpretative relationship that emerges between users and technology during their interaction within their lived environment. inFORM (Sean Follmer et al, 2013), which introduces dynamic physical affordances and constraints, is also a closely related work.

2.3 Hinged Dissection and Connection

Hinged dissection is a geometric problem. What inspired us most is the classic hinged dissection of an equilateral triangle into a square by Dudeney (1902) shown in Figure 1. Furthermore, Timothy G. Abbott et al. (2008) have proved that any finite collection of polygons of equal area has a common hinged dissection. That is, for any such collection of polygons there exists a chain of polygons hinged at vertices that can be folded in the plane continuously without self-intersection to form any polygon in the collection. This result guarantees that PolyHinge devices, with its hinged dissections and connections, have various forms it can transform between which can be used for various applications.

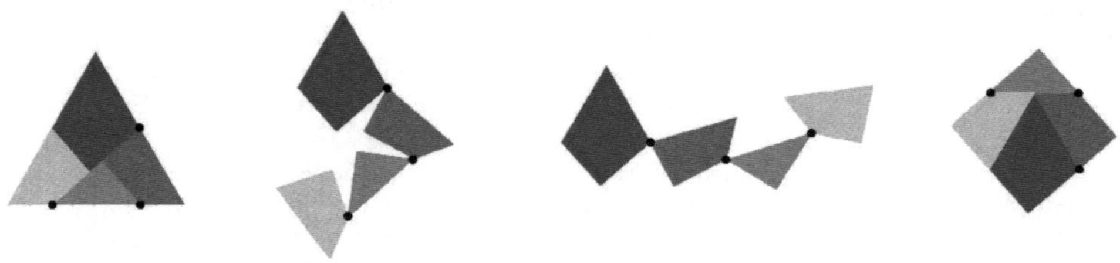

Figure 1. The classic hinged dissection of an equilateral triangle into a square by Dudeney

3. DESIGN

Inspired by Dudeney's hinged dissection of an equilateral triangle into a square as well as related research, we chose hinged dissection and connection as the method of changing the TUI's shape. This is a convenient way to change the TUI's geometric shape, and enables dynamic affordance and semantics in tangible interactions. We also made further research in adapting the concept of hinged dissection and connection on a triangle to a square presented by Dudeney onto polyominoes. In comparison with the classic hinged transformation between two shapes, polyominoes provide a way of performing a multi-state hinged transformation. We present an example of tetrominoes (a polyomino of order 4) transforming into 7 distinct shapes in Figure 2.

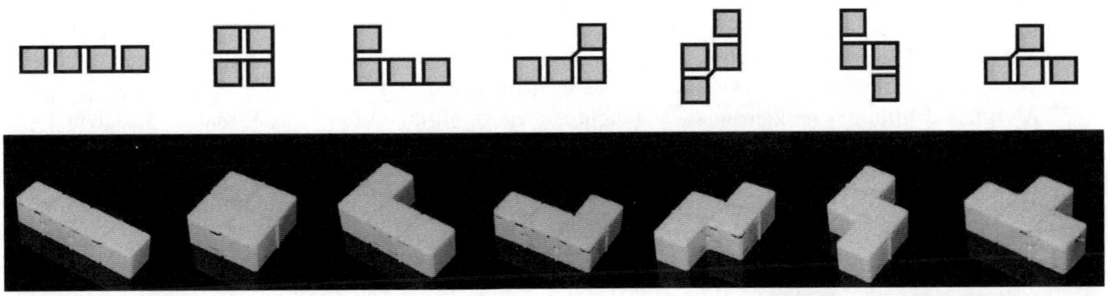

Figure 2. An example of a tetromino transforming into all of its distinct shapes—like Tetris

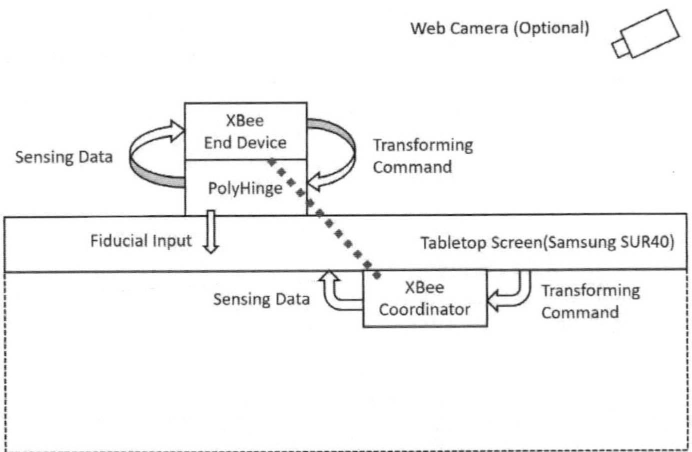

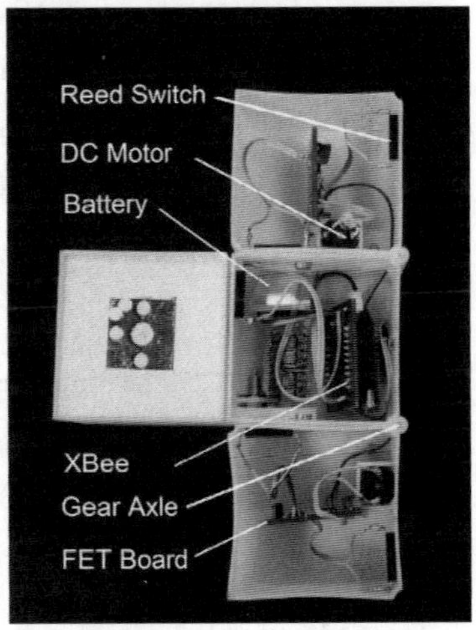

Figure 3. Left: The PolyHinge system architecture. Right: A typical PolyHinge hardware structure

3.1 Hardware

A typical PolyHinge hardware structure, shown in Figure 3 (Right), consists of several subunits connected together via hinges. A parent unit contains a DC motor which drives child units using gear axles fixed at hinge corners in order to execute rotations. Surfaces that may come into contact with each other during rotations contain magnet pairs and reed switches so as to detect contact and prevent over-rotation. FET (Field Effect Transistor) boards are used to amplify control signals from the XBee wireless receiver. Wires are routed through the hinged connections, carrying power and signals from one unit to another. The units are 3D printed with SLA, in a proper size that are very comfortable to grasp. In addition, fiducial tags are applied onto the bottom surfaces for optical tracking by the tabletop screen. Furthermore, there are extensible ports on the PCB for sensors to support functions such as tapping.

3.2 System

The PolyHinge system architecture is shown in Figure 3 (Left). We employed a multi-touch tabletop screen (Samsung SUR40 with Microsoft PixelSense) as a tracking demonstration platform for PolyHinge. In addition to traditional multi-touch interactions, the screen is capable of recognizing fiducial tags placed on its surface and detect their positions and orientations. An optional web camera can be used to support gesture input. We used XBee technology for bidirectional data communication between a PolyHinge device and the table. The PolyHinge uses an XBee end device while the table is connected to an XBee coordinator. This enables multiple PolyHinge devices to work with the table at the same time.

A typical dataflow is multichannel. The table gathers information from multi-touch input, fiducial input, sensing data from PolyHinge, and the optional web camera in order to recognize a correct input event according to the interaction scenario. Then a transforming command can be transmitted back to the PolyHinge which generates a physical shape output, as well as sound and visual information on the tabletop screen.

4. INTERACTION & APPLICATION

Together with a tabletop screen, PolyHinge is a mixed-reality system in which both physical and digital information is presented to the user. In addition to the active shape output, PolyHinge also serves as a multi-channel sensing interface that detects position, orientation, taps, and so on. Therefore, PolyHinge can provide unique interaction styles and applications in addition to ones provided by traditional rigid TUIs.

4.1 Hinge-Based Interaction

Users can physically manipulate PolyHinge devices beyond ways in which they can interact with traditional TUIs. Hinge-based interaction as an interaction style is simple and natural, as is shown in Figure 4. Users activate a hinge using a physical or a digital select, and then trigger a transformation using a virtual slide gesture on the tabletop screen. In this interaction, users naturally and directly manipulate the PolyHinge device's shape with individual control of each hinge.

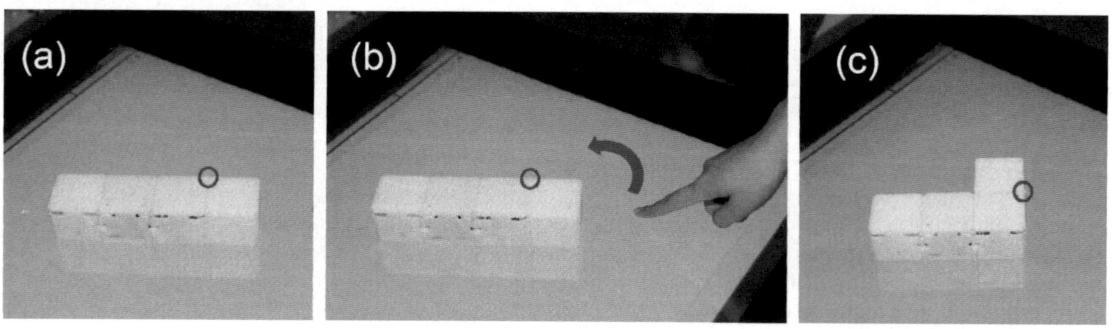

Figure 4. Hinge-based interaction, (a) a hinge is selected and activated; (b)(c) using a slide gesture on the tabletop screen to control the shape change

4.2 Shape-Based Interaction

For more complex PolyHinge geometric structures, indirect interactions are more natural. For example, for a PolyHinge device that transforms between a triangle and a square, users can outline a shape by hand and make the PolyHinge transform into the outlined shape (Figure 5). In such shape-based interactions, users control the device's shape with natural methods such as gestures, drawings, and so on.

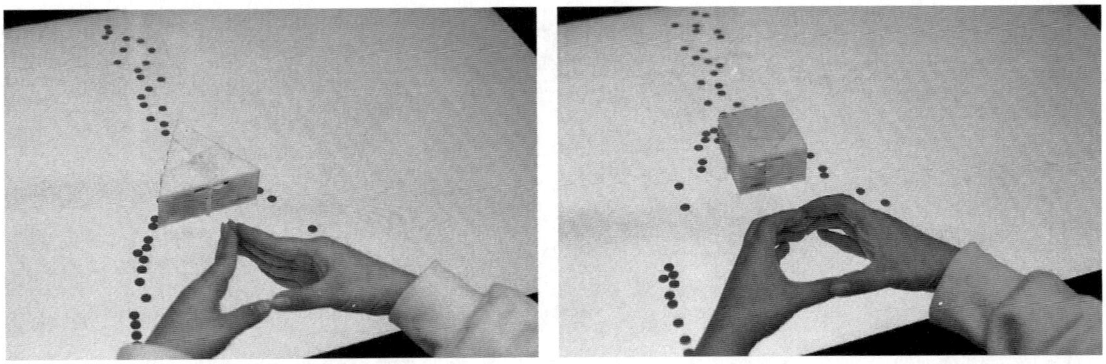

Figure 5. Shape-based interaction: outlining a shape by hands to control the shape of PolyHinge

4.3 Context-Based Interaction

In a complex real-world context-based interaction scenario with PolyHinge, users can perform a physical or a digital input and get both digital and physical outputs. There are a myriad of possibilities in designing the specific interaction style for different applications.

TUIs have persistent mappings (Shaer, O. and Hornecker, E, 2010) and thus the metaphor of a TUI has temporal and cognitive continuity. By making use of affordance and semantics in a TUI's appearance, its meaning or function as well as how to interact with it can be conveyed to the user. Affordance and semantics is an effective way to aid users in tangible interaction. This is similar to the use of metaphors in GUIs though TUIs are less malleable and less mutable than a purely digitally computer-controlled representation (Shaer, O. and Hornecker, E, 2010). In contrast with the static affordance and semantics of traditional TUIs, PolyHinge has a dynamic continuity and presents dynamic affordance and semantics as a characteristic of functional and bidirectional interface. This makes dynamic function and meaning accessible for physical TUIs, and expands the usage of TUIs in user cuing and many others ways.

PolyHinge can provide dynamic affordance for a user's input. This can be seen in a Tangible Tetris game that uses a transforming tetromino as a handheld device shown in Figure 6. Similar to traditional Tetris, the transforming tetromino will change its shape randomly each time after the user places it. In this case, dynamic affordance is used to cue users on how to interact with the TUI devices. The shape-changing property can indicate different interactions under the TUI's individual metaphor, and provide more possibilities for various scenarios.

Figure 6. Dynamic affordance in a Tangible Tetris game

PolyHinge can also provide dynamic semantics for multi-state metaphors. For instance, a PolyHinge transforming from an equilateral triangle to a square can be used as a physical play/stop button of a digital media player (in Figure 7). With the user's previous experience, the state indicated by the button can be easily recognized, and they can still move it around to control different movies like traditional TUIs. In this scenario, dynamic semantics is used to cue users on the state or result of an interaction.

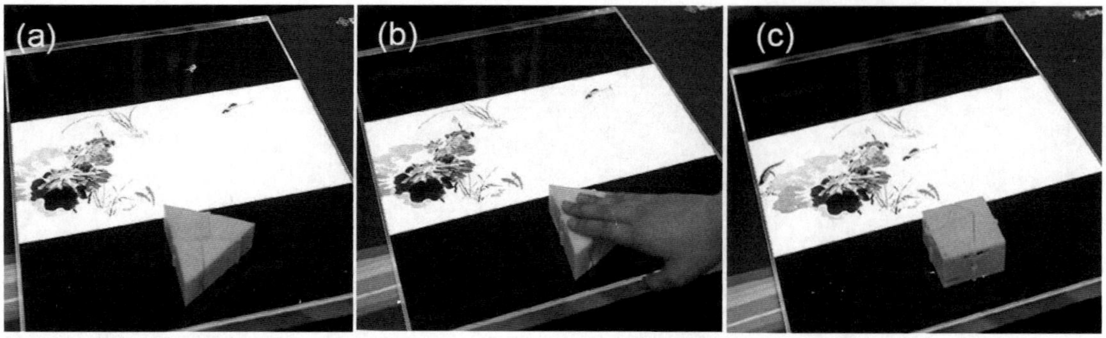

Figure 7. Dynamic semantics, (a) a physical play/stop button of a digital media player, (b) user tapping the button, (c) the movie playing and the button transforming to indicate its changed state and function.

5. USER STUDY

In our user study, we arranged 23 participants to play the Tangible Tetris game. After the game we distributed a questionnaire and conducted interviews to collect their impressions and thoughts.

According to the results of the questionnaire, the majority of the participants (N=18, 78.3%) thought the Tangible Tetris game was "really interesting", while a few (N=3, 13.0%) thought it was "a little uncomfortable" to play. In addition, the survey found that some (N=11, 47.8%) preferred the virtual Tetris, some (N=8, 34.8%) preferred the physical and a few were neutral (N=4, 17.4%). However, all except one of the participants (N=22, 95.7%) found the shape-changing TUI itself to be appealing. They felt that the shape-changing TUI is "effective", "accurate", and "attractive". In addition, many participants showed a strong curiosity to the transformation procedure and a great interest in the physical interaction. These results indicate that PolyHinge has a positive contribution to tangible interactions.

6. LIMITATIONS & FUTURE WORK

A decomino (a polyomino of order 10) has 9189 possible shapes (Redelmeijer D. H., 1981). However, when extending the structure from tetrominoes to higher order polyominoes, it does not seem to be possible to join 5 or more squares by hinges to form all possible shapes (Demaine, E. D. et al, 2005). This problem can be solved by dividing the polyomino subunits into smaller triangular pieces. Higher order polyominoes with such structures could be made into a physical pixel interface in which every subunit can perform a rotation and thus forming various pixel patterns as a whole.

Meanwhile, we are going to explore possibilities in swarm interactions, in which the PolyHinge devices act as modular tabletop robots, work collaboratively, and attach together using magnets. With the possibility of connecting multiple PolyHinges, more diverse and dynamic patterns can be formed. Such an interface is similar to modular robots, but with more exciting characteristics and greater possibilities in presentation and interaction.

7. CONCLUSION

In this paper we presented PolyHinge, a shape-changing TUI which enables active shape-changing output with dynamic affordance and semantics, thus inheriting the representative characteristics of a TUI while also extending its malleability and mutability. As PolyHinge is based on extended structures of hinged dissection and connection, its forms of transformation and interaction are highly diverse. The natural interaction styles allowed by PolyHinge are accessible and attractive to users.

ACKNOWLEDGEMENT

We thank Ms Qingyuan SHI, Ms. Jiawei LI, Mr. Fengyuan ZHU, and Mr. Qi LU for their support. Thanks for James Ronner and Mr Shaoen MA for proofreading English. This work is supported by National Natural Science Foundation of China under Grant No. 61402250, 61232013, and National Key Research & Development Plan of China under Grant No. 2016YFB1001402.

REFERENCES

Anne Roudaut, Rebecca Reed, Tianbo Hao, and Sriram Subramanian, 2014. Changibles: analyzing and designing shape changing constructive assembly. In *Proceedings of the SIGCHI Conference on Human Factors in Computing Systems* (CHI '14). ACM, New York, NY, USA, 2593-2596.

Abbott, T. G., Abel, Z., Charlton, D., Demaine, E. D., Demaine, M. L., & Kominers, S. D., 2008. Hinged dissections exist. *symposium on computational geometry*, 110-119.

Donald A. Norman, 1999. Affordance, conventions, and design. *Interactions* 6(3), 38-43.

Dhaval Vyas, Cristina M. Chisalita, and Gerrit C. van der Veer, 2006. Affordance in interaction. In *Proceedings of the 13th Eurpoean conference on Cognitive ergonomics: trust and control in complex socio-technical systems* (ECCE '06). ACM, New York, NY, USA, 92-99.

Demaine, E. D., Demaine, M. L., Eppstein, D., Frederickson, G. N., & Friedman, E, 2005. Hinged dissection of polyominoes and polyforms. *Computational Geometry*, *31*(3), 237-262.

Esben Warming Pedersen and Kasper Hornbæk, 2011. Tangible bots: interaction with active tangibles in tabletop interfaces. In *Proceedings of the SIGCHI Conference on Human Factors in Computing Systems* (CHI '11). ACM, New York, NY, USA, 2975-2984.

Henry E. Dudeney, 1902. Puzzles and prizes. *Weekly Dispatch.* The puzzle appeared in the April 6 issue of this column. An unusual discussion followed on April 20, and the solution appeared on May 4.

Hiroshi Ishii and Brygg Ullmer, 1997. Tangible bits: towards seamless interfaces between people, bits and atoms. In *Proceedings of the ACM SIGCHI Conference on Human factors in computing systems* (CHI '97). ACM, New York, NY, USA, 234-241.

Haipeng Mi and Masanori Sugimoto, 2011. HATs: interact using height-adjustable tangibles in tabletop interfaces. In *Proceedings of the ACM International Conference on Interactive Tabletops and Surfaces* (ITS '11). ACM, New York, NY, USA, 71-74.

Ivan Poupyrev, Tatsushi Nashida, and Makoto Okabe. 2007. Actuation and tangible user interfaces: the Vaucanson duck, robots, and shape displays. In *Proceedings of the 1st international conference on Tangible and embedded interaction* (TEI '07). ACM, New York, NY, USA, 205-212.

Lining Yao, Ryuma Niiyama, Jifei Ou, Sean Follmer, Clark Della Silva, and Hiroshi Ishii, 2013. PneUI: pneumatically actuated soft composite materials for shape changing interfaces. In *Proceedings of the 26th annual ACM symposium on User interface software and technology* (UIST '13). ACM, New York, NY, USA, 13-22.

Rong-Hao Liang, et al, 2014. GaussBricks: magnetic building blocks for constructive tangible interactions on portable displays. In *Proceedings of the SIGCHI Conference on Human Factors in Computing Systems* (CHI '14). ACM, New York, NY, USA, 3153-3162.

Redelmeijer, D. H., 1981. Counting polyominoes: yet another attack. *Discrete Mathematics*, *36*(3), 191-203.

Shaer, O., & Hornecker, E., 2010. Tangible user interfaces: past, present, and future directions. *Foundations and Trends in Human-Computer Interaction*, *3*(1–2), 1-137.

Sean Follmer, Daniel Leithinger, Alex Olwal, Akimitsu Hogge, and Hiroshi Ishii, 2013. inFORM: dynamic physical affordances and constraints through shape and object actuation. In *Proceedings of the 26th annual ACM symposium on User interface software and technology* (UIST '13). ACM, New York, NY, USA, 417-426.

STUDY ON DIGITAL STYLE DESIGN - ROBUST DESIGN SYSTEM FOR KANSEI USING MULTIVARIATE ANALYSIS AND TAGUCHI METHOD

Hideki Aoyama and Hitomi Yokoyama
Keio University, 3-14-1 Hiyoshi, Kohoku-ku, Yokohama, 223-8522, Japan

ABSTRACT

In recent years, aesthetic design is becoming increasingly important in industrial product development due to the growing maturity of product functions. The designer is required to reflect consumer needs in the aesthetic design while giving consideration to the applications and functions of the product. For this reason, effective techniques enabling design creation based on consumer preference and needs are indispensable. The Taguchi Method has been effectively used for the robust design of product functions. In this study, a design support method applying the Taguchi Method to robust aesthetic design in respect to the inconsistencies of human Kansei (sensitivity, emotion) is proposed. As an example using the method, it is applied for quantitatively analyzing the robustness of design solutions created in accordance with the design concept of a digital camera.

KEYWORDS

Taguchi Method, KANSEI, Robust design, Aesthetic design, Emotional design

1. INTRODUCTION

Through advances in manufacturing technology, it is becoming more difficult to differentiate products by their quality, and the relative contribution that the design of the appearance makes to the appeal of products is getting bigger. Appearance design largely depends on the Kansei (sensitivity, emotion) of the designer, and it is thought that creating designs based on scientific theory would be difficult [Hsin-Hsi Lai], [Sang W. Hong]. Nevertheless, to design products that will be well received by many consumers, what is needed is the analysis of the kinds of designs that are sought by consumers, and the development of methods that make it possible to create robust designs for the different Kansei of each consumer.

There have been many studies that aimed to analyze the relationship between form and Kansei, and to generate designs that correspond with designers' intended impressions [Chun-Chih Che], [Ezgi Aktar Demirtas], [Shana Smith], [Andreas K. NORDGREN], [Anitawati M. Lokman], [Fu Guo], [Hsin-Hsi Lai], [Mitsuo Nagamachi], [Pierre Lévy]. These studies are valid for analyzing the relationship between form and Kansei, but their analyses use averages of Kansei data, and do not take into account the differences in the Kansei of each person.

This study considers the differences in Kansei, and conducts an analysis of the relationship between form and Kansei. Based on survey information, the study analyzes users' Kansei of a target product with Hayashi's Quantification Method I and the Taguchi Method, and proposes methods for deducing designs that allow more people to experience the concept of the product along with quantitatively understanding customer preferences and needs. Furthermore, the study formulates a design support system based on the proposal methods. This system applies to the design of digital cameras that are coming under serious consideration for its designability.

In this paper, the words of "Kansei" and "Kansei-words" are used in various explanations. Here, "Kansei" is taken to mean "the impression obtained visually when viewing the target object," and "Kansei-words" is taken to mean "natural language expressing an impression."

2. ANALYZING KANSEI FOR SHAPE FACTORS

To aim for design optimization, it is essential to vary the design criteria and evaluate the relationship between those criteria and their output. This study analyzes the relationship between design parameters and Kansei assessment values in using digital camera shape design parameters for design criteria and output for Kansei assessment values.

2.1 Design Parameters

For design parameters, we used six exemplary parameters which have effects on Kansei: lens radius, corner radius, aspect ratio, hue, saturation, and brightness of the camera unit as shown in Figure 1.

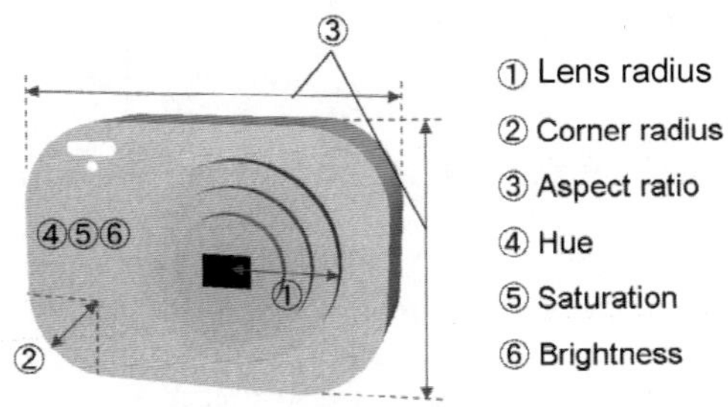

Figure 1. Design Parameters

The above six design parameters were each given six variations labeled Levels 1 through 6 as shown in Table 1. We then made samples shown in Figure 2 by using combinations of the different levels of each variable. The method for combining the levels referred to an orthogonal table which is a planning table for conducting experiments with relatively low frequency of evaluations concerning a large number of factors. We took a survey of impression assessments based on the samples shown in Figure 1, and collected Kansei data.

Table 1. Levels of Design Parameters

Parameter \ Level	1	2	3	4	5	6
Lens radius	3.0	2.7	2.4	2.1	1.8	1.5
Corner radius	0	0.48	0.96	1.44	1.92	2.40
Aspect ratio	1.0:1.0	1.0:1.2	1.0:1.4	1.0:1.6	1.0:1.8	1.0:2.0
Hue	0°	60°	120°	180°	240°	300°
Saturation	0%	20%	40%	60%	80%	100%
Brightness	0%	20%	40%	60%	80%	100%

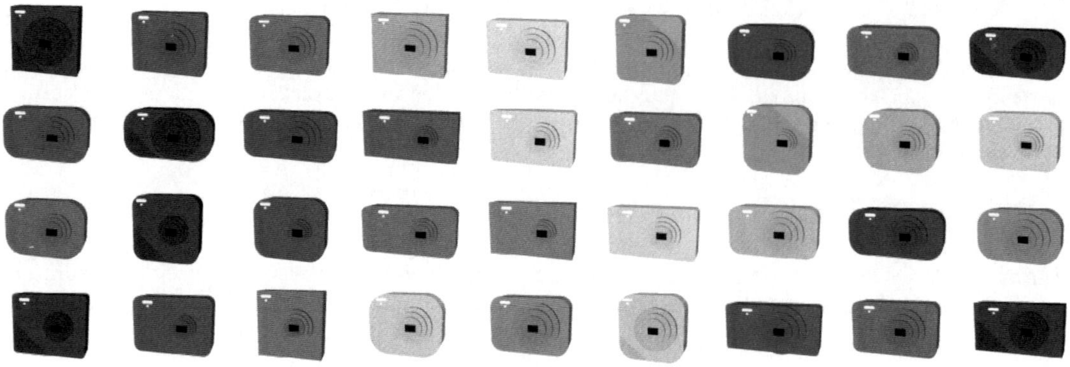

Figure 2. Examples of Digital Camera Design

2.2 Selecting Kansei-words for Expressing Impressions and Images of Product

Kansei data was collected through a survey. In the survey, several antonym-pairs of Kansei-words were shown to test subjects to evaluate the scale of impressions of each digital camera design shown in Figure 2. We selected several relevant antonym-pairs of Kansei-words to use on the survey from among a great number of Kansei-words to reduce the burden on the test subjects.

First, we chose 20 antonym-pairs of Kansei-words that can be used to express impressions of digital camera design from dictionaries and other sources. That is, we decided to describe impressions of digital camera appearances using 20 antonym-pairs of Kansei-words. In this instance, we excluded Kansei-words antonym-pairs describing the product quality: like "Good-Bad" and "Beautiful-Ugly," because they do not fit the intended goal of this system.

Next, we presented the digital camera shapes shown in Figure 2 to the subjects, and asked them about the impression of each camera shape to complete a survey of an 11-step scale on each of the 20 antonym-pairs of Kansei-words. The test subjects were 11 university students.

We conducted a cluster analysis of the survey result data, and classified four clusters that had close evaluation trends. Then we selected one antonym-pair of Kansei-words representing each cluster. As the result, the following antonym-pairs of Kansei-words: Unique-Orthodox, Cool-Cute, Formal-Casual, and New-Old were used for representing the impressions of digital cameras. The impression and image of digital camera shape is expressed according to these four Kansei-words antonym-pairs.

2.3 Collecting Kansei Data

We conducted an SD survey that had test subjects to evaluate the 36 samples shown in Figure 2 using an 11-step scale of the four selected antonym-pairs of Kansei-words as shown in Figure 3. The test subjects were 43 university students. We then conducted an analysis using the survey results as Kansei data.

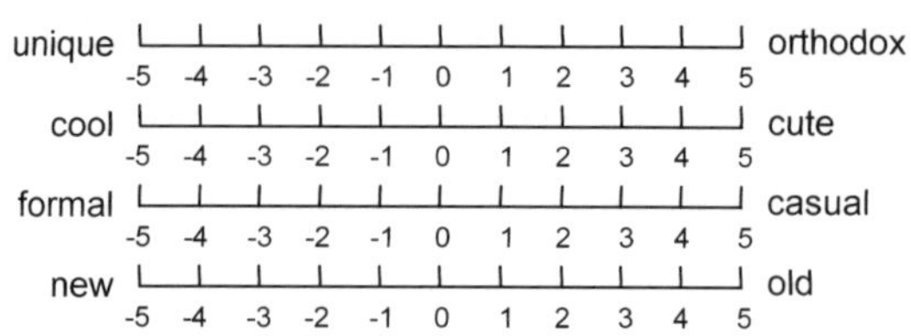

Figure 3. SD Scale of Evaluation

2.4 Analytical Methods

This study's analyses were conducted using Quantification Theory I (Hayashi's Quantification Method I) and the Taguchi Method. Each method is described below.

2.4.1 Quantification Theory I (Hayashi's Quantification Method I)

Hayashi's Quantification Method I is an analysis method in which the target variables are quantitative and the explanatory variables are qualitative, and is one method for analyzing by quantifying qualitative variables. Equation (1) expresses this with y for the target variable, x_i for the explanatory variable, and b_i for the coefficient. This study applies Hayashi's Quantification Method I using the Kansei assessment values for the target variables and the design parameters for the explanatory variables to quantify the effects that the design parameters have on Kansei assessment values.

$$y = b_o + b_1 x_1 + b_2 x_2 + \cdots + b_i x_i \tag{1}$$

2.4.2 Taguchi Method

The Taguchi Method is a technique for efficiently deducing robust design, and is used mainly in the design of functional products. This study creates robust designs for the dispersion of individual Kansei by applying the Taguchi Method to Kansei analysis. Equation (2) generally shows the output fluctuation (dispersion) S, the output average β, and the output standard deviation σ of the Taguchi Method.

$$S = \frac{\sigma}{\beta} \tag{2}$$

Generally, the output expands in the positive range as shown in the left part of Figure 4, and the output average β and output standard deviation σ are thought to be roughly proportional. Thus, normalizing the output standard deviation using the output average as in Equation (2) operates to avoid having a reduction of the output fluctuation (dispersion) merely reduce the output. Thus, the inverse of the output fluctuation is calculated with Equation (3). The η is called the SN ratio.

$$\eta = 10\log\left(\frac{\beta}{\sigma}\right)^2 \tag{3}$$

By increasing the SN ratio to get the inverse of the output fluctuation, the output dispersion decreases. In the Taguchi Method, optimal design solutions are found by setting standards that allow the SN ratio to increase.

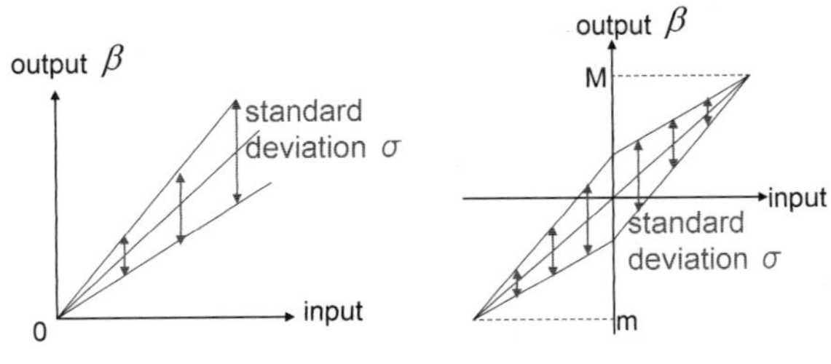

Figure 4. Relationship between the output and the standard deviation of the Taguchi method

In our method, the range of Kansei assessment values (outputs) is set from -5 to +5. In this way, when there are upper and lower limits to the output range, the relationship between output average β and output standard deviation σ is such that the upper and lower limit values of the output range, output average differences (expressed below as ℓ to simplify explanation), and output standard deviation σ are thought to have a proportional relationship as shown in the right side of Figure 4. This trend can be confirmed by the correlation between ℓ and σ shown in Figure 5. Because the relationship between the output average and output standard deviation differs from what was mentioned above, the SN ratio from Equation (3) cannot be used.

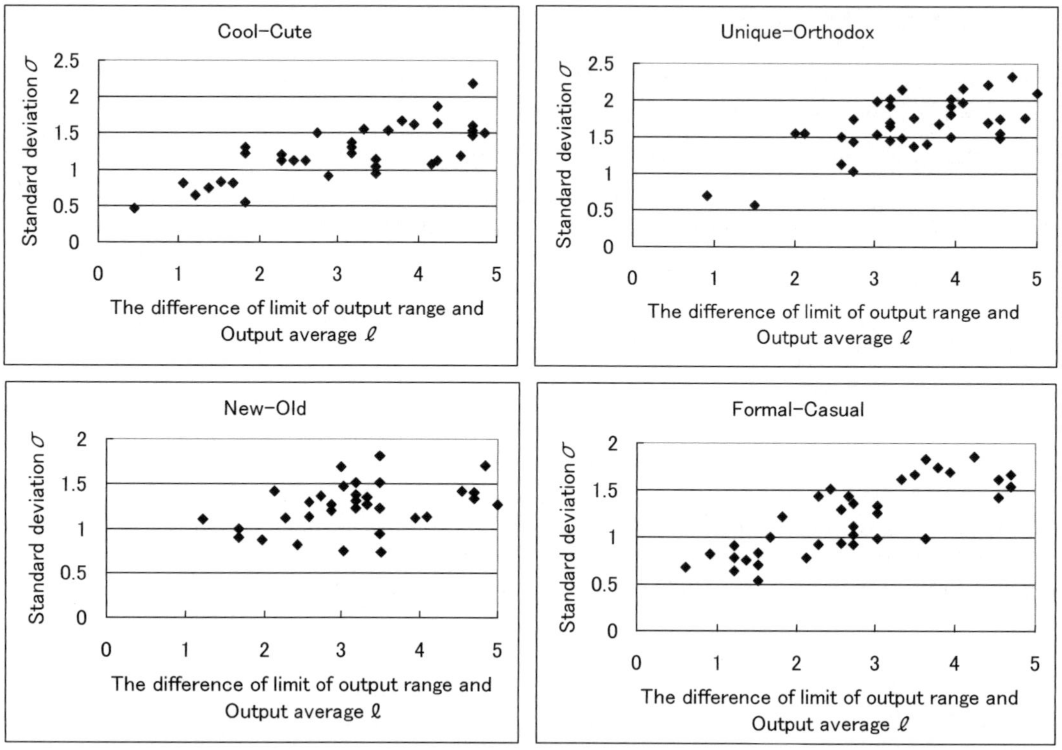

Figure 5. Relationship between σ and ℓ

Thus, this study defines output fluctuation S as in Equation (4). Reduction of the output fluctuation (dispersion) is kept from merely reducing the output by normalizing the output standard deviation σ with the denominator ℓ in Equation (4).

$$S = \frac{\sigma}{\frac{M-m}{2} - \left| \beta - \frac{M+m}{2} \right|} \tag{4}$$

Then, the output fluctuation inverse η that was obtained is used as the SN ratio in this method, as in Equation (5).

$$\eta = 10\log \left(\frac{\frac{M-m}{2} - \left| \beta - \frac{M+m}{2} \right|}{\sigma} \right)^2 \tag{5}$$

As with the conventional SN ratio in the Taguchi Method of Equation (3), as the SN ratio derived in our method increases the output dispersion decreases because the output fluctuation inverse has been taken. This study deduces the optimal design solution by setting standards that increase the SN ratio of Equation (5).

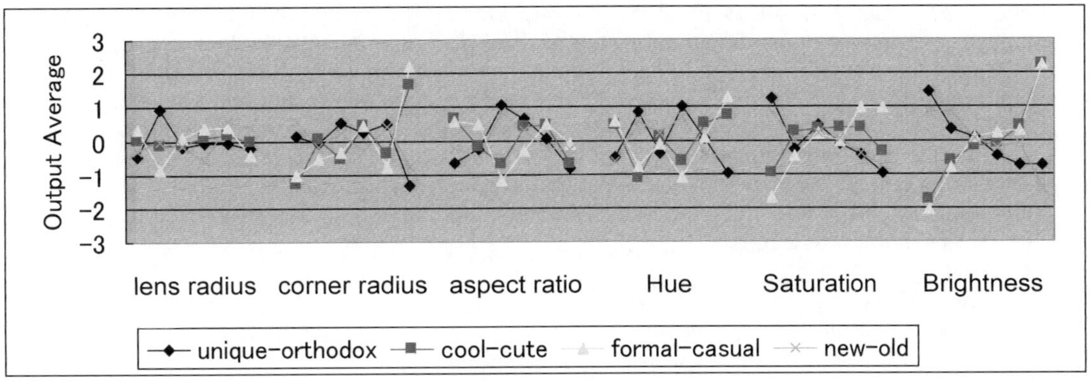

Figure 6. Output Average

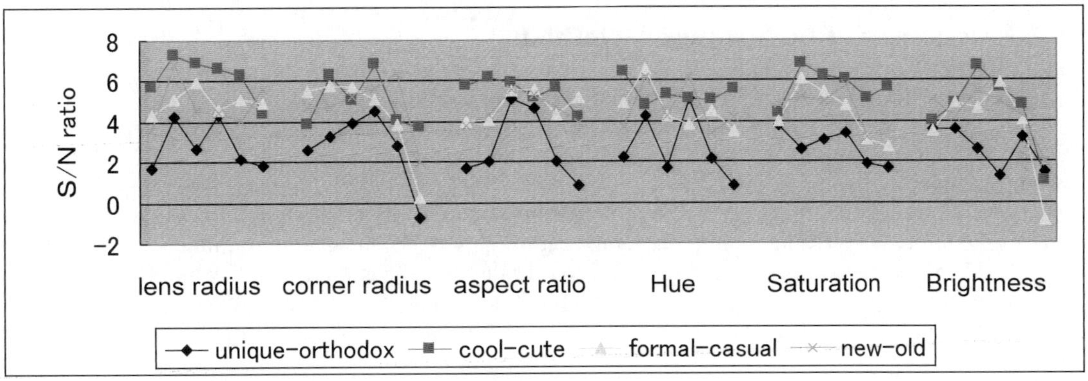

Figure 7. S/N ratio

2.5 Analysis Results

The output averages and the SN ratio accompanying changes of each parameter are shown in Figures 6 and 7, respectively. Based on these two sets of results, we deduce the robust design parameter values that fulfill the desired output values as well as have high SN ratios.

3. SYSTEM DEVELOPMENT AND PROPOSED METHOD ASSESSMENT

3.1 Developed System

Based on the above analysis methods and results, we developed a system for creating robust designs that suit the desired impression for customer Kansei. A system user (designer) first selects the impressions that he/she wishes to adjust from among the four antonym-pairs of Kansei-words. He/she then sets the target value for the impression assessment of the selected antonym-pairs of Kansei-words. Target values are set on the same -5 to +5 scale as the Kansei data collection survey.

Furthermore, to reflect a plans/idea of a system user in the design solution, the initial settings (design values) are entered. Entering initial settings is done by setting the initial levels as the levels that are closest to the design plan/idea for each parameter. Next, the user sets the maximum number of level modifications for the initial settings. This determines the number of level changes that will be permitted from the combination of levels chosen in the initial settings. Accordingly, the maximum number will be set low to give respect the initial design, and set high to prioritize enhancing robustness. The design solution is derived with the range of the number of level modifications. Furthermore, when the user has strong preferences about certain parts of the design, he/she can set those design parameters as fixed conditions in the initial level settings.

When the above settings are entered, the system selects all designs (level combinations) that comply with the input conditions (output fulfills the target values; modified number is within the maximum for the initial design; parameters set as fixed conditions are the same level as in the initial design) from among the enormous quantity of level combinations. The SN ratio is calculated for the selected design solutions, and the system puts forth those solutions with high SN ratios as the optimal solutions.

To summarize, the outline of this system is as follows:

1. Select Kansei-words pairs
2. Set target output values
3. Enter initial design settings (optional)
4. Enter fixed conditions (optional)
5. Extraction of design solutions that satisfy the conditions
6. Calculation of SN ratio
7. Output of optimal solution

3.2 Assessment of the Proposed Method

We reviewed the usefulness of this system by comparing the analytical results of the optimal solution extracted by the proposed system with other solutions. As an example, we will compare the analytical results when the selected conditions were a range of target output values from the scale 2.5-3.5 on the "Unique-Orthodox" antonym-pairs of Kansei-words. In the following explanation, Solution A is the optimal solution from the proposal system, and Solution B is the other solution. For Solution B, we used a solution that fit the target output values but had a somewhat low SN ratio. The degree of influence that Solutions A and B had on the SN ratio of each parameter's level for the design parameters is shown in Figure 8. In Figure 8, The red triangles are Solution A's levels and the blue triangles are Solution B's levels. Each parameter shown in Figure 8 shows the levels 1 through 6 from left to right. The actual form of Solutions A and B are shown in Figure 9.

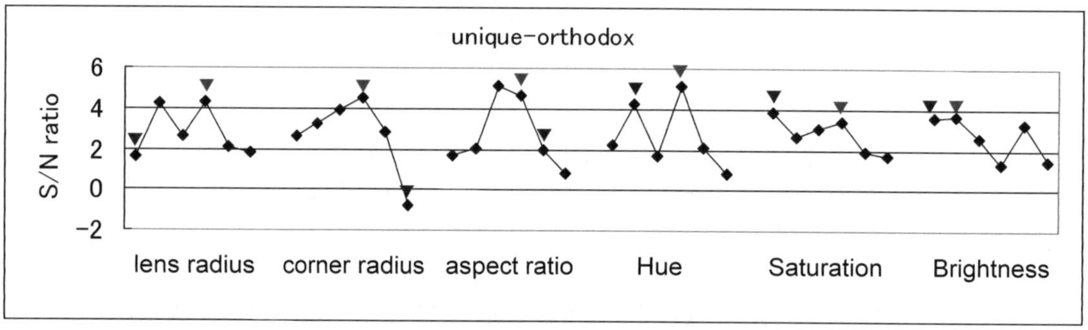

Figure 8. S/N ratio and levels of solution A and B

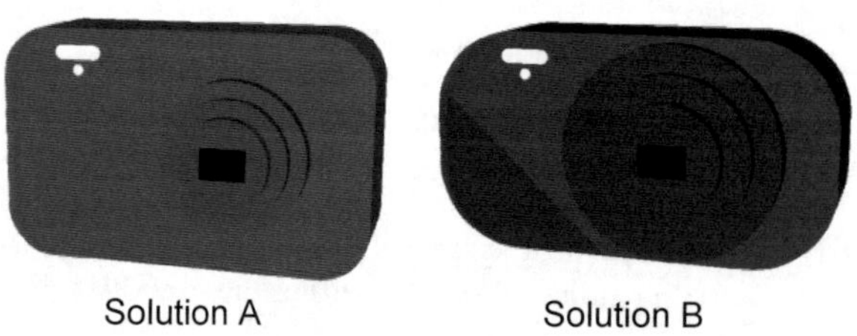

Figure 9. Shape of Solution A and B

As shown in Figure 8, when the SN ratios of the levels set for Solutions A and B are compared, Solution A has higher levels for most of the parameters, and a comprehensive assessment shows that Solution A selects for levels with higher SN ratios. This is because Solution A was deduced using the Taguchi Method. Furthermore, for Solution A as the optimal solution, not all parameter levels are set as the level with the highest SN ratio because the system operates to adjust within the target values for output average in parts in which the SN ratio fluctuation is small.

Figure 10 shows the analytical results of Solutions A and B. The vertical axis is the output, and it takes the standard deviation with the output average at center. The set target value range of 2.5-3.5 is shown in red.

The output average of Solution A is 3.25, and its output standard deviation is 2.88. On the other hand, the output average of Solution B is 2.83, and its output standard deviation is 6.78. As can be seen in Figure 10, the output average values for both Solutions A and B are within the range of target values, but the range of the output standard deviation is smaller for Solution A which was the optimal solution obtained by the developed system.

As we have shown above, it was confirmed that the proposal system was able to create robust design solutions for the variations in Kansei.

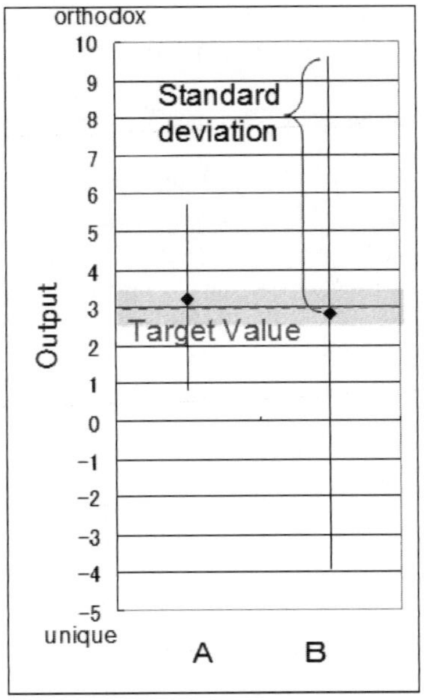

Figure 10. Analysis Results of Solutions A and B

4. CONCLUSION

This study conducted a proposal for a design support system aiming to create forms that meet a greater number of consumers' Kansei tendencies while also fitting the image that the designer intends. We analyzed the relationship between form and Kansei with consideration for the variability of Kansei, through multivariate analysis and the Taguchi Method. We formulated a system for creating robust designs for the variability of Kansei. We confirmed that through the proposal system, forms can be deduced that give the impression that the designer intends to a greater number of consumers. Furthermore, the following can be mentioned as topics for further study. The test subjects for both the Kansei-words selection survey and the Kansei data collection survey were university students. However, the Kansei of professional designers may differ from that of students. Therefore, it will be necessary to take the opinions of professional designers into account.

REFERENCES

Andreas Kjell Nordgren, Hideki Aoyama,2007, Implicit Shape Parameterization for Kansei Design Methodology, Journal of Advanced Mechanical Design, Systems, and Manufacturing, Vol. 1, No. 4, pp. 442-452.

Anitawati Mohd Lokman, 2010, Design & Emotion: The Kansei Engineering Methodology, Design & Emotion: The Kansei Engineering Methodology, Vol. 1, Issue 1, pp. 1-14.

Chun-Chih Chen, Ming-Chuen Chuang, 2008, Integrating the Kano model into a robust design approach to enhance customer satisfaction with product design, Int. J. Production Economics Vol. 114, pp. 667– 681.

Ezgi Aktar Demirtas, et al, 2009, Determination of optimal product styles by ordinal logistic regression versus conjoint analysis for kitchen faucets, International Journal of Industrial Ergonomics Vol. 39, pp. 866–875.

Fu Guo, Wei Lin Liu, Fan Tao Liu, Huan Wang, Tian Bo Wang, 2014, Emotional design method of product presented in multi-dimensional variables based on Kansei Engineering, Journal of Engineering Design, Vol. 25, issue 4-6, pp. 194-212.

Hsin-Hsi Lai, et al, 2005, A robust design for enhancing the feeling quality of a product: a car profile case study, International Journal of Industial Ergonomics Vol. 35, pp. 445-460.

Hsin-Hsi Lai, Yang-Cheng Lin, Chung-Hsing Yeh, 2005, Form design of product image using grey relational analysis and neural network models, Computers & Operations Research, Vol.32, No.10, pp.2689-2711.

Mitsuo Nagamachi, 1999, Kansei Engineering and its Applications in Automotive Design, SAE Technical Paper 1999-01-1265, pp. 1265-1275.

Pierre Lévy, 2013, Beyond Kansei Engineering: The Emancipation of Kansei Design, International Journal of Design, Vol. 7 No. 2. pp. 83-94.

Sang W. Hong, et al, 2008, Optimal balancing of multiple affective satisfaction dimensions: A case study on mobile phones, International Journal of Industrial Ergonomics, Vol. 38, Issues 3-4, pp. 272-279.

Shana Smith, Shih-Hang Fu, 2009, Factor Analysis of Head-Up Display Presentation Images, ASME 2009 International Design Engineering Technical Conferences and Computers and Information in Engineering Conference (IDETC/CIE2009), Vol. 2, pp1-8.

NOVEL APPROACHES IN HUMAN-VEHICLE INTERACTION INTERFACE OF A VEHICLE DRIVING ASSISTANCE SYSTEM

Manolo Dulva Hina[1], Hongyu Guan[2] and Amar Ramdane-Cherif[2]
[1]*ECE Paris School of Engineering, Bâtiment Pollux, 37 quai de Grenelle, 75015 Paris, France*
[2]*LISV Laboratory, Université de Versailles St-Quentin-en-Yvelines, 10-12 avenue de l'Europe, 78140 Vélizy, France*

ABSTRACT

Project CASA is a collaborative work of five industrial partners and one educational institution. Its goal is to contribute to the advancement of safe and green driving by proposing ADAS (advanced driving assistance system) based on smartphone. It is implemented by capturing and combining all the parameters related to the context of the driver, the vehicle, the environment and the infrastructure altogether to deduce the current driving situation. Based upon such driving situation, we may invoke driving assistance scheme in a form of an audio and visual message to notify or alert the driver. In the area of human-computer interaction, we have developed an interface that alerts or notifies a driver. We also work on the detection of level of stress of the driver. It is necessary on our part that a stressed driver should not be further stressed by our driving assistance messages. This work has been presented to the public and had been received warmly.

KEYWORDS

Multimodal interaction; context-aware system; intelligent transport system; stress-free messaging; affective interface

1. INTRODUCTION

The embedded features of ADAS (A. Armand, et al. 2014; Brioschi et al. 2017; Hina et al. 2016) are numerous and expensive to implement. These features are usually reserved for premium types of vehicles. Pending the deployment of these features on all vehicles, it is essential to propose an alternative, affordable and compatible solution for the existing and coming fleet. The goal of CASA project is to develop an innovative smartphone application, focusing on informative driving assistance functions (ADAS like). This solution is affordable since many solutions are done by the smartphone. The proposed solution is optimized and accurate because it is using real-time data from the vehicle, the driver and the environment. The expected results should improve safety, helping end users to use ADAS type functionalities. Moreover, based on user feedback, it is to improve and optimize future embedded solutions. The human-vehicle interaction (HCI) interface of Project CASA conveys messages and information to the driver. It notifies the driver of an incoming event and alerts the same when danger is detected. It has features that illustrate driver's behaviour, ability to drive, danger and monitoring of other parameters, such as detection of stress and fatigue. The HCI also features affective component wherein if the driver is detected to be stressed, it avoids adding stress in the way it conveys driving assistance messages.

2. RELATED WORKS

We looked at various types of driver assistance provided by different vehicle manufacturers. Formerly reserved for top-of-the-range vehicles, a lot of assistance is now available; others are optional and very costly. Advanced Driver Assistance Systems (ADAS) offer a means to enhance, among other things, active and integrated safety (Bengler et al. 2014). One of the first active assistance systems based on proprioceptive sensors was the anti-lock braking system (ABS) which started in 1978 (BOSCH 2016). The traction control system later improved the features of ABS system. With reference to the requirement on improving support for the driver, projects such as (SAFESPOT ; PREVENT ; CVIS), the number of safety-available functions on the vehicle is continuously increasing. This is in addition to already commercially available features such as anti-block brake system, electronic stability control, etc.

Many types of ADAS systems exist but are very expensive and therefore available only to limited number of vehicles. From a technical perspective, ADAS systems can be classified into three categories (see Figure 1):

- *Longitudinal Support Systems*: They constitute support to the driver in longitudinal driving tasks, preventing a collision with a vehicle ahead. In 1995, Mitsubishi developed "Preview Distance Control" (Motors) which continuously monitors inter-vehicle distance with vehicles ahead.
- *Lateral Support Systems*: They provide support to the driver by controlling the vehicle's position and velocity along the lateral axis. In 2001, Nissan built the first lane-keeping support installed in its Cima vehicle model (Nissan). In general, lateral supports can be categorized into three types: (i) lane-keeping systems, (ii) change-lane systems, and (iii) crossing-assistant systems.
- *Driver Vigilance Monitoring Systems*: They assist in constantly monitoring the driver's eyes, analyzing driver's vigilance and state of health, and intervention in case of stress, faint or alcohol consumption (Planing 2014). Data from steering wheel and driver behavior and features are analyzed using fuzzy classifier to determine the driver's vigilance (Vazquez Bergasa 2004). For example, in 2009, Mercedes-Benz's "Attention Assist" was developed to monitor the driver's fatigue level and drowsiness (Mercedes-Benz).

Most of technologies cited above are closed to proprietary constraints, reserved for premium cars and are costly. Our work, in contrast, is generic in nature that takes into consideration the ADAS features present in one vehicle brand and integrate them with those present in others. In our work, the intent is to consider the driving situation (S. Al-Sultan 2013) in determining the kind of assistance to be provided to the driver. Ours is a work in progress. As it evolves, added features such as machine learning will be incorporated.

3. THE CASA SYSTEM ARCHITECTURE

As stated, the Project CASA is an initiative of five industrial entities and one university in France. The goal is to create a low-cost ADAS based on smartphone, which is functional across various types of vehicles. The system view of Project CASA is shown in Figure 1(a). The Project's aim is to contribute to the advancement of safe and green driving. The task of each consortium partner is given below:

- *PSA-Peugeot-Citroen* – manufacturer of French vehicles Peugeot and Citroen. We use the cockpit of PSA vehicles as specimen means of navigation.
- *Continental* – a German-French industrial partner responsible for providing sensors and actuators in the project.
- *Oktal* – responsible for the design of car simulation program
- *Nexyad* – responsible for networking, scheduling, and transfer of data between project partners.
- *DPS* (Digital Product Simulation) – responsible for human-vehicle interface.
- *UVSQ* (University of Versailles St-Quentin-en-Yvelines) – responsible for combining various driving context parameters, detecting the actual driving situation and deducing the appropriate driving assistance actions appropriate for the situation.

Project CASA has two phases: as an ADAS simulated in the laboratory and as an ADAS simulated in the real vehicle. Here, we discuss Project CASA as an ADAS that is simulated in the laboratory. The interaction of CASA's system components is shown in Figure 1(b). A brief description is given below:

- The simulation uses a real vehicle cockpit. The cockpit is either that of a Peugeot or a Citroen vehicle. The various parameters representing the context of the vehicle (acceleration, brake, direction signal, etc.) are captured in real-time. They are sent and made available in the network. See Figure 2(a).
- We have a simulator that depicts a real-world driving environment. We can choose from various driving scenarios (i.e. city road, urban road, highway, etc.). In the simulator itself, various parameters representing the context of the environment (e.g. fog, visibility, pedestrian, stop sign, etc.) can be obtained and sent to the network. The simulator is shown in a large computer screen. Together, the cockpit and the simulator makes one feel that he/she is actually driving a vehicle, albeit inside the laboratory. See Figure 2(b).

- There is a common point of interaction – the repository called "DataNex". All the parameters representing the context of the environment, the vehicle and the driver are all made available in the DataNex repository.

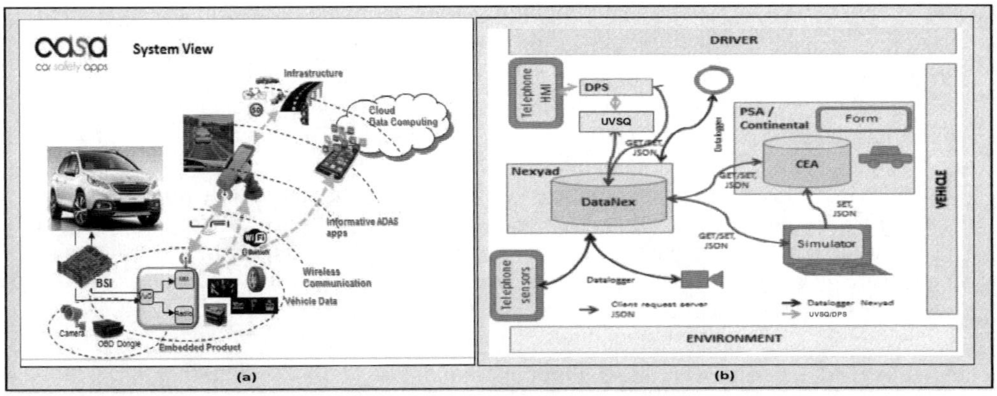

Figure 1. (a) CASA system view, (b) CASA sysem components interaction

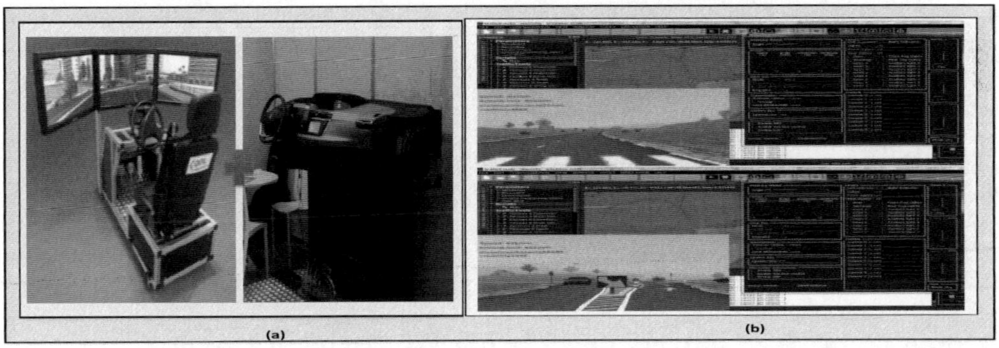

Figure 2. (a) Cockpit and driving simulator, (b) Driving scenario simulator

- The UVSQ group, through DataNex repository, collects the sample data coming from the vehicle (through the cockpit), the environment (through the simulator) and the driver himself. BSI (body systems interface) and OBD (on-board diagnostics) are vehicle gadgets that obtain parameters related to the vehicle. These data are fusioned together to detect the actual driving situation. Based upon the driving situation, there may be some actions that need to be implemented to assist the driver in the conduct of his driving. If there is a notification or alert message intended for the driver or an action intended to the vehicle itself, a message is sent to the DataNex repository.
- The message for the driver sent to the DataNex repository is recovered by the DPS's human-machine interface. It then broadcasts such message.
- The message that is intended for the vehicle is recovered from the DataNex repository and sent back to the vehicle, which then executes it. For example, the fog light needs to be activated in a foggy zone scenario. The CEA (see Figure 1(b)) component activates the signal corresponding to the fog light. The activated fog light is then manifested in the simulator.

4. ADAPTATION AND EVOLUTION OF DRIVER STATUS

This part is our work that is centered on the context of the driver, specifically the case of a stressed driver.

4.1 Driver Status

The driving context parameter of driver status is performed by consortium partner PSA. We will not deal here with the signal processing involved in the detection of such status. Instead, we receive this parameter and is already interpreted in the higher level of abstraction. Given below are the status of a driver:

- *Normal* – this generally refers to a relaxed driver who follows traffic rules and regulations.
- *Stressed* – this refers to a driver who appears somewhat focused yet driving is not normal. We consider three levels of stressed person: (i) *Low stressed* – manifested by irritation, (ii) *Medium stressed* – manifested by anger, and (iii) *Highly stressed* – manifested by being overly aggressive
- *Fatigued* – is an unfocused person, tired, one who might go to sleep while driving. We differentiate a fatigued person (coming from work) from one who just did physical exercise (fatigued from exercise). The one who comes from a physical activity has high heart beat rate and eyes well opened. The tired person coming from work has a normal heart beat rate but eyes are tired and might be detected as going to sleep. In this work, a fatigued person is limited to one who is exhausted from work.

4.2 Manifestation of a Stressed Driver

Stress has become one major factor that causes health problems. Hence, Kocielnik (Rafal Kocielnik 2013) et al attempted to present stress information, derived from sensors measurements in the context of a person's activities with an aim of achieving better stress balance. Rebolledo-Mendez et al (Genaro Rebolledo-Mendez 2014) proposes a detector of human emotions of which being tired and stress could be factors that are associated to traffic accidents.

According to New York State Vehicle and Traffic Law, a stressed driver does manifest in the following manners: (i) *excessive speed*, (ii) *frequent or unsafe lane changes*, (iii) *failure to signal*, (iv) *tailgating*, (v) *failure to yield the right of way*, (vi) *disregarding traffic controls*, and (vii) *driving under the influence of alcohol (impaired driving)*. We will use the two manifestations above – excessive speed and frequent or unsafe lane changes (events that describe others) – to determine the level of stress of a driver in our simulation

4.3 Sampling Driver's Stress Level Using Two Driving Events

Excessive speeding and frequent or unsafe lane changes are the two events that we consider to determine the stress level of a driver. We will consider each case accordingly. Consider a road with a speed limit (e.g. 50 km/h). A normal driver drives without over speeding (50 km/h or less). A stressed driver exceeds this limit. We create an association between subsets of stressed driver and the speed of a vehicle, as follows: (i) *low stressed*: speed within 10% in excess of speed limit, (ii) *medium stressed*: speed within 20% in excess of speed limit, and (iii) *highly stressed*: more than 20% in excess of speed limit.

We also consider the number of times the driver crosses the lane/white line within a road segment (i.e. road area located between two intersections). For our analysis, we divided this road into four zones (see Figure 3) and each zone's functionality is given below:

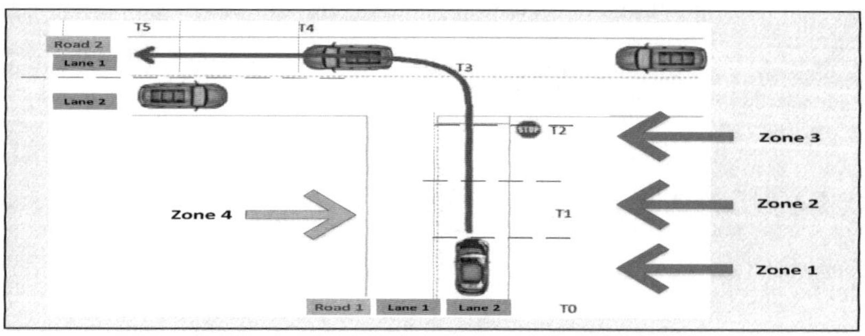

Figure 3. Partition of a road segment for the purpose of driving situation analysis

- Zone 1 – this zone is associated with notifying the driver (e.g. "*Turn left in 200 meters*")
- Zone 2 – this zone is associated with alerting the driver of what he has done (e.g. over speeding) or notifying him of what he has to do (e.g. *"Prepare to stop"*)
- Zone 3 – this zone is associated with assisting the driver on how to maneuver a complex task such as turning to the left in an intersection with many obstacles.
- Zone 4 – this zone is the traffic in the opposite direction and is associated with alerting the driver of being out of lane.

Siyaraman et al (Sayanan Siyaraman 2013) provided detailed work of lane and vehicle detection, localization and tracking. Petzoldt et al (Tibor Petzoldt 2014) noted the effect of changing lanes compromises the safety on the part of the driver. Concerning crossing white line/lane, we note that a normal driver does not cross the white line. A stressed driver, however, would cross the white line as follows: (i) *low stressed*: crossing the white line once; (ii) *medium stressed*: Crossing the white line twice; and (iii) *highly stressed*: Crossing the white line thrice or more. A driver crosses the white line if his vehicle moves from zone 1 to zone 4, from zone 2 to zone 4, or from zone 3 to zone 4.

4.4 Evolution of Stress Level due to Speeding

Given below is the evolution of the status of a driver with respect to over speeding. We consider four cases (S1 to S4). Each case describes a transition from the present status (any one status in the set) to a new status.

- Case 1: No over speeding: From (Normal | Low stressed | Medium stressed | Highly stressed) to Normal
- Case 2: Speeding in excess of up to 10% of speed limit: From (Normal | Low stressed | Medium stressed | Highly stressed) to Lowly stressed
- Case S3: Speeding in excess of up to 20% of speed limit: From (Normal | Low stressed | Medium stressed | Highly stressed) to Medium stressed
- Case S4: Speeding above 20% of speed limit: From (Normal | Low stressed | Medium stressed | Highly stressed) to Highly stressed

The state transition diagram that triggers the transition from one state to another due to variation in speeding is shown in Figure 4(Top).

4.5 Evolution of Stress Level due to Crossing Lane/White Line

Given below is the evolution of the status of a driver with respect to the number of times a driver crosses the white line within one turn left segment.

- Case 1: No crossing: From (Normal | Low stressed | Medium stressed | Highly stressed) to same status
- Case 2: Crossing once: From Normal to Low stressed; or From Low stressed to Low stressed; or From Medium stressed to Low stressed; or From Highly stressed to Medium stressed
- Case 3: Crossing twice: From (Normal | Low stressed | Medium stressed | Highly stressed) to Medium stressed
- Case 4: Crossing trice or more: From (Normal | Low stressed | Medium stressed | Highly stressed) to Highly stressed

The state transition diagram that triggers the transition from one state to another due to number of times a driver crosses the lane/white line that separates two traffic directions on the road is in Figure 4(Down).

4.6 Finding the New Status of the Driver

The new status of the driver is a function of his status evolution based on over speeding and on the number of times he crossed the lane/white line that separates two directions. The new driver's status is given below:

$$\text{New status} = \max(\text{New status due to over speeding}, \text{New status due to crossing white line}) \quad (1)$$

The above equation says that the new driver status is the higher of the new status due to over speeding and the new status due to crossing the white line. In order for this equation to hold, we need to assign numerical value to driver's status, hence the following: Normal = 0, Low Stressed = 1, Medium stressed = 2, Highly stressed = 3, and Fatigued = 4. To demonstrate the use of Equation 1, let us assume that at the beginning of the driving exercise, the user is "normal" (status 0). At the end of simulations of four turn-left segments, the driver status becomes "Highly stressed" (status = 3) with respect to crossing of the lanes/white lines. At the end of the driving exercise, however, the same driver did not overspeed, hence his status with respect to over speeding is normal (status = 0). His new status is calculated as follows:

- New status = max (New status due to overspeeding, New status due to crossing white line)
- New status = max (0, 3) = 3 = Highly stressed

In this sample case, our new driver status equation does not absolve a driver who crossed white lines several times just because he did not over speed.

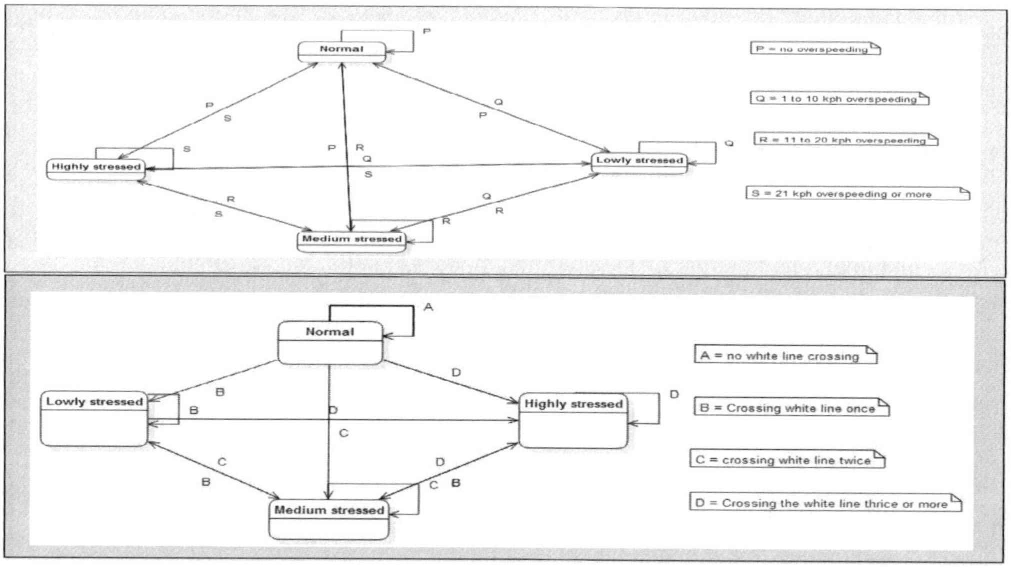

Figure 4. (Top) State transition diagram showing how speeding affects driver's status, (Down) State transition diagram showing how crossing the white line affects driver's status

4.7 Messages Not to Stress an Already Stressed Driver

In affective HCI, the emotional aspect of an interface is important. In our case, we have a stressed driver (Schießl 2007) and our goal is not to add further stress in conveying our driving assistance messages. To this end, we have consulted our colleagues (i.e. a psychologist and a driving instructor) to guide us in the type of messages that we can send to a stressed driver. We list down below the properties of these messages:

- A message of notification or alert must be short. A longer message is more appropriate to a normal driver.
- The voice in the notification or alert message should be calm.
- When available, a soft music background may be added to the driving assistance message
- When stress is manifested in a driver for a prolonged period (i.e. 15 minutes or more), a message informing the driver to take a break is sent.

For now, we are just dealing with two driver states: normal and stressed. Messages intended for fatigued driver will be implemented next.

4.8 Human-Vehicle Interaction Interface

Our HCI component receives messages from the fission component and such message needs to be relayed to the driver. The HCI interface is shown in Figure 5. As shown in Figure 5 (Top), the smartphone HCI home screen is shown. When a notification message is being broadcasted, it is manifested by a triangle with moving circles. A question to the driver is manifested by a square icon.

In Figure 5(Down), we are shown a snapshot of whether a certain feature should be on or off. In the diagram, we can see that monitoring a driver's capabilities and detection of fatigue are both set on. We are also shown the settings of the HCI interface.

For messages intended for the driver, we classify such message into two types:

1. *Notification* - a type of message that informs the driver of the event that is about to happen.
2. *Alert* - a type of message that warns the driver of an incoming hazard or the offense he has committed.

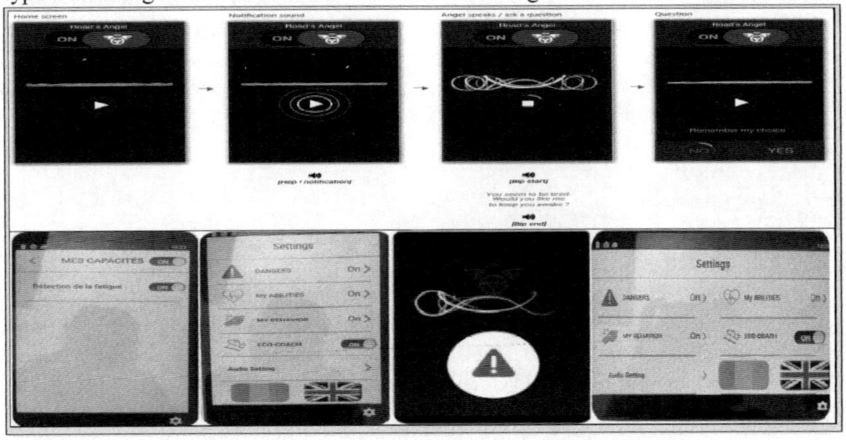

Figure 5. (Top) From left to right: Home screen, Notification sound, HCI asking the user a question and whether user answer should be remembered by the system. (Down) Form left to right: Fatigue Detection is on; Settings related to the driver's abilities, behaviour, green driving and danger; HCI danger alert

Regardless of the message classification, a driving situation requiring an assistance intervention may be in one of this category:

- *Behaviour* - a driving event is considered "behaviour" if this event happened because of the driver's action. For example, over speed. It is known that over speed will only occur if the driver exceeds the speed limit. As long as it is the driver that causes over speed, over speeding is a behavioural event. In general, in the behaviour category, the driver completely controls the situation.
- *Danger* - this category concerns a potential risk for the driver and all other players in the road. In this category, the danger is not under the control of the driver. For example, when entering a driving area with fog and low visibility, this situation is a "danger" event.
- *Ability* - this relates to the ability of the driver to continue driving. When the driver is detected fatigue, our system sends an alert message to inform him of his driving ability.

When two or more driving events occur at the same time, we know that it will be impossible to send two or more audio messages to the driver at the same time. To this end, we must determine the priorities of the messages and that the highest message is that to be sent to the driver: (i) "Notification" has a lower priority than the Alert; and (ii) "Behavior" has the lowest priority. "Ability" has absolute priority and "danger" is in the middle priority.

4.9 Public Reception

Project CASA was presented to the public during the European ITS[1] in Bordeaux, France on 5-9 October 2015. It was warmly received by the public that they were eager to know when this can be made available in the market. It was also received warmly that some journalists and experts in automobile featured it in their blogs, such as that of Laurent Meillaud's[2]. Project CASA is ongoing. The next phase will be its testing in the roads of Paris, France.

[1] http://2015.itsworldcongress.com/

[2] http://voituredufutur.blogspot.fr/

5. CONCLUSION

We have tested our CASA system using the simulation scheme in the laboratory and is shown in public. The public reaction is positive; some are asking when it will be completed and integrated into the actual vehicle. Preliminary test shows that by using our system, the driver's driving performance improves. When an infraction is committed and the driver is informed about it, he corrects his action, accordingly. The next time that the same user performs the test, previous infraction is no longer committed. Preliminary lab results indicate that our system helps in promoting safe driving environment. Our HCI interface is appropriate for an intelligent human-vehicle interaction. Future works include integrating machine learning capability, in particular, the cognitive user interface design (Peschl and Stary, 1998) and the cognitive component (John E. Kelley III, 2015) that learns new driving situation, reason with purpose and interact with humans naturally. This component will also learn from its experiences with the environment.

REFERENCES

A. Armand, et al. 2014. "Ontology-Based Context Awareness for Driving Assistance Systems." In *IEEE Intelligent Vehicles Symposium*, 227 – 33. Dearborn, MI, USA.

Bengler, Klaus, et al. 2014. "Three Decades of Driver Assistance Systems: Review and Future Perspectives." In *IEEE Intelligent Transportation Systems*, 6-32.

BOSCH. 2016. http://www.bosch.com/assets/en/company/innovation/theme03.htm.

Brioschi, Giacomo, et al. 2017. 'Computational intelligence on the cognition of driving context for a safe driving assistance system', *International Journal of Software Science and Computational Intelligence*, 9.

CVIS. http://www.cvisproject.org/.

Genaro Rebolledo-Mendez, Angelica Reyes, Sebastian Paszkowicz, Mari Carmen Domingo, Lee Skrypchuk. 2014. 'Developing a Body Sensor Network to Detect Emotions During Driving', *IEEE Transactions on Intelligent Transportation Systems*, 15: 1850 - 54.

Hina, Manolo Dulva, Hongyu Guan, Nan Deng, and Amar Ramdane-Cherif. "Secured Data Processing, Notification and Transmission for a Human-Vehicle Interaction System." In *ITSC 2016, IEEE Intelligent Transportation Systems Conference*. Rio de Janiero, Brazil.

John E. Kelly III. 2015. "Computing, cognition and the future of knowing: How humans and machines are forging a new age of understanding." In, 1-11.

Mercedes-Benz. 'Attention assist: protezione contro la stanchezza'. http://mercedes-benz.it/it_IT/attention-assist/detail.html.

Motors, Mitsubishi. 'Mitsubishi motors develops "new driver support system"'. http://www.mitsubishi-motors.com/en/corporate/pressrelease/corporate/detail429.html.

Nissan. 'Tmc develops collision avoidance assist system effective at high speeds'. https://www.jsae.or.jp/autotech/data_e/13-1e.html.

Peschl, Marcus F., and Chris Stary. 1998. 'The Role of Cognitive Modeling for User Interface Design Representations', *Mind and Machines*, 8: 203 - 36.

Planing, Patrick. 2014. 'The case of advance driver assistance systems.' in, *Innovation Acceptance* (Springer Gabler).

PREVENT. http://www.prevent-ip.org/.

Rafal Kocielnik, et al. 2013. "Smart Technologies for Long-Term Stress Monitoring At Work." In *26th IEEE International Symposium on Computer-based edical Systems*, 50 - 58. Poto, Portugal.

S. Al-Sultan, A. Al-Bayatti and H. Zedan. 2013. 'Context-Aware Driver Behavior Detection System in Intelligent Transportation Systems', *IEEE Transactions on Vehicular Technology*, 62: 4264 - 75.

SAFESPOT. www.safespot-eu.org.

Sayanan Siyaraman, Mohan Manubhai Trivedi. 2013. 'Integrated Lane and Vehicle Detection, Localization, and Tracking: A Synergistic Approach', *IEEE Transcations on Intelligent Transportation Systems*, 14: 906 - 17.

Schießl, Caroline. 2007. "Stress and Strain While Driving." In *Eurropean Conference of Transport Research Institutes*. Brno, Czech Republic.

Tibor Petzoldt, Stephanie Bruggemann, Josef F. Krems. 2014. 'Learning effects in the lane chnage task (LCT) - Realistic secondary tasks and transfer of learning', *Elsevier Applied Ergonomics*, 45: 639 - 46.

Vazquez Bergasa, Sotelo. 2004. "Real-time system for monitoring driver vigilance." In.: Departamento de Electronica Universidad de Alcala Madrid, Universidad Politecnica de Madrid.

THE EFFECTIVENESS AND USER SATISFACTION IN THE INTERFACE DESIGNED FOR DISABLED USERS – THE PILOT STUDY

Katarzyna Jach, Beata Bajcar and Anna Borkowska
Wrocław University of Science and Technology, Wybrzeże Wyspiańskiego 27, 50-370 Wrocław, Polamd

ABSTRACT

The main goal of this paper is the analysis of relations between usability of the tested system and its evaluation made by respondents from the target group. The system tested in the experiment, called Face Controller, is designed to operate the computer by head movements and facial expressions and it is dedicated to users with severe disabilities (i.e. spinal cord damages, tetraplegia). The users' effectiveness was measured by number of tasks done, and their satisfaction by ISO 9241-9 Device Assessment Questionnaire. To find the sources of discrepancy between the effectiveness achieved by the subjects (average level) and satisfaction (very high), the analysis of free answers categorized by three competent judges was done. Probably asymmetry of attribution of failure and success leads to conclusion that the failure or difficulty in using the system is attributed by disabled users rather internally (efficiency shortage), while success - externally.

KEYWORDS

Satisfaction, effectiveness, subjective usability, disabled users, Face Controller

1. INTRODUCTION

The main goal of this paper is an analysis of relations between usability of a tested system and its evaluation made by the respondents from the target group. The new system, called Face Controller (FC system) is dedicated for people with severe physical disability and its usability has not been assessed earlier. The basic variable analyzed in this project is usability of the system, also known as a quality of use. Usability testing was designed based on the definition contained in ISO 9241-11: "Usability is a measure of effectiveness, efficiency and user satisfaction with which the product can be used to achieve the purpose by users in a given context." Therefore, the study focused on measuring the effectiveness of the system, that is, finding the extent to which the evaluated system allows and helps users achieve their goals. It was also conducted to measure user satisfaction, that is, their subjective feelings related to the operation of the system (ISO 9241-11). To a lesser extent, studies were focused on measuring the effectiveness, i.e. relationship between outlays (eg. time) to effect, as an indicator less important both for the target group of users of the system, as well as to the context of use of the system.

Satisfaction is a broad and non-homogenous notion. In psychology, satisfaction is defined as subjective well-being, positive emotional and cognitive evaluation of certain object or area of functioning (eg. work) (Diener et al, 1985). In the previous version of ISO 9241-11 standard (1998), satisfaction used to be defined as "freedom from discomfort, and positive attitudes towards the use of the product". However, in the new draft version the satisfaction meaning was wider: "the extent to which attitudes related to the use of a system, product or service and the emotional and physiological effects arising from use are positive or negative" (Bevan et.al. 2015). Finally, in the current version of standard (still under development) satisfaction is defined as "person's perceptions and responses that result from the use of a system, product or service" with an additional note "'satisfaction is a component of usability and of user experience" (ISO/DIS 9241-11, 2015).

The relation between single characteristics of usability has been the investigation object since the very beginning of usability research. For example, Greene, et.al. (1992) reported that "user performance mirrored the preference data." Simultaneously, in the early nineties Nielsen and Levy (1994) analyzed over one hundred cases from 57 HCI studies and stated strong positive association between users' average performance and subjective satisfaction. However, in the same time Hufnagel (1990) doubted in use satisfaction of user ratings as measures of system effectiveness, which can be explained by differentiated attributions of success and failure (Weiner 1985). Hufnagel observed users with a high performance and he saw the source of their success in their own effort, while a weak performance was perceived as a result of poor system quality. Similarly, Bailey (1993) recommended separating clearly users' performance and preferences. Walker et al. noticed that users in the situation of choice between two different interfaces preferred more often the less effective one. This observation was interpreted by the authors in the context of users preferences determined not only by quantitative but qualitative aspects of interface as well (Walker at al. 1998).

Frøkjær et al. (2000) analyzed 19 usability studies and found the relations between three basic aspects of usability are not well understood and weakly related and therefore they recommend an independent analysis of the three mentioned usability areas in order to find the full usability assessment (Frøkjær et al 2000). More complex analysis was made by Kasper Hornbæk and Effie Lai-Chong Law in 2007. On the basis of the raw data from 73 surveys they found the correlations between different usability aspects relatively low. Pearson's product-moment correlation with 95% confidence interval between effectiveness and satisfaction one of 0.164 ± 0.062. Moreover, they found that users' perception of phenomena are generally not highly related with objective measures. On the other hand they stated that 86% of the analyzed studies show a positive correlation between effectiveness and satisfaction. It is worth noticing that their analysis was conducted on the very broad HCI domains, which can influence the final result. Much more higher correlations were stated in more specific researches. For example, Huffman and Hochster (2007) observed a strong correlation (over 0.7) between the relevance of results and user satisfaction in different search tasks. The similar highly correlated results were found between user's satisfaction and a system effectiveness by Thomas and Hawking (2006). Al-Maskari and Sanderson (2010) also confirmed their hypothesis that user effectiveness influences user satisfaction by showing a significant relation between these two variables ($r = .55$). The similar findings were made by Su (2003) and Law, Klobučar and Pipan (2006). Though, as in most cases the positive correlation between effectiveness and satisfaction is observed, all these findings show that a problem of relationship between these usability characteristics is ambiguous and complex and more investigation in this area is needed.

2. THE EVALUATED SYSTEM

The tested system, called Face Controller (FC), is dedicated to people with disabilities and it is an original solution created by Polish enterprise Risenbit. According to the creator's intentions, the system is designed for computer usage by people with severe disabilities that hinder using the computer in the standard configuration. Face Controller (FC) is a system for tracking the user's face and moving the cursor on the screen in response to head movements of the user. Additionally, Face Controller emulates a standard computer mouse by assigning chosen by user facial expressions (eye blinking, smile, mouth opening, etc.) to its different functions like left, right or double click. Disabled persons can therefore independently control the computer using head movements and facial expressions only. FC differs from other solutions of this type that makes use of the existing commercial game controllers Microsoft Kinect. The system works with both laptop and a traditional monitor. At the time of the software calibration, the user can assign some facial expressions to the basic functionalities and specify preferences sensitivity gestures. A set of cameras build in the Microsoft Kinect allows for precise tracking over 2000 points on the user's face with 30 Hz frequency. The schematic view of FC interface is shown on Figure 1.

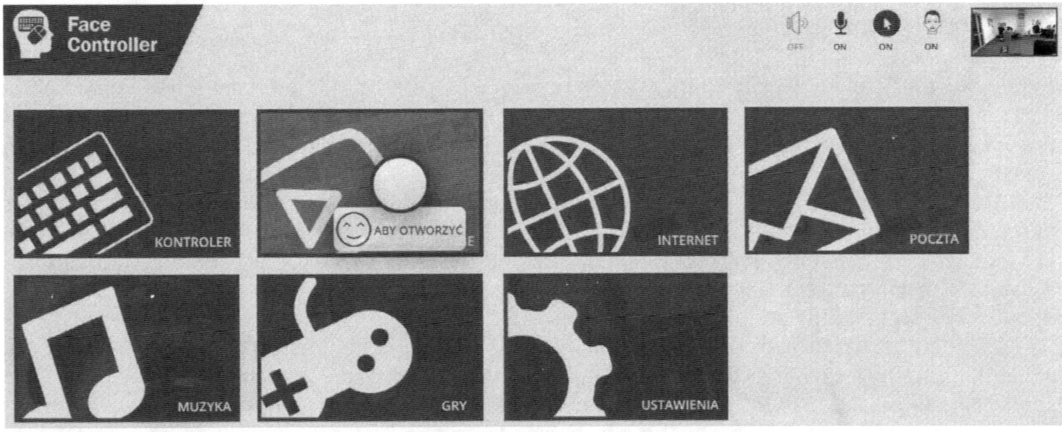

Figure 1. The schematic view of Face Controller interface with the cursor control (white dot) and a chosen gesture for click (a smile). Source: the image published with Risenbit consent

3. METHOD

3.1 Procedure and Measure

Before the first contact of participants with the FC system, their initial attitude toward system was checked, then they could acquaint with FC system. In the next step, we asked the participants about assessing their attitude toward FC (after the first contact/use and before FC testing). In the session of FC testing, participants performed four tasks. There were typical actions, which the user usually performs on the computer. The first task concerned the file operations (finding, opening and closing the file). In the second task, users performed arithmetic operation on the computer calculator. The third task was to check the information on a specific website (i.e., run a web browser, enter an online store, find and select a search product, check its price). In the fourth task, subjects wrote a short message via e-mail to a service online store. After tasks the user satisfaction and effectiveness of the task realization were assessed.

The effectiveness was measured by level of performance of the task with the use of FC system. The performance level is an aggregated result of the performed tasks. A score of 100 means performing all tasks, 25 score - one performed task, 50 score – two performed tasks, and 75 – three performed tasks, and the result of 0 means not performing any task

The satisfaction of the FC users was measured by questionnaire constructed on the basis of ISO 9241:9 standard. However, the original version of *ISO 9241-9 Device Assessment Questionnaire* includes questions about fatigue of some body parts which are not involved during work with Face Controller (finger, wrist, arm). Because of the adaptation of Device Assessment Questionnaire some modifications were needed. The questions about fatigue of eyes, mouth and face were added to the survey form. Participants rated specific aspects of the satisfaction on the 7-point scale. For the item referring to system ratings, there was used a bipolar scale used (*1 - too low; 4 – moderately; 7 - too high*), and to items describing fatigue, the unipolar scale was used (*1 – none; 4 – on average; 7 – very high*) (ISO 9241-9:2000).

A general evaluation of the system made by potential users was examined during the study, also in qualitative manner. After completing all the tasks, the participants were asked about the sources of satisfaction and dissatisfaction. These questions were open and the respondents had complete freedom in answering what they liked most about the tested system and what they did not like most. It was assumed that the source of satisfaction associated with using the new system may be of varied nature - can be either internal (such as efficiency of users or a level of their expectations) or external (such as quality of technical solutions or level of advancement of the prototype system). All free answers were recorded and categorized by three competent judges, who were experts in the field of ergonomics and psychology, experienced in the diagnosis of satisfaction, usability systems and the human-computer interaction. The detailed description of the procedure is available in the full research report (Bajcar et al 2017).

3.2 Participants

In the test of FC system, 30 physically disabled persons took part, including 4 women and 26 men aged 20 to 58 years (M_{age} = 33.0, SD_{age} = 9.38). The overrepresentation of men in the study sample may be due to the dominant type of disability. Among the causes of disability of participants had had trauma to the cervical spinal cord (mostly due to jump into the water, and a few cases of traffic accidents) and cerebral palsy (with the paresis of lower and upper limbs). In the tested sample 23.3% of participants use the computer almost every day, and 76.6% - for several hours a day. Moreover, they rated their computer skills as average (13.3%), good (30%) and very good (56.7%). Before the main session of FC testing, participants could acquaint with FC system. More than half of participants (53%) spent an average of about 1 hour, 33% - of from 1 to 3 hours, and the other - over three hours.

Moreover, the assessment of disability by Gross Motor Function Classification System (GMFCS) was made. This is a five level clinical classification system that describes the gross motor function of people with cerebral palsy on the basis of self-initiated movement abilities. Distinctions between levels are based on functional abilities, the need for walk supporting and the actual quality of movement (Palisano et al, 2008). All the test participants were classified at the 4th or 5th level of disability, which means they cannot independently walk, they use a wheelchair to move and they are impaired in all areas of motor function.

4. RESULTS

4.1 Effectiveness of Face Controller System Use

First, we checked the level of computer skills, including frequency, method and scope of computer use in everyday life. All the respondents use the computer every day or almost every day, usually for a few hours. Most of the respondents (27 people) do not require an assistant to the computer literacy. Almost half of the participants uses a traditional mouse and a keyboard (16 people) and a touchpad (13 persons), individuals use a joystick, a trackball or a tablet. On the five-point scale respondents rated their computer skills as high (M = 4.5, SD = 1,45). The participants highly evaluated their proficiency in performing common tasks in the field of computer literacy including confidence in saving files, use e-mail, search information, documents editing, a spreadsheet usage, online purchases and bank accounts handling. These results indicate that the limitations in the system usage are not the effect of poor computer skills.

In the context of the above data, we examined the level of the effectiveness of the task performance. The full effectiveness 53% of the respondents achieved, that is, they have done all the tasks. The others received a lower efficiency. Thus, 27% of people completed three, 3% - 2 tasks, 7% - one task of the four tasks. In addition, 10% of respondents performed no tasks (see Fig. 2). Therefore, for further analysis, the sample was divided into two subgroups; the first one – with a full effectiveness and the second one - with a limited effectiveness.

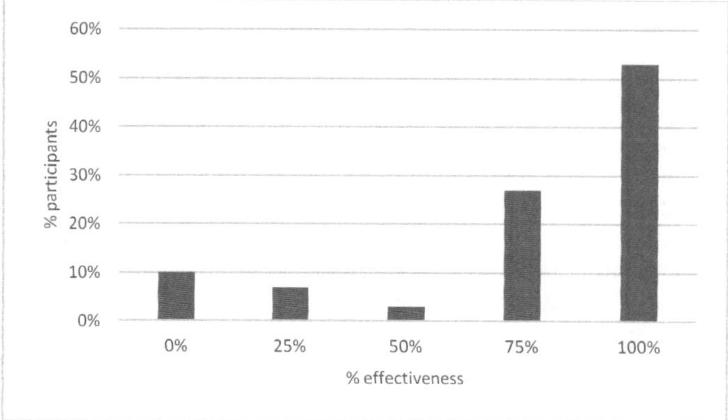

Figure 2. Effectiveness of FC users in task series performance (N = 29)

4.2 Effectiveness and User Comfort

As depicted in Table 1, assessment of specific aspects of comfort of FC system use (force to actuation, physical and mental effort, operation speed and smoothness, accurate pointing) are high, and aspects related to fatigue individual body parts (as face, mouth, eyes, shoulder, neck) are relatively low. Finally, the overall comfort and ease of use were also high.

Table 1. Mean, standard deviation, and rho Spearman's correlation coefficients between subjective usability dimensions and effectiveness and computer skills (N = 29)

	M	*SD*	Effectiveness	Computer skills
1. Force to actuation	4.21	1.08	-.44*	-.15
2. Smoothness during operation	4.29	1.08	-.37	-.28
3. Mental effort required for operation	4.28	.96	-.15	-.13
4. Physical effort required for operation	3.59	1.64	.01	-.33
5. Accurate pointing	4.79	1.61	.32	-.05
6. Operation speed	4.28	2.03	.47**	.17
7. Eyes fatigue	2.62	1.78	-.43*	-.34
8. Mouth fatigue	2.34	1.61	-.52**	-.38*
9. Face fatigue	2.69	1.95	-.54**	-.52**
10. Shoulder fatigue	2.45	1.96	-.39*	-.20
11. Neck fatigue	3.41	2.06	-.23	-.24
12. General comfort	5.34	1.59	.34	.01
13. Input device	5.52	1.79	.46*	.27
14. Effectiveness	76.67	33.43	-	.23

* $p < .05$, ** $p < .01$

The correlation analysis results shows that computer skills did not relate with usability dimensions, excluding the part of the body used more often in the testing of FC (as mouth, face and eyes). It means FC system is an adequate tool for people independently of their computer competencies level. The study identified some significant interrelationships between high effectiveness of the tasks performance and too low force to actuation, and high operation speed in the use of FC. On the other hand, low effectiveness was related with high fatigue of face, mouth, and eyes.

Analyzing the assessment of the FC before and after the test of system, it may be noted that there is no relationship between an attitude towards the system (measured before and after the first contact with the system) and effectiveness. There was also no relationship between attitudes toward system and post-testing ratings (ie. a general comfort and input device). Moreover, there was a significant and moderate correlation between effectiveness and general comfort of FC system use, and moderate but non-significant correlation between an input device and effectiveness (see Table 2).

Table 2. rho Spearman's correlations between attitude toward FC and general comfort, device and effectiveness (N = 29)

	1	*2*	*3*	*4*	*5*
1. Attitude toward FC (before first contact with system)	-				
2. Attitude toward FC (after first contact with system)	.50**	-			
3. General comfort of FC system use	.07	.29	-		
4. Input device of FC system	-.04	.20	.74**	-	
5. Effectiveness	.07	.08	.34	.46*	-

* $p < .05$, ** $p < .01$

When we compared the results on the dimensions of FC system evaluations, some significant differences between groups with total and limited effectiveness were revealed (Table 3). Persons with limited effectiveness manifested higher smoothness, but lower accuracy and speed operation than those with total effectiveness. In addition, limited effective participants declared higher fatigue of eyes, face, mouth, shoulder, than total effective persons. The input device and general comfort of FC system use were higher for the total than the limited effectiveness. These results showed that FC system was evaluated as good and not too tiring for. Generally, FC users were satisfied with the system use, evaluating highly the functions of the system and estimating low the level of fatigue and discomfort.

Table 3. Differences in the subjective usability dimensions in the dependence of level of effectiveness

	Limited effectiveness		Full effectiveness			
	M	*SD*	*M*	*SD*	U^a	*p*
Force to actuation	4.62	1.45	3.88	0.50	75,50	,077
Smoothness during operation	4.83	1.34	3.88	0.62	60,00	,044
Mental effort required for operation	4.54	1.33	4.06	0.44	77,00	,173
Physical effort required for operation	3.62	2.14	3.56	1.15	90,00	,529
Accurate pointing	4.08	1.80	5.38	1.20	56,00	,028
Operation speed	3.00	1.73	5.31	1.66	38,00	,003
Eyes fatigue	3.62	1.90	1.81	1.22	47,00	,008
Mouth fatigue	3.31	1.84	1.56	0.81	43,50	,005
Face fatigue	3.77	2.09	1.81	1.33	42,50	,004
Shoulder fatigue	3.31	2.29	1.75	1.34	60,00	,029
Neck fatigue	4.15	2.34	2.81	1.64	66,00	,088
General comfort	4.54	1.90	6.00	0.89	55,00	,027
Input device	4.38	1.98	6.44	0.89	41,00	,004

Note: ^{a} Mann–Whitney *U* test coefficient

4.3 Subjective Sources of User Satisfaction and Dissatisfaction

Beyond the quantitative variables, the qualitative data were also collected and analyzed. These data relate to general evaluations of the system. Categories indicated by respondents in free statements are interpreted as the source of their satisfaction of the system and of interaction with it. The following Tables 4 and 5, present categories created by the competent judges and describing the features and elements of the FC, which were most liked and most disliked by the participants, and examples of original answers to these categories.

Table 4. Categories of features and elements of the FC which most liked by the participants (N = 29)

Categories	Occurrences	Examples
Simplicity, intuitiveness, ease of use	*11*	*Control easy to understand*
Technical and social assumptions of the system dedicated to people with disabilities	*7*	*Idea of the project;* *The idea of using a computer for people with larger paralysis*
Autonomy for people with severe disabilities	*6*	*Finally, I will be able to operate in a sitting position without assistance; I can do it all myself*
Ability to customize functioning of the system	*3*	*Ability to customize*
Application versatility	*3*	*Variety of gestures that can be assigned to*

It seems that the categories used by the participants at the positive assessment and an expression of satisfaction refer rather to the principles of the system and the possibilities that it offers. Respondents focused less on technical and functional aspects, and more often talked about what might happen generally in everyday functioning of people with disabilities - in the context of their independence, efficiency and preventing exclusion.

Table 5. Categories of features and elements of the FC which most disliked by the participants (N = 29)

Categories	Occurrences	Examples
Difficulties in the operate and acquisition practice	*8*	*Hard to adapt in to operate the system*
Difficulties in handling small components	*4*	*Difficulty in targeting small buttons*
Technical problems on the side of the system	*4*	*As I turn, the system disconnects unnecessarily*
Problems with the recognition of gestures	*6*	*Errors in detecting gesture*
No possibility of voice text input	*3*	*Inability to write with voice*
No negatives	*8*	*I like everything*

In case of negative evaluations, the respondents focused on the features of the system, that generate specific technical problems (early, prototype version of the system, or lack of some functionalities). On the other hand, they referred to the difficulties associated with their condition and problems in the acquisition of practice (although it should be noted that almost all the participants had definitely little experience and a brief training with the new system). After a general qualitative analysis of categories used by the respondents to evaluate the system, in the next step the whole group of respondents was divided according to the criterion level of efficiency. Two groups were created: the first one consisting of people who have done all the tasks and the second one consisting of people who did not perform at least one task. Comparison of the two groups shows that they are also significantly different considering the quality categories used to provide a subjective evaluation of the tested system. The effective group generated more complex and varied responses. In positive assessments, the following categories prevailed: "simplicity, intuitiveness and ease of use" and " technical and social assumptions of the system dedicated to people with disabilities". Negative evaluations of respondents from this group referred rather to the internal attribution ("difficult to operate and acquisition practice"). They also pointed more often also to the category of "no negatives". The less effective individuals alluded in positive evaluations to general assumptions and the idea of the project, while the negative assessments focused on technical problems and problems with recognition of gestures.

5. CONCLUSIONS

In order to find the explanation for discrepancy between user's effectiveness and satisfaction we focused on psychological mechanisms. However, probably more factors need to be taken into account. Griffiths, Johnson and Hartley (2007) found that user satisfaction is not a single construct on the basis of user evaluation of system effectiveness, but it is influenced by different factors, connected with the system, its context of use and the user himself/herself. They notice influence of system output, system type, and task difficulty as well as user expectation and attitude, perceived ease of use and usefulness.

Interpretation of the results achieved in this study confirms the significant influence of psychological factors on the evaluation of computer systems. These mechanisms probably also cause a discrepancy between the effectiveness achieved by the subjects (average level) and satisfaction (high). In this particular case, (system dedicated to people with disabilities) probably asymmetry of attribution of failure and success leads to the fact that the failure or difficulty in using the system is attributed rather to internally (efficiency shortage), while success - externally. As it seems respondents may consider the success as a system idea itself, work on the improvement and intended it for the disabled and often neglected group of people.

It should be emphasized that other variables, analyzed throughout the project (eg. attitudes to study situation and expectations for the new system evaluated before the testing phase) and the context of research as well as the situation of the subjects, quite clearly indicate their impact on the positive assessment of the system. This might mean that the respondents did not assess the effectiveness and usability of the system, and even their own efficiency in handling it, but most of all the system as a support for the disadvantaged people and people threatened with a digital, social or professional exclusion. In this context, the results presented in the article are not surprising, however, they indicate a fairly high positive assessment of the system and high levels of satisfaction while moderate efficacy (half of the respondents did not passed all - a fairly simple, tasks). The high level of respondents satisfaction is not much due to expectation and conviction of the possibility of specific tasks completion and work with the system, as to the hope of strengthening their own autonomy, the overall efficiency of life (communication, social areas, etc.), and other possibilities of their own plans of using a computer. It also seems that part of the high positive evaluation system FC is connected with appreciating the fact of the idea of support for the disabled, recognizing and understanding their problems and attempting to solve them. Caring for people with disabilities, and combating their exclusion, unfortunately, is still not a standard and system solution in Poland.

In the analysis and interpretation of the results one should not forget about the particular context and how the research was conducted. First of all - besides the effectiveness - the majority of measures has subjective and declarative, not behavioral character. This may make participants' analyzed evaluations biased. Secondly, the level of difficulty of tasks used to measure the effectiveness was not validated on a group of disabled. Thirdly - the tested system is a prototype and research project - pilot studies conducted on a small, specific group of people interested in such systems (hence the significant number of men in the study group).

ACKNOWLEDGEMENT

The research was conducted at the Wroclaw University of Science and Technology, Poland in cooperation with Polish society "Association for Your New Opportunities".

REFERENCES

Al-Maskari, A. and Sanderson, M., 2010. A review of factors influencing user satisfaction in information retrieval. *Journal of the American Society for Information Science and Technology*. Vol. 61, No.5, pp. 859-868.

Bailey, R.W., 1993. Performance vs. Preference. *Proceedings of the Human Factors and Ergonomics Society Annual Meeting,* Vol. 37, No. 4, pp. 282 – 286.

Bajcar B., Borkowska A., Dzidowski A., Jach K., Kuliński M., Krzos P., Piwińska J., 2017. Raport z testów systemu Face Controller [Face Controller Testing Report], published 15.02.2017 at http://www.tnm.org.pl/facecontroler/2017/02/15/raport-z-testow-systemu-face-controller/.

Bevan N., Carter J., Harker S., 2015, ISO 9241-11 Revised: What Have We Learnt About Usability Since 1998?. In: Kurosu M. (eds) *Human-Computer Interaction: Design and Evaluation. HCI 2015. Lecture Notes in Computer Science*, vol 9169. Springer, Cham, pp.143-151.

Diener, E., Emmons, R. A., Larsen, R. J., GrifÞ n, S., 1985. The satisfaction with life scale. *Journal of Personality Assessment*, Vol. 49, No. 1, pp. 71–75.

Frøkjær E., Hertzum M., Hornbæk K., 2000. Measuring usability: are effectiveness, efficiency, and satisfaction really correlated? *Proceedings of the SIGCHI conference on Human Factors in Computing Systems (CHI '00)*. ACM, New York, NY, USA, pp. 345-352.

Griffiths J.R., Johnson F., Hartley R.J., 2007, User satisfaction as a measure of system performance. *Journal of Librarianship and Information Science*, Vol 39, No. 3, pp. 142 – 152.

Hornbæk, K. and Law, E. L-C., 2007. Meta-analysis of correlations among usability measures. *Proceedings of the SIGCHI Conference on Human Factors in Computing Systems (CHI '07).* ACM, New York, NY, USA, pp. 617-626.

Huffman, S.B., and Hochster, M., 2007. How well does result relevance predict session satisfaction? *Proceedings of the 30th Annual International ACM SIGIR Conference on Research and Development in Information Retrieval* (pp. 567–574). NewYork: ACM Press.

Hufnagel, E.M., 1990. User satisfaction - are we really measuring system effectiveness. *Proceedings of the 23rd Annual Hawaii International Conference on System Science* Piscataway, NJ: IEEE Computer Society. ISO 9241:9, pp. 237–446.

ISO 9241-11: 1998. Ergonomic requirements for office work with visual display terminals (VDTs) - Part 11 Guidance on usability.

ISO 9241-9:2000. Ergonomic requirements for office work with visual display terminals (VDTs) - Part 9: Requirements for non-keyboard input devices.

ISO/DIS 9241-11.2(en), 2015, Ergonomics of human-system interaction — Part 11: Usability: Definitions and concepts.

Law, E. L-C., Klobučar, T., Pipan, M., 2006. User Effect in Evaluating Personalized Information Retrieval Systems. *Proceedings of First European Conference on Technology-enhanced Learning (EC-TEL 2006),* Greece, Springer Lecture Notes on Computer Science (LNCS)

Nielsen, J. and Levy, J., 1994. Measuring usability: preference vs. performance. *Communications of the ACM* 37, Vol. 4, pp. 66-75.

Palisano, R., Rosenbaum, P., Walter, S., Russell, D., Wood, E., Galuppi, B., 2008. Development and reliability of a system to classify gross motor function in children with cerebral palsy. Developmental Medicine & Child Neurology. Vol. 39, No. 4, pp. 214–223.

Su, L.T., 2003. A comprehensive and systematic model of user evaluation of Web search engines: II. An evaluation by undergraduates. *Journal of the American Society for Information Science and Technology*, Vol.54, No.13, pp. 1193–1223.

Thomas, P., and Hawking, D., 2006. Evaluation by comparing result sets in context. *Proceedings of the Conference on Information and Knowledge Management (CIKM)* (pp. 94–101). NewYork: ACM Press.

Walker, M.A. et al, 1998. What can I say?: evaluating a spoken language interface to Email. In Karat, C.M. et al, (Eds.), *Proceedings of the SIGCHI Conference on Human Factors in Computing Systems* (CHI '98) (pp. 582-589). ACM Press/Addison-Wesley Publishing Co., New York, NY, USA.

Weiner, B.,1985. An attributional theory of achievement motivation and emotion. *Psychological Review*, Vol. 92, No. 4, pp. 548-573.

HANDS-FREE READING BRAILLE WITH A VIBROTACTILE WRISTBAND

Simon Schätzle[1], Bernhard Weber[1], and Benedikt Leichtmann[2]
[1]German Aerospace Center (DLR), Institute of Robotics and Mechatronics,
Muenchener Str. 20, 82234 Wessling, Germany
[2]Universität der Bundeswehr München, Human Factors Institute,
Werner-Heisenberg-Weg 39, 85579 Neubiberg, Germany

ABSTRACT

In this paper, a new approach to display Braille is presented. Braille dots are mapped to six tactors of a vibrotactile wristband. The dot patterns of characters are displayed with adequate vibrotactile stimuli generated by the tactors. Compared to the conventional way of reading Braille, the advantage of the proposed approach is that there is no need to commit a hand to active Braille dot scanning and thus, the hand is still free for other activities or tasks.

In a user study, different methods of mapping Braille to the wristband with respect to the assignment of cell dots to tactors as well as temporal aspects were evaluated using objective performance data and subjective ratings. Even with little training, promising results were obtained. Sequential mapping methods performed better than parallel methods and characters could be correctly recognized in up to 97% of cases.

KEYWORDS

Vibrotactile Feedback, Braille, Assistive Technology for Blind People.

1. INTRODUCTION

As a consequence of an impairment or loss of visual perception, blind or visually impaired people depend on their auditory and haptic channel for receiving information. It is well known that blind people can partially compensate the loss in visual channel by improving other senses like their haptic abilities. Several studies showed better tactile spatial acuity of blind in comparison to sighted people (Wong et al., 2011; Goldreich and Kanics, 2003; Goldreich and Kanics, 2006; Legge et al., 2008). Particularly for deaf-blind persons or when acoustic presentation of information to blind people is impossible or uncomfortable, using Braille is a common way to convey information. Braille is a tactile writing system with tiny palpable bumps used to represent letters through raised dot patterns. Each letter is coded with six dots in a matrix with two columns and three rows. Usually, embossed paper or electronic braille displays are used as output. In any case, the fingertip is necessary to feel the text which means that the hand cannot be used for other purposes while reading Braille.

In this paper, we introduce a new approach of presenting information to blind or visually impaired people without using their auditory channel and without blocking the hand for other activities or tasks. To this, tactile stimuli generated by a vibrotactile wristband are used. A review of the state-of-the-art reveals the potential of (vibro-)tactile feedback and the variety of applications such as sensory substitution, spatial orientation, navigation and motion guidance, exploration of virtual environments, communication, messages and multimedia in which tactile displays (Benali-Khoudja, 2004) have been deployed (Choi and Kuchenbecker, 2013; Jones and Sarter, 2008; Elliot et al., 2009). Depending on the application, the stimulation is applied to different locations such as fingertip (Galambos, 2012), hand (Yang et al., 2009), arm (Bark et al., 2011; Bosman et al., 2003; Kapur et al., 2010; Lehtinen et al. 2012; McDaniel, 2010; Piateske and Jones, 2005; Tadakuma and Howe, 2009), torso (Lindemann et al., 2006; Schroeder et al., 2015, Van Erp, 2004) or foot (Meier et al., 2015).

The design of vibrotactile displays and relevant issues such as the spatial and temporal resolution of the skin, the absolute and differential perception thresholds, spatial masking, apparent location, temporal enhancement, adaptation and frequency, amplitude and duration of stimuli have been intensively investigated and published in useful guidelines (Jones and Sarter, 2008; Cheung et al., 2008; Cholewiak and Collins, 2003; Cholewiak et al., 2001; Pongrac, 2006; Van Erp, 2002; Choi and Kuchenbecker, 2013). Furthermore, the conveyance of semantic information through vibrotactile stimuli has been explored with variations in the number and placement of tactors as well as in the modulation of signals (Pietrzak et al., 2009; Nicolau et al., 2013; Brown, 2007; Brewster and Brown, 2004; Yatani, 2009). The so-called "Vibratese" (Geldard, 1957) for example used five tactors on the upper body to encode information with variations in intensity and signal length. Similar to that, "Optohapt" used nine vibration motors that are scattered over the body (Geldard, 1966).

Besides the output of semantic information, displaying Braille with vibrotactile stimuli is not a novelty (Guerreiro, 2013). With UbiBraille, Nicolau et al. (2013) mapped Braille to six vibrotactile actuators that were attached to the user's index, middle and ring finger of both hands. Inspired by writing Braille characters, raised cell dots are displayed with vibrotactile stimuli on the fingers that are commonly used to write the given Braille character. Compared to this mapping, we pursue the idea of assigning cell dots to tactors based on a projection of the Braille cell into the cross section of the arm (see Fig. 1). Furthermore, in contrast to the simultaneously output of raised dots in the study of Nicolau et al., we also evaluated sequential and simultaneous methods.

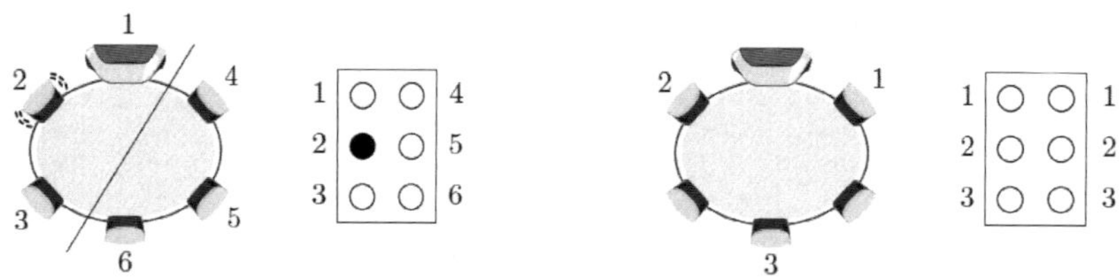

Figure 1. Assignment of Braille dots to the tactors if all tactors of VibroTac (left) or if only three tactors (right) are used

Other approaches known in the state-of-the-art uses touchscreens of mobile devices to display Braille vibrotactilly with the disadvantage that the hands are engaged in the reading process (Rantala, 2009; Jayant, 2010; Al-Quadah, 2011). Furthermore, individual encodings e.g. in the latter case (combinations of raised and unraised dots within a Braille character column is displayed through different encodings inspired by the Morse code) lead to high training effort.

In contrast to such approaches with own coding schemes, we use the well-known writing system Braille. Thus, only the mapping of the six dots to the six tactors of the wristband has to be learned. Compared to directly reading Braille with the fingertip, using VibroTac as a display for Braille is expected to be advantageous in situations where the user's hands need to be available for manipulative tasks (e.g. in the context of professional integration) or when usual tactile displays are complicated to use (e.g. while moving or as navigation hints e.g. "Caution, rotating door" on travel). Even though we expect the vibrotactile Braille reading to be slower than classical Braille reading, the proposed approach should be well suited to convey short messages.

This paper reports a user study we performed to evaluate the general usability of this approach and of VibroTac for displaying Braille characters. We designed different mapping methods that appeared reasonable to us and compared them in terms of performance data and subjective ratings. Due to the difficulty of recruiting blind people for such a time-consuming evaluation, we decided to conduct this study with sighted people. Consequently, the study was designed in a way that Braille literacy is not required: subjects had to reproduce the presented dot patterns on a print-out of blank characters without identifying the characters themselves. Though we expect better results for blind people as they are superior in tactile acuity and perception tasks than sighted people (Goldreich, 2003), further studies with blind people will be necessary (see section 6 for future work).

As the number of different methods claims high demand in terms of effort and required time of subjects, the evaluation experiments were split into two parts. In a pilot study (see section 4) with four subjects, we aimed at the evaluation of all presented methods in terms of usability and at the reduction of the number of methods. In the main study (see section 5), a selection of the best methods was investigated in detail with 18 subjects.

2. THE VIBROTACTILE WRISTBAND VIBROTAC

The vibrotactile output of Braille is realized with VibroTac (see Fig. 2), a tactile feedback device which was developed at the German Aerospace Center (DLR). This battery driven and wireless controllable wristband comprises six vibration motors (tactors) that are distributed around the arm in equal distances. Each of the tactors can be separately and continuously adjustable in frequency and shape (Schätzle et al., 2010).

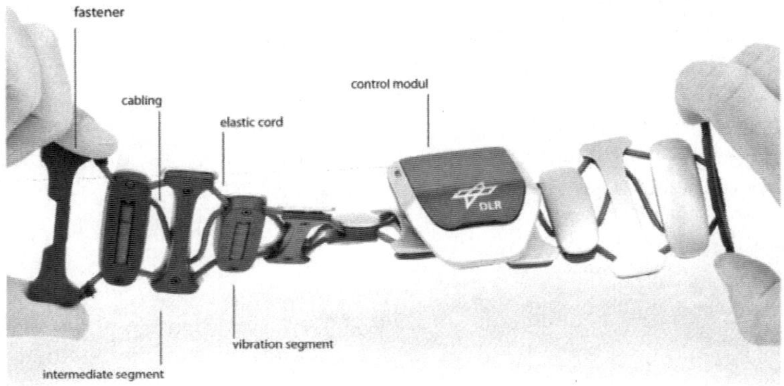

Figure 2. The vibrotactile wristband "VibroTac" with six tactors which is used to display Braille through vibrotactile stimuli

As the six dots of Braille cells are mapped to the six tactors of VibroTac, the spatial acuity with which the user is able to distinguish and localize the stimulation's position is crucial (for the user's performance). In a study with sighted people, even with very little training, a mean correct detection rate of approx. 95% was determined (Schätzle and Weber, 2015). It can be assumed that the tactile perception of blind people is more precise, resulting in even higher correct detection rates.

Besides the requirement of a reliable localization of activated tactors, the ability to present stimuli at different tactor locations that are perceived with equal magnitude is not less important. Information is not only transmitted by variations of signal shape and length but also by the intensity of the stimuli. As the perceived magnitude of stimuli with a certain frequency differ depending on the tactors' locations e.g. on the ulna, radius, muscle or fatty tissue, calibration factors for VibroTac were determined (Schätzle and Weber, 2015). Applying these factors to the commanded intensities allows for similar perception magnitudes of vibrotactile stimuli at the six different tactor locations around the human wrist.

Due to the ability of VibroTac to present spatially separated stimuli with six tactors that can be distinguished reliably and that can be controlled individually in signal shape and intensity, the device is well-suited as a haptic display for Braille.

3. MAPPING BRAILLE TO VIBROTAC

Mapping Braille to the six tactors of VibroTac can be realized in different ways. On the one hand, this concerns the assignment of cell dots to the single tactors, on the other hand the temporal aspects of stimuli patterns can be varied. We designed eight different mapping methods that appeared reasonable. Prior studies on VibroTac revealed that impulses with a signal length of approx. $T_{on} = 0.3$ s and with 30 % of maximum available intensity were perceived as pleasant. The resulting frequency of the stimulus is approx. 90 Hz.

As described below, unraised dots are displayed with signals of less intensity, resulting in stimuli with approx. 50 Hz and a perceived magnitude of approx. 25 % compared to the stimuli of raised dots. In two of the following methods, only three tactors were used in order to compare two configurations with different distances between the tactors and to check for potential better results due to a more reliable spatial distinction of activated tactors.

A) Sequential Methods

Braille cells are run through in a sequential way starting with the dot in the left column from first to third line followed by the right column from first to third line.

1) Sequential (SQ)

Raised dots are displayed with signal length T_{on} = 0.3 s and a subsequent signal pause T_{off} = 0.4 s. Before the next character is started, the output is paused for the duration T_{wait}.

2) Sequential rotated (SQ-ROT)

Analogous to method "SQ" but with VibroTac worn 30° rotated counterclockwise so that the separation line between the two columns is orientated vertically.

3) Sequential raised/unraised (SQ-R/UR)

Analogous to method "SQ" but additionally, unraised dots are presented with a signal of less intensity than the signal of a raised dot. Signal times for raised and unraised dots: T_{on} = 0.3 s, T_{off} = 0.15 s) and T_{wait} between characters.

4) Semi-sequential (SSQ)

Analogous to method "SQ" but with a short break T_{break}= 0.4 s between the columns of a character.

B) Parallel Methods

Several raised dots are displayed simultaneously.

5) Parallel (P)

All Raised dots are displayed with signal length T_{on} = 1.0 s and a break T_{wait} is inserted before the next character is started.

6) Semi-Parallel (SP)

First, all raised dots of the left column are displayed with signal length T_{on} = 1.0 s and after a break T_{break} = 1.0 s, all raised dots of the right column are displayed simultaneously and finally T_{wait} is added before the next character is started.

C) Three Tactors-Methods

In these methods, only three tactors (see Fig. 1, right) of the device are used. In consequence, the distances between the tactors are larger and hence better result might be obtained due to a more reliable distinction of the activation patterns.

7) Three Tactors Semi-Parallel (3SP)

Analogous to method "SP"

8) Three Tactors Sequential raised/unraised (3SQ-R/UR)

Analogous to method "SQ-R/UR"

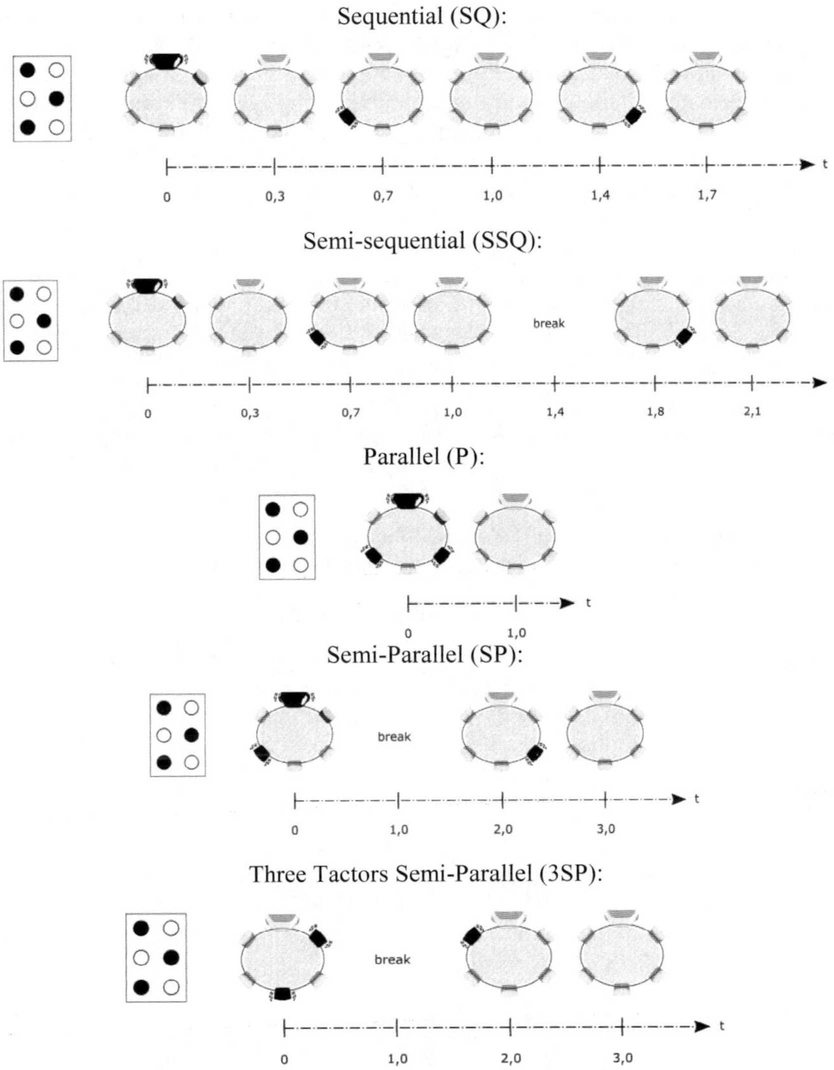

Figure 3. Schematic representation of mapping methods with different timing aspects

4. PILOT STUDY

In the pilot study, four sighted subjects (1 female, 3 male, with ages ranging from 22 to 34) participated.

4.1 Methods

The VibroTac was worn close to the wrist. The subjects sat on a chair and laid their hand relaxed onto the table such that the VibroTac did not touch the table surface. Ear protection generating white noise was worn in order to avoid acoustical influence of vibrating tactors. Calibration factors determined in a prior study (Schätzle and Weber, 2015) were applied to adjust the single tactor intensities so that perception magnitudes of vibrotactile stimuli are similar at all six different tactor locations, as information is also coded with the stimulus intensity.

Subjects were familiarized with VibroTac with three short impulses displayed successively at each tactor. Subsequently, the six dots of the Braille cell were presented sequentially with vibrotactile stimuli on the corresponding tactors in order to familiarize subjects with the dot-tactor assignment (see Fig. 1). Then, the recognition of complete characters was trained ten times by displaying different characters (from the set of characters depicted in Fig. 4) with the sequential (SQ) and the parallel (P) methods respectively. Each character was repeated three times before subjects had to mark the detected raised dots into a printed blank Braille cell and feedback was given by the investigator. Ear protection generating white noise was worn in the training phase and in the studies to avoid acoustical influence.

Each subject ran through a test series with all eight methods in randomized order and with nine different characters randomly chosen from a set of characters (see Fig. 4). The upcoming method was demonstrated with an example and was trained three times analogously to the training described above. Afterwards, a randomly selected character from the set of characters was displayed and subjects were asked to mark the recognized dots on the printed blank Braille without feedback of the investigator.

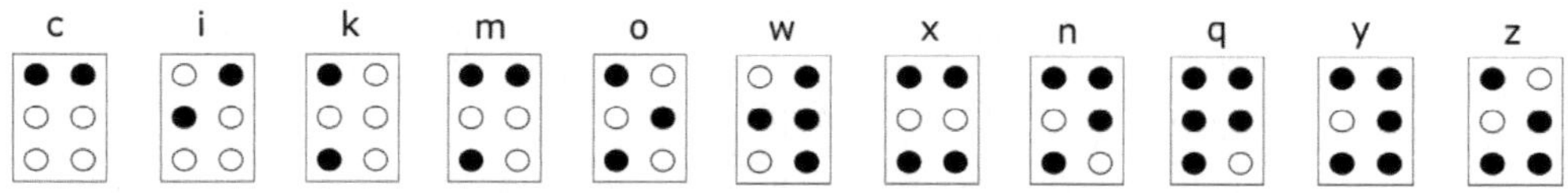

Figure 4. Braille codings of different characters as examples of dot patterns that were used in the studies. The characters were grouped into easy letters (only 2 raised dots) and in difficult letters (3 – 5 raised dots). Braille literacy is not required for the conduction of the studies as dot patterns had to be recognized only instead of identifying Braille characters

This procedure was conducted for nine characters per method. Besides objective data (e.g. correct recognition of raised and unraised dots), subjective ratings (e.g. difficulty and learnability) were gathered before the next method was started. After the third and sixth run, a recovery break was inserted in order to avoid adaptation effects and fatigue.

4.2 Results

As can be seen in Fig. 5, better results were obtained with sequential methods (1-4, 8) than with parallel methods (5-7) for the correct recognition of characters/dot patterns.

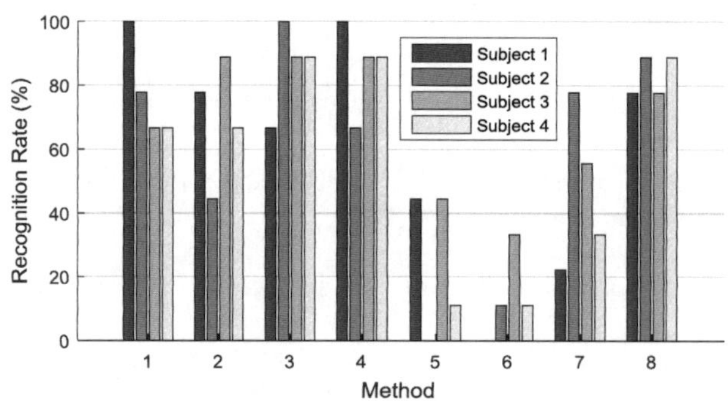

Figure 5. Correct recognition of vibrotactile displayed characters in Braille coding for eight different methods

Similarly, the subjective ratings of the different methods in terms of the difficulty to recognize characters (see Fig. 6, left) and the learnability (see Fig. 6, right) revealed the worst ratings for the parallel methods (5-7). Method 2 (SQ-ROT) with the rotated configuration of VibroTac did not improve performance compared to method 1 (SQ). Furthermore, the additional pause between left and right column in method 4 (SSQ) did not lead to a substantial improvement in the objective and subjective results.

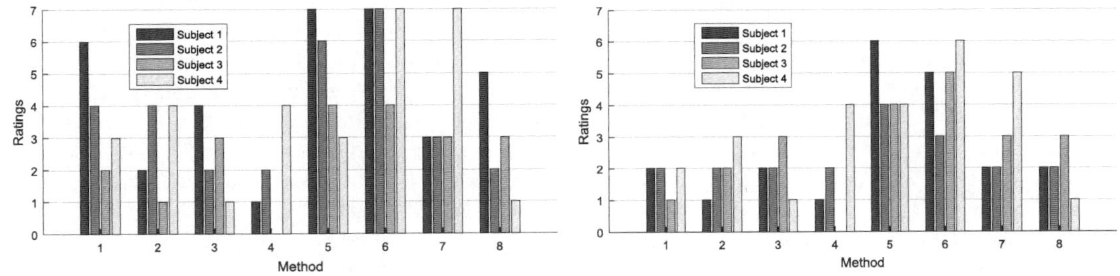

Figure 6. (left) Subjective ratings of the difficulty to recognize characters for different methods (Likert scale from 1 = very easy to 7 = very difficult) and (right) subjective ratings of the learnability to recognize characters for different methods (Likert scale from 1 = very easy to 7 = very difficult)

Method 3 (SQ-R/UR) and method 8 (3SQ-R/UR) yielded similar results. The increased distances between tactors when using three tactors only (method 8) compared to the method with same temporal condition but with six tactors (method 3), had no significant effect on the correct character recognition. The results indicate as expected that the parallel methods are more difficult to process and learn compared to the sequential methods.

4.3 Conclusion

In the pilot study, encouraging results were obtained for the mapping of Braille to a vibrotactile wristband with six tactors. With some methods very high recognition rates were obtained even without extensive training. The results indicate that the two sequential (SQ and SQ/R-UR) as well as the semi-parallel (3SQ) methods are the most promising methods and thus should be further evaluated in more details and with more subjects.

Despite of the moderate results in terms of character recognition and rated learnability obtained with parallel and semi-parallel methods, these variations of mapping should not be discarded completely. After initial difficulties, intensive training might lead to good results with the advantage of a high reading rate. Therefore, the method "Three Tactors Semi-Parallel" is also further investigated in the main study.

5. MAIN STUDY

In the main study, the mapping of Braille to the VibroTac is evaluated for three methods that have been selected in the pilot study. These are: "sequential", "sequential raised/ unraised" and "Three Tactors Semi-Parallel". Furthermore, the difficulty of the characters was varied to explore potential Method x Difficulty interaction effects.

5.1 Method

For the main study, N = 18 (7 female, 11 male) sighted individuals (employees of the German Aerospace Center; M_{age} = 28.4; SD =7.2 with an age range from 16 to 48 years) were recruited. None of them participated in the pilot study. First, a written description of the experiment was handed out and subjects signed an informed consent document. The experimental setup (posture, hand positioning and calibration factors) was the same as described in the pilot study.

Subjects were familiarized with the VibroTac and its tactor positions: successively, three impulses were displayed at each tactor (T_{on} = 0.6 s and T_{off} = 0.5 s) and a second time with T_{on} = 0.3 s and T_{off} = 0.4 s. Afterwards, vibrotactile stimuli according to method "SQ" were displayed in order to learn the assignment of Braille dots to the corresponding tactors. After this, each single dot was displayed in randomized order and had to be marked on a printed blank Braille cell. The experimenter fed back whether the answer was correct or not.

In a within-subject design with randomized condition order, eight randomly chosen characters were presented in each condition, two of those characters being easy (only two raised dots) and six being difficult (more than two raised dots). Again, subjects were asked to mark the detected dot pattern on the printed blank Braille without feedback of the experimenter. Before the test series was started, each upcoming method was demonstrated by an example and four different characters were trained with feedback of the investigator. As in the pilot study, ear protection generating white noise was worn in order to avoid acoustical influence. At the end of each condition, a questionnaire on mental workload and method appropriateness had to be filled out. For measuring mental workload, the item "mental demand" of the NASA-TLX (Hart and Staveland, 1988) was used ("How mentally demanding was the task? Was it simple or complex?"; Likert scale from 1 (very low/simple) to 20 (very high/ complex)). Method appropriateness was measured with the item "How appropriate is the method for displaying Braille characters?" (Likert scale from 1 (inappropriate) to 7 (very appropriate)).

5.2. Results - Objective Data

First, the number of correctly identified points for each character (see Tab. 1) was analyzed as the overall performance parameter. Repeated measures ANOVA with Method and Difficulty as within factors revealed a significant main effect of Method ($F(2, 34) = 5.27$, $p < .05$) and Difficulty ($F(1, 17) = 6.99$, $p < .05$) as well as a significant interaction of both factors ($F(2, 34) = 4.97$, $p < .05$). Pairwise comparisons with Bonferroni correction showed that the average number of correct points was significantly higher in the "SQ-R/UR" condition compared to the "SQ" ($p < .05$) and "3SP" condition ($p < .01$). As assumed, performance was better in the easy compared to the difficult character conditions. Interestingly, the significant interaction indicated that this difficulty effect varies across methods. Paired-samples T-tests indicated no significant difficulty effect for method "SQ" ($t(17) = .6$, ns.), a marginal trend for the method "SQ-R/UR" ($t(17) = 1.37$, $p <.10$, one-tailed testing) and a significant effect for method "3SP" ($t(17) = 4.18$, $p < .001$).

Table 1. Correctly identified points

Method	Difficulty	Mean (%)	SD (%)
SQ	Easy	0,92	0,12
SQ	Difficult	0,90	0,09
SQ-R/UR	Easy	0,98	0,05
SQ-R/UR	Difficult	0,97	0,06
3SP	Easy	0,96	0,05
3SP	Difficult	0,88	0,09

5.3 Results - Subjective Ratings

First, the subjective ratings listed in Tab. 2 were analyzed regarding mental workload ("How mentally demanding was the task? Was it simple or complex?"; Likert scale from 1 (very low/simple) to 20 (very high/ complex)). Repeated measures ANOVA with Method as within factor yielded a significant effect ($F(2, 34) = 12.68$, $p < .001$). Subsequent pairwise comparisons with Bonferroni correction showed that method "SQ-R/UR" was rated as being significantly less demanding or complex as the other methods (both ps < .01). No meaningful difference was found between "SQ" and "3SP" (see Tab. 2, left).

Finally, the overall appropriateness of the three methods for displaying characters was rated ("How appropriate is the method for displaying Braille characters"; Likert scale from 1 (inappropriate) to 7 (very appropriate)) and results are listed in Tab. 2, right). Again, ANOVA indicated a significant overall effect ($F(2, 34) = 5.34$, $p = .01$) and pairwise comparisons revealed that ratings for method "SQ-R/UR" were significantly higher compared to the other conditions (both ps < .05). The ratings for the other methods did not differ significantly.

Table 2. Subjective rating of mental workload (Likert scale from 1 (very low / easy) to 20 (very much / complex)) and of method appropriateness (Likert scale from 1 (inappropriate) to 7 (very appropriate))

Method	Workload		Appropriateness	
	Mean	SD	Mean	SD
SQ	10,94	4,77	4,83	1,38
SQ-R/UR	6,83	4,16	5,78	0,88
3SP	11,67	4,97	4,72	1,27

5.4 Discussion

The data of the main study showed clear evidence that the best performance is reached with the sequential method that presents all (raised and unraised) cell dots (SQ-R/UR). Recognition rates of 97-98% were obtained for easy as well as for difficult characters. In line with the objective data, subjects also rated this method best in terms of mental workload and appropriateness. Similar results (96%) were achieved with the semi-parallel method that uses 3 tactors (3SP) at least for easy characters whereas the recognition of characters with more than two raised dots within a column led to significant lower recognition performance.

Despite of the reliable distinction and localization of VibroTac's tactor positions (correct detection rate of approx. 95% for single tactor positions, determined in previous studies by Schätzle and Weber (2015)), the sequential method did not lead to convincing results. Obviously, subjects had problems to identify and memorize the single dot positions when these were presented in a quick sequence of vibrotactile stimuli. Perhaps intensive training could lead to similar results for the method "SQ" and "SQ-R/UR". Besides the difficulty to localize activated tactors, memorizing the sequence might also be challenging.

In the sequential method that presents all (raised and unraised) cell dots (SQ-R/UR), most information is transmitted to the user. This might be the reason for the superior results obtained with this method. Since unraised dots are also represented haptically, another recognition strategy is possible: subjects memorize the full haptic sequence (like a rhythm) rather than localizing the individual tactor positions. It seems that the haptic sequence can be recalled easily. This might work even retrospectively assumed that there is a short break before the next character is started. The disadvantage of the "SQ-R/UR" method is the additional time in comparison to method "SQ" in order to present the unraised dots.

Regarding the semi-parallel method "3SP", the correct detection of activated tactors is a major challenge. In comparison with the other two methods, the difficulty and thus the number of raised dots has a significant effect on the performance. The assignment of cell dots to the three tactors is not quite intuitive. However, this seems not to be the reason for the moderate results obtained for difficult characters as with the same method, convincing results are reached for easy characters.

6. CONCLUSION AND FUTURE WORK

In this paper, a new approach of displaying Braille through vibrotactile stimuli at the wrist was presented. Each of the six Braille cell dots is mapped to one of the six wristband's tactors. As the Braille coding itself is not altered, only the mapping between cell dots and tactors has to be learned. We performed a user study that aimed at evaluating the general usability of this approach and at the comparison of different mapping strategies (assignment of cell dots to tactors and temporal aspects). Due to the difficulty of recruiting blind people for such a time-consuming evaluation, the study was designed in a way that Braille literacy is not required. Thus, for a first evaluation of the approach we conducted the study with sighted people.

Even with little training, very promising results were obtained. The evaluation of eight different mapping methods with different assignments of cell dots to tactors as well as temporal aspects revealed significant differences in terms of objective performance (activation pattern recognition) and subjective ratings. The sequential presentation of raised and unraised dots turned out to be the best method. However, in further studies with more intensive training it should be investigated whether similar results can be achieved with the method using sequential presentation of raised dots only or with the method based on semi-parallel output of raised dots with three tactors or based on parallel output.

The results of this study indicate that the mapping of Braille code to six tactors at the wrist is a reasonable approach and that reading Braille without using the fingertip seems to be possible. We expect better results for blind people as they are superior in tactile acuity and perception tasks than sighted people. The feedback we received from a blind person in a preliminary test was positive and encouraging to further proceed with the presented approach. Anyway, future studies with blind subjects are essential to optimize and investigate relevant issues. First of all, the required time to output characters or words has to be shortened to allow for a natural communication. If stimuli are displayed in a fast sequence, one should have in mind that effects such as spatial masking, apparent location or temporal enhancement may affect correct localization of stimuli and deteriorate the performance. Furthermore, the recognition of several words or sentences and the robustness of vibrotactile Braille cues in the presence of distractors e.g. when engaged in another task or when lifting objects should be investigated. In addition, reading performance of blind people should be compared with a baseline condition e.g. traditional fingertip Braille reading or vibrational Morse code.

REFERENCES

Al-Qudah, Z. and Doush, I. A. and Alkhateeb, F. and Maghayreh, E. A. and Al-Khaleel, O., 2011. Reading Braille on mobile phones: A fast method with low battery power consumption. *International Conference on User Science and Engineering (i-USEr)*, Shah Alam, Selangor, 118-123.

Bark, K. and Khanna, P. and Irwin, R. and Kapur, P. and Jax, S. A. and Buxbaum, L. J. and Kuchenbecker, K. J., 2011. Lessons in using vibrotactile feedback to guide fast arm motions. *IEEE World Haptics Conference (WHC).* Istanbul, Turkey, 355-360.

Beck, K. and Ralph, J., 1994. Patterns Generates Architectures. *Proceedings of European Conference of Object-Oriented Programming.* Bologna, Italy, 139-149.

Benali-Khoudja, M. and Hafez, M. and Alexandre, J.-M. and Kheddar, A, 2004. Tactile interfaces: a State-of-the-Art Survey". *Int. Symposium on Robotics*. Bd. 31. Paris, France.

Bosman, S. and Groenendaal, B. and Findlater, J. W. and Visser, T. and de Graaf, M. and Markopoulos, P., 2003. GentleGuide: An Exploration of Haptic Output for Indoors Pedestrian Guidance. *5th Int. Symposium on Human-Computer Interaction with Mobile Devices and Services*. Hrsg. von L. Chittaro. Berlin Heidelberg: Springer Verlag, 358-362.

Brewster, S. and Brown, L. M., 2004. Tactons: structured tactile messages for non-visual information display. *5th Conf. on Australasian user interface (AUIC)*. Bd. 28. Dunedin, New Zealand, 15-23.

Brown, L. M., 2007. Tactons: Structured vibrotactile messages for non-visual information display. *Dissertation*. University of Glasgow.

Cheung, B. and Van Erp, J. B. F. and Cholewiak, R. W., 2008. Anatomical, neurophysiological and perceptual issues of tactile perception". *Tactile displays for orientation, navigation and communication in air, sea and land environments, NATO Research and Technology Organisation*, 1-18.

Choi, S. and Kuchenbecker, K. J., 2013. Vibrotactile Display: Perception, Technology, and Applications, *Proceedings of the IEEE*, vol. 101, no. 9, 2093-2104.

Cholewiak, R. W. and Collins, A. A., 2003. Vibrotactile localization on the arm: Effects of place, space, and age. *Perception & Psychophysics*, Bd. 65(7), 1058-1077.

Cholewiak, R. W. and Collins, A. A. and Brill, J. C., 2001. Spatial factors in vibrotactile pattern perception. *Eurohaptics*. Birmingham, UK, 1-7.

Elliott, L. R. and Coovert, M. D. and Prewett, M. and Walvord, A. G. and Saboe, K. and Johnson, R., 2009. A Review

and Meta Analysis of Vibrotactile and Visual Information Displays. *U.S. Army Research Laboratory*, Aberdeen Proving Ground, Aberdeen, MD

Galambos, P, 2012. Vibrotactile Feedback for Haptics and Telemanipulation: Survey, Concept and Experiment. *Acta Polytechnica Hungarica*, Bd. 9(1) (2012), 41-65.

Goldreich, D. and Kanics, I. M., 2003. Tactile acuity is enhanced in blindness. *Journal of Neuroscience*, 23(8), 3439-3445.

Goldreich, D. and Kanics, I. M., 2006. Performance of blind and sighted humans on a tactile grating detection task. *Perception & Psychophysics*, 68(8), 1363-1371.

Geldard, F. A., 1957. Adventures in tactile literacy. *American Psychologist.* 12(3).

Geldard, F. A., 1966. Cutaneous coding of optical signals: The optohapt. *Perception & Psychophysics.*, 377-381.

Guerreiro, J. and Gonçalves, D. and Marques, D. and Guerreiro, T. and Nicolau, H. and Montague, K., 2013. The today and tomorrow of Braille learning. *Proceedings of the 15th International ACM SIGACCESS Conference on Computers and Accessibility.*

Legge, G. E. and Madison, C. and Vaughn, B. N. and Cheong, A. M. and Miller, J. C., 2008. Retention of high tactile acuity throughout the life span in blindness. *Attention, Perception, & Psychophysics.* 70(8), 1471-1488.

Hart, S. G. and Staveland, L. E., 1988. Development of NASA-TLX (Task Load Index): Results of empirical and theoretical research. *Advances in Psychology*, 52, 139-183.

Jones, L. A. and Sarter, N. B, 2008.Tactile displays: guidance for their design and application. *Human Factors* 50(1), 90–111.

Kapur, P. and Jensen, M. and Buxbaum, L. J. and Jax, S. A. and Kuchenbecker, K. J., 2010. Spatially distributed tactile feedback for kinesthetic motion guidance. *IEEE Haptics Symposium*, 519-526.

Lehtinen, V. and Oulasvirta, A. and Salovaara, A. And Nurmi, P., 2012. Dynamic Tactile Guidance for Visual Search Tasks. *25th Annual ACM Symposium on User Interface Software and Technology.* Cambridge, Massachusetts, USA, 445-452.

Lindeman, R. W. and Yanagida, Y. and Noma, H. and Hosaka, K, 2006. Wearable vibrotactile fsystems for virtual contact and information display. *Virtual Reality*, Bd. 9(2), 203-213.

McDaniel, T. and Villanueva, D. and Krishna, S. and Panchanathan, S., 2010. MOVe- MENT: A framework for systematically mapping vibrotactile stimulations to fundamental body movements. *IEEE Int. Symposium on Haptic Audio Visual Environments and Games (HAVE).* Phoenix, AZ, USA, 1-6.

Meier, A. and Matthies, D. J. C. and Urban, B. and Wettach, R., 2015. Exploring Vibrotactile Feedback on the Body and Foot for the Purpose of Pedestrian Navigation". *2Nd Int. Workshop on Sensor-based Activity Recognition and Interaction (WOAR).* Rostock, Germany, 1-11.

Nicolau, H. and Guerreiro, J. and Guerreiro, T. and Carrico, L., 2013. UbiBraille: designing and evaluating a vibrotactile Braille-reading device. *15th Int. Conf. on Computers and Accessibility.*

Pongrac, H., 2006. Vibrotactile Perception: Dierential Effects of Frequency, Amplitude, and Acceleration. *IEEE Int. Workshop on Haptic AudioVisual Environments and their Applications (HAVE).* Ottawa, ON, Canada, 54-59.

Piateski, E. And Jones, L., 2005. Vibrotactile pattern recognition on the arm and torso. *First Joint Eurohaptics Conference and Symposium on Haptic Interfaces for Virtual Environment and Teleoperator Systems (WHC).* Pisa, Italy, 90-95.

Pietrzak, T. et al., 2009. Creating usable pin array tactons for nonvisual information. *IEEE Transactions on Haptics.* 61-72.

Rantala, J. et al., 2009. Methods for presenting braille characters on a mobile device with a touchscreen and tactile feedback. *IEEE Transactions on Haptics*. 28-39.

Schätzle, S. and Ende, T. and Wüsthoff, T. and Preusche, C., 2010. VibroTac: An ergonomic and versatile usable vibrotactile feedback device. *19th Int. Symposium in Robot and Human Interactive Communication (RO-MAN).* Viareggio, Italy, 670-675.

Schätzle, S. and Weber, B., 2015. Towards Vibrotactile Direction and Distance Information for Virtual Reality and Workstations for Blind People. *Int. Conf. on Universal Access in Human-Computer Interaction (HCI).* Los Angeles, CA, USA.

Schroeder, J. and Martin-Salvador, M. and Bakirov, M. and Straus, U., 2015. Tactile Satellite Navigation System: Using haptic technology to enhance the sense of orientation and direction. *66th Int. Astronautical Congress*. Jerusalem, Israel, 2015.

Tadakuma, R. and Howe, R. D., 2009. A whole-arm tactile display system. *World Haptics 2009 - Third Joint EuroHaptics conference and Symposium on Haptic Interfaces for Virtual Environment and Teleoperator Systems.* Salt Lake City, Utah, USA, 446-451.

Van Erp, J. B. F., 2002. Guidelines for the Use of Vibro-Tactile Displays in Human Computer Interaction. *EuroHaptics*. Edinburgh, UK, 18-22.

Van Erp, J. B. F. and Jansen, C. and Dobbins, T. and Van Veen, H. A. H. C., 2004. Vibrotactile waypoint navigation at sea and in the air: two case studies. *EuroHaptics*. Munich, Germany, 166-173.

Wong, M. and Gnanakumaran, V. and Goldreich, D., 2011. Tactile spatial acuity enhancement in blindness: evidence for experience-dependent mechanisms. *Journal of Neuroscience*, 31(19), 7028-7037.

Yang, G. H. and Ryu, D. and Kang, S., 2009. Vibrotactile display for hand-held input device providing spatial and directional information. *World Haptics - Third Joint EuroHaptics conference and Symposium on Haptic Interfaces for Virtual Environment and Teleoperator Systems*. Salt Lake, City, UT, USA, 79-84.

Yatani, K.and Khai, N. T., 2009. SemFeel: a user interface with semantic tactile feedback for mobile touch-screen devices. *Proceedings of the 22nd annual ACM symposium on User interface software and technology.*

THE USABILITY OF SYSTEM AND USERS' EMOTIONS DURING WORK WITH INTERFACE DESIGNED FOR DISABLED – THE PILOT STUDY

Beata Bajcar, Anna Borkowska and Katarzyna Jach
Wrocław University of Science and Technology, Wybrzeże Wyspiańskiego 27, 50-370 Wrocław, Poland

ABSTRACT

The main goal of this paper is to trace the relationships between emotional and descriptive aspects of assessments of users' satisfaction as one of the usability aspect. The usability test was done on a system called Face Controller dedicated to severely disabled users with limbs impaired. Using Face Controller, one can operate a computer with head movements and facial expressions only. Thirty disabled participants took part in the research. The users' satisfaction was measured by System Usability Score and Net Promoter Score and their emotional state three times during the testing procedure/system validation. It was found that respondents' positive emotional balance is related to their high FC system evaluation. Thus, the sources of users' satisfaction are not necessarily located on the side of the system itself, but on their initial emotional evaluations.

KEYWORDS

Face Controller, emotions, effectiveness, System Usability Score, Net Promoter Score

1. INTRODUCTION

The paper presents some results of usability tests made with users with severe disabilities on the system called Face Controller intended for operating a computer by head movements and facial expressions exclusively. We noted a huge discrepancy between different aspects of usability like users' satisfaction and their effectiveness (Jach et al. 2017). Therefore, the main goal of this paper is to find reasons of such a state by analyzing users' emotions before, during and after working with Face Controller.

Usability is defined in ISO 9241-11 (1998) standard as: "The extent to which a product can be used by specified users to achieve specified goals with effectiveness, efficiency and satisfaction in a specified context of use." Nielsen and Levy (1994) analyzed over one hundred cases from many studies and found the relations among different aspects of usability quite strong. Similar associations were stated by Sauro and Kindlund (2005). Kasper Hornbæk and Effie Lai-Chong Law in 2007 analyzed raw data from 73 HCI surveys and found the correlations between different usability aspects relatively low. On the other side they noticed that for most of the analyzed studies positive correlations among three aspects of usability were notified (Hornbæk, Law 2007). During the years, however, the emphasis on different aspects of usability has changed since the main attention was paid to efficiency and system effectiveness to the user satisfaction and pleasure of system use (MacDonald and Atwood 2013). Therefore, it can be assumed that relations observed between users' satisfaction and the total usability assessment appear to be stronger then stated in the past. Moreover, researchers agree that users' satisfaction is affected by different factors associated more with quality aspects than with users' performance. For example, Dillon (2001) shown the satisfaction is in relation to personal experience with technology, a preferred working style, and the aesthetics of system design. Similarly, Hassenzahl pointed emotional experiences during system usage and the aesthetics of system design as variables affecting a perceived quality of use (Hassenzahl, 2006). Thüring, and Mahlke (2005) proposed a model specifying three components of user experience and their interrelations called CUE-Model. The CUE-Model distinguishes two types of quality aspects which influence on a user. Instrumental qualities are connected with an experienced support and its ease of use. Non-instrumental qualities, like the visual aesthetics, concern the look and feel of the system. Though, instrumental qualities are related to the usability aspects of system effectiveness and efficiency and non-instrumental qualities are closely connected to the system appeal and attractiveness from a user's point of view (Thüring and Mahlke 2007).

Discussion on the cognitive and emotional aspects of evaluation of objects, people and events, is one of the most intense and long-term in psychology (Clore & Huntsinger 2007; Damasio, 1993; Haidt, 2012). In the debate psychologists consider that emotional reactions are specific assessments and bodily responses to changes in the environment and emerging stimuli. In turn, the cognitive assessment is the result of data processing and comprises an answer to the fundamental question: how the new stimuli and a changing situation can assist in the implementation individuals' current targets. Contemporary theories accept the priority of emotional evaluations also called intuitions. On the other hand, cognitive appraisals, verbalized, more or less conscious, generally constitute support for faster and more automated evaluations based on emotions. The presented study, among other things, is aimed at tracing the relationships between these aspects of human assessments – the emotional and descriptive ones. Also, what is important is discovering the causes of very high usability assessment results of the investigated system. It is assumed that they are not necessarily located on the side of the system itself and its characteristics, but on the initial emotional evaluations.

2. THE EVALUATED SYSTEM

The system under assessment has been developed in Poland by the enterprise Risenbit. The system is called Face Controller (FC) and it is dedicated to disabled people who are not able to move their limbs and therefore they cannot use standard computer devices. Originally, the system was designed for people with spinal cord damages, but nowadays it is used by people with other dysfunctionalities (myasthenia, tetraplegia). The main idea of Face Controller (FC) is tracking the user's head in order to move the cursor on the screen and controlling system actions by users' facial expressions (left or right eye blinking, smile, mouth opening, etc.). In that way a user can control a computer using his/her head movements and facial expressions only. Face Controller is a dedicated software which uses the game controller Microsoft Kinect, which is commercially available, for observing a user and recognizing the user's face. Face Controller uses sensitive cameras of Microsoft Kinect in order to track a user's face with the 30 Hz frequency. During the calibration process, a user can assign some selected facial expressions to specific computer actions and adjust their sensitivity.

2.1 Procedure and Measure

The validation of FC system consisted of two stages and three measures of different variables. First, the computer skills level, attitude toward the system, and emotional state were measured. Next, participants had a very first contact with Face Controller. They became acquainted with the system and could use it for an unlimited period of time. At the second stage persons participated in the FC system testing. The FC test took place in the presence of an assistant whose role was to provide a technical support and record the users responses. During the testing sessions subjects were supposed to do four different tasks. The scenario was built on the basis of an online shopping situation. Participants were asked for: (1) finding, opening and closing the file in order to find discount coupon; (2) checking the coupon value in a calculator; (3) checking the price of a chosen item in an online store; (4) writing a short email to the store. These four tasks encompass most of the typical major functionalities of a daily computer usage. Each task had individual maximum time duration, and it was broken by the assistant if the subject was not able to finish it on time. After that part of test, subjects assessed their satisfaction. The effectiveness was measured by a level of task performance. The performance level comprises an aggregated result of the performed tasks. Each tasks done by a subject means 25 points of the score, i.e. three performed tasks means 75 points.

In the validation of FC system, measures of the users emotions three times occurred: (1) before the first use of the system; (2) before testing the FC system; (3) after testing the FC system. To the measure of the same emotions in three time points we used a set of 10 adjectives, describing human emotions (five for positive emotions and five for negative ones). The items to the questionnaire used to measure experienced emotions were taken from the Polish adaptation of the 29 item UWIST Mood Adjective Checklist (UMACL) (Goryńska, 2005; Matthews, Jones, & Chamberlain, 1990). Participants were asked to assess their current mood by indicating terms of all emotions experienced at a given time. Additionally, after FC testing others emotions experienced during the test situation were measured. Thus, after FC testing there were implemented six items (describing positive emotions: encouraged, cheerful, positively surprised; and describing negative emotions: bored, disappointed, discouraged). The full procedure is described in the research report (Bajcar et al 2017).

The total usability of Face Controller system was assumed as the System Usability Score result. The System Usability Scale (SUS) has been known as usability metrics for over 30 years (Brooke, 1996) and it is widely applied in different language versions for usability tests all over the world (Brooke, 2013; Bangor et al. 2008). Currently, the System Usability Scale has been recognized as a reliable usability metrics, even for small sample tests (8-12 users) (Tullis and Stetson 2004). The Polish version of the original System Usability Score questionnaire was used (Borkowska, Jach 2016). The questionnaire comprised 10 statements scored on a 5-point Likert's scale with positive and negative statements placed alternately. The final score for the SUS can range from 0 to 100, where higher scores indicate a better usability (Brooke, 1996). Another indicator of the FC usability in the aspect of user's satisfaction used in the research was the Net Promoter Score. The Net Promoter Score was proposed as a single question for measuring the customer's satisfaction by Reichheld (2003). Users are asked "How likely is it that you would recommend the product to a friend or colleague?" and then provide a rating from 0 ("Not at all likely") to 10 ("Extremely likely"). Then, they are divided into three groups: promoters, neutrals or detractors. To be consistent with other questionnaires used in the research instead of the original eleven position scale, the ten position scale was used. Though, in that case respondents with 9 or 10 rating were classified as promotors and subjects with rating from 1 to 6 as detractors (Schneider et al. 2008). The metric has been constructed as a result of subtraction the percentage of detractors from the percentage of promoters. An interpretation of the Net Promoter Score in comparison to SUS score was made by Sauro (2009), who found a strong positive correlation (0.61) between these two variables.

2.2 Participants

In the research participated 30 physically impaired people aged 20 to 58 years (M_{age} = 33.0, SD_{age} = 9.38), mostly men (26 vs 4 women). All the subjects had severe disabilities due to some spinal cord damages, cerebral palsy or myasthenia. According to the Gross Motor Function Classification System (GMFCS) they were classified on the 4th or 5th level of disability (Palisano et al, 2008). All of the test participants use a wheelchair to move and they have been impaired in all areas of the motor function. In the tested sample 23.3% of participants use the computer almost every day, and 76.6% - for several hours a day. Moreover, they rated their computer skills as average (13.3%), good (30%) and very good (56.7%). Before the relevant test procedure most of the subjects (53%) use the investigated system not longer than an hour, 33% from 1 do 3 hours and 14% over three hours, which means a relatively short time of system usage on average.

3. RESULTS

3.1 Usability of the FC System

The data analysis showed the respondents evaluated Face Controller in terms of the System Usability Score relatively highly. Results are shown in Table 1. More than 60 percent of respondents assessed system over the average with SUS score over 67 (Brooke, 2013). At the same time, 30 percent of the participants received the SUS score at a minimum of 90, characterizes excellent systems in terms of usability (Brooke, 2013). The subjects particularly appreciate the ease of learning the system (average score of 4.4 on a scale of 1 to 5) and lack of its complexity. Most of the respondents used the FC for no longer than two hours, which confirms its ease of use. The analysis results showed that there were no significant differences in the usability level between GMFCS level IV and V (W = 52.0, ns).

Table 1. The distribution characteristics of the System Usability Score (SUS) for Face Controller

	Min	*Max*	*M*	*SD*
System Usability Score (SUS)	17	100	72.93	23.10

For the confirmation of the Face Controller assessment, the Net Promoter Score (NPS) popular in a marketing research was applied. Among the investigated subjects, the Net Promoter Score for Face Controller system is extremely high and equals to 62 (Reincheld, 2003), with the share of promoters, ie. people declaring a very high probability of recommendation (answer 9 or 10) as high as 79 percent (Table 2).

Table 2. Net Promoter Score for Face Controller

Indicator	score
Net Promoter Score (NPS)	62
Percent of promoters (rating 9 or 10)	79
Percent of detractors (rating 1 to 6)	17

In general, the standardized indicators of usability (SUS, NPS) showed that the users evaluations of FC system is high and positive. They were satisfied with the use of FC system and assessed its very highly. In addition, they predicted an increase in the level of satisfaction with longer FC usage and the increase of their assessment of FC usability, too.

3.2 Users Emotions in the FC System Validation

For the identification of the emotion changes in the FC system validation, the non-parametric Wilcoxon signed rank test was applied (McKenzie 2014). The first measure of emotions, before the first contact with FC showed clearly more positive than negative emotions, $W = 4.66, p < .001$. After the exploring stage of FC system re-measurement of the emotional state also showed the advantage of positive over negative emotions, $W = 4.57, p < .001$. After the stage of FC test participants indicated more positive than negative emotions, $W = 3.72, p < .001$.

Comparing an index of emotions in the three time points, there were no significant differences between before and after the first contact with FC in the negative emotions ($W = .63$, *ns*), and positive emotions indexes ($W = 1.27$, *ns*) (see Fig. 1). Between phases before and following FC testing we observed marginally significant differences in positive emotions index ($W = 1.74$, $p = .08$), but non-significant in the negative emotions ($W = 1.60$, *ns*). Moreover, there were no differences in the users positive affects between all measures; 1) between the first contact with FC and before FC testing ($W = .63$, *ns*); 2) between and after FC testing ($W = 1.60$, *ns*); 3) between the first contact with FC and after FC testing ($W = 1.07$, *ns*). In summary, negative emotions did not changed in the FC validation process, and in all the measures were low. Positive emotions in FC validation slightly decreased, but were still high.

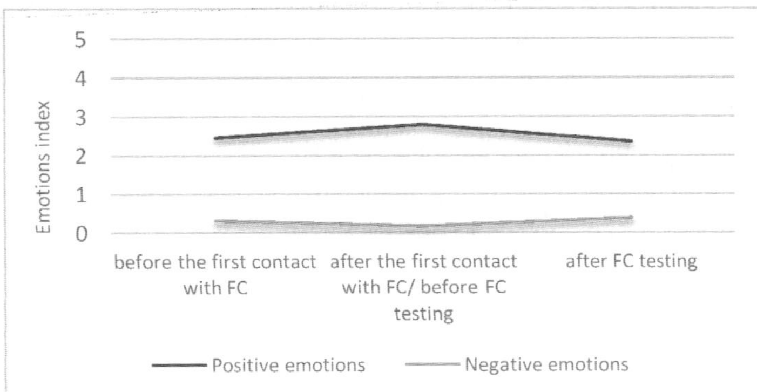

Figure 1. Emotions indexes of the users in FC system validation

In the second step we analyzed specific emotions experienced by respondents in all three measures. Results of these comparisons are presented in Fig 2. Before the first contact with FC system more than a half of the respondents indicated their interests (83 percent), calmness, and gladness. Less than a half of the people were calm and excited. Few respondents manifested stress (16.7 percent) and anxiety (6.7 percent). Other emotions were indicated by respondents occasionally. It means that before FC testing, and after the preliminary acquaint of FC, subjects had a similar positive emotional state as before the presentation. There were no significant differences (tested by Pearson's chi square test) in all emotions occurrence between before and after the first contact with FC system.

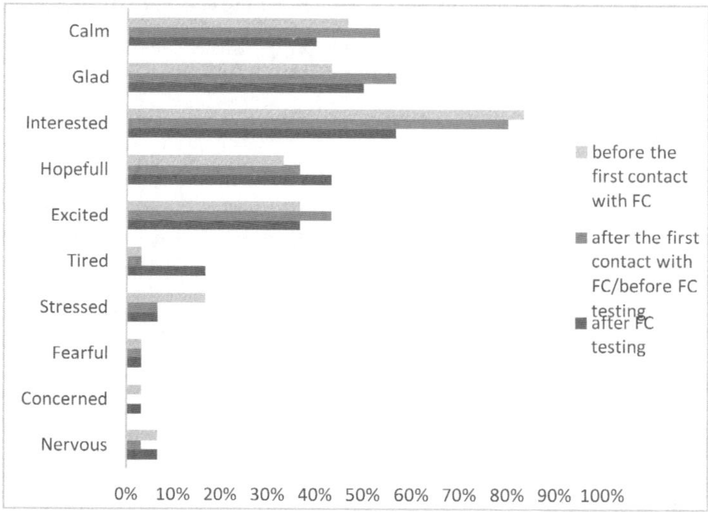

Figure 2. Percent of respondents expressed specific emotions in FC system validation

Comparing emotional states before and after the first contact with FC system a significant increase in the number of the following emotions has been observed: glad (χ^2 = 6.56, p < 0.05), excited (χ^2 = 7.64, p < 0.01), hopeful (χ^2 = 6.67, p < 0.05) and calm persons (χ^2 = 10.21, p < 0.01). The significant differences in the frequency of negative emotions and remained positive emotions were not observed. Besides, before and after testing of FC system, subjects significantly less declared calm (χ^2 = 6.56, p <.01), interest (χ^2 = 5.67, p <.05), and excitement (χ^2 = 9.81, p <.01). What is more, a greater number of participants felt hope (χ^2 = 9.81, p <.01). It is worth noting that there were no significant differences in the number of people declaring other emotions.

As depicted in Fig. 2, after FC system testing more than a half of participants was glad, interested, and about 40 percent calm, exited and hopeful. Moreover, 17 percent of sample experienced fatigue. Other negative emotions (such as fear, concern and anxiety) were declared by few people only. Comparing emotional states before and after FC testing subjects significantly less frequently declared calmness (χ^2 = 6.56, p < 0.05), interest (χ^2 = 5.67, p <.05), and excitement (χ^2 = 9.81, p <.01) than before the FC testing. In this situation a greater number of participants felt hope (χ^2 = 9.81, p <.01). It is worth noting that there were no significant differences in the occurrence of other emotions (both positive and negative ones) between before and after FC testing. This pattern of results suggests several important issues. Firstly, the respondents' mood (i.e. a pattern of emotions) confirms a positive attitude to FC system at all measures in all the steps of FC validation. Secondly, positive emotions prevailed over the negative emotions. Thirdly, the first contact with the FC system contributes a growing number of people in a positive affect. This means psychological factors had a limited impact of interfering the FC test stage. Despite the fact that after FC testing there was a decrease of positive emotions, most of the users still manifested many of the various positive emotions. Moreover, negative emotions were experienced by FC users less frequently independently of the situation.

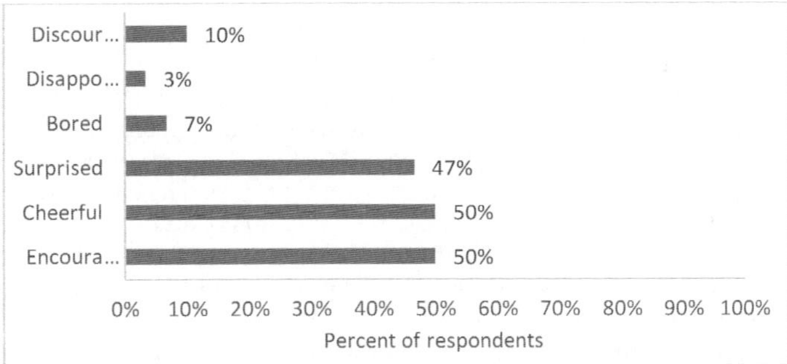

Figure 3. Percent of respondents expressed specific emotions only after FC system usage

In the next step we analyzed the specific emotions experienced only after the FC testing (Figure 3). In this situation half of FC users felt encourage, cheerfulness, and positive surprise (47 percent). Among negative emotions in the post-test situation there were isolated cases of discourage, disappointment, or boredom. In summary, an emotional balance measured after FC test was overwhelmingly positive. The results show that after FC test positive affect remains still high, although some emotions were experienced significantly less. Negative affect is still marginal. A number of tired and stressed users slightly increased after FC testing, but that was a natural effect after the task situation and does not affect the overall evaluation of FC system.

3.3 Emotional State of the FC Users and System Usability

To assess the overall evaluation of FC system we tested an interrelationship between usability indicators and positive and negative affect measured in three time points (before contact with FC, before, and after FC testing). Due to a small sample, *Spearman's* rank correlation coefficient was used.

From the correlation matrix of the results (Table 3) one can see high positive relationships between positive emotions before the first contact with FC, before FC testing, and after FC testing. Positive emotions (before the first FC contact and before FC testing) correlated positively at a moderate level. Whereas, negative emotions measured in different moments of FC validation were interrelated non-significantly. Positive and negative emotions interrelated negatively only after FC testing. It means that, the more positive emotions were experienced ,the less negative emotions were felt There were also a negative correlation between positive emotion before the first contact with FC and negative emotions after FC testing.

Table 3. The *rho* correlations between emotions and usability

	1	2	3	4	5	6	7
1.Usability	1						
2.Positive emotions (before contact with FC)	$.42^{*}$	1					
3.Positive emotions (before FC testing)	$.58^{**}$	$.37^{*}$	1				
4.Positive emotion (after FC testing)	$.64^{**}$	$.64^{**}$	$.65^{**}$	1			
5.Negative emotions (before contact with FC)	-.30	-.13	.09	-.15	1		
6.Negative emotions (before FC testing)	-.34	-.03	-.23	-.06	.20	1	
7.Negative emotions (after FC testing)	$-.73^{**}$	$-.43^{*}$	-.19	$-.55^{**}$	.16	.27	1

* $p < .05$, ** $p < .01$

Moreover, users positive emotions (measured in all time points) were positively related with usability at the moderate or high level. It is worth noticing that relation between positive affect and usability increases with a successive assessment of emotions. In contrast, usability was highly related with negative emotions only after FC testing. There was no significant correlation between usability and negative emotions before the first contact with FC and before FC testing.

4. CONCLUSIONS

As early as in 1983 Root and Draper stated that users feelings before they experience the assessed system were not a good indicator of their satisfaction after contact with the system in practice (Root, Draper 1983). That observation was proved later by Bailey, who found that even computer professionals expectations about users' performance and satisfaction can be inaccurate (Bailey 1993). The study assumed a strong relationship between users cognitive assessments of the FC system (evaluation of subjective usability) and their emotional evaluations (declared emotions). The resulting data fully confirm this relationship, though they are not entitled to the causality between these variables. The most important result is a positive emotional balance in evaluations of FC system at all stages of the study. A clear dominance of positive emotions over negative ones was evident. Despite a slight decrease in the indications of positive emotions experienced after an effectiveness test, it can be summarized that the subjects assessment shows a clearly positive system on the emotional aspects. The slight decrease in positive evaluations can be attributed to fatigue after extensive research or to creating more realistic assessments of the FC system. The low level of indications of negative emotions was constant for all three measurements. It could be consequence of consistency in assessments, but also a good-subject effect.

These different psychological mechanisms might be responsible for the dynamics of emotional assessments in different moments of the study. The subjects may assess the emotional dimensions alike the very idea of creation of the FC system , their own interaction (subjective effectiveness and satisfaction) with the FC system, and finally - the level of their motivation and confidence versus uncertainty in the new task situation (Locke & Latham 2002, Nicholls 1987, Bandura 1977). It may be considered that the affect changes in the FC validation are the effect of switching of emotional and cognitive evaluations or the effect of the emotional balance between positive and negative emotions. Investigating these dynamic (complementary or switching from one to another one) mechanisms is not possible on the basis of the collected data and requires a further research conducted on more representative and larger groups of subjects.

A very high cognitive evaluation (subjective usability) and the score of recommending the tested system (NPS) as well as a strong correlation between the declared emotions show a clear relation with cognitive assessments and experienced emotions. Based on psychological theories (Clore, 2007; Damasio, 1996; Epstein et al., 1996) concerning the affective and cognitive evaluations, it can be concluded that the determinant of a highly positive cognitive judgments is exactly emotions. It should be remembered that these emotions may have diverse sources in a particular situation. So a strong correlation of these ratings has not been noted in the area of efficiency or effectiveness aspects, which was in fact not the focus of this study.

The presented research has some limitations, which can have some implications for the final results. The variables analyzed, especially emotional feelings, are declared by respondents and due to their nature are not confirmed by other metrics. Moreover, the tasks used during the testing procedure were not validated on a group of disabled users. Although we made a pilot study on a sample of 20 healthy people at different levels of computer experience and literacy in order to estimate time limits for each task, but we were not able to conduct full study due to a limited access to the target group. This limitation can cause the reduction of emotions observed after the full testing procedure. Finally, we tested the system, which is still under development, on a small and specific sample.

ACKNOWLEDGEMENT

The research was conducted at the Wroclaw University of Science and Technology in cooperation with the Polish society "Association for Your New Opportunities".

REFERENCES

Bailey, R.W., 1993. Performance vs. Preference. *Proceedings of the Human Factors and Ergonomics Society Annual Meeting*, Vol. 37, No. 4, pp. 282–286.

Bajcar B., Borkowska A., Dzidowski A., Jach K., Kuliński M., Krzos P., Piwińska J., 2017. Raport z testów systemu Face Controller [Face Controller Testing Report], published at http://www.tnm.org.pl/facecontroler/2017/02/15/raport-z-testow-systemu-face-controller/.

Bandura A., 1977. Self-efficacy: Toward a unifying theory of behavioral change. *Psychological Review*, Vol.84, No.2, pp.191-215.

Bangor, A., Kortum, P. T., Miller, J. T., 2008. An empirical evaluation of the System Usability Scale. *International Journal of Human-Computer Interaction*, 24(6), pp. 574-594.

Borkowska A., Jach K., 2016. Pre-testing of Polish Translation of System Usability Scale (SUS), *Information Systems Architecture and Technology: Proceedings of 37th International Conference on Information Systems Architecture and Technology – ISAT 2016 – Part I*, pp.143-153.

Brooke, J., 1996. SUS: A "quick and dirty" usability scale. In P. W. Jordan, B. Thom-as, B. A. Weerdmeester, & A. L. McClelland (Eds.), Usability Evaluation in Industry. London: Taylor and Francis.

Brooke, J. , 2013. SUS: A retrospective. *Journal of Usability Studies* Vol. 8, No.2, pp. 29-40.

Clore, G.L., Huntsinger, J.R., 2007. How emotions inform judgment and regulate thought. *Trends in Cognitive Sciences,* Vol. 11, No. 9, pp. 393–399.

Damasio A.R., 1996. *Descartes' Error.* Macmillan, London, UK.

Dillon A., 2001. Beyond usability: Process, outcome and affect in human–computer interactions. *Canadian Journal of Library and Information Science*, Vol. 26, pp. 57–69.

Epstein, S., Pacini, R., Denes-Raj, V., Heier, H., 1996. Individual differences in intuitive-experiential and analytical-rational thinking styles. *Journal of Personality and Social Psychology*, Vol. 71, No. 2, pp. 390-405.

Goryńska, E., 2005. Przymiotnikowa Skala Nastroju UMACL Geralda Matthewsa, A. Grahama Chamberlaina, Dylana M. Jonesa. Podręcznik. [Mood Adjective Checklist UMACL Gerald Matthews, A. Graham Chamberlain, Dylan M. Jones. Manual]. Warszawa: Pracownia Testów Psychologicznych Polskiego Towarzystwa Psychologicznego.

Haidt, J., 2012. *The righteous mind.* Pantheon, New York, USA.

Hassenzahl, M., 2006. Hedonic, Emotional, and Experiential Perspectives on Product Quality. In C. Ghaoui (Ed.), Encyclopedia of Human Computer Interaction (pp. 266-272). Hershey, PA: IGI Global.

Hornbæk, K., Law, E. L-C., 2007. Meta-analysis of correlations among usability measures. *Proceedings of the SIGCHI Conference on Human Factors in Computing Systems (CHI '07).* ACM, New York, NY, USA, pp. 617-626.

ISO 9241-11: 1998. Ergonomic requirements for office work with visual display terminals (VDTs) - Part 11 Guidance on usability.

Jach K., Bajcar B., Borkowska A., 2017. The Effectiveness and User Satisfaction in the Interface Designed for Disabled Users – the Pilot Study.

Locke, E. A. & Latham, G. P., 2002. Building a practically useful theory of goal setting and task motivation. *American Psychologist*, Vol. 57, pp. 705–717.

MacDonald C.M., Atwood M.E., 2013. Changing perspectives on evaluation in HCI: past, present, and future. In CHI '13 Extended Abstracts on Human Factors in Computing Systems (CHI EA '13). ACM, New York, NY, USA, pp. 1969-1978.

McKenzie, S.I., 2014. Human-Computer Interaction: An Empirical Research Perspective. Waltham, MA: Morgan Kaufman.

Nicholls, J., G., 1984. Achievement motivation: conceptions of ability, subjective experience, task choice, and performance. *Psychological Review*, Vol. 91, No. 3, pp. 328-346.

Nielsen, J., Levy, J., 1994. Measuring usability: preference vs. performance. Communications of the ACM 37, Vol. 4, pp. 66-75.

Palisano, R., Rosenbaum, P., Walter, S., Russell, D., Wood, E., Galuppi, B., 2008. Development and reliability of a system to classify gross motor function in children with cerebral palsy. *Developmental Medicine & Child Neurology*, Vol. 39, No. 4, pp. 214–223.

Reichheld, F.F., 2003. The One Number You Need to Grow, *Harvard Business Review*, vol. 81, No. 12, pp. 46-54.

Root R.W., Draper S., 1983. Questionnaires as a software evaluation tool. In *Proceedings of the SIGCHI Conference on Human Factors in Computing Systems* (CHI '83), Ann Janda (Ed.). ACM, New York, NY, USA, pp. 83-87.

Sauro J., Kindlund E. 2005. A method to standardize usability metrics into a single score. In *Proceedings of the SIGCHI Conference on Human Factors in Computing Systems* (CHI '05). ACM, New York, NY, USA, pp. 401-409.

Sauro, J., 2009. Does better usability increase customer loyalty? The Net Promoter Score and the System Usability Scale (SUS). Retrieved 06.03.2016. from http://www.measuringu.com/usability-loyalty.php.

Schneider D., Berent M., Thomas R., Krosnick J., (2008). Measuring Customer Satisfaction and Loyalty: Improving the 'Net-Promoter' Score. Retrieved 10.03.2016 from http://van-haafen.nl/images/documents/pdf/Measuring%20customer%20satisfaction%20and%20loyalty.pdf

Thüring, M., Mahlke, S. 2007. Usability, aesthetics and emotions in human–technology interaction. *International Journal of Psychology,* Vol. 42, pp. 253–264.

Tullis, T. S., Stetson, J. N., 2004. A Comparison of Questionnaires for Assessing Website Usability. In Proceedings of, Usability Professionals Association (UPA) 2004 Conference (June 2004), pp. 7-11.

AR MUSEUM: A MOBILE AUGMENTED REALITY APPLICATION FOR INTERACTIVE PAINTING RECOLORING

Mattia Ryffel[1], Fabio Zünd[2], Yağız Aksoy[3], Alessia Marra[1], Maurizio Nitti[1], Tunç Ozan Aydın[1] and Bob Sumner[1]
[1]*Disney Research Zürich, Switzerland*
[2]*Game Technology Center, ETH Zürich, Switzerland*
[3]*ETH Zürich, Switzerland*

ABSTRACT

We present a mobile augmented reality application that allows its users to modify colors of paintings via simple touch interactions. Our method is intended for museums and art exhibitions and aims to provide an entertaining way for interacting with paintings in a non-intrusive manner. Plausible color edits are achieved by utilizing a set of layers with corresponding alpha channels, which needs to be generated for each individual painting in a pre-processing step. Manually performing such a layer decomposition is a tedious process and makes the entire system infeasible for most practical use cases. In this work, we propose the use of a fully automatic soft color segmentation algorithm for content generation for such an augmented reality application. This way, we significantly reduce the amount of manual labor needed for deploying our system and thus make our system feasible for real-world use.

KEYWORDS

Image Processing, Color Editing, Soft Color Segmentation, Augmented Reality

1. INTRODUCTION

Augmented reality represents a great opportunity to make everyday scenes more engaging to the user. In this work, we create an augmented reality application to make museums interactive and hence more engaging for visitors by letting them create personalized versions of the paintings via recoloring. We call our application AR Museum with the tagline Create your own masterpiece. Using our application that runs on mobile devices, users can change the colors of any painting via simple pointing at the color they wish to change on the mobile device. This way, we aim to attract the attention of especially young visitors to the art pieces in museums.

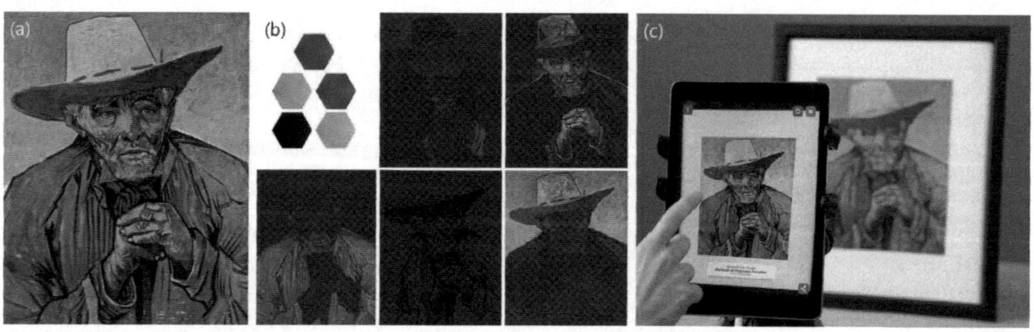

Figure 1. Given a digital image of a painting (a), we automatically determine a set of representative color distributions and corresponding so color segments (b). We present an augmented reality application aimed at museums that allows its users to change colors of the original painting in real-time (c). The content creation for such a system is streamlined through the use of soft color segments, which makes our application realizable for museums with large collections of paintings. The original painting is Portrait of Patience Escalier by Vincent van Gogh

Having a large number of paintings in a museum interactive instead of a small number of selected pieces is essential for a more effective application. However, manually creating the layers that are required for a seamless recolorization of complex paintings is a tedious task for an artist. We solve this scalability issue through the use of soft color segmentation. Figure 1 shows the automatically generated soft color segments and our recoloring application in action.

Decomposing an image into a set of constituent layers is one of the fundamental steps required in various image-editing applications. In fact, commonly used image editing tools (such as Adobe Photoshop, Gimp, among many others) take a layer-based approach to image editing. When creating compositions from scratch, it is common practice to create a layer structure where each layer contains a set of assets that will most likely receive similar edits. Equally important is to ensure that edits in one layer do not affect other layers, as well as not having an adverse effect on the overall image quality. In that sense, the layer structure of an image defines the demarcations between different image edits.

Unfortunately, in most cases, an artist does not have access to a corresponding layer structure while working with existing images. The application we present in this paper, namely interactively modifying colors of real-world paintings in an augmented reality environment, falls under this category. In our application, an existing image needs to be modified in a visually plausible manner in the absence of any accompanying layer structure. Creating such a layer structure is possible to a certain extent by manually drawing masks and utilizing range selection tools, but is often a very tedious and time-consuming task. Thus, automatically performing the layer decomposition is highly desirable, as this process is not a means for expressing artistic intention but merely a necessary step to make the final augmented reality system work.

In this production paper, we propose an end-to-end pipeline for locally changing colors of famous paintings interactively in real-time in an augmented reality environment. To refrain from color changes affecting the whole image, the paintings are decomposed into a set of layers that constitute similar colors in a pre-processing step. In order to ensure that changing the color of a layer does not produce visual artifacts such as abrupt transitions, the spatial extent of each layer is defined as an alpha channel instead of a binary edge. In our system, we perform this pre-computation step fully automatically using a recent soft color segmentation technique (Aksoy et al., 2017), significantly reducing the manual labor required in the process. As such, our paper demonstrates a novel use case of soft color segmentation in an augmented reality application.

2. RELATED WORK

Augmented Reality (AR) holds unique and promising potential to bridge between real-world activities and digital experiences, allowing users to engage their imagination and boost their creativity (Zhou et al., 2008). Combining different input modalities, such as touch and gestures, combined with the inherent intuitive camera control in AR applications empowers content creators to produce new forms of interactive experiences. Hence, the use of AR in museums has been attracting the research community for a long time. Through AR, the handheld museum guides can be enhanced in capability to provide a better flow of information to the user about the museum (Miyashita et al., 2008). Other work (Wojciechowski et al., 2004) created a system in early days of mobile AR that displays 3D versions of some of the pieces in museums. The positive effect of AR for an enhanced learning environment in museums has been shown in multiple studies (Wu et al., 2013) (Yoon et al., 2012). Other than an enhanced learning environment, Chang et al. (Chang et al. 2014) show that casual visitors can be guided to appreciate the art better through AR. On the other hand, reflections (Aydin et al., 2009) can have an adverse effect on presenting artwork in an AR environment. AR can also be used for personalized visits to the museum via creating stories (Keil et al., 2013). Recent work (Billinghurst et al. 2015) presents a comprehensive survey on applications on AR including its use in museums. In this work, we attempt to make museums more engageable especially for young visitors by allowing the users to personalize the color of paintings through the use of a mobile device. Recent work (Magnenat et al., 2015) (Zund et al., 2015) has shown how AR can be a host for enhancing creative real-world activities in a playful way. In this context, we employ AR to enhance the experience of visiting an art exhibition with an interaction component.

Soft color segmentation is defined as decomposition of an image into layers of homogeneous colors with opacity channels. Early work on the subject, notably the alternating optimization algorithm (Tai et al., 2007), show several applications of soft color segments for image editing. The alternating optimization algorithm takes the number of layers as input and iteratively solves for the color con- tent of the layers, referred as the color model, the opacity channels and the layer colors. Their approach especially lacks in terms of the smoothness of the opacity channels and homogeneity of layer colors. Recent work (Tan et al., 2016) (RGBSG) selects the color model before opacity estimation and fixes the layer colors to be solid. RGBSG requires the model colors to encompass the colors in the image from outside in the color space, which results in unrealistic colors in the model. This approach also suffers from prohibitively long run times as they optimize for the opacities of every pixel simultaneously, and requires the layer ordering beforehand, which is ill-defined and a nonintuitive task for a user. The unmixing-based approach (Aksoy et al., 2017) decreases the run time to around 1 minute per image by separating the opacity estimation and spatial smoothness problems. Their approach, which we use in our application, gives smooth layers with little variation in layer colors fully automatically, without requiring the number of layers of layer ordering. Algorithmic details for this method is discussed in detail in Section 3.

3. SOFT COLOR SEGMENTATION AND CONTENT GENERATION

In the proposed system the generation of layers is done automatically using the soft color segmentation algorithm (SCS) (Aksoy et al., 2017). SCS has two main steps: color model estimation and color unmixing. The color model is composed of a set of 3D RGB normal distributions representing the dominant colors in the image. It is constructed such that the colors of all the pixels are well represented, hence the number of layers depend on the color content of the image. The model is then given to the color unmixing algorithm for the estimation of layer colors and opacities for each pixel.

The color model estimation is done based on a voting scheme, where the most under-represented color is determined at each iteration. For a selected color, a seed pixel is selected from regions without strong edges in the image. From the local neighborhood of the selected seed pixel, a normal distribution is estimated. Figure 2 shows the seed pixels and the estimated color model for an example image.

We use the alpha add representation for overlaying opacity channels (Aksoy et al., 2017). As we assume purely opaque input paintings, our representation of opacities give two constraints for the opacities and layer colors to give us the original painting:

$$\sum_i \alpha_i^p \boldsymbol{u}_i^p = \boldsymbol{c}^p \quad \text{and} \quad \sum_i \alpha_i^p = 1 \quad \forall p, \tag{1}$$

where α_i^p and u_i^p represent the opacity and color of layer *i* at pixel *p*.

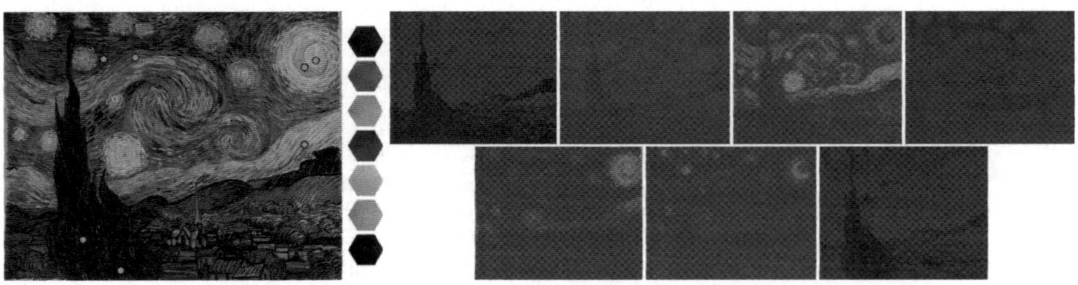

Figure 2. The unmixing-based soft color segmentation algorithm (Aksoy et al., 2017) first selects seed pixels (le) to determine a set of normal distributions in the RGB space to represent the colors in the input image. The hexagons show the color content of each normal distribution in the automatically estimated color model. This color model is then fed to the color unmixing algorithm to get spatially smooth layers of homogeneous colors, which is used for recoloring in our application. The original painting is The Starry Night by Vincent van Gogh

The opacities and colors for each layer are determined in two steps. The first step is the minimization of the sparse color unmixing energy (F_S).Given the color model, sparse color unmixing energy is minimized with respect to layer colors and opacities for each pixel independently:

$$\mathcal{F}_S = \sum_i \alpha_i^p \mathcal{D}_i(\boldsymbol{u}_i^p) + \sigma\left(\frac{\sum_i \alpha_i^p}{\sum_i (\alpha_i^p)^2} - 1\right), \tag{2}$$

where the layer color cost $D_i(u_i^p)$ is defined as the squared Mahalanobis distance of the layer color $u_i^p$to the layer distribution $N(\mu_i, \sum_i)$, and σ is the fixed sparsity weight. The energy minimization with constraints in Equation 1 is done via the algorithm used by (Aksoy et al., 2016).

As this energy minimization is defined independently for each pixel, the opacity channels are not necessarily spatially smooth. The second step addresses this issue by first smoothing the opacity channels using the guided filter (He et al., 2013) and then reestimating the layer colors to satisfy the first constraint in Equation 1.

The resulting layers, such as the ones presented in Figure 2, are characteristically of homogeneous colors and have smooth opacity transitions. Such layers make high-quality color editing straightforward: simply changing one of the colors in the color model results in natural color transitions in the image.

Before porting the layers to the mobile application, we define interaction regions as shown in Figure 3. These regions link the spatial extent of the user interaction with corresponding layers. Notice that we define these regions for layers with distinct hues and typically leave the black and white layers constant in order to preserve the luminance of the image constant.

4. INTERACTIVE COLOR EDITING APPLICATION

We developed a mobile app that allows users to play and interact with the colors of paintings by utilizing the soft color layers we discussed in the previous section and visualize their work through AR. To use the app, the user stands in front of a painting, holding a mobile device facing the painting. On the screen, a live video stream from the back-facing camera is presented to the user. As they point the mobile device at the painting, a virtual version of the same painting is shown, seamlessly integrated into the real world. To the user, the physical painting is replaced with a virtual, digitally enhanced version. The user can now click on different regions of the virtual painting to throw paint drops, which recolors regions of the virtual painting. The app allows the user to be creative and produce a personal, recolored version of the original painting. Figure 4 illustrates two individual examples. Figure 6 shows the application in action in a setup similar to a museum on a hand-held device for multiple paintings.

Figure 3. The regions for the user to interact with to change the color of a layer is roughly defined by the artist before the layers are ported to our mobile application

Figure 4. Our augmented reality application for interacting with paintings. The physical painting is seamlessly replaced on the mobile device with a digitally enhanced version, which allows the user to recolor regions and create their own masterpiece. The user recolored parts of Café Terrace at Night (left), and of Self-Portrait (right), both by Vincent Van Gogh

4.1 Implementation

In a preprocessing step, the virtual painting is divided into color layers using the soft color segmentation technique (Aksoy et al., 2017) to computationally provide a set of layers. For each layer, we manually define the collision regions as shown in Figure 3 that will allow the user to interact with the painting.

During runtime, the app analyzes the live camera stream and detects and tracks the templates of the paintings, which are registered in the app as image markers appearing in the camera image. As the virtual camera pose is estimated, the corresponding virtual painting is rendered on top of the camera image aligned with the image of the physical painting. When the user touches a region of the painting on the screen, a ray is cast to determine which layer is being activated. The app generates a random color and creates a visual effect of painting drops shooting from the virtual camera towards the painting. Upon impact, the drops recolor the selected corresponding layer by progressively shifting the hue to match the new color.

The app was realized using the Unity 5.5 game engine. The different layers of each painting were imported in the engine as ARGB textures. Each texture is then placed in the scene on different quads overlaid over the virtual painting marker. For each plane, we assign a set of colliders that match the corresponding colored regions of the painting. When the user taps on the tablet a ray is cast to identify the area of the painting that is activated. In addition, a custom shader is employed to create a smooth color shifting effect. Starting from the hue of the initial average color of the layer, whenever a new color is applied, it is converted to HSV space and the hue of each pixel is progressively shifted towards its difference from the initial value. In this way, we can preserve the individual features of each pixel without colorizing the whole layer. For the image marker tracking, we used Vuforia 6.2.6 as it provides a fast and reliable way to track the paintings and estimate the camera position.

Our application runs smoothly at 30 fps on second generation iPads, iPhones 5s, Nexus 7 (second generation), and Xperia Z tablets. A live video capture of our system is presented as supplemental material.

4.2 Automatic vs. Manual Layer Extraction

While it is certainly possible to produce the color layers manually instead of using the aforementioned soft color segmentation algorithm, the automatic method has significant advantages. In Figure 5, we show the manually generated soft color layers for the painting we present in our teaser image. The manually generated layers were produced by utilizing the color range selection tool in Adobe Photoshop CC. In order to obtain plausible layers, our artist had to adjust the fuzziness control of the tool, as well as performing additional manual edits. In general, a significant limitation of this tool is that it does not unmix the colors as the automatic soft color segmentation algorithm does. Performing the unmixing manually would have resulted in significant additional manual labor, which we did not attempt in this example. Even though we avoided manual unmixing, producing the layers in Figure 5 took roughly 10 minutes of artist time, versus approximately 1 minute fully-automatic processing time required by the automatic method. As a result, the use of the soft color segmentation method for our application makes the system scalable to a large number of paintings, making it possible to realize the AR application for a large collection of paintings with little cost.

Figure 5. Manually generated layers by an artist for the painting in the teaser

5. CONCLUSION

We presented an AR system for interacting with paintings by manipulating their colors. We demonstrated that the manual labor required for realizing such a system can significantly be reduced by utilizing automatic soft color segmentation. We presented various results captured using our prototype application, in addition to a live capture video provided as supplemental material. We believe that our production pipeline can be improved further by creating mesh colliders automatically from the alpha channel of the corresponding layers, therefore creating a fully automated process that can be easily deployed in any museum or exhibition.

Figure 6. Screen captures of our application when used on a hand-held device for recoloring multiple paintings

REFERENCES

Fabio Zünd et al. 2015. Augmented Creativity: Bridging the Real and Virtual Worlds to Enhance Creative Play. In SIGGRAPH Asia Mobile Graphics and Interactive Applications, Vol. 1, No. 1, Article 1. Publication date: April 2017.

Feng Zhou et al. 2008. Trends in augmented reality tracking, interaction and display: A review of ten years of ISMAR. In Proc. ISMAR.

J. Keil et al. 2013. A digital look at physical museum exhibits: Designing personalized stories with handheld Augmented Reality in museums. In Digital Heritage International Congress.

Jianchao Tan et al. 2016. Decomposing Images into Layers via RGB-space Geometry. ACM Trans. Graph. 36, 1 (2016), 7:1–7:14.

Kaiming He et al. 2013. Guided Image Filtering. IEEE Trans. Pattern Anal. Mach. Intell. 35, 6 (2013), 1397–1409.

Kuo-En Chang et al. 2014. Development and behavioral pattern analysis of a mobile guide system with augmented reality for painting appreciation instruction in an art museum. Computers & Education 71 (2014), 185 – 197.

Mark Billinghurst et al. 2015. A Survey of Augmented Reality. Foundations and Trends in Human-Computer Interaction 8, 2-3 (2015), 73–272.

Rafal Wojciechowski et al. 2004. Building Virtual and Augmented Reality Museum Exhibitions. In Proc. Web3D.

S. Magnenat et al. Live Texturing of Augmented Reality Characters from Colored Drawings. IEEE Trans. Vis. Comput. Graphics 21, 11 (2015), 1201–1210.

T. Miyashita et al. 2008. An Augmented Reality Museum Guide. In Proc. ISMAR.

Tai et al. 2007. Soft Color Segmentation and Its Applications. IEEE Trans. Pattern Anal. Mach. Intell. 29, 9 (2007), 1520–1537.

Tunç Ozan Aydın et al. 2015. Predicting display visibility under dynamically changing lighting conditions. Computer Graphics Forum (Proc. EUROGRAPHICS) (2009), vol 28, pp 173-182.

Yağız Aksoy et al. 2016. Interactive High-Quality Green-Screen Keying via Color Unmixing. ACM Trans. Graph. 35, 5 (2016), 152:1–152:12.

Yağız Aksoy et al. 2017. Unmixing-Based Soft Color Segmentation for Image Manipulation. ACM Trans. Graph. 36, 2 (2017), 19:1–19:19.

GESTURE-BASED LOCOMOTION IN IMMERSIVE VR WORLDS WITH THE LEAP MOTION CONTROLLER

Jorge C. S. Cardoso
CITAR - School of Arts, Portuguese Catholic University, Portugal
CISUC - Department of Informatics Engineering, University of Coimbra, Portugal

ABSTRACT

In this paper, we present a VR locomotion technique based on the Leap Motion device and compare it to other often-used locomotion techniques – gaze-directed locomotion and gamepad-based locomotion. We performed an exploratory user experiment to evaluate the three techniques based on their performance (time to complete the task), comfort (through the ISO 9241-9 assessment of comfort questionnaire), and simulation sickness (through the Simulation Sickness Questionnaire). Results indicate that the gamepad technique is both faster and more comfortable than either the Leap Motion-based or the gaze-directed techniques. These results suggest that the design of interaction techniques for the Leap Motion device should take into consideration the possible fatigue induced by the prolonged use of the device. For interaction tasks that require high performance, designers should look for alternatives to the Leap Motion device.

KEYWORDS

Interaction Device; Leap Motion; HCI; Virtual Reality; Locomotion; Performance Measurement

1. INTRODUCTION

Locomotion in virtual reality (VR) worlds is still an unresolved issue. Whether VR is experienced using head-mounted displays (HMD) or in CAVE rooms, locomotion presents various challenges and many techniques have been proposed and tested.

There have been many studies with real locomotion techniques where users of a VR world can physically move in the real world and produce an equivalent displacement in the virtual world. Real locomotion has the advantage of providing real proprioceptive and vestibular responses. In practice, however, real locomotion has a number of shortcomings: it requires a considerable unobstructed physical space to be useful (even with redirection techniques (Razzaque, Kohn and Whitton, 2001), the required area is larger than the typical living room); the VR equipment is usually not wireless, often requiring the use of cables hanging from the ceiling and help from operators to keep users free from entanglements (wireless solutions with portable computers do exist, but are usually heavy and bulky, or costly); it requires a tracking infrastructure. Simulated locomotion techniques like walking-in-place (WIP) have the advantage of not requiring a large physical area and of providing a physical experience similar to walking. However, they either require users to wear sensors on their feet or legs, or sensor equipped floors. Also, these techniques obviously require users to be standing up and exert themselves. Treadmills such as the Omni (Virtuix, 2016), Infinadeck (Infinadeck, 2016), are more expensive solutions and require additional setup and learning. Virtual locomotion techniques that make use of (typically) handheld controller are also often used. In these cases, locomotion is achieved by pressing buttons, moving joysticks, or gesturing in specific ways as one would do in a desktop or gaming scenario. These solutions have the advantage of being inexpensive and easy to use, but they generally result in a weaker feeling of presence than simulated or real locomotion techniques(Slater, Usoh and Steed, 1995; Usoh *et al.*, 1999).

In consumer VR, the most common approaches for locomotion are based on virtual locomotion techniques. Recently, new devices specifically designed for VR interaction have appeared. The HCT Vive VR controller or the Oculus Rift Touch controller for example, are handheld devices that are positionally and rotationally tracked in physical space. This allows the VR system to provide an exact match between the physical position and movement of the user's hands and the virtual representation of the hands. These controllers, however, require users to wear them in their hands at all times making it hard for users to use their hands to grasp or feel other physical objects in the physical environment (Steinicke *et al.*, 2008).

The Leap Motion (LM) controller is a 3D sensing device (Leap Motion Inc., 2016) for hand gesture interaction. The LM is a small input device controller (7.6 x 3 x 1.3 cm), which detects and recognizes user's hands posture and gestures (Figure 1). The LM can sense the position and orientation of the fingers of both hands, as well as the palm orientation and curvature. The device can be mounted on HMDs allowing users to use hand gestures to interact in VR worlds. At first sight, the LM appears as an interesting alternative to other controllers because it is worn in the HMD itself (users do not need to physically handle another device) and it allows free gestural interaction. Because it is a camera-based device, it also allows using the real image of the user's hands to be incorporated into the virtual world (although not in true color with the current version of the device). The LM can be attached to an HMD roughly in the same direction as the user's eyes providing a natural hands perspective in the VR world (see Figure 2).

Few studies have been conducted to evaluate the LM as a locomotion controller within HMD-based VR worlds. The objective of the current work is to provide an exploratory assessment of the LM device for locomotion in HMD-based VR and compare it with other techniques. Ultimately, this can help us design better locomotion interfaces that use the LM device by knowing the limitations of the device in an HMD-mounted setting and how users perform with it. For this, we have performed an experimental evaluation and comparison of three locomotion techniques – hand gestures with the LM device, gamepad-based locomotion, and gaze-directed locomotion. We measured the time it took for participants to complete the tasks, and we also gathered subjective feedback through the Simulation Sickness Questionnaire (Kennedy *et al.*, 1993) and the ISO 9241-9 assessment of comfort questionnaire (International Organization for Standardization, 2000).

The contributions of this paper are as follows: 1) A definition of a gesture-based locomotion technique for HMD-based VR using the LM device. 2) An assessment of the overall user experience and performance of using the LM for locomotion. 3)The evaluation of a gesture-based locomotion technique and comparison with gamepad-based and gaze-directed locomotion.

2. RELATED WORK

(Nabiyouni, Laha and Bowman, 2014) performed a usability testing to find which of five LM based 3D locomotion techniques was the most efficient in bare-hand interaction. The five techniques were tested in a set of three tasks and the interaction was performed using the LM controller. The techniques developed were based on the "Camera-in-hand" metaphor, in which the absolute position of the user's hand is directly mapped to the position of the virtual camera, simulating a situation where the user holds a camera in his hand; and on the "Airplane" metaphor, where the camera has a velocity controlled by the user. The three tasks devised for the evaluation of the locomotion techniques were "absolute travel", where the user was required to travel from a starting position to a known target position; "naive search", where the user was required to search for targets during a specific period; and "path following", where the user was required to follow a specific path by passing through rings. A 3D virtual scenario, modelled as a city, was used to perform the tests. This evaluation was performed in a desktop setting, i.e., not in an HMD-based VR setting. Results showed no difference between the techniques for the absolute travel task, but in the naive search the unimanual, camera-in-hand technique performed better than all the other techniques. In the path following task however, the four airplane metaphor techniques were significantly better than the unimanual camera-in-hand technique. In this study, the LM was positioned on top of the computer desk and the 3D world was visualized in the desktop monitor, which makes the results not directly applicable to an HMD setting. Also, no comparison with non-LM based techniques and no effort or comfort evaluation were done.

(McCullough *et al.*, 2015) developed a locomotion technique based on the Myo armband (Thalmic Labs Inc., 2016). The technique consisted in swinging the arms to initiate locomotion in the direction of the user's gaze. The faster the swinging, the faster the user moved in the virtual world. One advantage of the Myo device for gesture controls is that it is not vision-based: users can keep their arms in any position, unlike the LM which requires users' hands to be "visible" by the device. Another advantage of this technique is that users mimic more closely the (arm) movements of natural walking and thus potentially provides a more natural way of locomotion based on gestures. (McCullough *et al.*, 2015) compared their technique to joystick and real locomotion, however only turning errors and delay were measured. Results indicate a lower turning error for the Myo and real walking techniques when compared to the joystick technique. No effect of technique was found regarding the latency of turning. In this study, no evaluation of effort or comfort was done.

3. EXPERIMENT

The purpose of this study was to compare the efficiency and usability of the various locomotion techniques. For this, we created a simplified 3D world with two main areas, where users were asked to perform locomotion tasks, immersed in a first-person perspective, using three different locomotion techniques.

3.1 Locomotion Techniques

The Leap Motion locomotion technique (**LMTravel**) was designed for use with the Leap Motion controller positioned in the VR headset (see Figure 1). We used the VR mount for the Oculus Rift headset provided by Leap Inc. The LMTravel is based on hand gestures that allow us to control: 1) Movement start/stop. Opening both hands triggers the start of movement (Figure 2-a); closing both hands stops the movement (Figure 2-b). 2) Movement speed. The number of fingers stretched defined the movement speed: one finger corresponds to the lowest speed; all 5 fingers stretched corresponds to the highest speed (Figure 2-c). 3) Rotation. The tilt angle of the right hand is mapped to the camera's rotation.

The technique can also be used without rotation control by the right hand, using instead the rotation from the headset (i.e., the movement is directed by the user's gaze). In this case, once the movement has started, the right hand can be lowered and speed can be controlled by the left hand (Figure 2-d). In the experiment, the LMTravel technique was used without rotation control to give users a level of control like the other evaluated locomotion techniques.

The **Gamepad** locomotion technique uses a standard gamepad controller. Users control the direction of movement using the gamepad's joystick button. In this technique, we opted to allow movement in eight directions. Besides the usual forward, backward, left strafe and right strafe directions, we also allow diagonal directions. This is more in line with what gamepad users would expect from the controller. Again, the forward movement is relative to the user's gaze.

The **Gaze-based** locomotion technique places a "cursor" in the center of the screen and a corresponding target icon (a white cylinder) in the floor in case the user's gaze intersects the floor. By pressing a button (for implementation simplicity, we used a wireless mouse) the user moves to the target location. This technique is like the one used by (Grasset, Lamb and Billinghurst, 2005), but in our implementation users can move to any point in the ground plane provided they can look at it, instead of moving only a step in one of eight directions. In case there are obstacles in the way, our implementation chooses the shortest path. In the Gaze technique, users are free to look anywhere while the movement is in progress.

3.2 Tasks

Figure 1. Leap Motion mounted on the Oculus Rift

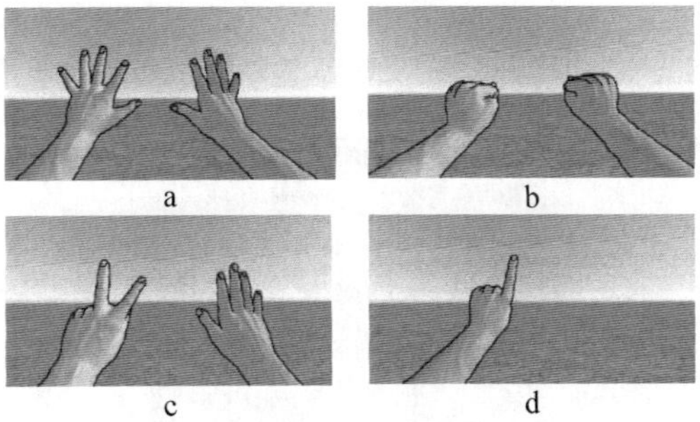

Figure 2. Hand poses for the LMTravel technique

Task 1 was a simple path following task that took place in an open area composed of 7 circular platforms on the ground. The next platform that the user should get to was indicated by a large purple sphere in the air over the platform. Figure 3 shows a perspective view of the area for task 1, with the purple sphere over platform number 1. Platforms were logically numbered 1 to 7 and participants were asked to follow the purple sphere (i.e., to reach the corresponding platform). Participants were asked to make 6 sequences, where one sequence would correspond to the following platform sequence: 1-2-5-6-7-4-3-1-3-4-7-6-5-2-1.

Task 2 consisted in searching for a red vase inside each of the 8 houses in area 2 of the virtual world (see Figure 4). Each house was identified by a number clearly visible from the front door of any house. The order in which participants had to visit each house was indicated by the researcher and it was different for each locomotion technique (but the same for every participant). Participants performed task 2 once.

3.3 Procedure

The experiment was a within-subjects design where all participants were subjected to the three locomotion techniques. To balance the order in which the techniques were given to participants we generated all 6 permutations and sequentially assigned participants to each permutation. Participants were introduced to the experiment with a brief description of what they would be asked to do, and with an initial training phase. In the training phase, we equipped participants with the VR headset and Leap Motion and explained how the various locomotion techniques worked. We then asked participants to explore the VR world inside and outside a house, informally asking participants to accomplish simple tasks such as entering a specific room. This training phase would end when users said to be comfortable with the workings of the various techniques. Participants sat on a swivel with no armrests, to make it easier to rotate. The computer that drove the VR world (and to which the VR headset was attached) was in a standard computer desk in front of the participant.

After the training phase, we asked participants to go to the starting point of task 1 (platform number 1) and briefly explained the task. After task 1 was completed (all 6 sequences) we explained and asked participants to accomplish task 2. The time it took to complete each task was automatically recorded by the VR world software.

After both tasks were completed for a given interaction technique, we asked participants to remove the headset and fill in the Simulation Sickness Questionnaire (SSQ) (Kennedy *et al.*, 1993) and the ISO 9241-9 assessment of comfort (International Organization for Standardization, 2000) questionnaires in a computer that was setup and dedicated to the questionnaires in the laboratory. We also allowed participants to take a break before or after filling in the questionnaires (we did not measure the break time). After the last locomotion technique experimented, we additionally asked the participant to fill in a two-question questionnaire where they would state which technique they liked best and which one they disliked the most. A complete session would last for about 45 minutes.

3.4 Participants and Apparatus

We gathered a convenience sample of thirty-nine participants, recruited from the university department, mostly MSc students. However, the final experimental data consists of only 31 participants (6 female, 25 male). The reasons for excluding participants include: not finishing the experiment due to extreme motion sickness, and experimenter error while collecting the log files. The headset was an Oculus Rift DK2 and the computer that ran the VR world was an iMac capable of driving the Rift at 70 fps. The VR scenarios and logging software was programmed in Unity 3D. We used a Leap Motion device version 1.2.1+10992.

Figure 3. Area for task 1

Figure 4. Inside of house in task 2

4. RESULTS AND DISCUSSION

In this section, we report the results from the experiment. In the analysis of these results, it should be noted that the LMTravel technique was the only technique that allowed users to control the movement speed by raising a different number of fingers. We did not record the speed selection of participants along the experiment, but it is safe to assume that participants were not always moving at the highest speed possible when experimenting with the LMTravel technique. (Both the Gaze and Gamepad techniques moved the user at the highest speed.)

During the experiments, we noticed a problem with the physical setup: as users rotated in their chair, the headset cable would sometimes get entangled with the chair and users had to rotate back to a standard position. We did not try to solve this issue during the experiment so that all participants experienced the same conditions.

4.1 Trajectories

Looking at the resulting trajectories from the different techniques, we observe noticeable differences between them. Figure 5 shows a top view of the trajectories performed in task 1 by a single participant. With gaze-directed locomotion, trajectories are essentially straight lines (except in the cases where participants select a different target location before the current movement finishes), but participants often overshoot their targets. This may be because the selection cursor of the gaze technique gets smaller as it is placed farther away from the user. Also, at higher distances, the same angular displacement of the head causes a higher linear displacement of the selection cursor, making it harder to position accurately. This issue might have been alleviated with a better visual feedback on the selected target position, for example, by highlighting the objects on which the cursor rests.

In terms of trajectory, the LMTravel results in straight lines, indicating that users have control over the trajectory.

We calculated the distance traveled in each sequence and the average distance per sequence per locomotion technique. In task 1, the LMTravel technique resulted in the shortest average distance per sequence (Table 1). Inspection of the 95% confidence intervals shows that the differences were significant between all locomotion techniques, but the Gamepad technique resulted in only about 3.5% higher average sequence distances than the LMTravel technique.

The gamepad technique resulted in jagged trajectories. This may be due to inadvertent changes in direction (users may position the joystick a bit to the sides causing a side short movement) or simply because movement corrections must be made in a discrete way - the gamepad technique supported only 8 discrete movement directions. Even though users could change direction of movement by changing their gaze direction, gamepad users might be accustomed to using only the gamepad's joystick. This may have created some confusion while controlling the locomotion. However, overall it did not result a substantially higher distance when compared to the LMTravel.

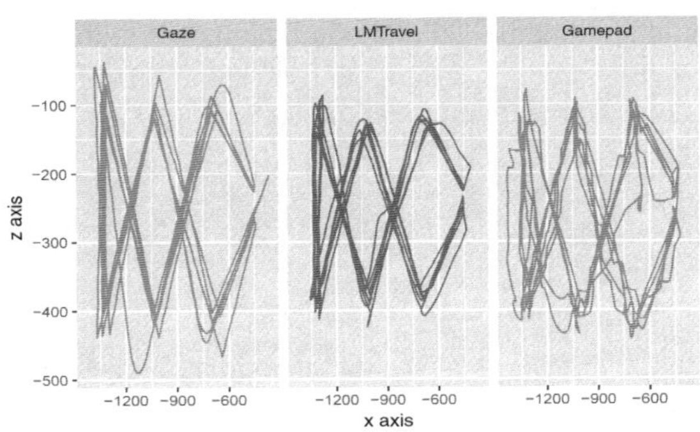

Figure 5. Illustrative trajectories from task 1

Table 1. Average sequence distances for task 1 (VR World units)

Technique	Mean [95% conf. int.]	SD	Min	Max
Gaze	3083 [3031, 3136]	328	2592	4324
LMTravel	2737 [2714, 2762]	152	2424	3368
Gamepad	2833 [2810, 2858]	153	2500	3365

4.2 Movement Time

We measured how long participants took to complete each sequence in task 1, and how long it took them to complete task 2. For task 1, Figure 6 shows the average sequence movement duration for the 6 sequences, per locomotion technique.

There seem to be an obvious learning effect for Gaze and LMTravel. It is also apparent that the Gamepad technique far exceeds the others in terms of movement performance. In the next comparisons, we have removed sequence number 1 from the data because the learning effect is most obvious for that sequence.

Table 2 shows the average movement duration for both tasks. The differences between the techniques in both task 1 and task 2 are very similar. Inspection of the confidence intervals shows that there is a significant difference between Gamepad and both LMTravel and Gaze. Users are much faster with the gamepad, spending about 20% less time in either task, than with Gaze or LMTravel techniques. Paired t-tests between LMTravel and Gaze showed a marginally significant difference in task 1 ($t(30)=1.9217$, $p = 0.06419$), but no significant difference task 2 ($t(30)=0.70495$, $p = 0.4863$).

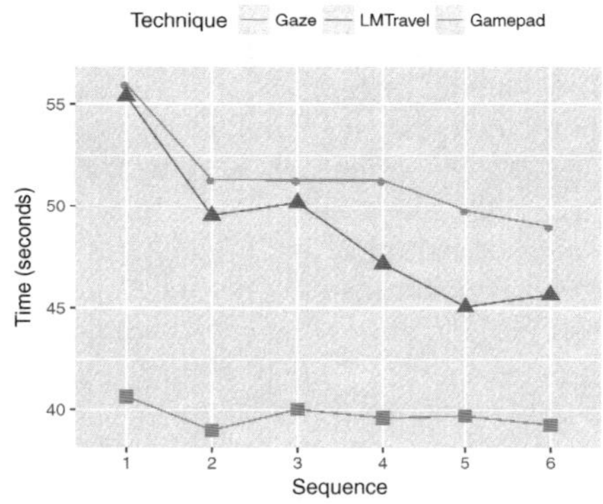

Figure 6. Average sequence movement duration per technique.

Table 2. Movement duration (in seconds). For task 1, the values correspond to the average sequence duration. For task 2, the values correspond to the average time for completion of the task

Technique	Mean [95% conf. int.]	SD	Min	Max
Task 1				
Gaze	51.2 [49.8, 52.6]	8.6	39.3	94.7
LMTravel	48.2 [46.4, 50.1]	11.5	32.3	90.0
Gamepad	40.1 [38.6, 41.6]	9.6	24.7	67.0
Task 2				
Gaze	218.7 [202.0, 235.5]	47.5	148.0	339.4
LMTravel	213.3 [203.2, 223.3]	28.6	164.2	274.4
Gamepad	165.9 [153.0, 178.8]	37.2	116.5	259.8

4.3 Questionnaires

4.3.1 ISO 9241-9

The results from the ISO 9241-9 assessment of comfort questionnaire are presented in Figure 7. The Gaze and Gamepad techniques are rated very similarly by the participants of the study (in general, Gaze is rated only slightly lower than the Gamepad technique).

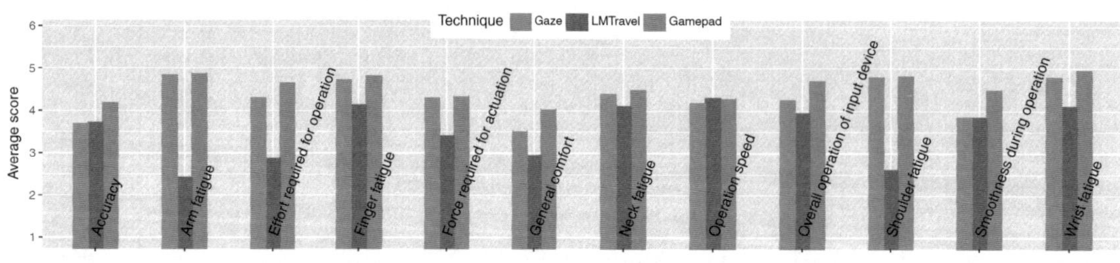

Figure 7. Results from the ISO 9241-9 assessment of comfort questionnaire

The LMTravel technique however, scores negatively in various of the questions, specifically the ones related to the fatigue of the upper limbs. The arm fatigue, effort required for operation, general comfort, and shoulder fatigue items have been rated lower than 3, on average. These results are in line with other assessments of the LM device in other situations: (Seixas, Cardoso and Dias, 2015) evaluated the LM device for desktop 2D pointing and the results of the ISO 9241-9 questionnaire in that study also show low scores in these items. These results are expected as the LMTravel technique requires users to keep their arms lifted for them to be detected by the LM device. Without any physical support, the required position is not comfortable and prolonged use results in fatigue – similar to the gorilla arm effect with prolonged use of vertical touch screens.

4.3.2 SSQ

The results from the Simulation Sickness Questionnaire (SSQ) are presented in Figure 8. For these questionnaires, we used the data from all 39 study participants, since all of them experienced the three techniques long enough to be able to evaluate them in the SSQ. Although results show slightly higher values for the Gaze technique than the Gamepad (with the LMTravel generally in between), paired Wilcoxon signed rank tests on total score revealed no statistically significant difference.

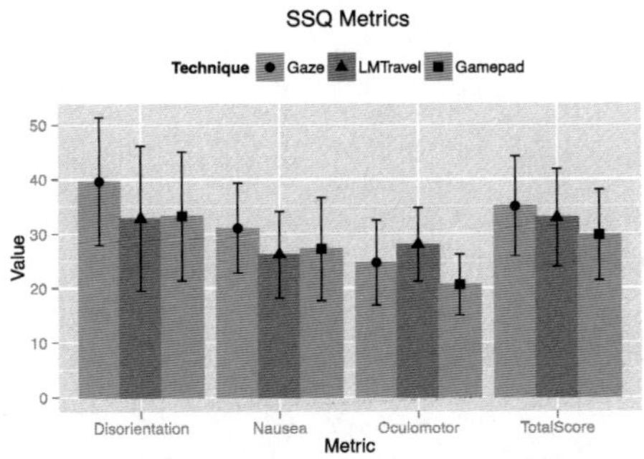

Figure 8. SSQ calculated metrics

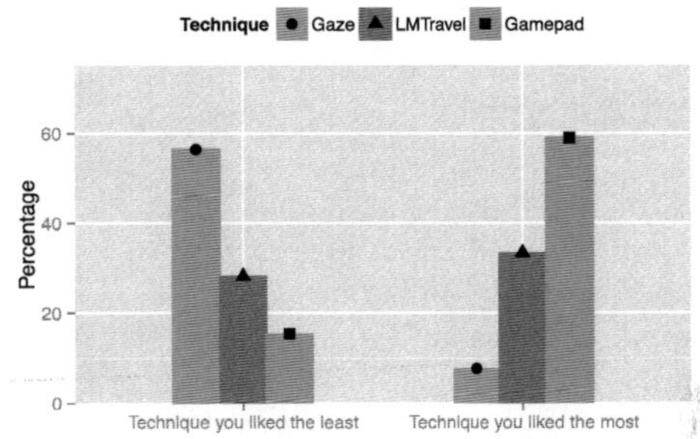

Figure 9. Technique preference

4.3.3 Preferred Technique

We also asked participants to explicitly tell us which technique they liked best and which one they disliked most. The percentages for each technique are shown in Figure 9.

Clearly, the Gamepad technique was the favorite: it was chosen as the preferred technique by almost 60% of the participants. The Gaze-directed technique was the least liked: chosen by 56%. The preference for the LMTravel technique was more divided: 33% chose it as the preferred technique, and 28% chose it as the least preferred technique. Unfortunately, we did not follow up the responses to this last questionnaire to determine the reasons for the participants' preferences.

5. CONCLUSION

The development of the LM device has recently been targeted especially towards VR interaction where the device is attached to the HMD. Our study provides an initial observation of the user experience while using the device in its proposed HMD-attached setting for locomotion.

We have presented the results from an experiment designed to study the Leap Motion device as a locomotion controller for HMD-based VR worlds and compared it with more standard techniques such as Gaze-based locomotion and Gamepad locomotion. We compared the performance (movement speed), as well as the effort required, and the simulation sickness effect for the three techniques.

The results indicate that the Leap Motion gestures we chose perform marginally better than the Gaze technique but worse than the Gamepad technique, in terms of movement speed. Also, results show that the effort required to operate the Leap Motion in these conditions is considerably higher than the effort required to operate the Gamepad or the Gaze-based techniques.

Our study did not pretend to provide an in-breadth evaluation of the LM. Our results can only be interpreted in light of the fact that the LM was attached to the HMD and that we asked users to perform a locomotion task, which generally required users to be looking straight at the horizon. In this setting, the main implication of our study is that care should be taken to ensure that users don't get too tired while interacting. The envisioned interaction should not require prolonged use of the same hand and arm poses. In situations where users are interacting with objects such that they are facing down or slightly down, the fatigue effect may not be as pronounced as in our study.

In this study, we did not refine the LMTravel technique, as we wanted to get an initial feedback on the possibilities of the device for locomotion within VR. It may be possible to conceive locomotion interaction techniques for the LM device that do not require users to keep their arms extended for long periods, hence reducing the effort of using the device. Additionally, interaction designers may try using the LM device in a position other that the HMD itself, which may allow for more comfortable hand and arm poses.

While our LMTravel technique was not as performant as the Gamepad technique, the use of the LM device in the HMD-attached setting is still worth considering in many situations. The LM device has the obvious advantage of not requiring users to hold a physical device, making their hands free to pick up physical objects, in situations where the user is not locomoting.

REFERENCES

Grasset, R., Lamb, P. and Billinghurst, M. (2005) 'Evaluation of mixed-space collaboration', *Proceedings - Fourth IEEE and ACM International Symposium on Symposium on Mixed and Augmented Reality, ISMAR 2005*, 2005, pp. 90–99. doi: 10.1109/ISMAR.2005.30.

Infinadeck (2016) *Infinadeck*. Available at: http://www.infinadeck.com/ (Accessed: 20 June 2011).

International Organization for Standardization (2000) *Ergonomic Requirements for Office Work with Visual Display Terminals (VDTs): Requirements for non-keyboard input devices*. ISO. Available at: http://www.iso.org/iso/home/store/catalogue_ics/catalogue_detail_ics.htm?csnumber=30030 (Accessed: 30 April 2014).

Kennedy, R. S., Lane, N. E., Berbaum, K. S. and Lilienthal, M. G. (1993) 'Simulator Sickness Questionnaire: An Enhanced Method for Quantifying Simulator Sickness', *The International Journal of Aviation Psychology*, pp. 203–220. doi: 10.1207/s15327108ijap0303_3.

Leap Motion Inc. (2016) *Leap Motion*. Available at: https://www.leapmotion.com/ (Accessed: 1 January 2016).

McCullough, M., Xu, H., Michelson, J., Jackoski, M., Pease, W., Cobb, W., Kalescky, W., Ladd, J. and Williams, B. (2015) 'Myo Arm–Swinging to explore a VE', in *Proceedings of the ACM SIGGRAPH Symposium on Applied Perception - SAP '15*. New York, New York, USA: ACM Press, pp. 107–113. doi: 10.1145/2804408.2804416.

Nabiyouni, M., Laha, B. and Bowman, D. A. (2014) 'Poster: Designing Effective Travel Techniques with Bare-hand Interaction', in *EEE Symposium on 3D User Interfaces (3DUI)*. Center for Human - Computer Interaction and Department of Computer Science, Virginia Tech, pp. 139–140. Available at: http://people.cs.vt.edu/blaha/docs/Poster - Designing Effective Travel Techniques with Bare-hand Interaction.pdf (Accessed: 23 January 2014).

Razzaque, S., Kohn, Z. and Whitton, M. C. (2001) 'Redirected Walking', *Proceedings of EUROGRAPHICS*, pp. 289–294. doi: 10.1017/CBO9781107415324.004.

Seixas, M. C. B., Cardoso, J. C. S. and Dias, M. T. G. (2015) 'The Leap Motion movement for 2D pointing tasks: Characterisation and comparison to other devices', in *Proceedings of the 5th International Conference on Pervasive and Embedded Computing and Communication Systems (PECCS-2015)*. SCITEPRESS Science and Technology Publications, Lda. doi: 10.5220/0005206100150024.

Slater, M., Usoh, M. and Steed, A. (1995) 'Taking steps: the influence of a walking technique on presence in virtual reality', *ACM Transactions on Computer-Human Interaction*, 2(3), pp. 201–219. doi: 10.1145/210079.210084.

Steinicke, F., Bruder, G., Kohli, L., Jerald, J. and Hinrichs, K. (2008) 'Taxonomy and implementation of redirection techniques for ubiquitous passive haptic feedback', *Proceedings of the 2008 International Conference on Cyberworlds, CW 2008*, pp. 217–223. doi: 10.1109/CW.2008.53.

Thalmic Labs Inc. (2016) *Myo*. Available at: https://www.myo.com/ (Accessed: 1 June 2016).

Usoh, M., Arthur, K., Whitton, M. C., Bastos, R., Steed, A., Slater, M. and Brooks, F. P. (1999) 'Walking > walking-in-place > flying, in virtual environments', *Proceedings of the 26th annual conference on Computer graphics and interactive techniques - SIGGRAPH '99*, pp. 359–364. doi: 10.1145/311535.311589.

Virtuix (2016) *Virtuix Omni*. Available at: http://www.virtuix.com/ (Accessed: 1 January 2016).

Webel, S., Olbrich, M., Franke, T. and Keil, J. (2013) 'Immersive experience of current and ancient reconstructed cultural attractions', *Proceedings of the DigitalHeritage 2013 - Federating the 19th Int'l VSMM, 10th Eurographics GCH, and 2nd UNESCO Memory of the World Conferences, Plus Special Sessions fromCAA, Arqueologica 2.0 et al.*, 1, pp. 395–398. doi: 10.1109/DigitalHeritage.2013.6743766.

GESTURES IN HUMAN-COMPUTER INTERACTION – WHICH SHAPE AND HOW MANY?

Lisa Graichen[1], Matthias Graichen[2] and Josef F. Krems[1]
[1]*Chemnitz University of Technology, Cognitive and Engineering Psychology, Germany*
[2] *Universität der Bundeswehr Munich, Human Factors Institute, Germany*

ABSTRACT

Due to the paradigm of Natural User Interaction gestures came into focus of HCI. When using gesture interaction in an approach to make HCI more natural, the questions of which gestures and how many gestures can be used in an interface is important to answer. In this paper two experiments are described, one concerning an assessment of two different gesture sets, one being more adapted to human communication, one being more adapted to communication with technical devices. The second experiment focuses on the number of gestures, using three different interfaces, one with two, one with four and one with six different gestures. Results show no clear differences of the participants, however interfaces with six gestures and with human-centered gestures were assessed slightly more positive.

KEYWORDS

NUI, Gesture-based interaction, Gestures, Acceptance, User Experience, Workload

1. INTRODUCTION

1.1 Gestures in Human-Computer Interaction

Gestures are usually considered as being a “nonverbal” form of communication. Scientists doing research in the field of grammar normally focus on written and spoken language. These two facts show the imagination that gestures are something separated from verbal speech and communication. It comes that in the last years this imagination started to change. Now researchers are engaged in the pretty young field of gesture use, trying to understand how gesture accompanies human speech. Speech is now seen as something multimodal including gestures (Fricke, 2013), which can be described on a continuum from gestures accompanying speech to sign language (McNeill, 1992).

Speakers deliberately use gestures to show the appearance of an object, point to objects or persons or make clear their attitude towards something. The process of gesturing begins with the hand in a relaxed position, which is then moved in front of the body to perform the meaningful part of the gesture and then moved back into a relaxed position. Gestures can be classified in two global categories: autonomous and co-verbal gestures. Autonomous gestures replace speech, stand alone and can be understood without co-verbal clarification. Co-verbal gestures occur together with other modalities, typically with speech (Bressem & Ladewig, 2011).

In the last years, gestures were also considered in the design process of modern human-computer-interaction (HCI) aiming at facilitating complex operation processes and offering entirely new interaction strategies. Saffer (2009) divides modern gestural interfaces in two categories: Touch-based interfaces and free-form interfaces. To interact with a touch-based interface the user needs to touch the screen of the device directly, e.g. with his fingertips. To interact with a free-form interface (or gesture-based interface; GBI) the user is not required to touch the device. The user either has to operate using an input device like a glove or controller, or must perform the gestural input operations within the near range of sensors (e.g. depth sensing cameras and infrared sensors), which track movements of the body (e.g. hand and fingers) and convert them into 3D input. Referring to touch-based interaction (TBI) often the term gesture is used as well for describing different input movements carried out on the screen, like swiping the screen with one or two fingers. Additional to Saffer (2009), a free-form interface would also be an interface being controlled by gaze or emotions. In the following sections and experiments the term of "gesture-based interaction" and "gesture" in general as reference to an in-air hand movement respective manipulating the interface by in-air gestures without touching the interaction device.

For the traditional way of interaction with mouse and keyboard, the WIMP-paradigm (acronym for windows, icons, menus, and pointing devices) was developed (e.g. Kortum, 2008). When using the mouse, there is only one input possibility (besides the two-dimensional targeting of the cursor), namely clicking. Users need to learn, when, how and where to click with which mouse button to get the desired outcome. Hereof, TBI is similar by using fingers instead of the mouse. But in contrast, there can be completely new ways when using in-air gestures. The known paradigm is still possible by using fingers for cursor targeting and action performing, but differing from TBI as fingers will not touch the display and remain in the air. It follows that there will be no direct feedback for succeeding in the intended action like perceiving the mouse click or the contact with the display. There can be also a new way of using a specified gesture for a specified action (cf. the gesture of drawing a circle is used for repeating something, see below). In this case the user needs new knowledge on what kind of gesture stands for which action. On the other hand, there will be no need for visually searching an item on the display, as the gesture can simply be performed in the air and the computer will translate the recognized movement into a predefined operation. Being combined with voice output it would be possible to interact with the system completely without looking on the display. That makes gesture-based interaction especially interesting for drivers interacting with IVIS.

In recent publications of modern HCI the term "natural" often comes up. Usually it is used as a synonym referring to the "real world" when designing HCI more like people would actually interact in their everyday life, e.g. with things or other people. Natural User Interaction (NUI) is then often thought as being realized by changing the input modes in HCI. Thereby, one can think of TBI, GBI, voice commands, gaze control, and so on. But of course, this conception falls short as input (and output) mode can be a first step in creating a more natural interfaces, but is not a guaranteed to create one. All in all, the term "natural" describes the behavior and experience of the user, not the actual product of the interface (Wigdor & Wixon, 2011).

1.2 Research Question

There have been several experiments conducted using GBI, most of them with a narrowly defined scope or using gestures adapted from TBI (for an overview see Graichen & Metzner, 2014). For this reason, the present study aims to have a broader view on GBI. For creating any kind of gestural interface (may it be for smartphones, smart home environments, or in-vehicle technologies), it is necessary to know what gestures should be used and how many gestures users are likely (to remember and) to use. For TBI there is a set of gestures that is used by nearly every interface. To create such a widely accepted set of gestures likewise for GBI, the question arises, how these gestures should be designed. Do users have special preferences or do they simply learn whatever is provided? Moreover the number of gestures is important as well. When having few gestures, the learning effort will be low, but gestures cannot be that well adapted to the represented action. When having more gestures, the learning demand will be higher, but the gesture will suit the represented action better. As there is no literature comprising this question, the present work aimed at exploring rather than evaluating user preferences and to provide an initial guideline for designing GBI. Two experiments are described in this paper. The first experiment focuses on the shape of gestures, the second experiment on the number of gestures when interacting with a fictional user interface.

2. METHOD

2.1 Participants

Participants (mostly students) for both experiments were recruited via mailing lists of TU Chemnitz. In total 30 (19 female) people took part in the first experiment with a mean age of 25.27 years (SD = 6.4). Eleven people said, they already had experience in using GBI, 19 said they would not have any experience yet. Ten participants indicated they would be strongly interested in GBI, twelve indicated medium and eight low interest.

In the second experiment, a total of 88 people (61 female) took part, with a mean age of 23.99 (SD = 5.1 years), and were assigned to the experimental groups as follows: 29 of them operated with two gestures, 29 with four gestures and 30 six gestures (as these participants were the same as in experiment 1). Concerning previous experience, 25 people said, they already would have used GBI, 63 said they would not have any experience yet. Concerning the general interest in GBI, 32 participants indicated they would be strongly interested, 39 indicated medium and 17 low interest.

2.2 Research Design

To preclude inter-individual differences and to get the possibility of a direct comparison, a within-subject design was chosen for the first experiment. Each participant operated with the interface using 1) six gestures, developed to be as natural as possible (NUI, close to interpersonal communication and real-world-actions) and 2) six gestures, developed to be special for human-machine interaction (abbreviated as TI for technical interaction.

For the second experiment, a between-subject design was chosen. Every participant encountered the interface with either two, four, or six gestures taken from the designed NUI-gesture set (see Figure 5 and Table 1). This design was chosen to avoid confusion of the participants when interacting with the same interface using a changing number of gestures.

2.3 Procedure

Participants were first instructed to the interface and its functionalities. By that, participants were reminded that the whole experiment aimed at rating the type of interaction, not the aesthetic or usability of the user interface. After that, they were asked, if it would be ok to film the experiment for later evaluation. If they agreed, video recording was started. Afterwards they familiarized with the user interface by mouse as long as they wanted. Then, the instructor showed all the gestures and use cases according to the experimental conditions, and participants were required to repeat them. When all questions were clarified, a training session followed. Only in this training session, participants could monitor on a second screen what the gesture recognition device would detect, in order to get used to the detection performance and learn how to conduct the gestures correctly. The instructor observed the participant in this phase to ensure that the gestures were performed correctly and to give tips otherwise. When the participant felt confident in the usage of gestures, they were asked to accomplish a set of use cases, while the instructor counted occurring errors or special problems. Sequence of use cases has not been randomized in order to increase content-related coherence. An error was defined as every action that did not lead to the correct result, for example an erroneous detection of the leap or a deficient conduction of the gesture and so on.

Participants of the first experiment learned first one of the two gesture sets and then the other one. After using each gesture set, participants assessed the acceptance, workload, and user experience and decided which gestures they liked more for each action. Overall, the experiment took each participant about 90 minutes.

2.4 Facilities and Apparatus

2.4.1 User Interface

Participants operated with a self-developed web-based interface on a 14" laptop (Pentium 5 processor), which represented simple tasks from everyday use when interacting with a computer and responded to user inputs via the gesture recognition device (see below). These actions comprised 1) open and close something, 2) move to the next page (or scroll up or down), 3) zoom, 4) rotate and 5) grab and move an object (similarly to drag & drop, or copy an object). The first screen was designed with different tiles with symbols or pictures on their surface (similar to Windows 8 tile interface), which could be simply opened and closed (see Figure 1). By doing so another picture, a small text or a map appeared on the screen. On the second screen, the user could choose a picture from a list by activating them through the buttons on the left side. The selected picture appeared on the middle of the interface, and could then be rotated and zoomed (see Figure 2). The third screen showed a large white ball on red background, which could be grabbed and moved by the user anywhere on the screen (see Figure 3). When grabbing, a blue ring around the ball signalized the successful grabbing. The current position of the cursor was indicated by a red dot. On both sides of each screen, arrows indicated that one could move to the next or a previous screen. To move forward or backwards the user had to use the corresponding (swiping sideways, e.g. see Figure 5). The pictures used in the first two screens showed mostly cars. The interface was the same for both experiments and all experimental conditions, to make sure occurring differences could be attributed to differences in gestures sets.

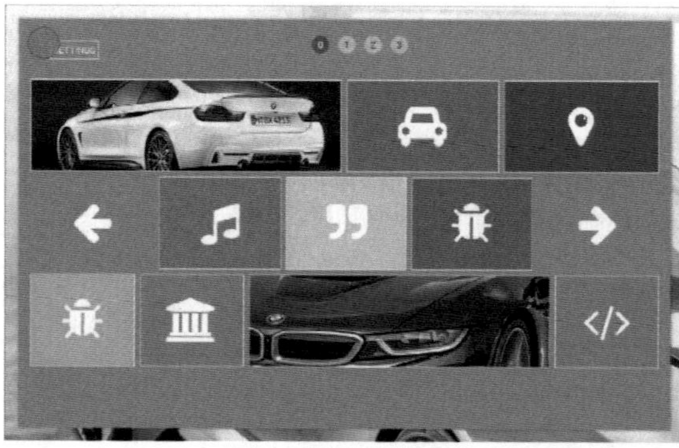

Figure 1. Screen 1: Open and close

Figure 2. Zoom and rotate

Figure 3. Grab and move

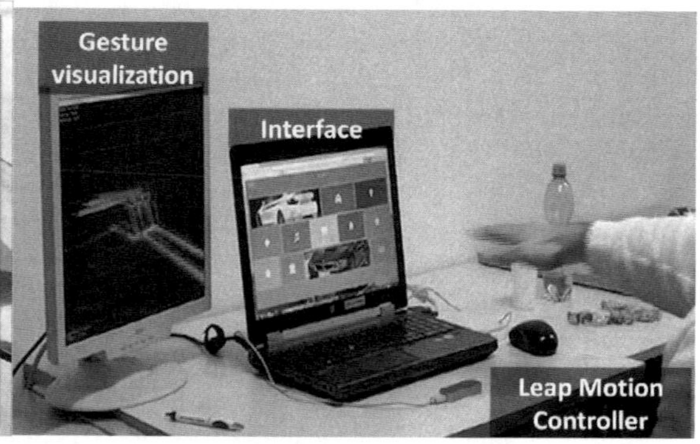

Figure 4. Experimental setup

2.4.2 Gesture Recognition

For the detection of gestures in open space Leap Motion was used (e.g. Marin, Dominio, & Zanuttigh, 2014). The controller was placed in front of the laptop (see Figure 4), but participants were free to place it, wherever it would suit them best. A second screen was placed next to the laptop showing the Leap Motion Visualizer. This visualizer displayed a grid with an abstracted hand model for showing what the controller detects at each moment. During the training session the screen was rotated towards the attendees, during the experimental session it was rotated to the camera. Video camera was placed next to the participants, so that faces would not be visible, but the screen with Leap Motion Visualizer for later evaluation (e.g. errors in gesture recognition).

2.4.3 Gesture Sets for Experiment 1

For the first experiment, two different gesture sets have been designed (see figure 2) for 1) natural interaction (NUI) and 2) technical interaction (TI). The design process was guided by general literature on gestural human-human-communication, but was also restricted by the detection quality of the gesture recognition device (all gesture have to base on swiping or circle-drawing movements). While gestures for 'Open', 'Close', 'Zoom' and 'Rotate' differ between the both sets, gestures for 'Move' and "Drag & Drop' are the same in both sets, as there was no other useful alternative for these actions.

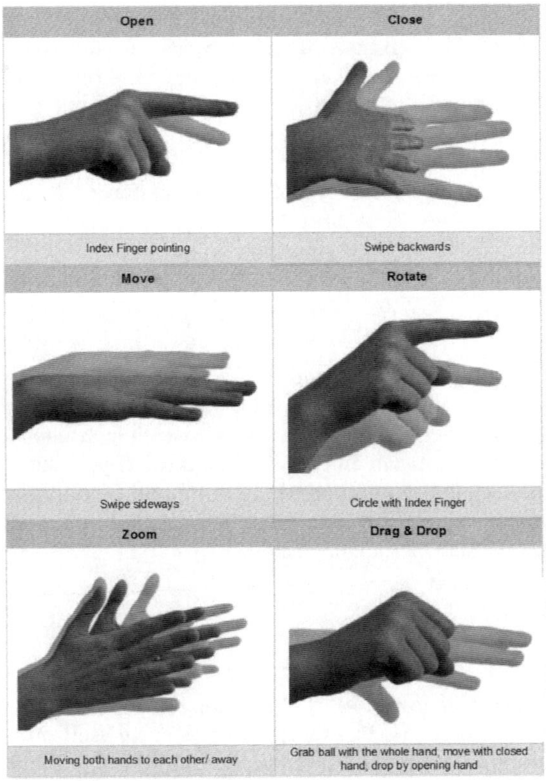

Figure 5. NUI-Gestures used in experiment 1

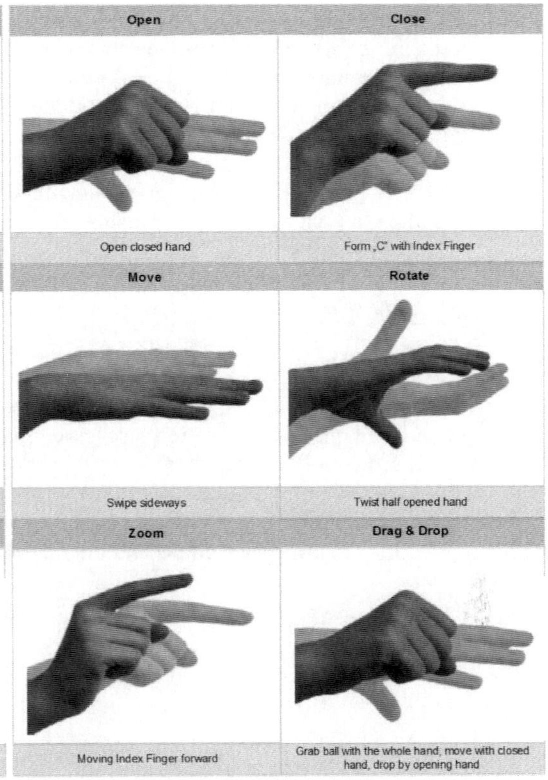

Figure 6. TI-Gestures used in experiment 1

2.4.4 Gesture Sets for Experiment 2

In the second experiment the number of NUI-gestures (see experiment 1) has been manipulated as can be seen in table 1. For the two-gesture-interface and the four-gesture-interface some actions do not have their own adapted gesture (like close or zoom). In this case the gesture for "open something" was used, that means participants had to tap on a button, which showed an "x" in the upper right corner for "close something" or on a button having written "zoom" on it.

Table 1. Gesture sets in experiment 2

	Two gestures	Four gestures	Six gestures
Open	Index finger pointing	Index finger pointing	Index finger pointing
Close	-	Swipe backwards	Swipe backwards
Drag & Drop	-	-	Grab ball with the whole hand
Move	Swipe sideways	Swipe sideways	Swipe sideways
Zoom	-	Moving both hands apart	Moving both hands to each other
Rotate	-	-	Circle with Index Finger

2.5 Subjective Data

Acceptance was measured by a 9-item questionnaire (using a 5-point rating scale ranging from -2 to 2) of Van der Laan, Heino, and Waard (1997). It consist of the two subscales 'usefulness' (five items) and 'satisfying' (four items). Workload was assessed using the 6-item NASA-TLX by Hart and Staveland (1988). It estimates the level of 'mental demand', 'physical demand', 'temporal demand', 'effort', 'performance', and 'frustration level' with one item each using a rating scale ranging from 0 to 20 (with a maximum total score of 120).

User experience was assessed for the experimental factor of interaction type using the 'AttrakDiff' questionnaire by Hassenzahl, Burmester, and Koller (2003). It consists of four subscales (with seven items each): 1) 'pragmatic quality' (PQ; pertaining to usability criteria), 2) 'stimulation' (pertaining to interestingness and voluptuousness), 3) 'identity' (pertaining to identification with the product) and 4) 'attractiveness'. The subscales 'stimulation' and 'identity' form together the general subscale of 'hedonic quality' (HQ).

In the first experiment, a short questionnaire was used to assess which of the both gestures (NUI vs. TI) corresponding to each use case participants preferred most.

3. RESULTS

The overall workload score has been obtained by averaging the subscales of NASA-TLX without weighting (often referred as raw TLX; in accordance with Hart (2006). For the interpretation of the results HQ and PQ of AttrakDiff the classification scheme by the questionnaire authors were consulted (see www.attrakdiff.com). For statistical analysis (two-sided) t-tests have been conducted for experiment 1 and ANOVAs with independent measures for experiment 2, including appropriate effect size calculation. None of the groups showed significant differences and the effects were small. Therefore, the detailed values will not be reported in the following sections and only descriptive statistics are presented.

3.1 Experiment 1

For acceptance, the usefulness and the satisfying scale values were higher for NUI gestures (0.75 and 0.65) than for TI gestures (0.38 and 0.39). NASA-TLX score was lower for NUI gestures, which means slightly lower workload reported (9.63 vs. 10.04). For AttrakDiff both interfaces were rated as being "self-oriented". Attractiveness subscale was again higher for NUI gestures (1.19) than for TI gestures (0.85). See Table 2 for detailed values.

Table 2. Results for subjective data of experiment 1

Score	Set 1 NUI		Set 2 TI	
	M	*SD*	*M*	*SD*
Usefulness	0.75	0.82	0.58	0.83
Satisfying	0.65	0.95	0.39	1.01
TLX	9.63	2.71	10.04	3.43
HQ	1.66	0.64	1.44	0.64
PQ	0.22	1.18	-0.09	1.36
Attractiveness	1.19	1.19	0.85	1.27

When being asked what gestures they liked most participants preferred NUI gesture for 'close' and for 'zoom', for 'open' there was no difference in the preference of the participants and for 'rotate' TI gesture was slightly preferred (see Table 3).

Table 3. User preferences concerning NUI or TI gestures for each use case

Gesture	Open		Close		Zoom		Rotate	
	NUI	TI	NUI	TI	NUI	TI	NUI	TI
Number	15	15	26	4	22	8	14	16

3.2 Experiment 2

For acceptance, the usefulness and satisfying scale were similar for two and four gestures (0.49 and 0.41 vs. 0.25 and 0.28) and higher for six gestures (0.75 and 0.65). Workload was similar for all interfaces the lowest score was reported for the four-gesture-interface with 9.27. For AttrakDiff all interfaces were assessed self-oriented. Attractiveness was again similar for two and four gestures (0.80 and 0.81) and higher for six gestures (1.18). See Table 4 for detailed values.

Table 4. Results for subjective data of experiment 2

Score	Two Gestures		Four Gestures		Six Gestures	
	M	*SD*	*M*	*SD*	*M*	*SD*
Usefulness	0.49	0.78	0.41	0.81	0.75	0.82
Satisfying	0.25	0.98	0.28	0.82	0.65	0.95
TLX	10.59	3.50	9.27	3.21	9.63	2.71
HQ	1.55	0.89	1.36	0.67	1.66	0.64
PQ	0.03	0.89	-0.26	1.05	0.22	1.18
Attractiveness	0.80	0.88	0.81	1.04	1.19	1.19

4. DISCUSSION

The present study aimed at the investigation of user preferences regarding the type and number of gestures when operating with an (computer) interface. Therefore, a simple experimental setup using a freely available gesture recognition device and a self-developed web-interface was set up. As there is no common state of the art, which could be aggregated from literature regarding these questions, the present study was conducted for exploratory reasons, and no assumptions were made in prior. Though no significant results could be found, still interesting insights could be gained from the user interactions.

User ratings regarding acceptance were highest for NUI-gestures and the set of six gestures (but on a relatively low level, with higher values of the perceived usability than for satisfaction). Similarly, the perceived workload was assessed lowest for NUI-gestures, but was lowest for the set of four gestures. Most interestingly, while the perceived pragmatic quality (which can be understood as an usability evaluation) was indifferent regarding both NUI- and BI-gestures, the hedonic quality was relatively high for both gesture sets, indicating that the general usage of GBI is experienced as highly stimulating. This is also reflected in the ratings for attractiveness, which is highest for the set of six gestures. These results may be attributed to the initial contact with an innovative technology as such, but this would not hold true for participants with prior experience with GBI. The general positive results with both gesture designs might indicate an overall unlocked potential of user experience with GBI in HCI.

However the investigated use cases represent only a small number of basic interaction tasks. But the preference comparisons also reveal, that a general statement in favor of NUI or TI cannot be made. This might imply, that the design of GBI should maybe not be generally guided by maximizing the naturalness of gestural movement mappings on related real-world-tasks.

When it comes to the number of different gestures, there seems to be no downside for the users. A slight preference for the six-gesture alternative could be found, indicating that there might be room for even more gestures.

Further research has the potential of creating a standard set of gestures that is widely accepted for different use cases, contexts and devices (like smartphones, smart environments or in-vehicle interfaces) and represents a number of useful and transferable actions. But this also requires a gesture recognition device which inheres less restrictions concerning the gesture design. The presented results give first directions towards these standards. Moreover more research on the usefulness of GBI in a realistic situation (like in-vehicle interaction or at home) is needed to determine the concrete user demands and the user experience of this new type of interaction. As younger persons may tend to be more flexible and open to new technologies further research could be investigating if there are differences when having older participants.

REFERENCES

Bressem, J., & Ladewig, S. H., 2011. Rethinking gesture phases: Articulatory features of gestural movement? *Semiotica, 2011*(184). doi:10.1515/semi.2011.022.

Fricke, E., 2013. Towards a unified grammar of gesture and speed: A multimodal approach. In C. Müller, A. Cienki, E. Fricke, S. Ladewig, D. McNeill, & S. Teßendorf (Eds.), *Handbücher zur Sprachund Kommunikationswissenschaft: Band 38.2. Body - Language - Communication. An international handbook on multimodality in human interaction. Volume 1.* Berlin Germany, Boston Massachusetts: Walter de Gruyter GmbH.

Graichen, L., & Metzner, M., 2014. Gestures in human-computer interaction - A review from a psychological point of view. In K. Blashki & Y. Xiao (Eds.), *Proceedings of the International Conferences on Interfaces and Human Computer Interaction 2014, Game and Entertainment Technologies 2014 and Computer Graphics, Visualization, Computer Vision and Image Processing 2014. Lisbon, Portugal, July 15 - 19, 2014 (part of the Multi Conference on Computer Science and Information Systems 2014)* (pp. 243–248). Lisbon: IADIS Press.

Hart, S. G., 2006. Nasa-Task Load Index (NASA-TLX); 20 Years Later. *Proceedings of the Human Factors and Ergonomics Society Annual Meeting*, *50*(9), 904–908. doi:10.1177/154193120605000909

Hart, S. G., & Staveland, L. E., 1988. Development of NASA-TLX (Task Load Index): Results of empirical and theoretical research. In *Advances in Psychology. Human Mental Workload* (Vol. 52, pp. 139–183). Elsevier. doi:10.1016/S0166-4115(08)62386-9

Hassenzahl, M., Burmester, M., & Koller, F., 2003. AttrakDiff: Ein Fragebogen zur Messung wahrgenommfener hedonischer und pragmatischer Qualität. In G. Szwillus & J. Ziegler (Eds.), *Berichte des German Chapter of the ACM: Vol. 57. Mensch & Computer 2003. Interaktion in Bewegung* (pp. 187–196). Stuttgart, Leipzig: B.G. Teubner.

Kortum, P. (Ed.)., 2008. *HCI beyond the GUI: Design for haptic, speech, olfactory and other nontraditional interfaces*. Amsterdam, Boston: Elsevier/Morgan Kaufmann.

Marin, G., Dominio, F., & Zanuttigh, P. (2014). Hand gesture recognition with leap motion and kinect devices. In *IEEE International Conference on Image Processing (ICIP), 2014. Paris, France, 27 - 30 Oct. 2014* (pp. 1565–1569). Piscataway, NJ: IEEE. doi:10.1109/ICIP.2014.7025313

McNeill, D. (Ed.)., 1992. *Hand and mind: What gestures reveal about thought*. Chicago: The University of Chicago Press.

Saffer, D., 2009. *Designing gestural interfaces*. Sebastopol, CA: O'Reilly Media, Inc.

Van der Laan, J. D., Heino, A., & Waard, D. de., 1997. A simple procedure for the assessment of acceptance of advanced transport telematics. *Transportation Research Part C: Emerging Technologies*, *5*(1), 1–10. doi:10.1016/S0968-090X(96)00025-3

Wigdor, D., & Wixon, D. (Eds.)., 2011. *Safari Tech Books Online. Brave NUI world: Designing natural user interfaces for touch and gesture*. Amsterdam: Morgan Kaufmann/Elsevier.

SUITABLE PARAMETERS FOR TACTON DESIGN IN TOUCH SCREEN INTERACTION

Tobias Stein, Martin Seeger, Bernd-Burkhard Borys and Ludger Schmidt
Human-Machine Systems Engineering Group,
Mechanical Engineering Department, University of Kassel, 34125 Kassel, Germany

ABSTRACT

Tactons are structured tactile messages and used to transmit information to users via the haptic sense. Common parameters (i.e. frequency, amplitude, rhythm, roughness, waveform, and duration) were examined and tested for discriminability to get valid information for tacton design in a touch screen interaction scenario. 51 participants took part in the experiment, which consisted of 98 randomized tasks. In each task, participants were presented two vibration signals via a touch screen and had to decide, whether signals were identical or different. Various combinations showed recognition rates above 90 % and it became clear that some parameters are more suitable in tacton design than others. Frequency and roughness achieved the best results, involving all paired comparisons, which were correctly distinguished by each participant. Distinguishable levels of parameters and design recommendations were derived from the results of the experiment, and considerations about future tacton design are presented.

KEYWORDS

Human-machine interaction, haptic feedback, coding information, tacton parameters.

1. INTRODUCTION

Touch screens are increasingly used in mobile devices such as smartphones or tablet computers, as well as in stationary systems like ticket vending machines or information terminals. Using touch screens, it is possible to perform complex interactions in a small area while remaining flexible at low cost. Compared to mechanical keyboards, touch screens show the disadvantage, that haptic feedback and familiar feeling provided by mechanical keys, transmitted via the sense of touch, is lost. Typing on a touch screen interface is more difficult and may result in a lower input speed (Hoggan et al. 2008). To address this problem, artificially generated vibrations provide tactile feedback in numerous devices. In addition to that, using the haptic sense to convey information is a promising approach to improve human-machine interaction (El Saddik 2007), in particular when the visual or auditory channel is overloaded or not available (Brewster and Brown 2004a).

1.1 Related Work

In recent studies, haptic feedback was successfully used, e. g. to present directional cues on participants' torso (van Erp et al. 2005, van Erp 2005, Tan et al. 2003). Other researchers found, that haptic feedback can increase situational awareness (Tan et al. 2003, Sklar and Sarter 1999), also in changed gravity conditions (Rochlis and Newman 2000). In these studies, haptic signals were rather simple, comprising mostly of a single signal with a frequency around 250 to 300 Hz. Moreover, it was shown that haptic feedback could help to estimate distance-to-obstacle in the absence of vision (Hartcher-O'Brien et al. 2015) and even can be used to improve the level of surgical precision during laser surgery procedures (Fichera et al. 2016).

While interacting on a flat steady surface like a touch screen or a flat virtual or real keyboard, haptic feedback can improve typing speed and reduce error rate, especially when haptic feedback is provided local rather than global (Kim and Tan 2014, Ma et al. 2015), and facilitate typing performance (Sim et al. 2016). Similar results can be found for mobile applications (Yatani and Truong 2009, Hoggan et al. 2008). In an eyes-free setup, better results concerning the error rate were achieved when the haptic feedback was given in a precise way matching participants' contact point on the touch screen (Yatani and Truong 2009). Research and design recommendations exist concerning a simple touch screen interaction like a button click, e. g. about providing a tactile "click" feeling when users touch the virtual buttons on a touch screen (Fukumoto and Sugimura 2001), the most pleasant tactile feedback for mobile (Koskinen et al. 2008) and stationary (Stein et al. 2016) touch-sensitive screens, and artificially created button edges on a touch screen (Pakkanen et al. 2010, Nashel and Razzaque 2003).

For transmitting more complex information using the haptic sense, Brewster & Brown (2004b) suggested the use of tactons. Tactons are structured tactile messages (Brewster and Brown 2004a), in which parameters of the vibration signal like frequency, amplitude, duration, etc. are modulated to encode information and transmit it to the user via the haptic sense. Compared to simple vibrations, the design of tactons is flexible, and depends on the information they encode. The application areas of tactons are diverse. Tactons can be presented via a computer mouse (Chan et al. 2008, Klatzky and Lederman 2006), a "PHANTOM" that is a high performance, 3D haptic interface (SensAble Technologies) (Lederman et al. 2006, Sjöström 2001), waist belts (van Erp et al. 2005) or torso displays (van Erp 2005, Tan et al. 2003), a vibrotactile wristband (Arab et al. 2015), and touch screens.

As an example, tactons presented progress information during file download while the user worked on other tasks (Brewster and King 2005). Three different haptic signals, all with the same frequency of 250 Hz but different durations and rhythms, informed the user about the status of the current download (i. e. start of a new download, current position of the process, and end of the task) and led to a significant improvement of performance as well as an overall preference for the tactile display (Brewster and King 2005).

In another study, tactons were used to inform the user about type and priority of an incoming message (Brown et al. 2005). Three different types (i. e. voice call, text message, multimedia message) were encoded by different rhythms, while the priority (i. e. low, medium, high) was encoded by the roughness of the vibration signal. Roughness is created by multiplying a sine wave of a given frequency by a sine wave of another frequency, thus modulating the amplitude of the base signal by the second frequency (Brown et al. 2005). Here, an unmodulated sine wave, a 250 Hz sine wave modulated by a 50 Hz sine wave and a 250 Hz sine wave modulated by a 30 Hz sine wave were used. Results showed that type of message (encoded by rhythm) was recognized on average 93 % and the priority (roughness) showed an average recognition rate of 80 % (Brown et al. 2005).

In a similar experiment, the encoded information was increased to three dimensions represented by a tacton (Brown et al. 2006). Type of, importance of, and time until an upcoming appointment (each with three different levels) were encoded by rhythm, roughness and spatial location, respectively. While rhythm and roughness were the same characteristics as above, time was encoded by the location of three tactors, which were attached at the wrist of the participant, the elbow and a point equidistant between them. Results showed a recognition rate of 96.7 % for appointment type (represented by rhythm), 50.2 % for importance (roughness) and 95.5 % for remaining time (location). To improve the recognition of roughness, the experiment was repeated with only two different levels of roughness, while rhythm and spatial location were kept. Appointment types (99.1 %) and remaining time (98.8 %) showed no significant differences compared to the primary experiment, but roughness recognition rate improved significantly (82.4 %) (Brown et al. 2006).

To examine the use of tactons to provide ambient information on a mobile device, e. g. while the user is typing a message, another set of tactons was designed (Constantin and Brewster 2010). Tactons encoded proximity events of two different groups of persons (friend or child, represented by the two different levels of roughness used in the latter experiment) and three current locations (far, close, and in office/school, represented by rhythm using a one-note, two-note and four-note signal respectively). This setting was challenging because tactons need to be short (300 ms duration) but still distinguishable. Results showed an overall recognition rate of 87.7 %. Reducing the number of events to be recognized during the experiment led to an improved recognition rate of 98.3 % (Constantin and Brewster 2010).

1.2 Aim of the Proposed Study

To summarize these findings, rhythm and roughness seem to be suitable parameters to transmit information via the haptic sense even when signal duration is very short. In each of these studies, the tactor was placed on a non-interacting part of the participants, a finger, hand or forearm. However, in future applications, e. g. when tactons are used in touch screen interaction, the device itself the user is interacting with will probably generate the haptic feedback providing it to the user's interacting finger. In this case, it is important to investigate whether existing empirical findings are transferable to situations where a user is interacting with flat surfaces like a touch screen interface. Thus, it is reasonable to examine all possible parameters for encoding information via tactile feedback in such a scenario to generate valid design recommendations based on findings with a large number of participants.

The aim of the study described below is to examine the given parameters for a touch screen interaction scenario. For the described scenario, locations as well as spatiotemporal patterns are unsuitable parameters because there is only one location to provide haptic feedback, namely the user's interacting finger. In this regard, the parameters frequency, amplitude, rhythm, roughness, waveform, and duration of tactile feedback were examined. The results of this experiment will help to derive distinguishable levels of parameters for tacton design.

2. METHOD

2.1 Experimental Setup

A stationary touch screen mock-up was built up using aluminum profiles (Figure 1, left). A 15-inch LC-display, adjustable in height and tilt angle, was attached. A 19-inch surface capacitive touch screen panel (3M ClearTek II with an USB-Controller 3M EXII-7760UC; Figure 1, right) was installed above the display, carried by four single piezoelectric actuators (PI Ceramic's P-820.3B), each mounted with a preload force using a spring, in the screen corners. These actuators were controlled by a multifunction data acquisition device (National Instruments' USB-6002) and powered by four separated working amplifiers (PI Ceramic's E-617.00F) providing synchronous tactile feedback across the whole screen. An optical laser displacement sensor (Keyence LK-32) was installed below the touch screen to measure the surface movement of the panel. Data recording of the displacement sensor was executed by the measuring system BioPac MP 150 with a recording frequency of 1000 Hz. The place of the researcher on the opposite consists of a common computer with keyboard, mouse and monitor where the software for the study is played. The software for this experiment was programmed using National Instrument's LabVIEW software.

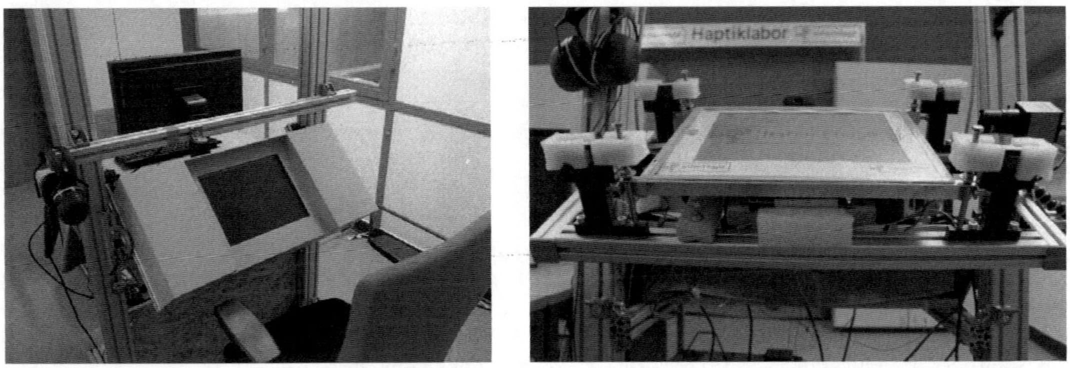

Figure 1. Stationary touch screen mock-up used in this experiment (left) and its technological components (right)

2.2 Tactile Feedback Parameters

While only one parameter was altered in a single comparison, the other parameters were set to standard values. Table 1 lists all parameters of the haptic feedback and their values examined in this study as well as the values used for the standard signal. Each value of one parameter was compared with all the other values of the same parameter. Example: Six different frequency levels (L_{freq}) led to

$$N_{freq} = L_{freq} \cdot (L_{freq} - 1) / 2 = 15$$

paired comparisons of the parameter frequency. A total of 87 different paired comparisons were presented. In addition to that, 11 control pair signals were added in a random selection comprising identical signals while ensuring that an identical comparison of each parameter was involved. Hence, the experiment consisted of 98 tasks which were presented once to the participants in a randomized way. The following list explains parameters used and values taken.

Table 1. Parameters and values examined in this study

Frequency (N = 15)	**Amplitude** (N = 21)	**Rhythm** (N = 15)	**Roughness** (N = 15)	**Waveform** (N = 6)	**Duration** (N = 15)
120 Hz					
144 Hz	8 µm				
173 Hz	10 µm				450 ms
208 Hz	12,5 µm				475 ms
250 Hz	15 µm	continuous	not applied	sine wave	500 ms
290 Hz	18 µm	short short	50 Hz / 6 Hz	triangle wave	525 ms
	22 µm	short short short	50 Hz / 10 Hz	square wave	550 ms
	26,5 µm	short short long	100 Hz / 12 Hz	sawtooth wave	600 ms
		short long short	100 Hz / 20 Hz		
		short long long	250 Hz / 30 Hz		
		long long	250 Hz / 50 Hz		standard signal

Frequency. The fingertip is most sensitive for vibration at frequencies close to 250 Hz (e. g. Gescheider et al. 2004, Verrillo and Gescheider 1992). In recent experiments with haptic feedback on flat surfaces, the authors identified a preferred frequency of 150 Hz and frequencies of 100 Hz, 200 Hz and 250 Hz to be pleasant as well (Stein et al. 2016). Therefore, frequencies between 100 Hz and 300 Hz were examined to cover this range. Differences between the frequencies were determined to be at least 20 % (van Erp 2002). The standard signal was set to 250 Hz satisfying the maximum fingertip sensitivity criterion. Because of technical restriction – the actuators were not able to generate an accurate 300 Hz vibration signal at an amplitude of 15 µm (required for the standard signal) – the upper frequency was set to 290 Hz.

Amplitude. Values of the amplitude were all set in the perceptual pleasant spectrum (see Stein et al. 2016, Stein and Schmidt 2015) while the differences between the single amplitudes were derived from the suggestion of Pongrac (2008).

Rhythm. To design different rhythms, a short (50 ms) and a long (150 ms) signal were combined in various combinations using two or three single signals. Derived from van Erp's indication (2002), a pause of 50 ms was set between the different signals. Example: "short long short" in Table 1 stands for "short signal (50 ms) – pause (50 ms) – long signal (150 ms) – pause (50 ms) – short signal (50 ms)".

Roughness. In several experiments of Brewster's Human-Computer Interaction Group (Brown et al. 2006, Brown et al. 2005) a 250 Hz sine wave, modulated by a 50 Hz as well as a 30 Hz sine wave was determined as suitable for tacton design. To investigate whether signals with other frequencies but the same ratio between base signal and second signal are distinguishable, too, the frequencies 100 Hz and 50 Hz were chosen and modulated by a signal with 20 % and 12 % of its value.

Waveform. On the one hand, some recent works state that waveform seems not to be a suitable parameter for tacton design (Constantin and Brewster 2010, Brewster and Brown 2004a, Brewster and Brown 2004b) and that a sine, triangle and sine^2 stimuli are considered to feel little different, as well as a square and a sawtooth stimuli (Merchel and Altinsoy 2009). On the other hand, waveform was found to deliver recognition rates about 94 % when comparing sine, square and sawtooth wave (Hoggan and Brewster 2007). Therefore, sine, triangle, square, and sawtooth waves were tested in this study to examine which suggestion is valid for the application scenario regarding a touch screen interaction.

Duration. Duration is an important parameter in tacton design because signals need to last long enough that the user can receive the encoded information but not too long making information transfer slow. The duration of a single touch screen input in consideration of various influencing factors is already known and amounts to 169 ms on average (Seeger et al. 2015). However, for complex information transmitted via tactons, duration presumably needs to be longer. Several durations ranging from 450 ms to 600 ms were used and their comparisons led to differences between 25 ms and 150 ms.

2.3 Participants

51 (22 female, 29 male) participants took part in this study. Their mean age was 30 years (± 9 years, range 21 – 64) and 48 of them (94 %) used the right hand for writing, though carried out the experiment with their right hand, 3 participants (6 %) used their left hand.

2.4 Experimental Procedure

The setting of the experiment was rather simple. Basically, participants were presented two vibration signals on the index finger of their dominant hand via a touch screen and had to decide, whether signals were identical or different. The overall time required by one participant to complete the 98 tasks comprising 87 different and 11 identical paired signals was 25 to 30 minutes.

Before the start of the experiment, participants got a short introduction and signed the experimental agreement. They were indicated to work as accurate as possible regardless of the time required to make their decision, motivated by an incentive for the best three results (15 €, 10 € and 5 €). After a short test run to become familiar with the setting and the user interface, participants started the experiment. By touching two test buttons, the first two different haptic feedback signals were presented to the participants who had to decide if the signals were identical or different. When both test buttons were touched at least once, two answer buttons ("identical", colored green, and "different", red) appeared. After this decision, the next paired comparison appeared and the answer buttons disappeared until the test buttons were activated once again and so on. Participants were allowed to replay the two signals as often as they liked before making their decision.

During the experiment, they had to wear in-ear headphones playing white noise and additional hearing protectors to avoid acoustical inducements caused by the noise generation of the piezoelectric actuators.

3. RESULTS

3.1 Recognition Rates

The overall recognition rate was 0.69 ± 0.15. In Table 2, the recognition rates and the standard deviations of the parameters examined are summarized. A t-test found a significant difference when comparing the recognition rates of the identical signals and the different signals ($p < 0.001$, $df = 50$), indicating that identical signals were correctly identified more frequently. T-tests showed that there were no significant differences in the results of men and women ($p = 0.931$, $df = 49$) as well as in the results of younger and older participants ($p = 0.871$, $df = 23$) comparing the lower and upper quartile.

Table 2. Recognition rates and standard deviations of the parameters

	Frequency	Amplitude	Rhythm	Roughness	Waveform	Duration	Identical signals	Overall
Recognition rate	0.89	0.65	0.79	0.90	0.40	0.27	0.83	0.69
Standard deviation	0.11	0.24	0.16	0.18	0.12	0.07	0.07	0.15

Comparing the single recognition rates of the parameters is not practical because some paired comparisons within one parameter are more suited than others so that an overall comparability of the single parameters seems not to be feasible.

3.2 Stimulus Pairs Identified as Suitable

Table 3 lists all pairs participants were able to discriminate in at least 90 % of the cases. Recognition rates above 90 % are seen as "close to perfect" (Brown and Brewster 2006) and therefore defined as the threshold for suitable combinations. All other pairs failed in reaching this threshold. In Table 3, only the discriminating parameters and its values are listed, other parameters were set to standard signal (see Table 1). In this experiment, nine paired comparisons were correctly distinguished by all 54 participants (recognition rate = 1), namely two comparisons of the parameter frequency and seven comparisons of the parameter roughness.

Table 3. Suitable paired comparisons with recognition rates ≥ 90 %

	Paired comparisons	Recognition rate
Frequency	120 Hz / 144 Hz	0.90
	120 Hz / 208 Hz	1
	120 Hz / 250 Hz	0.92
	120 Hz / 290 Hz	1
	144 Hz / 250 Hz	0.92
	144 Hz / 290 Hz	0.98
	173 Hz / 250 Hz	0.94
	173 Hz / 290 Hz	0.90
	208 Hz / 250 Hz	0.92
	250 Hz / 290 Hz	0.96
Amplitude	8 µm / 18 µm	0.92
	8 µm / 22 µm	0.94
	8 µm / 26.5 µm	0.96
	10 µm / 26.5 µm	0.90
	12.5 µm / 26.5 µm	0.94
Rhythm	short short short / short long long	0.92
	short short long / short short	0.98
	short long short / short short	0.98
	short long long / short short	0.98
	short long long / long long	0.92
	short short / long long	0.96
Roughness	250 Hz, 50 Hz / 100 Hz, 20 Hz	0.98
	250 Hz, 50 Hz / 100 Hz, 12 Hz	0.98
	250 Hz, 50 Hz / 50 Hz, 10 Hz	1
	250 Hz, 50 Hz / 50 Hz, 6 Hz	1
	250 Hz, 30 Hz / 100 Hz, 20 Hz	1
	250 Hz, 30 Hz / 100 Hz, 12 Hz	1
	250 Hz, 30 Hz / 50 Hz, 10 Hz	1
	250 Hz, 30 Hz / 50 Hz, 6 Hz	1
	100 Hz, 20 Hz / 50 Hz, 10 Hz	0.96
	100 Hz, 20 Hz / 50 Hz, 6 Hz	1
	100 Hz, 12 Hz / 50 Hz, 10 Hz	0.94
	100 Hz, 12 Hz / 50 Hz, 6 Hz	0.96

3.3 Ratios of Frequency and Amplitude

Figure 2 shows the recognition rate dependent on the ratio of the two compared frequencies (left) and amplitudes (right) respectively. It is obvious, that an increasing ratio leads to higher recognition rates for frequency as well as for amplitude. Regarding duration, a similar effect cannot be detected.

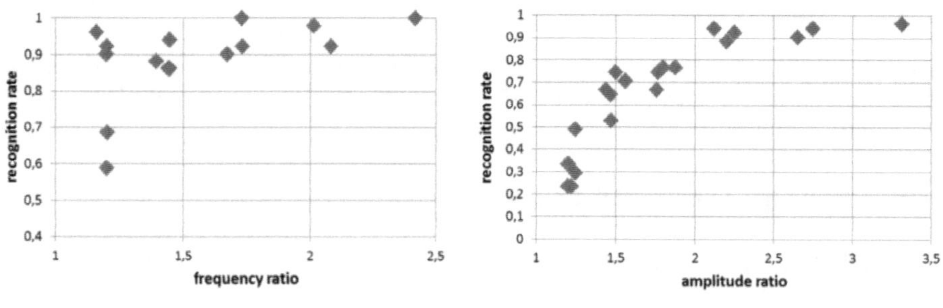

Figure 2. Recognition rate dependent on frequency ratio (left) and amplitude ratio (right)

4. DISCUSSION

4.1 Interaction of Parameters

It is necessary to mention, that altering one parameter of a vibration signal could influence the perception of other parameters. For example, a change in amplitude leads to a change in the perception of frequency, which has an impact on the use of frequency as a cue (Brewster and Brown 2004b). The various rhythms used in this experiment were also different in their length of time (i. e. 150 ms – 450 ms), thus interact with duration. Therefore, even if only one parameter of a vibration signal is altered, one has to be aware that there could be an effect on other parameters, too.

4.2 Absolute and Relative Discriminability

Making relative comparisons between stimuli is much easier than absolute identification (Brewster and Brown 2004a). In this study, the different parameter levels were discriminated in a relative way, which means that participants always had the possibility to compare two signals before making their decision. In future tacton design, it will be important to generate tactons that can be identified clearly without any comparison.

4.3 Design Recommendations

Frequency. For the parameter frequency, the ratio should be at least 1.5 (see Figure 2, left) – using this threshold, participants in this experiment were able to discriminate the presented signals in more than 90 % regardless of the frequency values used. Furthermore, it is known that no more than nine different levels of frequency should be used for coding information (van Erp 2002).

Amplitude. Only four of the 21 combinations of amplitude were discriminated correctly by more than 90 %. As shown in Figure 2, right, a ratio of 2.5 can clearly be discriminated by more than 90 % and should therefore be chosen for tacton design when using amplitude as a parameter. In addition to that, no more than four levels should be used when encoding information by amplitude (van Erp 2002). Another suggestion is to leave amplitude under the control of the user (Brown et al. 2005, Pakkanen 2010) because of their different perception thresholds, individual preferences and possible impairment of other parameters' perception. But in particular, when coding different safety levels, e. g. the state of a process of an industrial system, different levels of amplitude should be used to indicate danger, warning or safety (VDI/VDE 3850-1).

Rhythm. Concerning the rhythm, the rather similar signals were deliberately chosen to find out if even these similar rhythms are distinguishable. Based on the findings of this experiment, rhythm seems to be a suitable parameter for this scenario and opens a wide range for tacton designs. In a former study, Summers (2000) figured out that participants used temporal pattern information rather than information from frequency/amplitude modulation for decoding speech information from vibration signals indicating that rhythm could be a dominant parameter for tacton design.

Roughness. Roughness was already supposed to be a suitable parameter, which was confirmed. However, only when the base signals of the paired comparison had different frequencies, the recognition rate was adequate. This contrasts to former findings where two signals using the same base signal and merely other second signals for roughness creation led to acceptable recognition rates, too (Brown et al. 2006, Brown et al. 2005). Physiological (e. g. location and size of the contact area where the tacton is applied) as well as technological aspects (e. g. technology used for tacton generation) may explain this difference, which cannot finally be answered. Nevertheless, roughness can be used to encode information and, moreover, other base signals besides 250 Hz can be chosen, which makes tacton design using roughness more diversely.

Waveform. In a touch screen interaction scenario, waveform seems to be an inappropriate parameter for encoding information and should therefore not be used in tacton design. The best recognition rate occurred by comparing a sine and a sawtooth wave (54.9 %), but the result is still far from being a suitable combination according the defined threshold of 90 %.

Duration. Duration has to be more diverse than the values applied in this experiment when using it to encode information. None of the paired comparisons of the parameter duration achieved a suitable recognition rate. Nevertheless, choosing more diverging values, duration could still be a suitable parameter in tacton design.

4.4 Intuitive Tacton Design

A promising approach for tacton design is proposed by Chan et al. (2008, 2005). They designed tactons for a turn-taking protocol in remote collaboration and defined three different tacton families (i. e. changes in control, being in control, waiting for control). The tactons were presented to the users via their computer mouses. The design of the tactons is based on metaphors, e. g. waiting for control is coded as a pulse sensation to the users suggesting a person tapping or drumming her fingers while waiting (Chan et al. 2005). Using such metaphors should make the tactons intuitive to learn and help users to understand and memorize the particular meaning of the tactons more easily. This suggestion reaches its limits when the number of tactons increases and one metaphor could stand for different functions. A possible solution could be to design groups of general valid tactons, e. g. rough, unpleasant vibration signals which encode functions that are connoted negatively (like wrong input, interruption of operation, etc.) and smooth, comfortable tactons for functions with positive associations (like entry confirmed, process completed, etc.).

Another approach could be to define a set of tactons for recurrent functions in computer application menues (e. g. OK, delete, volume up or down). This standard set of tactons could be extended with other tactons while the subfunctions are encoded by a similar tacton like their superior standard function, thus, remaining in the same tacton family.

5. CONCLUSION

In this research, regarding an input on a flat surface, common parameters for encoding information were examined. Suitable values and distinguishable levels for single parameters became clearer and design recommendations were derived. Based on the experimental findings, a variety of possible applications could be examined, and tactons for many different applications and devices can be designed.

Furthermore, by comparing the results of this experiment with former research, it becomes clear that findings cannot simply be transferred to other application scenarios but should rather be tested under the particular conditions.

In future tacton design for touch screen applications, using the parameters and thresholds proposed in this study, it is also desirable to find appropriate metaphors for the encoded function to help users understand the tactons and make them easier to learn.

It will also be interesting to find out how the findings of this study can be translated for a user-held device like a smartphone or a tablet and if the signals received in the other hand impact perception on the interacting finger.

REFERENCES

Arab, F. et al., 2015. Haptic patterns and older adults: To repeat or not to repeat?. *IEEE World Haptics Conference 2015,* pp. 248-253.

Brewster, S. A. and Brown, L. M., 2004a. Tactons: Structured Tactile Messages for Non-Visual Information Display. *Proceedings of the fifth conference on Australasian user interface*, vol. 28, pp. 15–23.

Brewster, S. A. and Brown, L. M., 2004b. Non-Visual Information Display Using Tactons. *CHI'04 extended abstracts on Human factors in computing systems*, pp. 787–788.

Brewster, S. A. and King, A., 2005. An Investigation into the Use of Tactons to Present Progress Information. *Human-Computer Interaction – INTERACT 2005*, pp. 6–17.

Brown, L. M. et al., 2005. A First Investigation into the Effectiveness of Tactons. *Eurohaptics Conference and Symposium on Haptic Interfaces for Virtual Environment and Teleoperator Systems*, IEEE World Haptic Conference, pp. 167–176.

Brown, L. M. et al., 2006. Multidimensional Tactons for Non-Visual Information Presentation in Mobile Devices. *Proceedings of the 8th Conference on Human-Computer Interaction with Mobile Devices and Services*, pp. 231–238.

Chan, A. et al., 2005. Learning and Identifying Haptic Icons under Workload. *Eurohaptics Conference and Symposium on Haptic Interfaces for Virtual Environment and Teleoperator Systems*, IEEE World Haptic Conference, pp. 432–439.

Chan, A. et al., 2008. Designing haptic icons to support collaborative turn-taking. *International Journal of Human-Computer Studies*, vol. 66, no. 5, pp. 333–355.

Constantin, A. and Brewster, S. A., 2010. Tactile Feedback for Ambient Awareness in Mobile Interactions. *Proceedings of the 24th BCS Interaction Specialist Group Conference*, pp. 412–417.

Fichera, L. et al., 2016. Kinesthetic and vibrotactile haptic feedback improves the performance of laser microsurgery. *IEEE Haptics Symposium (HAPTICS),* pp. 59-64.

Fukumoto, M. and Sugimura, T., 2001. Active Click: Tactile Feedback for Touch Panels. *CHI 2001: Extended Abstracts on Human Factors in Computing Systems*, pp. 121–122

Gescheider, G. A. et al., 2004. Some characteristics of tactile channels. *Behavioural Brain Research*, vol. 148, no. 1, pp. 35–40.

Hartcher-O'Brien, J. et al., 2015. Perception of distance-to-obstacle through time-delayed tactile feedback. *IEEE World Haptics Conference 2015,* pp. 7-12.

Hoggan, E. and Brewster, S. A., 2007. New Parameters for Tacton Design. *CHI '07 Extended Abstracts on Human Factors in Computing Systems*, pp. 2417–2422.

Hoggan, E. et al., 2008. Investigating the Effectiveness of Tactile Feedback for Mobile Touchscreens. *Proceedings of the SIGCHI Conference on Human Factors in Computing Systems*, pp. 1573–1582.

Kim, J. R. and Tan, H. Z., 2014. A study of touch typing performance with keyclick feedback. *IEEE Haptics Symposium (HAPTICS),* pp. 227-233.

Klatzky, R. L. and Lederman, S. J., 2006. The Perceived Roughness of Resistive Virtual Textures: I. Rendering by a Force-Feedback Mouse. *ACM Transactions on Applied Perception*, vol. 3, no. 1, pp. 1–14.

Koskinen, E. et al., 2008. Feel-Good Touch: Finding the Most Pleasant Tactile Feedback for a Mobile Touch Screen Button. *Proceedings of the 10th international conference on Multimodal interfaces*, pp. 297–304.

Lederman, S. J. et al., 2006. The Perceived Roughness of Resistive Virtual Textures: II. Effects of Varying Viscosity with a Force-Feedback Device. *ACM Transactions on Applied Perception*, vol. 3, no. 1, pp. 15–30.

Ma, Z. et al., 2015. Haptic Keyclick Feedback Improves Typing Speed and Reduces Typing Errors on a Flat Keyboard. *IEEE World Haptics Conference*, pp. 220–227.

Merchel, S. and Altinsoy, M. E., 2009. Audiotactile feedback design for touch screens. *International Conference on Haptic and Audio Interaction Design*, Berlin, Heidelberg: Springer, pp. 136–144.

Nashel, A. and Razzaque, S., 2003. Tactile virtual buttons for mobile devices. *CHI'03 extended abstracts on Human factors in computing systems*, pp. 854–855.

Pakkanen, T. et al., 2010. Comparison of Three Designs for Haptic Button Edges on Touchscreen. *Proceedings of the IEEE Haptic Symposium*, pp. 219–225

Pongrac, H., 2008. Vibrotactile perception: examining the coding of vibrations and the just noticeable difference under various conditions. *Multimedia Systems*, vol. 13, no. 4, pp. 297–307.

Rochlis, J. L. and Newman, D. J., 2000. A tactile display for international space station (ISS) extravehicular activity (EVA). *Aviation, Space and Environmental Medicine*, vol. 71, no. 6, pp. 571–578.

El Saddik, A., 2007. The Potential of Haptics Technologies. *IEEE Instrumentation & Measurement Magazine*, vol. 10, no. 1, pp. 10–17.

Seeger, M. et al., 2015. Die Berührungsdauer eines Button- Klicks bei stationären Touchscreens. *Mensch und Computer 2015 – Tagungsband*, pp. 243–252.

Sim, S. H. et al., 2016. Improved typing on a flat keyboard via tactile key-identity feedback. *IEEE Haptics Symposium (HAPTICS),* pp. 319-324.

Sjöström, C., 2001. Using Haptics in Computer Interfaces for Blind People. *CHI'01 Extended Abstracts on Human Factors in Computing Systems*, pp. 245–246.

Sklar, A. E. and Sarter, N. B., 1999. Good Vibrations: Tactile Feedback in Support of Attention Allocation and Human-Automation Coordination in Event-Driven Domains. *Human Factors: The Journal of the Human Factors and Ergonomics Society*, vol. 41, no. 4, pp. 543–552.

Summers, R., 2000. Single Channel Information Transfer Through The Skin: Limitations and Possibilities. *Proceedings of ISAC 2000.*

Stein, T. and Schmidt, L., 2015. Die vibrotaktile Wahrnehmung von Amplituden bei unterschiedlichen Frequenzen an einer ebenen Platte. *Forum Arbeitsphysiologie: 19. Symposium Arbeitsmedizin und Arbeitswissenschaft für Nachwuchswissenschaftler*, p. 11.

Stein, T. et al., 2016. Die vibrotaktile Wahrnehmung des Menschen an einer ebenen Oberfläche. *Arbeit in komplexen Systemen – Digital, vernetzt, human?! 62. Kongress der Gesellschaft für Arbeitswissenschaft*, pp. 1-6 (A.4.24).

Tan, H. Z. et al., 2003. A Haptic Back Display for Attentional and Directional Cueing. *Haptics-e*, vol. 3, no. 1, pp. 1–20.

van Erp, J. B., 2002. Guidelines for the Use of Vibro-Tactile Displays in Human Computer Interaction. *Eurohaptics 2002: Conference Proceedings*, pp. 18–22.

van Erp, J. B. et al., 2005. Waypoint Navigation with a Vibrotactile Waist Belt. *ACM Transactions on Applied Perception*, vol. 2, no. 2, pp. 106–117.

van Erp, J. B., 2005. Presenting directions with a vibrotactile torso display. *Ergonomics*, vol. 48, no. 3, pp. 302–313.

Verrillo, R. T. and Gescheider, G. A., 1992. Perception via the sense of touch. *Tactile Aids for the Hearing Impaired*, pp. 1–36.

VDI/VDE 3850, 2014. Development of usable user interfaces for technical plants – Part 1: Concepts, principles and fundamental recommendations.

Yatani, K. and Truong, K. N., 2009. SemFeel: A User Interface with Semantic Tactile Feedback for Mobile Touch-screen Devices. *Proceedings of the 22nd annual ACM symposium on User interface software and technology*, pp. 111–120.

CREATION OF ARTIFACTS: STATE OF ART OF DESIGN

Ismael Gaião Filho[1] and Fabio Campos[2]
[1]UFPE, Brazil
[2]UFPE / Bolsista CAPES - Proc.88881.120765/2016-01, Brazil

ABSTRACT

For the State of the Art research, Theoretical Rationale was used as a conceptual basis for all methodological applications and scientific terms and addresses all research content related to bibliography, process definitions and methodologies and academic reports. Ideally, it is conceivable that this document clearly shows the concepts, objectives, references, with background information. The Design Methodologies, which are the basis for this research, are detailed below. This point of detail level was considered important because they serve as a basis, referencing the same authors, of great importance in the area of design. Finally, the state of the art is presented, updating the levels of research applied today and how the current academy is based and produces studies on the subject, and how the status quo of these researches complement this dissertation, to update concepts and possible paradigms found in the last Years, for the methodological teaching of design.

KEYWORDS

Methodology, Creativity, History, Design Methods

1. INTRODUCTION

Creating an artifact includes identifying a problem - which can also be an opportunity, understanding your market, analyzing competitions and the like, observing its usage characteristics, predicting future trends, understanding its technical aspects, understanding its users, The ancient mantra of form and function.

However, the methods used to exploit the problem often take a lot of time and effort to develop and classify it. In industrial practice, the focus of the project and avoiding extensive, linear and inflexible schedules, and for that, several of the research activities should be conducted outside the production process of the product (Norman, 2006).

The process is broad and consists of several phases and stages, capable of conducting the production work of several professionals in an appropriate way, through design models (Basseto, 2004). These factors include the collection of data and information necessary to identify the public and the market, through the production and use of the product, as well as its disposal (Back et al., 2008).

Romano (2003) indicates that the artifact creation process can be described through three macrophases, which are decomposed into eight other divisions: Planning, Projection and Implementation.

The planning considers the actions for the development of a project plan, which will serve as a case for the following; The project seeks to transform customer needs into technical and detailed solutions; The implementation consists of the application of the models from the design phase to the launch and final validation of the project (Basseto, 2004).

Macrophases require a strong knowledge base of different natures on design, such as marketing, industrial production, methods of supporting creativity, selection of solutions, etc. Some skills are needed for each of the phases, such as exploration, analysis, interpretation and decision making. The end of each phase includes an evaluation of the result obtained, which if positive, guarantees the transition to the next phase (Basseto, 2004).

The cost of designing is of fundamental importance in relation to competitive frameworks, as it is directly reflected in the product price (Basseto, 2004). In order to contribute to the design, which is on the rise in the market of performance (De Moraes, 1997), creative techniques act as fundamental to have a greater margin of safety and accuracy in the conceptual design decisions.

According to Baxter (2000), "the early stages are the most important in the process of developing new products." Baxter also developed a spend model involved in the phases, and proves that the cost is lower at first, because the research only takes place on paper and the design works are limited to cheap designs and models. In the following phases it entails a series of costs, besides the loss of time with rework.

Therefore, it is possible to affirm that creativity interferes mainly in the initial phases of design - mainly in the conceptual phase - in which the identity of the product is defined (Basseto, 2004). Baxter (2000) states that "the key to success in product development is to invest more time and talent in the early stages."

An addition to the elaborate and diffused forms of these ancient concepts was championed by Henry Petroski. "The form follows the failures" (Petroski, 1992) is a variation of this thought, but that represents the same concept. Petroski argued that the shortcomings of a project were also important in the sense of the creation process, because even flaws had their uses.

Evolution of the function of the artifact, so Petroski develops that:

"Here is the central idea: the shape of artifacts is always subject to change in response to their actual or imagined shortcomings, the inability to function properly. This principle drives inventions, innovations and ingenuity. And that moves all inventors, innovators and engineers, and it follows a corollary: since nothing is perfect and that, in fact, our ideas about perfection are also not static, everything is subject to change over time. Impossible for an artifact to be perfected. The more-than-perfect can only be a tense, never a thing ".

Another researcher who focused on the flaws of the products and evolution of the generation processes was the architect Christopher Alexander. According to Alexander (1964), designers should look to failures if we ever want to succeed in project improvement. From the idea that people used projected artifacts, the starting point would be use, "any element that can be designed is a problem to be solved" (Alexander, 1964).

As a clipping of the research, the evidence of some concepts used and that are necessary for a better future understanding, the application of this dissertation project and how the experiments were carried out. Always with the theoretical basis for the use of each application, study and experiment performed.

In this way, there are concepts of space and environment, structural. Design concepts that explain methodologies, methods and techniques, what they mean and how they are applied, and forms of project activity to use.

To solve a problem, the formulation and its appropriateness of the possibilities are of high importance for the success of creativity in the process of designing artifacts. Baxter (2000) lists three ways of using the problem, generating solutions for it: Reducing the problem, Expansion of the problem, Digression of the dilemma.

Reduction of the problem: is to examine the characteristics of the problem and seek to solve it by modifying one or more of these characteristics. It focuses attention on the existing product, not on it.

Expansion of the problem: it intends to broaden the perspective of the problem, opening up a range of new solutions that are not restricted to the product in question.

Problem-finding: seeks the "escape" of anxiety from the immediate domain of the problem, using lateral thinking, so as to move away from the initial conditions of the problem, or even to move to something completely different from it and then approach again.

It is with the intention of facilitating the application of these processes that the methodologies, methods and techniques apply. Each of them with identifications in these forms of treatment of the problem. The way to ramble or blur about the problem is an attempt to approach the way each person thinks, structuring thought.

2. METHODOLOGY OF DESIGN

In recent years, the theme Methodology has been gaining importance as a central design theory, strengthening its use as a strategy for research and development in design (Dechamps & Naya, 1997). Research projects aim to improve, adapt and / or create methods, building models for problem solving and product development.

A study on important developments for the subject, authors such as Bruce Archer (Bonsiepe et al 1984), Bruno Munari (1998), Morris Asimow (1968), Christopher Jones (1992), Briggs and Havlick (Dubberly, 2009), Bernhard Bürdek (2006), and Bernd Löbach (2001) classify their methods and tools for collecting information and user data - mostly through different approaches. However, design methodologies differ according to their authors, however, they have in common as an initial step the data collection.

For the expansion of the discussion about project methodology or method, it is fundamental to define the general concept, since many different definitions can be found on the term. This lack of a formal and unified concept, collaborates with the development of different methodological models for the project (Vasconcelos, 2009).

As a reference to the Oxford dictionary, the term "design" dates back to 1588, having 3 possible definitions for the term. The first of these defines design as a plan developed by men or by a possible scheme of achievement. The second classification dictates design as the first graphic sketch of a work of art. The last one is the definition of design as an object of applied arts or a tool for the execution of a work (Bürdek, 2006). In this context, the methodology in design can be understood as a set of methods or processes that support the designer about his activities.

For Alexander (1964), the process of conception refers to the act of structuring real objects that present a new physical order, form and organization, in response to the function.

Löbach (2001) defines that the project could be deduced as an idea, plan or project for a solution of a problem. Therefore, design - as a verb - sets formalize an idea and pass it on to other people.

Cross classifies the design methodology as being characterized for the study of principles, procedures and the exercise of design, as the focus on the final objective, to improve the practice of design, presenting a strongly focused orientation in the creation process (Cross, 1993; Kroes, 2002).

Bomfim (1995) defends methodology as the science that deals with the study of methods, techniques and tools and their applications in the definition, organization and solution of practical and theoretical problems, thus defining the methodology of design as the discipline that lends itself to Application of methods for specific and concrete problems.

Concluding this stage of analysis and conceptualization it is possible to develop an understanding for the design methodology of appropriate projects for this research. From this step, it is concrete the thought of a schematic process involving several stages of design, with the objective of supporting the designer (or the design team) about the development or the concept of solutions to a given problem, such as an artifact, a Product or service.

2.1 History of Methodologies

Historical research on the evidence of design theory dates back to the 1950s design was generally done by individuals and the methods applied were not exactly clear, being known as the "black box" meaning that it is not visible (Hileman, 1998). From that point on, the development of design methods began, as is known today (Jones, 1992), especially in countries where industrialization had already reached significant levels, such as England and Germany (Bonfim, 1995).

In September 1962, the Conference on Systematic, Intuitive Methods in Engineering, Industrial Design, Architecture and Communication was held at Imperial College in London and can be considered as the main brand for further discussion of design methods and Development (Jones, 2001).

Concomitantly, the Ulm School (Hochschule für Gestaltung) played a key role in the development of these methods by applying extensive research in design theory and formulation based on functionalism. The increased activities offered to Designers in industry in the mid-twentieth century is seen as a prime cause for progress in design methods (Bürdek, 2006).

Aligned with research development factors, the increasing complexity of functional problems and the inability of Designers to solve them, coupled with the need for a profound result of activities or attitudes that has become even more complex to solve intuitively (Alexander, 1964), all strong arguments for the need to develop logical structures as design methodologies. Jones, using questioning, argued mainly about the high complexity of new problems, unlike the old way of designing traditionally (Jones, 1992).

After Ulm, it is remarkable not only the serious acceptance of a more scientific and objective approach to studies in design. Rational determinism prevailed; There was an attempt to determine the entire process and its minimum components. It was believed that the design process could be explicitly stated, the relevant data collected and, consequently, a projected ideal artifact (Dubberly, 2009).

Throughout the 1970s, design methods took different paths. The annulment of the belief that a single method should be accepted as a general model. On the other hand, new researchers have sought to develop methodological models, new approaches such as studies and concerns about the user, ergonomic needs and cost (Jones, 1992). The design began to be established as a science once it found support in scientific methodology for an autonomous design methodology to be designed.

The following decade continued to develop several studies, following the changes of previous years. The rational and deterministic model encountered increasing opposition, especially when postmodernism brought new trends (Bürdek, 2006). Design altered its concept by merging with diverse areas to meet the needs of the time and future problems such as ecology and ecosystem, which represented the paradigm shift between design as a natural science for a social science.

The 1990s represented a period in which the context of insertion of a product became more important than the artifact itself. New directions for the processes have been necessary since significant technological advances, such as the increasing digitalization of the products. The old functionalism has dissolved into new immaterial themes, such as usability and interface design, which lack modern procedures (Bürdek, 2006).

Nowadays, the models are often adapted or even created by companies to local apparatus, and no longer developed by scholars or researchers of the design. Van Aken argues that design methodology should not be self-centered but should be constantly adapted to designers to support design needs (Van Aken, 2005).

It is possible to visualize that the researches and the design methodologies were developed in a considerable way and can be classified as a scientific proof of the importance of the studies. However, in the case of research that deals with the development of the concept with the focus on the activities and how to exploit them to present benefits and better use there is still much research to be addressed.

2.2 Methodologies of Creation Projects

Based on the conceptualization of design methodologies and their researches, in order to understand conception processes in a simple way, it was possible to classify the steps, based on the studies of Bruno Munari (1998) and Neves et al. (2008), in a compilation for If we use 5 methods of information collection, applied in the disciplines.

Market research: a method that seeks to demonstrate the economic relevance of the project and establish a business opportunity through the identification of market niches;

Historical evolution: method that allows to gather a vast amount of information about the origins and evolution of a certain product or similar over the years;

Analysis of Similar or Competitive: A method that investigates similar products and potential competitors to identify their positive and negative aspects;

Trend analysis: a method that seeks and identifies inclinations regarding use, technology, public, etc., predicting possible unfolding;

Personas: A method that creates detailed user profiles to represent larger audiences and avoid personal biases during development.

According to Neves et al. (2008), designers should define users based on all the information collected during the process of exploring the problem, in order to describe and formulate personas with social and cultural characteristics of these users.

Pruitt (2006) develops the thought that everyone who participates in the design of a product should keep in mind the needs of each person who will use it. In theory, all decisions and the end result would fully satisfy all consumers. However, it is very difficult to get the whole team thinking about users.

To address this problem, Cooper (1999) suggests the personas tool to organize and present information about the target group of a project. The author defines personas as imaginary people who represent the real ones throughout the design process. Even though they are imaginary, personas must be defined with rigor and significant precision, they should perfectly figure out archetypes as hypothetical of actual users.

Pruitt (2006) suggests reasons that support the use of the technique of people:

- The first: as conception, the most natural tendency is to be self-centered, not user-centered. People generally tend to approach a product based on their own needs and desires, even when they themselves are not really the potential users for the designed product;
- Secondly, as users are very varied, it takes great effort to understand their needs, desires, preferences and behaviors.

The persona needs a profile and a face, a physical materialization that will be observed and a detailed list of hobbies, activities, musical preferences, eating habits, etc.

These methods consolidate and complete all research for the information process. The entire process covered both product and user aspects with the goal of providing a vast and reliable amount of information to the people involved in a design project.

2.3 Development in Creativity

It is understandable from the common sense that creativity is a natural quality, however, it has been concluded by philosophers and psychologists that creativity can be stimulated. In this way, everyone can be creative, provided they apply an effort and some specific technique to do so (Baxter, 2000).

Torrance argues that "creative thinking is the process of perceiving gaps or missing and disturbing elements" and that we develop and evaluate ideas or hypotheses about them. It can also be classified as "adventurous thinking, moving away from the main line, allowing one thing to lead to the other"; "To deviate from the habitual sequence of thought, to have a synthetic, selective and inquisitive mind" (Torrance, 1976).

For other authors, creativity is directly related to reasoning, being a unique characteristic of the human being, related to the senses and emotions, that allow us to acquire and classify data (Alves et al., 2007).

Alves, Campos and Neves (2007) argue against standard thinking with the concept that creative techniques are "heuristic ways of accelerating the creative process." In addition to promoting a better interaction between the components of a creative team, they "uniformize / balance the creativity of all", without dependence on those considered "naturally creative". Thus, creative techniques are capable of generating solutions at the time and place where they are needed, independent of "spontaneous creativity", making possible the creative potential of each team member (Alves et al., 2007).

Bernhard Bürdek (2006), Cal Briggs and Spencer Havlick (Dubberly, 2009), Bernd Löbach (2001), Gui Bonsiepe (1998), and others, such as Morris Asimow (1968), John Chris Jones (1992), Donald Koberg and James Bagnall (1984), Bruno Munari (1998), John Gero (1990 & 2007), Nigel Cross (Dubberly, 2009) and Neves et al. (2008) define a specific stage for creating solutions, generating alternatives. This step is given considerable importance in the process.

According to Back et al. (2008), the generation of design alternatives aims to create several alternative solutions to the same problem, leading to the comparison and combination of possible solutions so that, in the end, one can select the most appropriate and innovative concept.

Idea-generating participants should be prepared and well-informed about the problem they need to solve. During the process of ideation, one should not use judgments and criticisms of others' ideas, so that they do not cause inhibition or blockage in the creative process to the most withdrawn people, especially in brainstorming (Baxter, 2000).

"Design is the link between creativity and innovation" (Cruickshank, 2010), using the techniques can improve the creation of the artifact and can give it a longer useful life, in order to make the artifact really fulfill its role and Become useful and tangible for the user to carry out their actions and desires.

Bürdek (2006) states that in design there is a connection between the experience of years of developing analog products and the new world of digital products. Being the transition from matter to the digital language, and then from its visualization. From this type of concept connect groups of people to achieve better solutions and opportunities for qualified and well-evaluated use.

The link between the theory, proposal and methodology of Design practice in search of better and innovative solutions is based on a question as to how it is applied and on what occasions it can be used and how it will contribute to the process.

According to Bomfim (1995), the techniques are capable of increasing creativity in order to accelerate the data generation process of ideas. Over the years, these techniques have been improved and even new methods have been developed derived from the ancients. In addition, these techniques can be divided between those who explore the creative process and those focused on exploring the logical process.

For Baxter (2000), in designing the designer's focus must be on ideas. Practical restrictions should be set aside for a future step. Neves et al. (2008) affirm that the main objective of the techniques for the generation of alternatives is to widen the range of possible solutions for an artifact.

3. CONCLUSION

Although the use of such methods has relevant support in the design literature (Bonsiepe et al, 1984, Bruno Munari, 1998, Morris Asimow, 1968, Christopher Jones, 1992, Bernd Löbach, 2001; Scientists attesting, in fact, the gain of performance with its use.

Nowadays, techniques are still not used in the way that has been idealized in the past. Several factors interfere with practice as a standard tool. The research of the techniques adds knowledge and advantages both for the industry and for the design, since each of them brings with it own characteristics of its structure. The inclusion of the methods, techniques and fundamentals of the Design that can be used as a standard / everyday way to search for the best solutions and innovation of the artifacts produced, which in practice offers the opportunity for the creation teams to increase production and development capacity of ideas.

This research project looks at the theme of the creation of Artifacts improvements and that with the use of this resource can evolve in the process of problem solving methodology based on the concepts of Design. At the end of the research it is intended to observe the benefits generated by the use of this type of study and it meets the defined objective and contribution in a positive and positive way to these processes of ideation.

The main intention of this type of research is to improve the use of methods, to make better their applications and to prove useful and facilitating factor, so that any user can and obtain the desired benefits that the methods used in the design intend to offer. Its facilitating factor aims to be independent of study area, medium or place of use, thus showing a cultural social value for both professionals and contribution to industry.

Recent research already indicates the gains in using creative techniques to generate alternatives (Ferreira, 2010). Although Bomfim (1984) has already suggested that design methodology supports designers, but their adoption does not guarantee success, it is not possible to identify specifications and gain metrics in design literature when performing structured procedures.

For Cavalucci, Lutz and Kucharavy (2002), there is an outdated classification of creative techniques, which makes it difficult to choose the appropriate techniques to solve a given design problem. The authors assert that the usual classification of creative techniques into systematic and non-systematic has been consecrated and useful according to the needs of the twentieth century, but a new classification is necessary that embraces new characteristics, technologies, innovation and competitiveness, so fundamental To the reality of the 21st century.

REFERENCES

Alexander, C., 1964. *Notes on the Synesthesis of Form.* Harvard University Press, Cambridge.

Alves, H. D. A.; Campos, F.; Neves, A., 2007. *Aplicação da técnica criativa "Brainstorming Clássico" na geração de alternativas na criação de games.* Depto. de Design - UFPE, Recife.

Arias, E. et al., 2000. *Transcending the individual human mind-creating shared understanding through collaborative design.* ACM Transactions on Computer-Human Interaction (TOCHI) 7.1

Asimow, M., 1968. *Introdução ao Projeto de engenharia.* Editora Mestre Jou, São Paulo.

Back, N. et al., 2008. *Projeto integrado de produtos: planejamento, concepção e modelagem.* Manole, Barueri.

Basseto, E. L., 2004. *Proposta de Metodologia para o Ensino das Fases de Projeto Informacional e Projeto Conceitual.* UFSC, Santa Catarina.

Baxter, M. R., 2000. *Projeto de produto: guia prático para design de novos produtos.* São Paulo:Editora Blucher, São Paulo.

Bonfim, G., 1995. *Ideias e Formas na história do design: uma investigação estética.* Universidade Federal da Paraíba, João Pessoa.

Bonsiepe, G., 2011. *Design, cultura e sociedade.* Editora Blucher, São Paulo.

Bonsiepe, G; Kellner, P; Poessnecker, H., 1984. *Metodologia experimental: desenho industrial.* Coordenação CNPq/Editorial, Brasília.

Bürdek, B. E., 2006. *História, teoria e prática do design de produtos.* Editora Blucher, São Paulo.

Campos, F.; Neves, A. M.; Souza, R., 2007. *O Processo de Design e a Incerteza Subjetiva.* Annals of the 4th International Conference on Design Research. Anais, Rio de Janeiro.

Cavallucci, D.; Lutz, P.; Kucharavy, D., 2002. *Converging in problem formulation: a different path in Design.* Proceedings of DETC/DTM 2002 ASME Design Engineering Technical Conferences, Montreal.

Cooper, A., 1999. *The Inmates Are Running the Asylum.* Macmillan, New York.

Cross, N., 2011. *Design Thinking: Understanding How Designers Think and Work.* Bloomsbury Academic, London.

Cruickshank, L., 2010. *The Innovation Dimension.* Design Issues, Massachusetts Institute of Technology, Massachusetts.

De Moraes, D., 1997. *Limites do Design.* Studio Nobel, São Paulo.

Dechamps, J.P.; NAYA, P.R., 1997. *Produtos irresistíveis.* Markron Books, São Paulo.

Dubberly, H. 2009. *How do you design? A compendium of Models.* Available at: http://www.dubberly.com/wp-content/uploads/2008/06/ddo_Designprocess.pdf.

Dubberly, H. 2010. *The space of design.* Available at: http://www.dubberly.com/wp-content/uploads/2010/07/ddo_article_TheSpaceOfDesign.pdf.

Ferreira, R. A., 2010. *Performance das Técnicas de Geração e sua Medição.* Universidade Federal de Pernambuco, Recife.

Gero, J. S., 1990. *Design Prototypes: a knowledge representation schema for design.* AI Magazine.

Gero, J. S., 2007. *FBS Model and the perspective aims of design methodology.* Design Studies.

Hileman, R. 1998. *An introductory lecture for digital designers by Rhodes.* Available at: http://www.smsys.com/pub/dsgnmeth.pdf.

Jones, J. C., 1992. *Design Methods.* Willey, Indianapolis.

Jones, J. C. 2001. *Softopia version 2.2.* Available at: http://www.softopia.demon.co.uk /2.2/index.html

Löbach, B., 2001. *Design Industrial, base para configuração dos produtos industriais.* Edgar Blucher, São Paulo.

Kroes, P., 2002. *Design Methodology and the nature of technical artefacts.* Design Studies. vol. 23.

Munari, B., 1998. *Das coisas nascem as coisas.* Martins Fontes, São Paulo.

Neves, A., 2014. *Design Thinking Canvas.* Recife.

Neves, A. M. M.; Campos, F. F. C.; Barros, S. G.; Campello, S. B.; Aragão, I; Castillo, L., 2008. *XDM Métodos Extensíveis de Design.* 8o Brazilian Congress of Research & Development in Design. Senac, São Paulo.

Norman, D., 2006. *Why doing user observations first is wrong.* ACM Interactions.

Petroski, H., 1992. *The evolution of the useful things.* Vintage Books.

Pruitt, J.; ADLIN, T., 2006. *The persona lifecycle: keeping people in mind throughout product design.* Elsevier Inc, San Francisco.

Romano, L. N., 2003. *Modelo de Referência para o Processo de Desenvolvimento de Máquinas Agrícolas.* UFSC, Florianópolis.

Torrance, E. P., 1963. *Education and the creative potential.* University of Minnesota, Minneapolis.

Torrance, E. P., 1976 *Criatividade: medidas, teses e avaliações.* IBRASA, São Paulo.

Vasconcelos, L. A. L., 2009. *Uma Investigação em Metodologias de Design.* Federal University of Pernambuco, Recife.

Vasconcelos, Luis A. L. 2012. *The Designer's Perception and Expert's Evaluation: Testing Techiniques for Problem Exploration on a Design Methodology Framework.* Federal University, Recife.

Van Aken, J. E., 2005. *Valid knowledge for the professional design of large and complex design processes.* Design Studies, Great Britain.

DO USERS WANT ADDITIONAL FEEDBACK WHEN USING A GESTURE-BASED SYSTEM?

Lisa Graichen[1], Matthias Graichen[2] and Josef F. Krems[1]
[1]*Chemnitz University of Technology, Cognitive and Engineering Psychology*
[2] *Universität der Bundeswehr Munich, Human Factors Institute*

ABSTRACT

With the aim of making human-computer interaction more natural and enjoyable to use gestures came into focus of HCI. When using gesture interaction the question of whether there should be an additional form of feedback is needed is important to answer. In this paper an experiment is described, concerning an assessment of three different forms of feedback, representing different levels of information (low information level with only the cursor changing, medium level of information with the detected gesture being displayed and high level of information with the detected movement of hand being displayed). Results show a preference of the users for the feedback form with the highest level of information. However, feedback with the lowest level of information was assessed nearly as positive, so both variants seem to be possible to use.

KEYWORDS

HCI, NUI, Gesture-based interaction, Gestures, User experience

1. INTRODUCTION

1.1 Gestures in Human-Computer Interaction

A pretty new approach in human-computer interaction (HCI) is the idea of designing the user experience more natural by adapting the interaction with a computer or technical device more similar to face-to-face communication between humans (cf. Wigdor & Wixon, 2011). By doing so, interaction is supposed to get more pleasant and stress-free for the user and action accuracy will increase (e.g. Gonzalez, 1996; Tavanti & Lind, 2001; Oh, Robinson, & Lee, 2013). There are two starting points when changing interaction modes: the input mode, which the user adopts for feeding the system with entries and the output mode, which the system uses to get information to the user (e.g. Schomaker et al., 1995). As the input mode can be varied more easily and the effect can be conceived more distinctly by the user the following paper will be concentrating on the input mode.

One way of reaching more naturalness is the use of gestures, which are considered of being one of the most natural forms of interaction in literature (e.g. Karam & Schraefel, 2005; Quek et al., 2002). Of course also other modalities can be used like touch or haptics, voice commands or auditive outputs, gaze control, emotion control and so on. But of course changing input (or output) mode can only be a first step in creating a more natural interface, but does not automatically creating one. All in all, the term “natural” describes more the experience and behavior of the user, not the sheer product of the interface (Wigdor & Wixon, 2011).

A gesture is a process beginning with the hand in a relaxed position, which is then moved in relation of the body to perform the meaningful part of the gesture and then moved back into a relaxed position. There are two categories of gestures: Autonomous gestures and co-verbal gestures. Autonomous gestures are used instead of speech, stand alone and can be understood without co-verbal clarification. Co-verbal gestures occur together with other modalities, usually with speech (Bressem & Ladewig, 2011).

When using gestures in modern HCI, interfaces can be divided into two categories (Saffer, 2009): Touch-based interfaces and free-form interfaces. When using a touch-based interface (touch-based interaction; TBI) the user needs to directly touch the screen of the device, typically with his fingertips. To interact with a free-form interface (or gesture-based interface; GBI) the user is not required to touch the device but conducts the movement in the air. The user either has to perform the movement while using an input device like a glove or controller, or has to perform the gesture within the near range of sensors (e.g. depth sensing cameras and infrared sensors). These sensors will track movements of the body (e.g. hand and fingers, or whole body) and convert the 3D information into specific input. The term gesture is often used as well referring to touch-based interaction for describing different input movements carried out on the screen, like swiping with one or two fingers. In the following sections and experiments the term of "gesture-based interaction" and "gesture" in general is used as reference to an in-air hand movement respective manipulation of the interface by in-air gestures without touching the interaction device.

The WIMP-paradigm (acronym for windows, icons, menus, and pointing devices) can be used to describe the traditional types of HCI using mouse and keyboard in combination with a display (e.g. Kortum, 2008). With a computer mouse, there are two possible input modes: Two-dimensional movements of the cursor, and clicking (pressing mouse buttons). The user can easily obtain feedback information of his input actions by visually tracking the cursor and mentally comparing its changes in position to his movements of the hand and fingers. TBI follows a similar idea of movement by using fingertips instead of the computer mouse, which likewise increases naturalness and eases access to the system.

Regarding GBI, the known paradigm can still be addressed by using the fingers for targeting the cursor and executing an action. But in contrast to TBI fingers do not touch the display and will remain in the air, which means that there is an additional gap between the user and the device. This might reduce the usual experience (e.g. learned from mouse or touch interaction) to obtain direct feedback indicating a successful interaction (cf. the perception of the clicking mouse or the haptic feeling when touching the display screen). Furthermore, gestural interaction also enables the user to perform particular task-related gestures, which otherwise would require several steps of point-and-click- or touch-interaction, and can be more versatile but also complex to perform. For example, a specified gesture for a pre-defined action can be used (cf. the gesture of drawing a circle is used for rotating an image). It follows that users need to learn which gesture stands for which action. On the other hand there is no need to visually search for an item on a display which is required to be selected for the intended task (e.g. the rotation button). The gesture can be performed and the computer will translate the detected movement into the predefined operation. Being combined with acoustic feedback it would be possible to interact with the system without having to look on a display at all, which makes it especially interesting for drivers interacting with in-vehicle information systems (IVIS).

1.2 Research Question

Several studies have been conducted using GBI, most of them with a narrowly defined scope or using gestures adapted from TBI (for an overview see Graichen & Metzner, 2014). For this reason, the present study aims to gain a broader view on GBI. The general importance of having feedback in HCI has been emphasized by several design guidelines (cf. Kortum, 2008; Shneiderman & Plaisant, 2005; Wigdor & Wixon, 2011). Moreover, Renaud and Cooper (2000) stated that graphical feedback would be especially useful. Therefore it is necessary to know if there should be any kind of additional feedback when designing a gestural interface (e.g. for smartphones, smart home environments, or IVIS). When using TBI or a mouse, users usually get a direct feedback that any plain input action was correctly performed in form of the haptic of a screen or the click of a mouse. For in-air gestures there would be no comparable feedback beyond seeing the intended action is being performed on the screen or not. Therefore, it is important to investigate, whether users actually need a special type of feedback for successful GBI, or if it is appropriate to get a lagged feedback otherwise (that means the feedback can be seen when the action was already performed). In the present work, three levels of visual information depth were used to give feedback to the user: 1) A simple feedback providing only few information, but being less cognitively demanding, 2) a feedback with medium complexity, and 3) a feedback providing a high amount of information, but being highly demanding when being constantly monitored. As this topic of designing GBI is relatively new to HCI, there are no concrete hypotheses for this experiment (i.e. in favor of one feedback version), so the study was conducted with an explorative character.

2. METHOD

2.1 Participants

Participants (mostly students) were recruited via mailing lists of TU Chemnitz. In total 29 (20 female) people took part in the experiment with a mean age of 23.01 years (SD = 4.27). 21 people said, they already had experience in using GBI, eight said they would not have any experience yet. Twelve participants indicated they would be strongly interested in GBI, twelve indicated medium and five low interest.

2.2 Research Design and Feedback Conditions

To preclude inter-individual differences and to allow for a direct comparison of feedback information level, a within-subject design was chosen. Each participant operated with the interface three times using 1) feedback 1 with a low level of information, that means only the cursor was highlighted (short magnification of the red circle) when a gesture was detected, 2) feedback 2 with a medium level of information by displaying, the detected gesture in written form (e.g. "Rotation"; see Figure 2) and 3) feedback 3 with a high level of information by a simplified (abstracted) animated figure of the actual hand and finger movements (similar to the gesture visualizer as can be seen in Figure 4), so that users could always see what the Leap Motion as detecting at every moment (see Figure 3).

3. PROCEDURE

Participants were first instructed to the interface and its functionalities. By that, participants were reminded that the whole experiment aimed at rating the type of interaction, not the aesthetic or usability of the user interface. After that, they were asked, if it would be ok to film the experiment for later evaluation. If they agreed, video recording was started. Afterwards they familiarized themselves with the user interface by mouse as long as they wanted. Then, the instructor showed all the gestures and use cases according to the experimental conditions, and participants were required to repeat them. When all questions were clarified, a training session followed. Only in this training session, participants could monitor on a second screen (see Figure 4) what the gesture recognition device would detect, in order to get used to the detection performance and learn how to conduct the gestures correctly. The instructor observed the participant in this phase to ensure that the gestures were performed correctly and to give tips otherwise. When the participant felt confident in the usage of gestures, they were asked to accomplish a set of use cases, while the instructor counted occurring errors or special problems. An error was defined as every action that did not lead to the correct result, for example an erroneous detection of the leap or a deficient conduction of the gesture and so on.

Participants first used one of the three feedback version and then the other two, sequence was randomized. After using each gesture set, participants assessed the acceptance, workload and adequacy of feedback. Overall, the experiment took each participant about 90 minutes.

3.1 Facilities and Apparatus

3.1.1 User Interface

Participants operated with a self-developed web-based interface on a 14" laptop (Pentium 5 processor), which represented simple tasks from everyday use when interacting with a computer and responded to user inputs via the gesture recognition device (see Figure 1 to Figure 3).

These actions comprised 1) open and close something, 2) move to the next page (or scroll up or down), 3) zoom, 4) rotate and 5) grab and move an object (similarly to drag & drop, or copy an object). The first screen was designed with different tiles with symbols or pictures on their surface (similar to Windows 8 tile interface), which could be simply opened and closed (see Figure 1). By doing so another picture, a small text or a map appeared on the screen. On the second screen, the user could choose a picture from a list by activating them through the buttons on the left side. The selected picture appeared on the middle of the interface, and could then be rotated and zoomed (see Figure 2). The third screen showed a large white ball on red background, which could be grabbed and moved by the user anywhere on the screen (see Figure 3). When grabbing, a blue ring around the ball signalized the successful grabbing. The current position of the cursor was indicated by a red dot. On both sides of each screen, arrows indicated that one could move to the next or a previous screen. To move forward or backwards the user had to use the corresponding gesture (swiping sideways, e.g. see Figure 5). To display the information from feedback 2 and 3 a small window was placed in the upper left area (see Figure 2 and Figure 3).

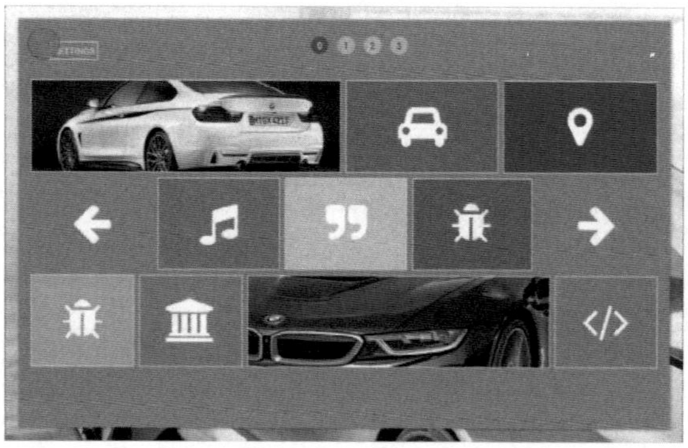

Figure 1. Screen 1: Open and close

Figure 2. Zoom and rotate

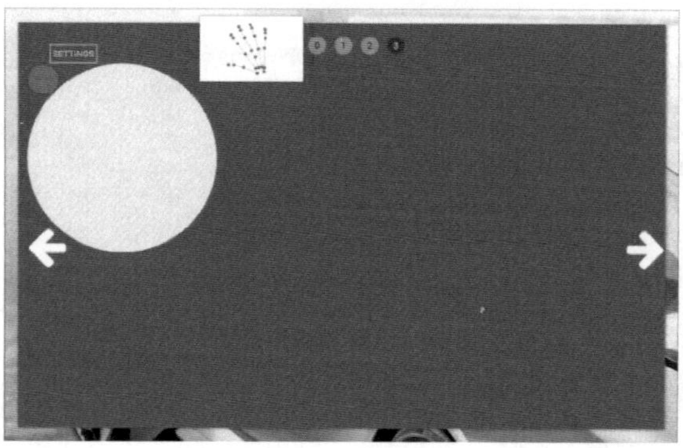

Figure 3. Grab and move

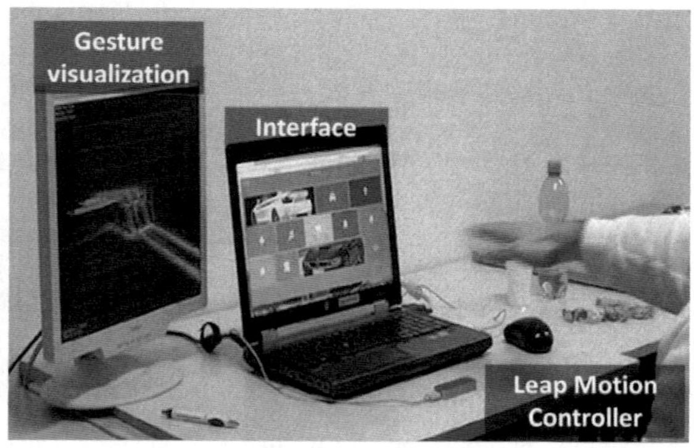

Figure 4. Experimental setup

3.1.2 Gesture Recognition

For the detection of gestures in open space Leap Motion was used (e.g. Marin, Dominio, & Zanuttigh, 2014), which recognizes hand gestures in top of the device within a limited infrared corridor. The controller was placed in front of the laptop (see Figure 4), but participants were free to place it, wherever it would suit them best. A second screen was placed next to the laptop showing the Leap Motion Visualizer. This visualizer displayed a grid with an abstracted hand model for showing what the controller detects at each moment. During the training session the screen was rotated towards the attendees, during the experimental session it was rotated to the camera. Video camera was placed next to the participants, so that faces would not be visible, but the screen with Leap Motion Visualizer for later evaluation (e.g. detection of errors in gesture recognition).

3.1.3 Gesture Set

For the experiment a gesture set has been designed (see Figure 5). The design process was guided by general literature on gestural human-human-communication, but was also restricted by the detection quality of the gesture recognition device (all gesture have to base on swiping or circle-drawing movements).

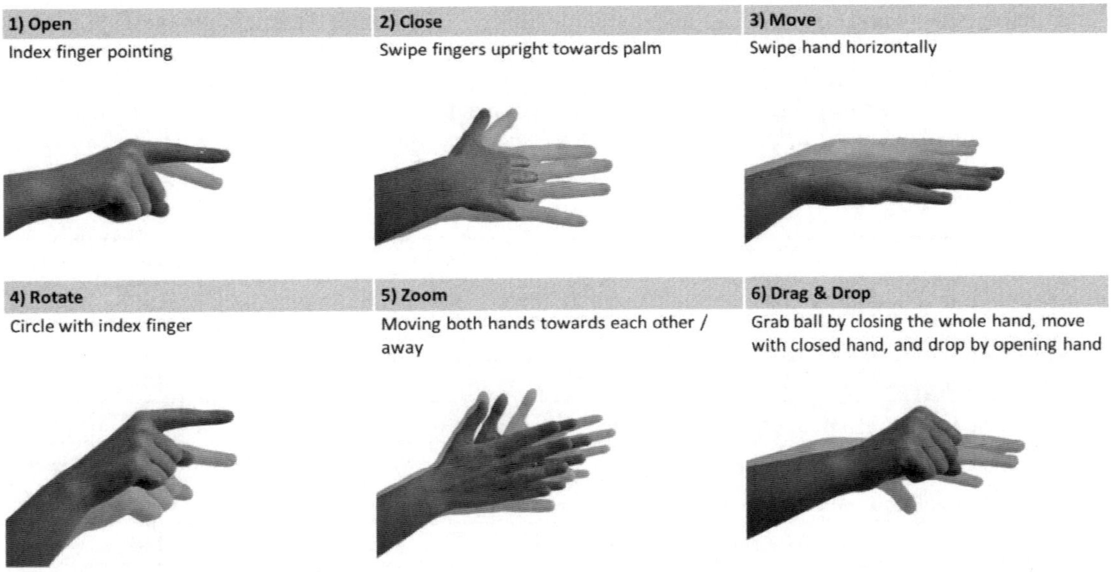

Figure 5. Gesture set

3.2 Subjective Data

Acceptance was measured by a 9-item questionnaire (using a 5-point rating scale ranging from -2 to 2) of Van der Laan, Heino, and Waard (1997). It consist of the two subscales 'usefulness' (five items) and 'satisfying' (four items). Workload was assessed using the 6-item NASA-TLX by Hart and Staveland (1988). It estimates the level of 'mental demand', 'physical demand', 'temporal demand', 'effort', 'performance', and 'frustration level' with one item each using a rating scale ranging from 0 to 20 (with a maximum total score of 120).

For the assessment of feedback more detailed a self-developed questionnaire with 13 items was used (see table 2). Participants were asked to assess each feedback version on a 5-point Likert scale.

4. RESULTS

The overall workload score has been obtained by averaging the subscales of NASA-TLX without weighting (often referred as raw TLX; in accordance with Hart (2006). For statistical analysis ANOVAs with repeated measures, including appropriate effect size calculation were conducted. Only for the subjective feedback assessment no ANOVA was conducted, as this questionnaire was self-developed.

Table 1. Results of subjective data

Score	Feedback 1		Feedback 2		Feedback 3	
	M	*SD*	*M*	*SD*	*M*	*SD*
Usefulness	0.67	0.75	0.14	0.83	0.63	0.89
Satisfying	0.61	0.74	0.41	0.63	0.55	0.88
TLX	8.47	3.13	7.23	2.75	6.67	3.21

For acceptance, means of the usefulness scale were comparable for feedback 1 and feedback 3 (0.67 vs. 0.63), feedback 2 was assessed lower (0.14). This difference is significant ($F(2, 56) = 4.739$; $p = .013$; $\eta_G^2 = 0.081$). For satisfying scale values were similar for all feedback versions (0.71 vs. 0.41 and 0.55), this difference is not significant ($F(2, 56) = 4.079$; $p = .46$; $\eta_G^2 = 0.012$). NASA-TLX score was lowest for feedback 3 (6.67) and highest for feedback 1 (8.47). This difference is significant as well ($F(2, 56) = 17.296$; $p < .001$; $\eta_G^2 = 0.06$). See Table 1 for detailed values.

Results of the detailed assessment of the feedback versions can be seen in Table 2. For most items feedback 3 was assessed highest. For example, results indicate that feedback 3 is appropriate, conveys relevant information and helps using the interface. The impression of feeling distracted was lowest when using feedback 3. However, participants seem to constantly monitor the small figure when using feedback 3.

Table 2. Detailed assessment of feedback versions

Question	Fb 1	Fb 2	Fb 3
The feedback is appropriate	3.22	2.97	3.52
The feedback conveys all relevant information	3.24	3.21	3.24
The feedback helps to use the interface	2.95	2.21	3.48
Due to the feedback I know exactly what I am doing	3.17	3.14	3.52
The feedback shows me what the Leap Motion detects	3.64	4.14	3.69
Due to the feedback I know I performed the right action	3.25	3.76	3.00
Due to the feedback I know exactly what will happen next	2.41	2.03	2.45
I would like to get more information by the feedback	2.52	2.86	2.69
I am overly distracted by the feedback	3.86	4.03	3.38
I monitored the feedback constantly	3.10	2.69	3.69
The feedback would help to understand constraints of the system	3.08	2.83	3.41
The feedback would help to realize the detection performance	3.61	4.03	3.79
The feedback would help to understand occurring errors	3.02	2.69	3.14

5. CONCLUSION

The present study aimed at the investigation of user preferences regarding the question if there should be an additional form of feedback when operating with an (computer) interface using gestural interaction. Therefore, a simple experimental setup using a freely available gesture recognition device and a self-developed web-interface was set up. As there is no common state of the art, which could be aggregated from literature regarding these questions, the present study was conducted for exploratory reasons, and no assumptions were made in prior regarding the design of an appropriate feedback.

User ratings regarding acceptance were highest for feedback 1 and feedback 3, with feedback 2 being rated significantly lower. However, the perceived workload was assessed lowest for feedback 3 and highest for feedback 1. The detailed assessment concerning the three feedback versions showed interesting results. Feedback 3 was rated as the most informative. Moreover it was seen to help understanding the interface with its constraints and letting users know what they are doing. Another advantage is the improved understanding of occurring errors, as users can permanently see what the Leap Motion is detecting. On the other hand users were monitoring the screen a lot.

However the investigated use cases represent only a small number of basic interaction tasks. But the preference comparisons also reveal, that a general statement on the general necessity of an additional feedback cannot be made. User ratings of feedback 3 (with a high information level) were similar to those for feedback 1 (with nearly no information). This might imply, that the design of GBI should maybe not be generally guided by implementing an additional feedback But it might be useful to increase the acceptance and the understanding (cf. building appropriate mental models on how the systems works) when this new interaction technology is introduced to a new domain.

Further research has the potential of creating a standard set of gestures that is widely accepted for different use cases, contexts and devices (like smartphones, smart environments or in-vehicle interfaces) and represents a number of useful and transferable actions. But this also requires a gesture recognition device which inheres less restrictions concerning the gesture design. The presented results give first directions towards these standards. Moreover more research on the usefulness of GBI in a realistic setting (like in-vehicle interaction or at home) is needed to determine the concrete user demands and the user experience of this new type of interaction.

REFERENCES

Bressem, J., & Ladewig, S. H. (2011). Rethinking gesture phases: Articulatory features of gestural movement? *Semiotica, 2011*(184). https://doi.org/10.1515/semi.2011.022

Gonzalez, C. (1996). Does animation in user interfaces improve decision making? In M. J. Tauber, B. Nardi, & G. C. van der Veer (Eds.), *Proceedings of the SIGCHI conference on Human factors in computing systems common ground - CHI '96* (pp. 27–34). New York, New York, USA: ACM Press. https://doi.org/10.1145/238386.238396

Graichen, L., & Metzner, M. (2014). Gestures in human-computer interaction - A review from a psychological point of view. In K. Blashki & Y. Xiao (Eds.), *Proceedings of the International Conferences on Interfaces and Human Computer Interaction 2014, Game and Entertainment Technologies 2014 and Computer Graphics, Visualization, Computer Vision and Image Processing 2014. Lisbon, Portugal, July 15 - 19, 2014 (part of the Multi Conference on Computer Science and Information Systems 2014)* (pp. 243–248). Lisbon: IADIS Press.

Hart, S. G. (2006). Nasa-Task Load Index (NASA-TLX); 20 Years Later. *Proceedings of the Human Factors and Ergonomics Society Annual Meeting, 50*(9), 904–908. https://doi.org/10.1177/154193120605000909

Hart, S. G., & Staveland, L. E. (1988). Development of NASA-TLX (Task Load Index): Results of empirical and theoretical research. In *Advances in Psychology. Human Mental Workload* (Vol. 52, pp. 139–183). Elsevier. https://doi.org/10.1016/S0166-4115(08)62386-9

Karam, M., & Schraefel, M. C. (2005). *A taxonomy of gestures in human computer interaction*. Technical report, Electronics and Computer Science. University of Southampton. Retrieved from http://eprints.soton.ac.uk/261149/

Kortum, P. (Ed.). (2008). *HCI beyond the GUI: Design for haptic, speech, olfactory and other nontraditional interfaces*. Amsterdam, Boston: Elsevier/Morgan Kaufmann.

Marin, G., Dominio, F., & Zanuttigh, P. (2014). Hand gesture recognition with leap motion and kinect devices. In *IEEE International Conference on Image Processing (ICIP), 2014. Paris, France, 27 - 30 Oct. 2014* (pp. 1565–1569). Piscataway, NJ: IEEE. https://doi.org/10.1109/ICIP.2014.7025313

Oh, J., Robinson, H. R., & Lee, J. Y. (2013). Page flipping vs. clicking: The impact of naturally mapped interaction technique on user learning and attitudes. *Computers in Human Behavior, 29*(4), 1334–1341. https://doi.org/10.1016/j.chb.2013.01.011

Quek, F., McNeill, D., Bryll, R., Duncan, S., Ma, X.-F., Kirbas, C.,. Ansari, R. (2002). Multimodal human discourse: Gesture and speech. *ACM Transactions on Computer-Human Interaction, 9*(3), 171–193. https://doi.org/10.1145/568513.568514

Renaud, K., & Cooper, R. L. (2000). Feedback in human-computer interaction - characteristics and recommendations. *South African Computer Journal, 26*, 105–114.

Saffer, D. (2009). *Designing gestural interfaces*. Sebastopol, CA: O'Reilly Media, Inc.

Schomaker, L., Nijtmans, Camurri, A., Lavagetto F., Morasso, P., Benoit, C.,. Blauert, J. (1995). *A taxonomy of multimodal interaction in the human information processing system* (A report of the Esprit Project 8579 MIAMI No. WP 1). Retrieved from http://www.ai.rug.nl/~lambert/projects/miami/taxonomy/taxonomy.html

Shneiderman, B., & Plaisant, C. (2005). *Designing the user interface: Strategies for effective human-computer interaction* (4. ed.). Boston, Mass.: Pearson.

Tavanti, M., & Lind, M. (2001). 2D vs 3D, implications on spatial memory. In K. Andrews, S. Roth, & P. C. Wong (Eds.), *IEEE Symposium on Information Visualization 2001 (InfoVis 2001). 22-23 October 2001, San Diego, California, USA* (pp. 139–145). Piscataway, NJ: IEEE. https://doi.org/10.1109/INFVIS.2001.963291

Van der Laan, J. D., Heino, A., & Waard, D. de. (1997). A simple procedure for the assessment of acceptance of advanced transport telematics. *Transportation Research Part C: Emerging Technologies, 5*(1), 1–10. https://doi.org/10.1016/S0968-090X(96)00025-3

Wigdor, D., & Wixon, D. (Eds.). (2011). *Safari Tech Books Online. Brave NUI world: Designing natural user interfaces for touch and gesture*. Amsterdam: Morgan Kaufmann/Elsevier.

THE EFFECT OF INTERACTION ON VISUAL APPEAL AND TRUST IN ONLINE HEALTH INFORMATION

Marian McDonnell and Tara O'Reilly
Institute of Art, Design & Technology, Kill Avenue, Dun Laoghaire, Co Dublin, Ireland

ABSTRACT

64% of the Irish population use the internet as a health information resource (Gallagher, Tedstone, Moran and Kartalova-O'Doherty, 2008). This health information is used to self-diagnose and check symptoms, but anyone can upload information online, making it difficult to regulate trustworthy and untrustworthy information. When users trust inaccurate information, it can cause anxiety and unnecessary financial cost. Previous research has found online users depend on the visual appeal of a website as an indicator of trust. This impression can be formed within 50 milliseconds; regardless of information quality. The purpose of this study was to examine if trust after a short exposure (200 milliseconds) and trust after a long exposure (7 seconds) were predictors of trust after interaction. Furthermore the effect of website genre on trust and visual appeal was analysed. 25 participants rated visual appeal and 73 rated trustworthiness. There was a significant relationship between trust short and trust interaction, with trust short accounting for 36.8% of the variation in trustworthiness ratings after interaction. Website genre influences visual appeal rating but not trustworthiness ratings. From these results, it was concluded that impressions formed in 50 milliseconds can be extended to impressions formed after interaction.

KEYWORDS

Visual Appeal, Trustworthiness, Interaction, Website First Impressions, Online Health Information, Website Genre

1. INTRODUCTION

The internet allows users to complete a plethora of activities online, improving quality of life (Liang, 2011). However, there are downsides to relying on the internet. There is low cost and low skill required to produce and share information online, which makes it more liable to inaccuracies, due to the possibility of anyone, regardless of expertise being able to post online (Metzger & Flanagin, 2015). One subject that falls prey to inaccuracies is health information. People seek out health information to self-diagnose, read journal articles, watch videos, search for diet advice, and extra information after a visit to the doctor (Moretti, Oliveira & Silva, 2012). Although this information is not always correct, 29% of participants go against doctors' advice in favor of online advice (Zaini, Fakeh, Shahibi, Dollah, Ibrahim & Paiman , 2013). Responsibility to correctly evaluate information falls on the information seeker. Information seeking is a behaviour describing the way in which an individual collects and sources information for personal or academic purposes. This information and the website on which it is hosted must be correctly evaluated for its trustworthiness (Kakai, Ikoja- Odongo & Kigongo-Bukenya, 2004). Trust has been defined as the expectation that the word, promise, oral or written statement of an individual is reliable (Costante, den Hartog & Petkovic, 2011). Trustworthy information is subjective and described as fair and unbiased. Identifying trustworthy information can be difficult due to the lack of professional gatekeepers regulating the quality of information (Metzger and Flanagin, 2007). The way in which individuals evaluate information can be made clear by models of information processing.

1.1 Models of Information Processing

Information processing theory (Severin & Tankyard, 2001) states that information is sent, the receiver knows, understands and agrees with it and as a result forms a new opinion. In relation to online health information, this theory explains the process of accepting information from online health websites, choosing a website, gaining trust and making one's own choice based on this trust. The elaboration likelihood model of persuasion, dual processing and mere exposure effect can offer a description on how information is processed. The elaboration likelihood model (ELM) of persuasion argues that the amount of cognitive effort used to process a message depends on individual and situational factors. The theory states that information is processed centrally (active and conscious processing) or peripherally (use of simple cues/ heuristics), and depends on the level of effort used to understand a piece of information. When motivation and ability to process is high, the central route is used; when motivation and ability to process is low, the peripheral route is taken (Chiang and Jackson, 2013). ELM explains the ways in which attitudes change throughout encountering messages and sources of these messages. Another theory which supports ELM is the dual processing model of credibility assessment proposed by Metzger (2007). Metzger hypothesized highly motivated users will apply an analytical process to assessment whereas low motivated users will apply a heuristic assessment. This motivation derives from the consequences of trusting inaccurate information. However, on the contrary, Lucassen, Muilwijk, Noordzij & Schraagen (2012) argue that credibility evaluation is heuristic to some extent, given that full systematic evaluation is not always feasible. Furthermore, trust involves risk but full systematic evaluation reduces rick to zero. Therefore, information evaluation implies that there is always some level of heuristic evaluation.

Finally, the mere exposure effect can be extended to online information processing. When a stimulus is viewed on more than one occasion it is considered more favorably (Zajonc, 2001). This phenomenon was reported in trust and visual appeal studies (Tractinsky, Katz & Ikar, 2000, Lindgaard,

2011). Tractinksy et al. (2000) highlighted a correlation between perception of visual appeal (VA) and perception of the usability of the system as a whole. Perception of the systems usability was influenced by VA and not by the actual usability of the system. This implies users rely on visual appearance.

Research has found individual differences in evaluating information. Liao & Fu (2011) reported the effects of age and individual differences in young adults and older adults by measuring the cognitive abilities, internet experience and domain knowledge by asking participants to evaluate the content and contextual features. Older adults were less able to differentiate between credible and less credible information in comparison to younger adults. Older adults were reported as reading the content passively and therefore being more open to being misled. Nielson and Molich (1990) introduced the concept of heuristic evaluation. This is a strategy which involves viewing the interface and commenting subjectively on the strengths and weaknesses. As a result, the user is influenced by their intuition, devoid of any guidelines.

1.2 Visual Appeal

Visual Appeal (VA) has been described as a pleasurable and harmonic experience. VA occurs at a visceral level before the brain even has time to appraise the stimulus at a cognitive level (Lindgaard, 2007). Visual complexity, colorfulness (Reinecke et al., 2013), density, contrast and graphics (Lindgaard, 2011) on a webpage have been attributed to high VA. Furthermore heat map analysis research has shown that users are more drawn to images than text due to less cognitive effort involved (Sarathy & Pengnate, 2013). Additionally mobile phones with a high visually appealing design are perceived as efficient and less prone to errors (Sonderegger & Sauer, 2010). Previous VA research has indicated the leverage that VA has on perceptions of usability.

Tractinsky, Katz & Ikar (2000) created a computer simulated auto teller machine, requiring participants to rate the usability prior and post use. Visually appealing interfaces were rated high in usability. Manipulation of loading times and responsiveness had no effect on perceived usability and perceived visual appeal. This study led to the postulation of what is beautiful is usable, regardless of actual usability. Tractinsky et al (2000) proposed a halo effect, whereby one attribute overrules other attributes.

Following this, VA has been extended as influencing first impressions and trustworthiness. It takes just 50 milliseconds for a user to create a reliable first impression of a webpage. Lindgaard, Dudek, Fernades & Brown (2006) had participants rate a number of homepages on visual appeal in 50ms and 500ms, finding consistency between these two time scales, concluding that 50ms is sufficient for reliable first impressions. These first impressions are vital for developing opinions and furthering actions on a website. Further research by Lindgaard (2011) indicated first impressions of VA can be extended to perceived trustworthiness and usability. Participants rated homepages on VA, trustworthiness and usability; the ratings indicated that trustworthiness scores and usability scores were influenced by VA. Response scores also indicated participants were more comfortable rating VA than trustworthiness and usability. It is possible that these results were a consequence of the mere exposure effect (Zajonc, 2001). This study only used static images and did not consider how interaction with the webpage would affect the outcome. Lee & McDonnell (2016) reported visual appeal impressions are formed through precognitive processes and users use careful reasoning during trust formation. Participants rated 30 static webpages on VA and trust, but did not include interaction. There is no focus on one specific genre, which raises the question whether some genres are more or less likely to be trusted by users.

1.3 Trustworthiness and Online Health Information

Trust online is difficult to achieve in comparison to human to human trust, where body language and other physical signals can be used. It is open to editorial and structural changes which make it less reliable (Metzger and Flanagin, 2007). A decision to choose a website from a search engine list is rarely based on careful analysis of the content, but more on the visual appeal of the website, regardless of the quality of the information (Van der Geest & van Dongelen, 2009). A two stage experiment was conducted whereby websites hosted the same information content but were manipulated to have high visual appeal or low visual appeal. Participants first viewed the site for 750ms and then in stage two viewed the site for 5 seconds, and gave it a visual appeal rating. Participants expected the high visual appeal sites to have higher quality information than the low visual appeal sites. Similarly, Briggs (2008) reported guidelines that effect trust in online health information. The webpage must make a good first impression with VA. Content must not be commercially focused and should be personally tailored to users. Although this study confirms that online health information is processed similarly to other content, the methodology was not without flaws. Participants gave their opinions on the websites one week after viewing them. Therefore, this may have affected recall of the websites and consequently effect ratings. Although VA is a strong predictor of trustworthiness perceptions, research has indicated the need for other methods to evaluate trustworthy information. Metzger and Flanagin (2007) stated five criteria to consider when evaluating online information. These include accuracy, author credentials, objectivity, scope and how current the information is. The presence of a street address, privacy policy and endorsements (Rains & Karmickel, 2009) are also significant. Appropriate evaluation of online information is particularly important in e-health.

Online health information websites are increasingly being used to diagnose numerous symptoms. Inaccuracy to correctly evaluate online health information can lead to anxiety, unnecessary financial cost and distractions (White, 2009). The web as a health resource is an important tool for individuals within a low income bracket. Individuals with low income tend to prioritize basic daily items over visits to the doctor and thus use the internet as a resource to ease health anxieties (Kim, 2015). Although online health information can help people of low income, physicians feel that it can be a hindrance during a visit to a clinic.

Kim and Kim (2009) conducted a survey of 493 Korean physicians on their opinions and experiences with online health information. The physicians believed most of the information online is inaccurate or the patient incorrectly judges the information in accordance with their symptoms which can lead the patient to question the physician's advice or not follow treatment. Although the majority of physicians in the study felt online health information had mostly negative effects, they did state it can improve patients' understanding of medical terms and gives them confidence. This study focused on physicians' opinions of how patients judge information, which may have been misinterpreted. Furthermore Kim & Kim (2009) did not consider why patients reject the physicians' advice in favor of the internet.

1.4 Website Genre

Perception of trust is perceived differently across website genres. News and e-commerce websites were perceived as more credible than interest group and personal websites. Specifically news websites were perceived more credible when assessing sponsor and message credibility (Flanagin & Metzger, 2007). Furthermore in e-banking sites, brand name, security, reliability and availability were the top trust aspects. In e-commerce reliability and availability, brand name and appearance were considered to be the most important (Costante, den Hartog & Petkovic, 2011). Websites from official sources such as government bodies were considered to be of higher quality and reliability than sites with a commercial and persuasive focus (Young, Komoldi, Rózsa & Chu,2015). This highlights how some website genres can effect trust, but there is a lack of research that focuses on health websites and trust.

1.5 The Current Study

Research has shown that visual appeal has a significant influence on trust (Lee & McDonnell, 2016) and accounts for first impressions formed when using a website (Metzger et al, 2015). 64% of the Irish population uses the internet as a health information resource, making it important for users to accurately decipher trustworthy sites to benefit from the information instead of raising health anxiety (Gallagher et al., 2008). However, there is a lack of research surrounding how interaction with a webpage influences trustworthiness evaluation. The current study aims to fill in the gap in the literature by comparing and examining the effect of visual appeal and trust after allowing participants to engage with 3 main genres of health websites (government, insurance and general health). Furthermore the current study will compare 3 different healthcare genres on visual appeal and trust. From the aforementioned research gaps, the following research questions and hypothesis are proposed:

Research Questions:

1. Does interaction with a webpage influence trustworthiness rating compared to a short and long exposure time?

2. Does the website genre affect impressions of visual appeal or trustworthiness.

Hypotheses:

1. There will be a difference in trust ratings after interaction with the webpage compared to a short exposure time (200 milliseconds).

2. There will be a difference in trust ratings after interaction with the webpage compared to a long exposure time (7 seconds).

3. There will be a difference in visual appeal ratings across the 3 different genres.

2. METHOD

2.1 Design

The design of part one of the experiment is a correlational repeated measures design, investigating the relationship between three independent variables and one dependent variable. The independent variables are visual appeal (VA), trustworthiness rating after short exposure (TS) and trustworthiness rating after a long exposure (TL). The dependent variable is trustworthiness rating after interaction with webpage (TIN). The design of part two is a quasi-experimental, repeated measures design, investigating the effect of website genre (k=3, health insurance, government health information, general health information) on the variables visual appeal, TS, TL, TIN.

The sample consisted of 73 participants, all 3rd level students of Dun Laoghaire Institute of Art, Design & Technology (IADT). To obtain visual appeal ratings, 23 creative computing students were selected by purposive sampling due to their understanding of the research topic. To obtain trustworthiness ratings, 73 participants (male = 47, female = 26) were selected through convenience sampling and were all students of IADT studying Applied Psychology (n = 23), Creative Computing (n = 38), and User Experience (n = 12). Ages ranged from 18 – 54, with 73% falling within the 18 – 24 age band.

The treatment of all participants was in accordance with the ethical standards of the Psychological Society of Ireland. The study was approved by the Department of Technology and Psychology Ethics Committee (DTPEC) at IADT.

2.2 Materials and Apparatus

A total of 30 webpages were selected. All websites fell within the website genre of health. Three health subgenres were selected; (1) health insurance, (2) government and (3) general health information. Each website was checked on free online software hosted on http://checkpagerank.net/. This software checked websites for popularity and website were excluded if the worldwide rank was more than 1,000,000 (McDonnell & Lee, 2016).

Each phase of the experiment required participants to rate each webpage using a Likert scale rating system. A task sheet was supplied for phase 3 of the experiment, detailing 30 minor tasks. There was one task per website. The participant completed each one in order to interact with the website. For example, task 1 was for Halligans.ie which instructed the participant to 'Find the Eircom AVC group scheme'. When the task was completed, a box was ticked as evidence of interaction. The experimental program was adapted from McDonnell & Lee (2016) Axure RP Pro7 version number 7.0.0.3187. Further adaptations by the researcher were constructed in the same program to facilitate phase three of the experiment and the focus on health websites. A pilot study was conducted with 6 participants, two weeks before data collection. Problems such as typos in the information pack and broken links in the prototype were identified and fixed. Pilot participants found the task sheet too time consuming. Written answers were replaced with check boxes. The information pack was updated from paper to online format and included the prototype link to make it more user friendly.

2.3 Procedure

2.3.1 Part 1: Obtaining Ratings For Part One (Visual Appeal)

23 Creative computing students were approached in a computer lab. Participants were given the hyperlink to the online information sheet, consent form, demographic survey and hyperlink to experiment. Furthermore, each participant was handed an instruction sheet. Participants viewed 30 static images of webpages selected by the researcher. Participants viewed the webpage for any amount of time they required; furthering this, each site was rated on visual appeal from 1 (extremely unappealing) to 7 (extremely appealing). After participants rated the webpages they were debriefed and thanked for their participation.

2.3.2 Part 2: Trustworthiness Ratings

73 participants were approached in lab classes and provided with an information pack similar to that in 2.2.1 with the addition of an adapted instruction sheet and task sheet for phase 3. Participants were again given five practice images/ tasks before viewing and rating the 30 test images/websites. Images were shown in random orders across phase 1, phase 2 and phase 3 to control for the order effect. Across the three phases, participants viewed each webpage three times. Ratings for trustworthiness were collected in three phases; Phase 1: a white mask was displayed for one second, followed by an image of the website homepage for 200ms, and then a white mask for one second. Participants were then asked to provide a self-entered rating of trustworthiness from 1 (extremely untrustworthy) to 7 (extremely trustworthy). Once all 30 test images were rated in phase 1, phase 2 of the experiment began. Phase 2: images were displayed for a time of seven seconds, and similar to above participants were asked to provide a rating of trustworthiness from 1 to 7. Once all 30 images were rated in phase 2, phase 3 began. Phase 3: participants were asked to interact with each of the 30 websites by completing a task for each website. Once each task was completed, participants were required to provide a self-entered rating of trustworthiness from 1 (extremely untrustworthy) to 7 (extremely trustworthy). Once the experiment was completed, participants were thanked and debriefed.

3. RESULTS

3.1. Trustworthiness Short and Trustworthiness Long as Predictors of Trustworthiness after Interaction

Descriptive statistics for the variables TS, TL and TIN are displayed in table 1.

Table 1. Decriptive Statistics

Variable	N	Mean	Standard Deviation
Trust Short	30	3.64	3.64
Trust Long	30	3.89	.54
Trust Interaction	30	4.24	.543

There was an excellent ICC value for all 3 variables. This shows a very high level of agreement between raters for all three variable TS, TL and TIN.

A hierarchical multiple regression was conducted to determine if the addition of variables TS and then TL obtained from online test improved the prediction of TIN. H1 looked to examine if trust after a short exposure time is a predictor of trust after interaction. This was tested using a Hierarchical Multiple Regression. TS explains a significant amount of variation in TIN,$F(1,28) = 16.327$, $p <.000$, $R2 =.368$. That is an increase of .368, meaning there is an increase of 36.8% predictability of TIN. H1 can be accepted.

H2 looked to examine if trust after long exposure time is a predictor of trust after interaction. TL did not explain a significant amount of variation in TIN, $F(2, 27) = 6.910$, $p=.014$, $R2 =.460$. That is an increase of .460, meaning there is an increase of 46% predictability of TIN. This is not significant. H2 can be rejected. All assumptions of hierarchical multiple regression were met. There was linearity as assessed by partial regression plots and a plot of studentized residuals against the predicted values. There was independence of residuals, as assessed by a Durbin-Watson statistic of 2.262. There was homoscedasticity, as assessed by visual inspection of a plot of studentized residuals versus unstandardized predicted values. Tests were conducted to see if the data met the assumptions of collinearity (TS, Tolerance = 2.90, VIF = 3.447; TL Tolerance = 2.90, VIF 3.447). There were no leverage values greater than 0.2, and values for Cook's distance above 1. There assumption of normality was met, as assessed by Q-Q Plot.

3.2 The Effect of Website Genre on Ratings of VA, TS, TL And TIN.

The independent variable, genre, consisted of three levels; insurance, general and government. There were ten websites in each genre. H3 proposed website genre would have a significant effect on VA ratings, while H4 proposed website genre would have a significant effect on trust ratings. To investigate H3 and H4, a series of one-way ANOVAS were conducted.

There were no outliers in the data, as visually assessed by inspection of a boxplot. All data was normally distributed as assessed by Shapiro's Wilk test ($p > .05$). There was homogeneity of variances, as assessed by Levenes test for equality of variances. There was a significant difference in Visual Appeal Ratings across genres, $F (2, 27) = 3.84$, $p = .034$. H3 can be accepted. Post Hoc analysis using Tukey HSD revealed an increase for VA between genres insurance ($M = 4.03$, $SD = .887$) government ($M = 3.11$, $SD = .876$), a mean increase of .923, 95% CI [.072, 1.77], which was statistically significant ($p =.032$). There was an increase from government to general ($M = 3.37$, $SD = .463$), a mean increase of .261, 95% CI [-.59, 1.11]. This was not statistically significant ($p = .730$). A second within subjects ANOVA was conducted to test for the effect of the independent variable website genre on TS. There was no significant differences across genres, $F (2, 27) =1.93$, $p = .164$. A third within subjects ANOVA was conducted to test for the effect of website genre on TL. There was no significant differences across genres, $F (2, 27) = 1.07$, $p = .358$. A fourth within subjects ANOVA was conducted to test for the effect of website genre on TIN. There was no significant difference across genres, $F (2, 27) = 1.93$, $p = .164$. Hypothesis 4 was rejected.

4. DISCUSSION

The current study investigated the relationship between variables VA, TS, & TL on TIN. The effect of website genre on VA and Trust was also investigated. A hierarchical multiple regression was conducted to examine hypotheses 1 and hypotheses 2. The results revealed that trustworthiness after short exposure (TS) was a predictor of trustworthiness after interaction (TIN), but trust worthiness after a long exposure (TL) was not a predictor of TIN. This was partially expected based on previous research (Tractinsky et al., 2000, Lindgaard et al., 2011).Four one way within group ANOVAS were conducted to examine hypotheses 3 and hypotheses 4. Results showed that VA was significantly affected by website genre but TS, TL and TIN were not affected by website genre.

4.1 Interpretation of Results

Results of the hierarchical multiple regression illustrate that trust after a short exposure is a significant predictor of trust scores after interaction. This indicates that first impressions have a significant positive impact on longer exposure. This adds support that first impressions are based on precognitive judgements (McDonnell & Lee, 2016), and critical for opinions and furthering actions on websites (Lindgaard et al., 2011). This could be a result of the mere exposure effect (Zajonc, 2001). From phase 1 to phase 3, participants viewed each webpage a total of three times. According to the mere exposure effect, the more a website is viewed the more favorable it is considered (Tractinsky, Katz & Ikar, 2000., Lindgaard, 2011). Interestingly, when trust scores after a short exposure were joined with trust scores after a long exposure ,they were not significant predictors on trust scores after interaction. It is important to look at the mean trust scores which show that two thirds of the scores increased from trust long to trust interaction. Although there was no significant effect, participants did briefly increase their trust scores from TS to TL and then TL to TIN. This illustrates participants opinion of trust improved after each condition, albeit not significantly. This finding is supported by the mere exposure effect (Zajonc, 2001) and the halo effect which was also found in Tractinsky et al.,(2000).

The lack of increase may be due to the participants not feeling motivated. Metzger stated motivated and non-motivated users apply different analysis. Phase 1 and 2 required a rating based on the participants own opinion. Phase 3 required the use of a task sheet. The task sheet may have motivated the users to analyse the websites more thoroughly and therefore increasing their perceptions of trustworthiness.

Website genre had a significant effect on VA. Insurance websites were rated as the most visual appealing genre. This supports previous research reporting that different genres of websites have different VA perceptions (Costante, den Hartog, J. & Petkovic, 2011). Previous research found that websites with a commercial focus such as insurance websites negatively affected VA (Young et al., 2015). Most of the websites in the insurance category were aimed at Irish customers. This may have caused cultural implications, considering the majority of websites in other genres were international.

Website genre had no significant effect on trust, which contradicts previous research stating different genres are perceived as more trustworthy (Flanagin & Metzger, 2007). However, the mean scores indicate that the genre insurance was rated more favourably on trust than government and general websites. This finding does not support Young et al., (2015) who reported government websites are considered more reliable and of higher quality than sites with a business focus. Insurance websites were rated the most visually appealing. Therefore, this possibly explains why a commercially focused website gained more trust than a government website.

4.2 Limitations

The method for phase three (rating trust scores after interaction) required participants to use a task sheet and mark when they completed each task. Some participants may have rated TIN on whether they completed each task and not on the content of the website. Additionally each phase was self-report, and due to phase 3 not having a time constraint, participants could have fabricated the result without interacting with the webpage to finish the experiment faster. Although websites were checked online for rank, it is still possible that participants in the sample were familiar with the websites. Furthermore the majority of websites were not aimed at an Irish audience and therefore there may be cultural implications of using international websites. The samples used in this study were all students and the majority was between 18 to 25 years of age. This makes the results difficult to generalize to the population. Additionally the sample was non-target. Previous research has found that motivated and non-motivated users apply different analysis. Another weakness was the complete experiment took approximately 45 minutes to one hour to complete. From observations made by the researcher, during the experiment it was evident some of the participants were becoming frustrated with the lengthy experiment. This may have affected their ratings. Due to the already lengthy time, only 30 websites could be used with 10 websites in each genre. Results might have been more substantial if more websites were used.

4.3 Strengths

The current study regarded previous criticisms on trustworthiness raised by McDonnell & Lee (2016), by branching away from only static websites and requiring participants to interact with websites, and then rate for trustworthiness. Additionally focusing on one genre, online health information, identified how subgenres were perceived differently, whereas previous research had a broader genre focus (McDonnell & Lee, 2016., Flanagin & Metzger, 2007). The pilot study significantly helped the final experiment by identifying issues and overall improving the methodology. Each variable had high levels of interrater reliability as measured by ICC values. All assumptions of the hierarchical multiple regression and one way ANOVA was met. All participants were studying at least two IT modules, and understood the importance of the research. This means that there was a high degree of internal validity.

4.4 Future Research

The sample in this study was non-targeted. Motivated users apply different analysis to a website than non-motivated users (Metzger & Flanigin, 2007). Future research could investigate the difference between motivated and non-motivated user perceptions of visual appeal and trust, using the same methodology as the current research. Website evaluation criteria should be used as a guideline when identifying trustworthy material to gain more insight into what makes one online health website genre more trustworthy than another. Eye tracking software could be implemented to examine hotspots of a webpage that users are drawn to when making their first impression on trustworthiness. Research has found websites with faces are more visually appealing than logos. More research needs to be conducted on website elements with regard to first impressions and trust.

4.5 Conclusion and Implications

This study has shown that first impressions of trustworthiness can be extended to trustworthiness opinions after interaction, meaning that visual appeal is an important contributor to trusting online health information. This study also highlighted that website genre has a significant effect on VA. The genre of Insurance was the highest rated in VA and trustworthiness. Gaps within previous literature were explored, as research in trust after interaction is scarce. This information is of value to creators of online health websites. Highly appealing website design is what create trust in information hosted online. This result can help designers create a website which users can instantly trust. Further research should compare motivated and non-motivated online health information seekers.

REFERENCES

Briggs, P. (2008). Designing effective health websites. Towards Persuasive Adaptation, 1-2.

Chiang K. & Jackson, A. (2013). Health literacy and its outcomes: Application and extension of elaboration likelihood model. International Journal of Healthcare Management, 6(3), 152-157.

Costante, E. den Hartog, J. & Petkovic, M. (2011). On-line Trust Perception: What Really Matters. In Proceedings of the First Workshop on Socio-Technical Aspects in Security and Trust, 52-59.

Djamasbi, S., Siegel, M. & Tullis, T. (2014). Can fixation on main images predict visual appeal of homepages?. 47th Annual Hawaii International Conference on System Sciences (HICSS), Computer Society Press.

Flanagin, J.A. & Metzger, J. M.(2007). The role of site features, user attributes, and information verification behaviours on the perceived credibility of web-based information. New Media Society, 9(2), 319 – 342.

Gallagher S, Tedstone Doherty D., Moran R and Kartalova-O'Doherty, Y. (2008). Internet use and seeking health information online in Ireland: Demographic characteristics and mental health characteristics of users and non-users. HRB Research Series 4. Dublin: Health Research Board.

Kim, Y. (2015). Is seeking health information online different from seeking general information online? Journal of Information Science, 41(2) 228–241

Kim, J. & Kim, S. (2009). Physicians' perception of the effects of internet health information on the doctor–patient relationship. Informatics for Health & Social Care, 34(3): 136–148

Li, Y., Gao, J., Meng, C., Li, Q., Su, L., Zhao, B., Fan, W. & Han, J. (2015) A survey on truth discovery. ACM SIGKDD Explorations Newsletter, 17(2), 1-16.

Liang, T. (2011). Association between Use of Internet Services and Quality of Life in Taiwan. Journal of Data Science, 9, 83-92.

Liao, V & Fu, W. (2011). Effects of Aging and Individual Differences on Credibility Judgment of Online Health Information. Proceedings of the 29th international conference on Human factors in computing systems (CHI).

Lindgaard, G. (2007). Aesthetics, Visual Appeal, Usability and User Satisfaction: What Do the User's Eyes Tell the User's Brain? Australian Journal of Emerging Technologies and Society, 5(1), 1-14.

Lindgaard, G., Dudek, C., Sen, D., Sumegi, L. & Noonan, P. (2011). An exploration of relations between visual appeal, trustworthiness and perceived usability of homepages. ACM Transactions on Computer-Human Interaction, 18(1). Lindgaard, G., Fernandes, G., Dudek, C. & Brown, J. (2006). Attention web designers: You have 50 milliseconds to make a good first impression! Behaviour & information technology, 25(2), 115-126.

Lucassen, T., Muilwijk, R., Noordzij, L.M. & Schraagen, M.J. (2012). Topic familiarity and information skills in online credibility evaluation. Journal Of The Association For Information Science And Technology, 64(2), 254-264.

Metzger, M. J. (2007). Making sense of credibility on the Web: Models for evaluating online information and recommendations for future research. Journal of the American Society of Information Science and Technology, 58, 2078–2091.

Metzger, J. M., & Flanagin, J. A. (2015). Psychological approaches to credibility assessment online. The Handbook of the Psychology of Communication Technology, 445-466.

Moretti, A. F., Oliveira, Silva, K.M.E (2016). Access to health information on the internet: a public health issue? Rev Assoc Med Bras, 58(6):650-658.

Nielsen, J. & Molich, R. (1990). Heuristic evaluation of user interfaces. CHI '90 Proceedings of the SIGCHI Conference on Human Factors in Computing Systems, 249-256.

Rains, A.S. & Karmikel, D.C. (2009). Health information-seeking and perceptions of website credibility: Examining Web-use orientation, message characteristics, and structural features of websites. Computers in Human Behaviour, 25, 544 – 553.

Reinecke, K., Yeh, T., Miratrix, L., Mardiko, R., Zhao, Y., Liu, J. & Gajos, Z.K. (2013). Predicting Users' First Impressions of Website Aesthetics With a Quantification of Perceived Visual Complexity and Colorfulness Proceedings of the SIGCHI Conference on Human Factors in Computing Systems. ACM, 2049–2058.

Sarathy, R. & Pengnate, S. (2013)Visual appeal of websites: The durability of initial impressions. *46th Hawaii International Conference on System Sciences*, 480-489.

Severin, J.W. & Tankyard, W.J. (2001) Communication Theories: Origins, Methods and Use in Mass Media. New York, NY: Pearson.

Sonderegger, A. & Sauer, J. (2010). The influence of design aesthetics in usability testing: effects on user performance and perceived usability. Applied Ergonomics, 41(3), 403–410.

Tractinsky, N. & Katz, S.A. & Ikar, D. (2000). What is beautiful is usable. Interacting with Computers, 13, 127 – 145.

Van der Geest, T. & van Dongelen, R. (2009). What is beautiful is useful - Visual appeal and expected information quality. IEEE International Professional Communication Conference, 1-5.

Wells, J., Valacich, S.J.& Hess, J.T. (2011). What signal are you sending? How website quality influences perceptions of product quality and purchase intentions. Management Information Systems Quarterly, 35 (2), 373-396

White, W.R. & Horvitz, E. (2009). Cyberchondria: Studies of the escalation of medical concerns in web search. ACM Transactions on Information Systems, 27,(4).

Zajonc, B.R. (2001). Mere Exposure: A Gateway to the Subliminal. Current Directions inPsychological Science, 10(6), 224-228.

AN INTERACTIVE ACTION SET DETECTION IN NATURAL LANGUAGE HYBRID SYSTEM

Alexander Wachtel, Jonas Paczia and Walter F. Tichy
Karlsruhe Institute of Technology, Chair for Programming Systems Prof. Walter F. Tichy, Am Fasanengarten 5, 76131 Karlsruhe, Germany

ABSTRACT

In this paper, we introduce an interface for natural language dialog system and the Microsoft Excel API. This interface enables users to describe actions in unrestricted natural language interactively and run these actions in the technical domain like Microsoft Excel. We implement a hybrid system that supports natural language interactions similar as a chat bot and gesture control to follow the user's showing actions. For this purpose and also to avoid the lack of inconsistent code documentation, we dynamically export the provided documentation for coding in Visual Studio and provide it in the xml-format to the hybrid system. Users can use already existing actions and provide new action sets to the hybrid system at runtime. For our first prototype of the hybrid system, we concentrate on extending for handling graphs and charts. Evaluated by a user study the hybrid system can successfully resolve more that 80 % of the given user tasks.

KEYWORDS

Natural Language Processing; End User Development; Natural Language Interfaces; Human Computer Interaction; Programming in Natural Language; Dialog Systems

1. INTRODUCTION

Many dialog systems have already been developed. Commercially successful systems, such as Apple's Siri, actually based on active ontology (Guzzoni, 2006), and Google's Voice Search (Bellegarda, 2014) or (Williams, 2009) cover many domains. Reference resolution makes the systems act natural. However, there is no dialog interaction. The Mercury system (Seneff, 2002) designed by the MIT research group is a telephone hotline for automated booking of airline tickets. Mercury guides the user through a mixed initiative dialog towards the selection of a suitable flight based on date, time and preferred airline. Furthermore, Allen (2007) describes a system called PLOW. As a collaborative task agent PLOW can learn to perform certain tasks, such as extracting specific information from the internet, by demonstration, explanation, and dialog.

Myers (2006) and Scaffidi (2005) compared the number of end users and professional programmers in the United States. Nearly 90 million people use computers at work and 50 million of them use spreadsheets. In a self-assessment, 12 million considered themselves as programmers, but only 3 million people are professional programmers. According to Liberman (2006), the main question in the End User Development (EUD) area of research is, how to allow non-programming users who have no access to source code, to program a computer system or extend the functionality of an existing system. In general, spreadsheets have been used for at least 7000 years (Hurst, 2000). The created spreadsheets are not only the traditional tabular representation of relational data that convey information space efficiently, but also allow a continuous revision and formula-based data manipulation. It is estimated that each year hundreds of millions of spreadsheets are created (Abraham, 2004).

We work is based on Natural Language User Interface (NLUI) (Wachtel, 2017) that should enable users to describe algorithms in their natural language and provide a valid output by the dialog system for given user description. First, we implemented a dialog component (Wachtel, 2015) that enables users to interact with our system and manipulate spreadsheet data via natural language (Wachtel, 2016a). Furthermore, we already support control flows, conditional and loop statements (Wachtel, 2016b). This paper presents our work on a hybrid system and is structured as following: section 2 describes our work on the hybrid system, action sets and API import. Section 3 evaluates the hybrid system in a user study. Section 4 presents related work in the research areas of programming in natural language, End User Programming and natural language dialog systems. Finally, section 5 presents a conclusion of our topic and future work.

1.1 Related Work

NLyze, an Add-In for Microsoft Excel that has been developed by Gulwani (2014) at the same time as our system. It enables end users to manipulate spreadsheet data by using natural language. It uses a separate domain-specific language for logical interpretation of the user input. Instead of recognizing the tables automatically, it uses canonical tables which should be marked by the end user. Another of Gulwani's tool QuickCode (Gulwani, 2011) deals with the production of the program code in spreadsheets through input-output examples provided by the end user (Cypher, 1993). It automates string processing in spreadsheets using input-output examples and splits the manipulations in spreadsheet by entering examples. The focus of his work is on the synthesizing of programs that consist of text operations.

Paternò (2013) introduces the motivations behind end user programming defined by Liberman (2006) and discusses its basic concepts, and reviews the current state of art. Various approaches are discussed and classified in terms of their main features and the technologies and platforms for which they have been developed. In 2006, Myers (2006) provides an overview of the research in the area of End User Programming. As he summarized, many different systems for EUD have already been realized (Ko, 2014) or (Gulwani, 2012) or (Cypher, 1993). However, there is no system such as our prototype that can be controlled with natural language. During a study in 2006, Ko (2014) identifies six learning barriers in End User Programming: design, selection, coordination, use, understanding and information barriers. Dorner (2008) describes and classifies EUD approaches taken from the literature, which are suitable approaches for different groups of end users. Implementing the right mixture of these approaches leads to embedded design environments, having a gentle slope of complexity.

Such environments enable differently skilled end users to perform system adaptations on their own. Sestoft (2013) increases expressiveness and emphasizing execution speed of the functions thus defined by supporting recursive and higher order functions, and fast execution by a careful choice of data representation and compiler technology. Cunha (2012) realizes techniques for model-driven spreadsheet engineering that employs bidirectional transformations to maintain spreadsheet models and synchronized instances. Begel (2005) introduces voice recognition to the software development process. His approach uses program analysis to dictate code in natural language, thereby enabling the creation of a program editor that supports voice-based programming.

The idea of programming in natural language was first proposed by Sammet (1966), but enormous difficulties have resulted in disappointingly slow progress. One of the difficulties is that natural language programming requires a domain-aware counterpart that asks for clarification, thereby overcoming the chief disadvantages of natural language, namely ambiguity and imprecision. In recent years, significant advances in natural language techniques have been made, leading, for instance, to IBM's Watson (Ferrucci, 2010) computer winning against the two Jeopardy! world champions, Apple's Siri routinely answering wide-ranging, spoken queries, and automated translation services such as Google's becoming usable (Liu, 2004) or (Ortiz, 2014).

Ballard (1979) and Biermann (1980, 1983) introduced their Natural Language Computer (NLC) that enables users to program simple arithmetic calculations using natural language. Our prototype extends the idea with a dialog system component for step-by-step construction of complex expression and enables users to perform tasks they otherwise would not be able to accomplish. Although NLC resolves references as well, there is no dialog system. Metafor introduced by Liu (2005) has a different orientation. Based on user stories, the system tries to derive program structures to support software design. A different approach regarding software design via natural language is taken by RECAA (Körner, 2014). RECAA can automatically derive UML models from the text and also keep model and specification consistent through an automatic feedback component. A limited domain end-to-end programming is introduced by Le (2013). SmartSynth allows synthesizing smartphone automation scripts from natural language description. However, there is no dialog interaction besides the results output and error messages.

2. HYBRID SYSTEM

Due to the potential complexity and dimensions of action sets we extended the dialog component (Wachtel, 2017) by a hybrid system. This hybrid system extends the consisting natural language approach that manages the interaction through the dialog system and introduces a new graphical user interface providing a better overview and more interaction choices. During runtime, users can switch at any time between these systems.

2.1 Dialog System

Each interaction increases the associated probability that is used for an assumption about interactions. On each interaction, the dialog system presents the user a limited amount of options, chosen regarding to its probability. To simplify the process for the user only interactions with the last object are available, so no reference is needed. After each interaction the user is asked, if more interactions are welcome, and if so another iteration will be started. If there are no new interaction, the recent set of actions can be saved using an arbitrary name. To avoid duplicate action sets, the module compares the current one with saved sets. If it is duplicate, the user is informed, but still able to save it under new name.

2.2 Graphical User Interface

Using the graphical user interface, called APIDialog, users have access to all options of each object (See Figure 1). The displayed information is from the Microsoft documentation. The *Value*-column (marked as 3 in Figure 1) contains the default values for C# and are determined by the module. Using the *Add*- and *Remove*-Button (marker 1 and 2) the user can change the current action set. The middle of the APIDialog presents all retrieved information about the selected element. The fields *Return Type*, *Read-Only* and *Parameter* are filled by properties and methods. If an object is selected, these fields stay empty. In Figure 1 the method *ApplyLayout* is selected, for each parameter is stated if it is optional. More information can be displayed by double clicking on the parameter. After clicking on a cell in the column *Value*, the user can enter the desired *parameter value*. Further implementation for methods has not been done yet.

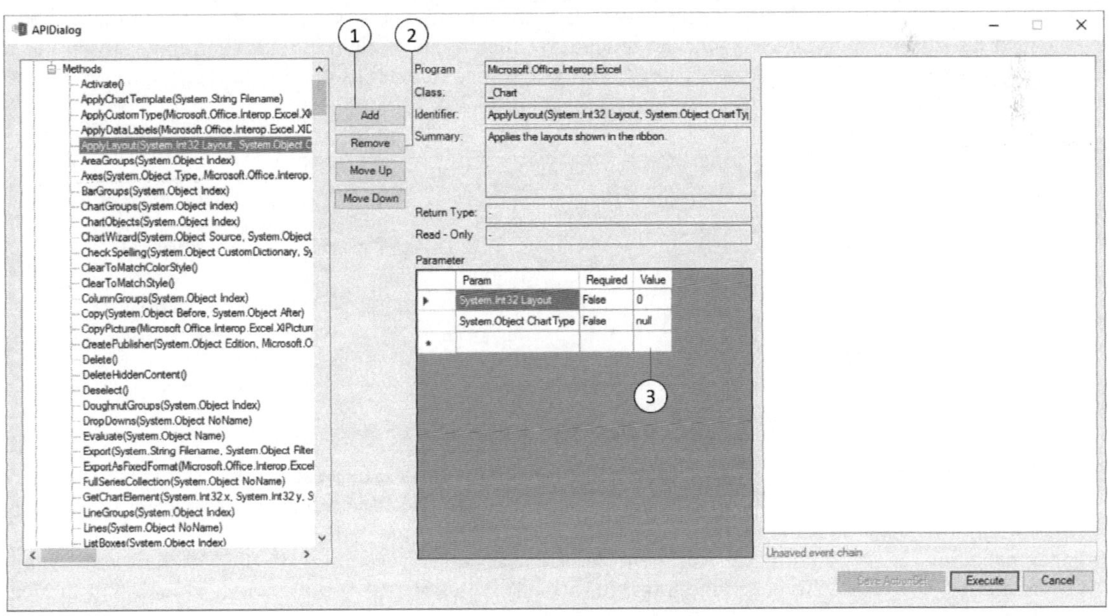

Figure 1. Graphical user interface

When user adds a new property, a new view is shown in Figure 2. All imported information about the property are presented and a compatible object (marker 1) and new property-value (marker 2) can be chosen. The *Preview*-Button in the *PropertyDialog* changes the property temporarily, to give the user an impression of the change.

The action is discarded in case it is not confirmed with the *OK*-Button. Confirming the action adds it to the current action set (right column in the APIDIalog). A non-empty set with a name different than the default (Unsaved action set) can be added to the interaction options of the object and used in the future.

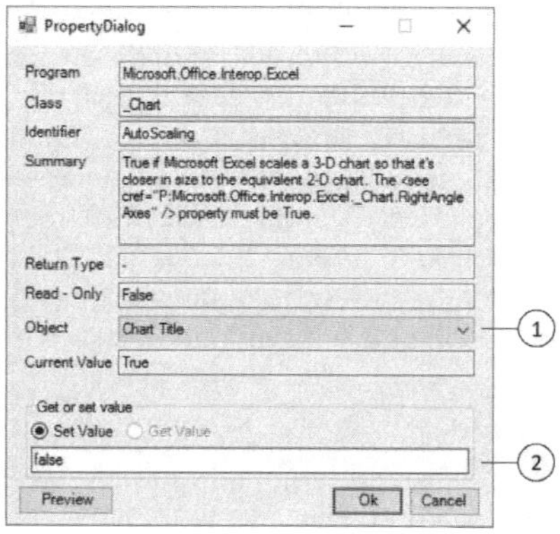

Figure 2. Property dialog

2.3 Action Sets

In this work, we define action sets as arbitrary sets of API calls learned and executed during runtime. The system can learn a new action set during runtime from the user via two options: the established dialog system and a graphical user interface. Both systems have the same basic functionality, although the dialog system reduces the options for interactions in each iteration. The dialog system target group are unexperienced users who need more advice from the system and who are quicker using natural language. Advanced users can pick the next interaction freely or users who are quicker by clicking the system provides a graphical user interface. In case of user input "Please, draw a chart", the system tries to detect some implicit steps and asks user for data and chart type to execute this command (See Figure 3).

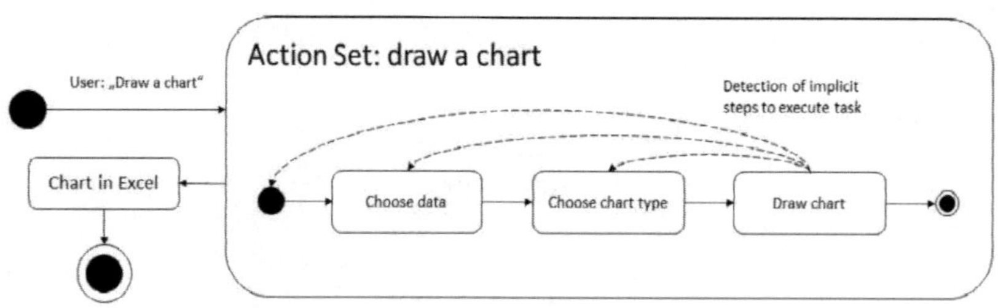

Figure 3. Action set for a simple use input

In our first implementation step the system focuses on properties, because a single value is easier to enter for users. Methods often require more values for parameters and the correct input order is crucial for the execution. The usage is additionally complicated because some methods have optional parameters and the documentation does not provide sufficient information for all parameters. The system only supports properties with basic data types at the moment, because end users have not enough information to create a complex object and complex constructs are difficult to provide.

2.4 API Import

On each startup of the program the API import tool is executed to obtain the latest information about the API. This is necessary for the system being aware of the options provided by the API. Developing the API import of the Excel API documentation had two approaches, the first was to use the documentation found in the internet on the official Microsoft development website. This approach was discarded quickly because export of the website is slow and inconvenient. All objects had to be marked manually and only 200 elements could be exported at once. With a total of 1111 objects this is time consuming and provides inconsistent results, considering future content updates by API documentation developer. Additionally, these HTML-based documentation pages are designed to be easily understood by humans, but not to be readable by machines. The structure of documentation pages depends on its content that complicates developing a suitable and long-term algorithm.

Therefore, the import uses a XML documentation file that can easily be utilized by an algorithm. Every object, property, method and event is stored in a unique XML element and the type can be identified by a specific prefix (See Table 1). To enhance the chance of presenting relevant interactions to the user through the dialog system, a system to detect and label these was created. Properties and methods with a specific identifier seem to be more interesting to end users. Terms like *Name* or *Title* are easier to grasp than cryptic ones like *Column3DGroup* or *DisplayBlankAs*.

Table 1. Prefix types

Prefix	Element type
T	Object
P	Property
M	Method
E	Event
F	Others

Possible values for properties and method are not defined by the documentation. They have to be extracted from other resources. The used values are chosen randomly, e.g. *XLChartType*-Enumeration (Microsoft, 2017), the lowest value for nearly 70 elements is -4169 and the highest is 112, and are not included in the XML documentation. Also, the XML documentation contains duplicated objects, e.g. *T:Microsoft.Office. Interop.Excel.Chart* and *T:Microsoft.Office.Interop.Excel._Chart* – both objects have equal summaries, but not the same properties, and methods.

3. EVALUATION

The system quality was evaluated by a user study. Nine participants were given tasks to solve with the developed system. All persons were non-native English speakers. Five participants were new to our system – we called them beginners, and four have already used our dialog system without APIDialog – called experts. Two participants have never used Excel before, four uses it rarely and three regularly. The evaluation consisted of five tasks to compare APIDialog and dialog system implementation (See Figure 4, right):

- Task 1: creating a diagram
- Task 2: checking for more interaction options with the diagram
- Task 3: changing some diagram properties
- Task 4: saving an action set with an arbitrary name
- Task 5: controlling the available interaction options for action sets

For comparing the two elements of the hybrid system, the participants were split randomly in two groups. Group A used the GUI and group B the dialog system (See Figure 4, left). The tasks of the groups were different at two points, based on the different structure. The first difference is, that group A used the standard excel function to create a chart because the system only provides this functionality through the dialog system.

The second difference is the amount of interaction choices. Group A can freely choose between all available options (both properties and methods), but group B is limited to the preselection choice of the dialog system. Additionally, group A is not restricted to the "chart" object because all possible objects are available by the GUI system (See Figure 1). The results are separated in the two groups because of the different approach. The success quota for the beginners is 73.3% and for the expert users 83.3%.

Furthermore, we asked the participants to find information about a property that they have found in the GUI one task earlier. In this case, we wanted to know if they can solve a task manually without our system via internet research on developer documentation websites. Only two of nine participants were able to solve this task by searching the standard online developer documentation. Two other users were able to find the required information with the VBA reference. All other participants failed to complete this task – with our system all of participants could complete it one task earlier.

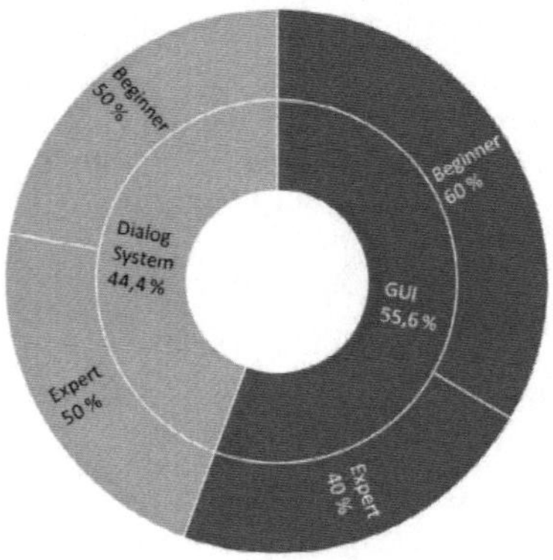

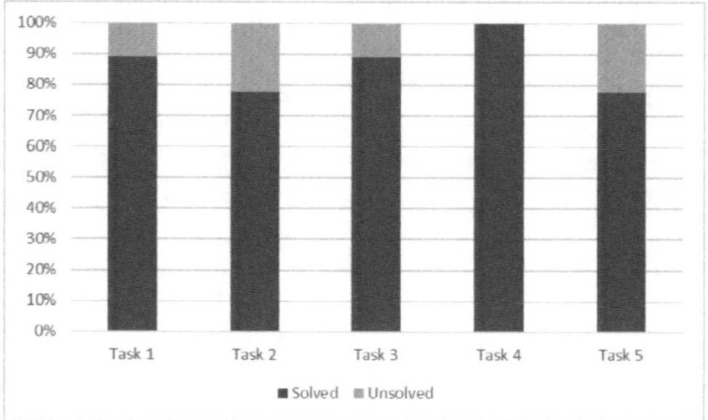

Figure 4. Participant's distribution on study groups (left) and task results (right)

3.1 Group A: GUI

Group A had five participants who were able to solve 86.7% of given tasks. Surprisingly, some participants struggled to find the standard excel function to insert a diagram. The APIDialog was found and opened intuitively. Finding the *chart* object, which is needed to interact with the diagram caused some problems because sometimes the underscore in the task description was not read. This problem continued, some participants complained about the difficult names. Also, the descriptions of objects, properties and methods was perceived as to short and just partially comprehensible. Adding interactions to the action set which is going to be executed made aware of a potential error-problem reason. Some participants expected the *Add*-Button to add new interactions to the existing ones and not to add actions to the current action set. The element representation of the current action set was described as clear and reasonable. Saving the action set irritated some participants because the default text has to be replaced to enable the save button. The overall impression of the GUI was denoted as intuitive and helpful. The input interpretation and the output were also rated positive, 60% of the participants would use our system, and all of them attest a good overall system quality and natural answers. Also, the complete group estimates the time to solve the tasks without being supported by the system to be as long as with it. Just 40% expect to be able to finish the assignments without the system (See Figure 5, left).

3.2 Group B: Dialog System

Group B had four participants who were able to solve 83.3% of the tasks. Two problems were noticed: the first was the way unexperienced users interacted with the system. Instead of engaging in a dialog, they were inserting a command sequence. For example, some users did not answer to questions of the dialog system directly, as they would do in a human conversation. Another hurdle were counter questions, because they are not expected by the system. Both cases let the system lose the context and the planned process was aborted. The system did not understand the situation anymore which made it necessary to repeat the previous input. This also explains the rating of the system. Participants who answered the questions of the system directly, rated it positive. In case of unexpected answers, the system was not able to determine the meaning and was therefore not able to react as expected. This can also be seen, 55% think their input was understood and 60% of the answers were described as useful. Multiple participants requested a more detailed tutorial for the future, to understand the basic vocabulary and proper usage. Also, an auto correct function was asked for, so non-natives are supported a little more. About 25% of group B would use our system, although 50% testify a good overall quality and 75% of the answers as natural. Furthermore, 25% of the participants guess to need at least as much time to solve the tasks without our system, as they needed with it. Also 25% of the participants think the tasks are not solvable without our system (See Figure 5, right).

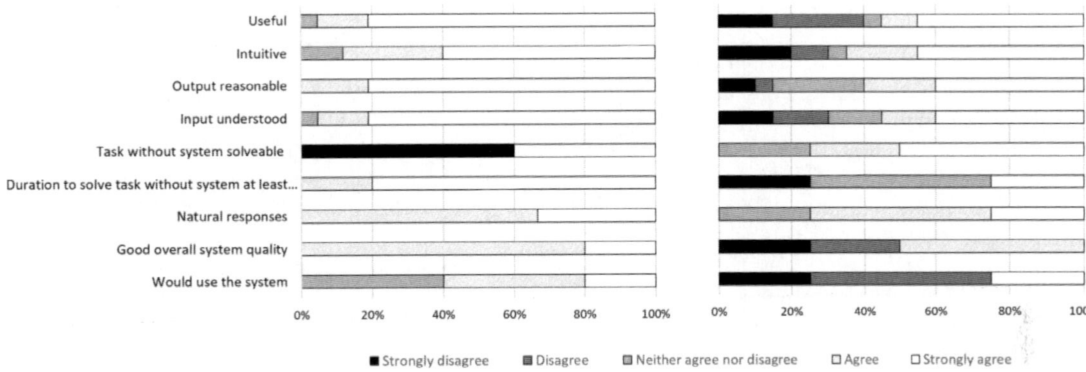

Figure 5. Ratings of the hybrid system by the participants of group A (left) and group B (right)

4. CONCLUSION AND FUTURE WORK

In this paper, we presented a hybrid system that supports natural language interactions similar as a chat bot and gesture control to follow the user's click actions. For this purpose and also to avoid the lack of inconsistent code documentation, we dynamically export the provided documentation for coding in Visual Studio and provide it in the xml-format to the hybrid system. The results of the user study can be summed up as very positive. Both components of the hybrid system could achieve high success rates with more than 80% solved tasks. Participants of both test groups quickly gained a better understanding of the system, especially in the dialog system.

Users could use already existing actions and provide new action sets to the hybrid system at runtime. Nowadays, users can easily give descriptions (Tichy, 2013) for algorithms including statements, conditionals, and loops. To enable the system for end user development, these parts should be recognized correctly by the system. In the current version of our prototype, the system supports control flows, such as conditionals and loops, but the challenge is to understand the user input at runtime and put the different statements in the right order. There is a lot of work on our system still needs to be done. The goal is to implement valid code snippets from natural language input that describes algorithms. We are also exploring ways to extend the system functionality with the help of the dialog. Due to the unrestricted natural language of end users the system needs to be extended for handling descriptions that use different words, e.g. synonyms, for descriptions that can be already handled by the system.

REFERENCES

Guzzoni, D. (2006) *Active: A unified platform for building intelligent web interaction assistants.* In Web Intelligence and Intelligent Agent Technology Workshops, IEEE/WIC/ACM International Conference.

Bellegarda, J. R. (2014) *Spoken Language Understanding for Natural Interaction: The Siri Experience*. Springer NY.

Williams, J. D. (2009) *Spoken dialogue systems: challenges and opportunities for research*. AT&T Labs – Research.

Seneff, S. (2002) *Response planning and generation in the MERCURY flight reservation system*. MIT.

Allen, J. (2007) *PLOW: A Collaborative Task Learning Agent*. Association for the Advancement of Artificial Intelligence.

Myers, B.A. (2006) *Invited Research: Overview End-User Programming*. CHI.

Scaffidi, C. (2005) *Estimating the numbers of end users and end user programmers*. Proceedings of the IEEE Symposium on Visual Languages and Human-Centric Computing, ser. VLHCC '05, IEEE Computer Society.

Liberman, H. (2006) *End-User Development: An Emerging Paradigm*, in End User Development, Kluwer Academic Publishers, pp.1-8.

Hurst, M (2000) *The interpretation of tables in texts*. University of Edinburgh, Ph.D.

Abraham, R. (2004) *Header and Unit Inference for Spreadsheets Through Spatial Analyses*. IEEE Symposium on Visual Languages – Human Centric Computing.

Wachtel, A (2017) *Natural Language User Interface For Software Engineering Tasks*. 10th International Conference on Advances in Computer-Human Interactions.

Wachtel, A (2015) *Initial implementation of natural language turn-based dialog system*. International Conference on Intelligent Human Computer Interaction (IHCI).

Wachtel, A (2016a) *Context Detection in Spreadsheets Based on Automatically Inferred Table Schema*. 18th International Conference on Human-Computer Interaction, rated with Best Paper Award.

Wachtel, A (2016b) *A Natural Language Dialog System Based on Active Ontologies*. 9th International Conference on Advances in Computer-Human Interactions.

Microsoft (2017) *XLChartType-Enumeration*, Available at: https://msdn.microsoft.com/en-us/library/office/ff838409.aspx (Accessed: 7. May 2017).

Gulwani, S. (2014) *NLyze: Interactive programming by natural language for spreadsheet data analysis and manipulation*. SIGMOD.

Gulwani, S. (2011) *Automating string processing in spreadsheets using input-output examples*. ACM SIGPLAN.

Cypher, A. (1993) *Watch what I do: programming by demonstration*. MIT Press.

Paternò, F. (2013) *End user development: Survey of an emerging field for empowering people*. ISRN Software Engineering.

Ko, A. (2004) *Designing the Whyline: A Debugging Interface for Asking Questions About Program Failures*. CHI.

Gulwani, S. (2012) *Spreadsheet data manipulation using examples*. ACM.

Dorner, C. (2008) *End user development: Approaches towards a flexible software design*. European Conference on Information Systems.

Sestoft, P. (2013) *Sheet-defined functions: Implementation and initial evaluation*. End-User Development. IS-EUD 2013

Cunha, J. (2012) *Bidirectional Transformation of Model-Driven Spreadsheets*. Springer Lecture Notes in Computer Science.

Begel, A. (2005) *Spoken Language Support for Software Development*. Ph.D. Thesis, Berkeley.

Sammet, J.E. (1966) *The Use of English as a Programming Language*. Communication of the ACM.

Ferrucci, D. (2010) *Building Watson: An Overview of the DeepQA Project*. Association for the Advancement of Artificial Intelligence.

Liu, H. (2004). *Toward a programmatic semantics of natural language*. Visual Languages and Human Centric Computing.

Ortiz, C. L. (2014) *The Road to Natural Conversational Speech Interfaces*. IEEE Internet Computing.

Ballard, B. (1979) *Programming in natural language: NLC as a prototype*. Association for Computing Machinery (ACM).

Biermann, A (1980) *Toward Natural Language Computation*. American Journal of Computational Linguistics. Volume 6 Issue 2, pp. 71-86.

Biermann, A (1983) *An experimental study of natural language programming*. International journal on Man-Machine Studies. Volume 18, Issue 1, pp. 71-87.

Liu, H (2005) *Metafor: Visualizing stories as code*. 10th international conference on Intelligent user interfaces.

Körner, S. (2014) *Transferring Research Into the Real World - How to Improve RE with AI in the Automotive Industry*. IEEE 1st International Workshop on Artificial Intelligence for Requirements Engineering.

Le, V. (2013) *SmartSynth: Synthesizing Smartphone Automation Scripts from Natural Language*. MobiSys.

Tichy, W. F. (2013) *Universal Programmability - How AI Can Help*. Artificial Intelligence Synergies in Software Engineering.

USER ELICITATION FOR COGNITIVE CONSONANCE IN THE DESIGN OF DIGITAL ARTIFACTS

Rui Belfort[1], Fábio Campos[2] and Juliana Gonçalves[1]
[1]UFPE
[2]UFPE / Bolsista CAPES – Proc. 88881.120765/2016-01
Recife, Brazil

ABSTRACT

This paper presents the concept of using knowledge elicitation to help users seek cognitive consonance. The aim is to build a framework to involve in the design process those who are going to use the digital artifact, especially when prototypes or under development products are available to use. That way, authors offer a tool to collect relevant data and prevent interrupting experiences with dissonant interactions, involving users in the design, keeping the designer as facilitator of the whole process.

KEYWORDS

Knowledge elicitation, cognitive dissonance, user experience; digital artifact design

1. INTRODUCTION

The Design focus has migrated from products and services to "ways of think and do", models, methods, frameworks, tools, design culture (Manzini, 2016). There are at least a hundred methods of Design available (Martin & Hanington, 2012) and for each specific product or service, some method or methods can be a better choice (Blomkvist & Segelström, 2014). The critical think of the Designer it's fundamental to make those choices without seeing those methods as "cookie cutters process that can be used universally", but analyzing the context (Forlano, 2016).

The discussion on how, when and where is better to assess users during the process of designing is still contemporary and relevant (Law, 2007; Friess, 2010; Hokkanen, 2015; Taffe, 2015). The traditional design project begins with a brief and requirements, determined by research to set strategy, evaluate through usability tests and 'use in field' observation (Sanders & Stappers, 2014). The Designer ideation involves fetching information and sketching words and draws (Cheng, 2016), but users can be part of the process from the beginning (Taffe, 2015), consciously, through questionnaires to increase efficiency of quantitative measurement (Laugwitz et. al., 2008); on prototype evaluation while physically monitored through eye tracking, and in this case, user's consciousness cannot hinder the process (Bergstrom & Shall, 2014); or by remote usability tests, applied with users at home using personal computer (Tullis, 2007); and many others.

Even though there are different ways of approaching this matter, it is unquestionable the importance of understanding how much can a design affect the user and vice-versa; there is a lot, still, to be acknowledged on this. From a neuroscience perspective, the coding of emotional stimulus properties depends on the cognitive context, and there is, generally, a dynamic balance between emotional and cognitive neural processes (Pallesen, 2008). That means the right context and emotions arising from spontaneous behavior could make a difference on project results.

Eliciting users, then, should never go against cognitive consonance, what happens very commonly in the digital industry and academia. We cannot take the risk of making participants rationalize the experience (Csíkszentmihályi, 1997) and, consequently, assess invalid information. We believe that data collection should be unnoticed by those who are its object, to generate valid results. Accessing users data isn't a new practice, there are methods as automated remote research (Martin & Hanington, 2012), seeking more assertive results through data collection without the user notice (Belfort, 2013).

Per the Theory of Cognitive Dissonance (Festinger, 1957), there are three states of cognition: dissonance, irrelevance or consonance. Dissonance happens when an individual faces information that goes against existing beliefs, an inconsistency; the problem is that is very often the case considering the only constant in contemporary world is change (Hall, 2006). Naturally, people seek to fix dissonance. For example, on Puean Program, and educational effort in which student-teachers from Japan teach English in Thailand's secondary school; they experienced conflicts between theory and practice, such as: in theory, the teachers should provide ample opportunities to the students speaking in English on class; on practice, keeping little communication has better results maintaining the order (Hall, 2012). The conflict mentioned is a dissonance, and after years of observation, the cognitive dissonance is not necessarily negative, from conflicts could emerge practices and promote teacher development (Hall, 2017).

This is very relevant in digital artifact design. The most established paradigms are built around the idea of these must never being 100% done (Ries, 2011). If everything changes, so do digital artifacts, to provide up to date potential user experience. Otherwise, they can easily become outdated and, of course, lose the interest of whoever should be looking forward to use. But is it even possible to assess users real time, so they won't need to rely on memory, natural context of use, so there won't be environmental influence and directly, without the need of any human mediation? Evidences point that the answer is yes (Belfort, 2013), but still it is very hard to measure the negative or positive influence of it on the experience.

Although, in digital artifacts, the interaction with each interface elements could take seconds, and any negative feeling or conflict, such as a cognitive dissonance, could make the user go for a similar digital artifact; the options are abundant and for that reason digital producers cannot take risk of providing inconsistent. Emotional processes have many attributes including motor-expressive, sensory-perceptual, autonomic-hormonal, cognitive-attentional, and affective-feeling aspects (Panksepp, 2003) and all of them affects user experience. Trying to bring this into disciplinary design, as a tool for all phases of the process, is a first step to a theoretical-methodological advance in involving users without losing quality of data collection and take the conduction off from the designer.

It is our main hypothesis that it is not only possible to elicit users during the process of designing a digital artifact, without interfering on experience, but also it can be used to boost cognitive consonance. For that to be achieved, besides balancing the users' expectations and the artifact potential use, as theory suggests, assessment must dynamically give the opportunity to drive inconsistencies into consonance. This paper presents the concept of using knowledge elicitation to help users seek cognitive consonance. The aim is to build a framework to involve in the design process those who are going to use the digital artifact, especially when prototypes or under development products are available to use. That way, we also offer a tool to collect relevant data and prevent interrupting experiences with dissonant interactions.

1.1 Theoretical Basis

The importance of correctly approaching the involvement of users in the design process, without manipulating (consciously or not) feedback, to extract accurate data on their experience, and make it relevant to the project, is quite consensual (Krippendorff, 2000). A whole branch of scientific thinking named knowledge elicitation (Diaper, 1989) deals with the peculiarities and difficulties of it.

Since 2010, we have been doing many experiments with the purpose of eliciting users in the design process, without losing quality of data collected (Belfort, 2011b; Belfort, 2012; Belfort, 2013). The main result of those lies in the discovery of principles of experience and the importance of considering them in any user assessment, to minimize possibility of invalid data collection.

Basically, user experience has three main principles (Isomorsu, 2008; Law, 2007; Smith, 2015).

- Every experience is subjective. Observers (researchers) can interpret it from their backgrounds. The best way of assessing it, then, is from the user himself;
- Every experience is ephemeral. That means once it is over, it cannot be repeated. Each occurrence is different. So, it is not good to rely on users' memory;
- Every experience is situated. In other words, is not good to analyze it outside (in a lab, for example) the usual context of use.

A lot of work was put in enabling user elicitation as dynamic call to action. What we mean is that to validate the idea of principles being essential to experience data collection, a testable implementation was demanded; that is TR2UE (Tracking Real-time, Real-context User Experience) (Belfort, 2011a); a framework in which theory and practice of user experience come together as an assessment tool.

Throughout the whole process of designing and developing it, the idea of almost no interference on user experience was the main concern to be addressed. In that sense, we dealt with the scientific problem presented here in a general way, which was, until now, important to bring the matter to the disciplinary design field. This is quite an advance, but get into details of it is now necessary, as a natural step for research evolution.

In the pursuit of that, we understood inconsistency starts with a break (Activity Theory) (Leont'ev, 1978), leading to dissonance (Cognitive Dissonance Theory) (Festinger, 1957), and breaking flow (Flow Theory) (Csíkszentmihályi, 1997) of user experience. So the stimuli should help fixing breaks, offering potential consonance and reestablishing flow.

2. EXPERIMENT

As an effort to contribute with the matter presented on this paper, we did an empirical experiment to gather information, formulate hypothesis, deduce potential results, test and evaluate data with an A / B procedure (Eisenberg, 2008). The two equivalent groups (Brazilian men and women, from 21 to 35 years old, under graduation, graduated and masters, in areas related to digital design and development) of 5 people (Nielsen, 2015) were asked to perform a simple task, on an iPhone 6, while think aloud (Lewis, 1982) the whole process. The experimental, was exposed to the variable under study; stimuli for consonance.

To simulate an actual digital artifact use, a mockup of Stryd[1] was built with POP[2]. We chose those two tools because their functionalities apply perfectly for experimentation. It gave participants the impression that they were using the real software on their smartphones. The audio was recorded using the native app for voice memo, on the same device used by participants, in a way that no one could notice the experiment was being conducted. People were approached as if we had a problem and were asking for help. We applied experiment in similar conditions (place, time, environment, etc.). Instructions were given printed, as bellow.

INSTRUCTIONS

Follow every step as asked bellow. During the process, say everything you are doing. You have to go from beginning to end, without any help.

Beginning.

Step 1
Access Settings.

Step 2
Select option Weight.

Step 3
Change Body Weight, from 10 to 70 KGs, then Update it.

Step 4
Go back to Settings.

Step 5
Select option Software Update.

Step 6
Upgrade it.

End.

Figure 1. Instructions card

[1] https://www.stryd.com
[2] https://popapp.in

Actual Stryd has inconsistencies both in Body Weight Update and Software Upgrade interactions. It does not show any status after user performs the task, causing the impression it wasn't processed, when user tries it. Control group had to deal with the inconsistent version, while we prototyped a consistent one, with clear result status, was to be used by the experimental group. Details can be seen in the following Figure 4 and Figure 5, displayed below.

Actual Stryd does not show any status when both tasks are performed, by clicking Update or Upgrade buttons. User expects to receive a feedback (for example, a status message) when perform a task, and that is why dissonance takes place. Prototyped Stryd show status with a simple flash message: "Your weight was updated" and "Your device is up to date" when Update or Upgrade buttons are clicked. Because of that, user understands what is happening and consonance is installed.

Figure 2. Actual Stryd

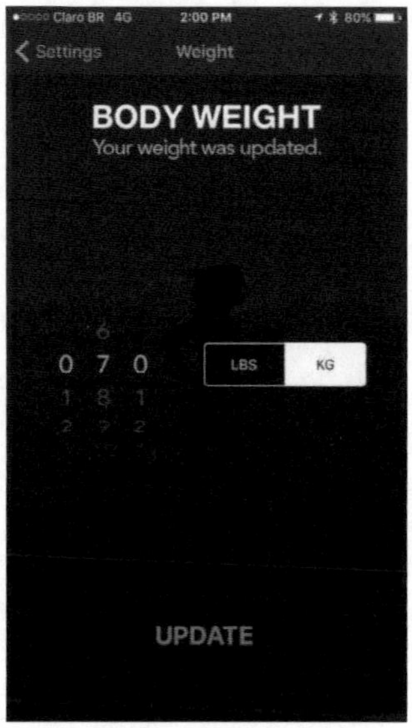

Figure 3. Prototyped Stryd

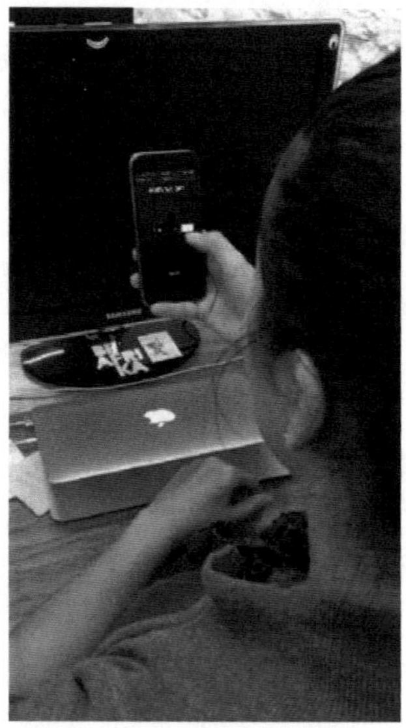

Figure 4. Partcicipants

While participants perform tasks, we were following three dimensions: #1 number of dissonant occurrences; #2 time to perform the whole task, without assistance; and #3 number of people getting to end without any dissonant action. The idea, as explained, is to find evidence that correct stimuli, as simple as it may be, can help users to fix inconsistency and find consonance, to use it as a design resource. And this can be used as a design procedure, to involve them, without taking designer off from conduction.

3. RESULTS ANALYSIS

It is important to point out that this is an exploration study. In the phase we are right now, it was very clear, through the experiment, that there is correlation between unclear dissonant interactions with worse results and more clear and consonant driven flash messages with better use performance, in the dimensions we are using to evaluate experience, as expected. This is going to be outspread in other experiments, with variations on the object, until this evidence become strong enough to sustain the hypothesis.

It is very common that a digital artifact must receive an upgrade and as result it may cause to users inconsistent experience; it takes time and effort for them to feel consonance, when most of the time a new change takes place. Some upgrades can be very time and budget consuming, so getting back to last version, or fixing what is wrong, when dissonance is too bad for users, is not always the most productive approach. So, these findings configure an opportunity on that matter.

More specifically, in the experiment, control group, that used dissonant actual app, committed 325% more errors (3.4 average) than the experimental group (0.8 average). Also, they spent 66% more time on solving the tasks, in comparison to the ones who used consonant prototyped version. Only one person, from all participants, from the experimental group, did the whole routine without any mistake captured. There is a clear tendency showed in the results.

In this experiment, we dealt with actual and obvious inconsistencies, specifically picked for the research needs of verification. There are a big range of dissonant interactions, much more complex, that could be addressed, as we are preliminarily doing here, without necessarily changing the digital artifact, but offering user the opportunity to seek consonance through clear and consistent potential interaction. There are many variables we can test to strengthen the argument of research.

Achieving this in a specific matter is not difficult, but imagine dealing with dissonant interactions in a procedural way. That is the long-term goal of this research. And more specifically, we aim to use it as a design tool to assess users and enhance experience and engagement at same time, by offering consonance opportunity as cognitive stimuli, when digital artifact is in constant change. The issue is clear, but as we can attest with Stryd, and many other contemporary digital artifacts, is still not resolved.

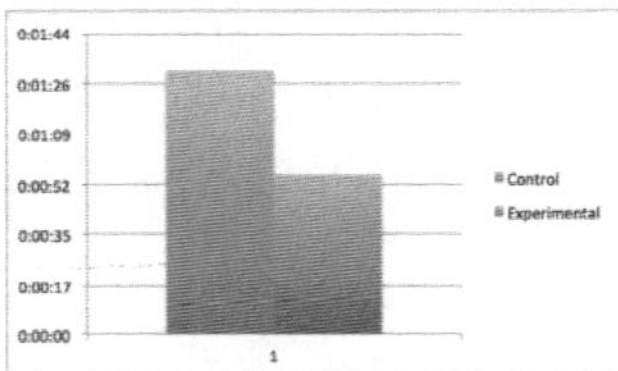

Figure 5. Average time spent to complete tasks

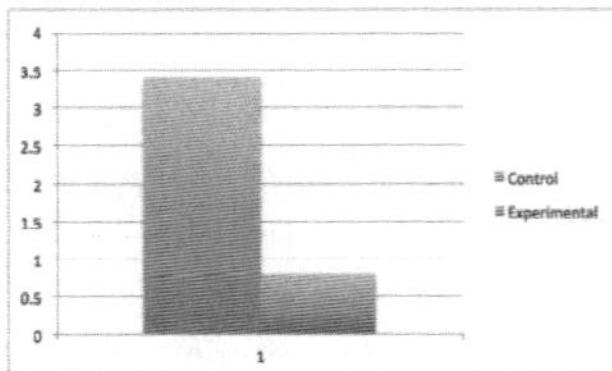

Figure 6. Average number of dissonant occurrences

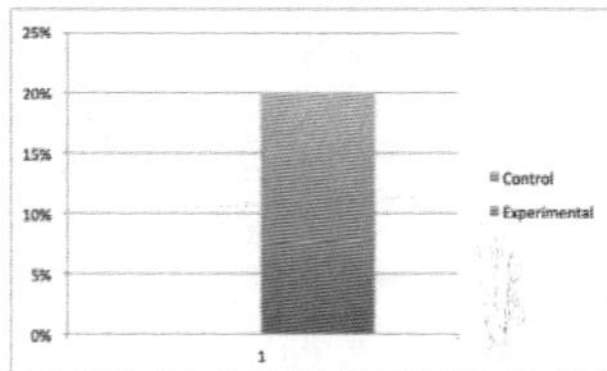

Figure 7. % of people who did not commit any mistakes

4. CONCLUSIONS

In 14 years of practice and 8 of research in Porto Digital (DIGITAL, 2010, via www), working in world class projects, products and services, side by side with highly qualified professionals and in collaboration with leading organizations, became evident that even design being identified as a processual work for transformation, it is inclined to empiric decision-making in the production process of digital artifacts, while other disciplines seek to balance intuition matters with rigor and protocol.

> *"If [...] designers were asked to think of the qualities that indicate a successful product or service, amongst the most common would surely be "intuitive". For a design to be regarded as intuitive is almost the highest praise it can receive."* (CAMILO, 2016).

Even considering how the praxis of digital producers functions, the configuration process, and its phases, techniques and tools, still is key-element of design. Designing is a methodology with transformational potential. Even when it uses subjective data, creative tools, or intuitive decision-making, still is a protocolled activity. The nature of projecting artifacts, in a disciplinary perspective, it's structured, not the opposite. And this is an intrinsic mark of design, that shall not be disconsidered.

> *"It is a shift from the aim of creating a 'design science' to that of creating a 'design discipline'. The focus is now on understanding the design process through an understanding of design cognition, or the 'designerly' ways of knowing and thinking."* (CROSS, 2007).

All of this will be helped by this investigation, that aims to end up building a framework that enables user elicitation as a cognitive consonance booster, and as a tool for involving users in the design process, without taking the designer off the conduction. Also, research aim to balance data and intuition, through the design process; enabling procedures for each one. Next steps are to implement and test it with a bigger sample and in different and more complex digital artifacts. Also, it is important to structure framework in a way anyone can use; conceptually and pragmatically speaking, for both academia and market purposes.

REFERENCES

Belfort, Rui. *Investigações Teórico-Metodológicas sobre Experiência de Usuário no Âmbito do Design.* UFPE, 2011a;

Belfort, Rui et. al. *Comparando o desempenho de escalas Likert e Pictórica, para acessar experiência de usuário.* Anais do Congresso Internacional de Design da Informação (CIDI), 2011b;

Belfort, Rui et. al. *Comparing Likert and Pictorial scales to assess user feedback.* Proceedings of International Conference on Applied Human Factors and Ergonomics (AHFE), 2012;

Belfort, Rui et. al. *The Role of Scales in Knowledge Elicitation.* Proceedings of Probabilistic Safety Assessment and Management (PSAM), 2013;

Bergstrom, R., Shall, A. *Eye Tracking in User Experience Design.* Morgan Kaufmann, 2014;

Blomkvist, J; Segelström, F. *Benefits of External Representations in Service Design: A Distributed Cognition Perspective.* In: The Design Journal.Vol. 17. Issue 3. Taylor & Fancis, 2014;

Cheng, P. *Development of a mobile app for generating creative ideas based on exploring designers' on-line resource searching and retrieval behavior.* In: Design Issues. Volume 44. MIT Press, 2016;

Csíkszentmihályi, Mihály. *Finding Flow. The Psychology of Engagement With Every Day Life.* Harper Collins Publishers, 1997;

Diaper, D. *Knowledge elicitation: Principles, techniques and applications.* Ellis Horwood Ltd., 1989;

Eisenberg, Bryan. *Always Be Testing: The Complete Guide to Google Website Optimizer.* Wiley Publishing, 2008;

Festinger, Leon. *A Theory of Cognitive Dissonance.* Stanford University Press, 1957;

Forlano, L. *Decentering the Human in the Design of Collaborative Cities.* In: Design Issues: Volume 32 Number 3. MIT Press, 2016.

Friess, E. *The Sword of Data: Does Human-Centered Design Fulfill Its Rhetorical Responsibility?* In: Design Issues: Volume 26, Number 3. MIT Press, 2010;

Hall, Stuart. *A identidade cultural na pós-modernidade.* DP&A, 2006;

Hall, J. M. *Report on the Puan Program: Hints for teaching about the Japanese culture in English*. Bulletin of English Education Iwate University, 2012.

Hall, J. M.; TOWSEND. *Using critical incidents and E-Portfolios to understand the emergent practice of Japanese student-teachers of English*. Elsevier, 2017;

Hokkanen, L. et. al. *Early Product Design in Startups: Towards a UX Strategy. In Product-Focused Software Process Improvement.* Proceedings of PROFES, 2015;

Isomorsu, Minna. *User experience evaluation with experimental pilots.* Proceedings of CHI, 2008;

Krippendorff, K. *Propositions of Human-centeredness: A Philosophy for Design.* In: Durling, D.; Friedman, K. (Eds.). Doctoral Education in Design: Foundations for the Future. Staffordshire University Press, 2000;

Laugwitz, B. et al. *Construction and Evaluation of a User Experience Questionnaire.* In: HCI and Usability for Education and Work. Springer Berlin Heidelberg, 2008;

Law, Elffie et. al. *Towards a UX Manifesto.* Proceedings of HCI, 2007;

Leont'ev, A. *Activity, consciousness, and personality.* Prentice- Hall, Inc., 1978;

Lewis, C. *Using the "Thinking Aloud" Method In Cognitive Interface Design (Technical report).* IBM, 1982;

Manders-Huits, N. *Practical versus moral identities in identity management.* Springer, 2010;

Manzini, E. *Design Culture and Dialogic Design.* In: Design Issues. Volume 32, Number. MIT Press, 2016;

Martin, B; HANNINGTON, B. *Universal methods of design.* Rockport Publishers, 2012;

Nielsen, Jakob. *Why You Only Need to Test with 5 Users.* (http://www.nngroup.com/articles/why-you-only-need-to-test-with-5-users). March, 2017;

Pallesen, K. et al. *Cognitive and Emotional Modulation of Brain Default Operation.* In: Journal of Cognitive Neuroscience. MIT Press, 2008;

Panksepp, J. *At the interface of the affective, behavioral, and cognitive neurosciences: Decoding the emotional feelings of the brain.* Bowling Green, 2003;

Pouivet, R. *On the Cognitive Functioning of Aesthetic Emotions.* In: LEONARDO, Vol. 33, No. 1. MIT Press, 2000;

Ries, Eric. *The Lean Startup: How Constant Innovation Creates Radically Successful Businesses.* Crown Business, 2011;

Roto, Virpi et. al. *User Experience Evaluation Methods in Academic and Industrial Contexts.* Proceedings of Interact, 2009;

Sanders, E. B.-N., & STAPPERS, P. J. *Probes, toolkits and prototypes: three approaches to making in codesigning.* In: CoDesign. Taylor & Francis, 2014;

Smith, Tech. *UX 2.0: Any User, Any Time, Any Channel* (http://download.techsmith.com/morae/docs/UserExperience2_0.pdf). March, 2017;

Taffe, S. *The hybrid designer/end-user: Revealing paradoxes in co-design.* In: Design Issues: Volume 40. MIT Press, 2015;

Tullis, T. et al. *An Empirical Comparison of Lab and Remote Usability Testing of Web Sites.* Proceedings of Usability Professionals Association Conference, 2007.

TRIGGERING YOUR CREATIVITY WHILE WRITING: CREATIVEWALL - A NOVEL CROWDSOURCING PLATFORM

Frederica Gonçalves[1], Igor Sousa[2] and Pedro Campos[3]
[1]*Madeira-ITI/University of Madeira, Polo Científico e Tecnológico da Madeira. Piso -2, 9020-105 Funchal, Portugal*
[2]*University of Madeira, Campus Universitário da Penteada, , 9020-105 Funchal, Portugal*
[3]*Madeira-ITI/University of Madeira, Polo Científico e Tecnológico da Madeira. Piso -2, 9020-105 Funchal, Portugal*
+351 291 721 006
ORCID: 0000-0001-7706-5038

ABSTRACT

This paper presents a novel crowdsourcing platform called CreativeWall, where users can preserve their creative writings and share them with the community, thus creating an interactive way for users to develop their abilities in writing. CreativeWall has also a Microsoft Word Add-In that helps writers to trigger their creativity while writing. We show that for a creative task such as writing, our creativity support tool can enhance the creativity and mental well-being of its users. To support this argument we highlight some results triangulating qualitative and quantitative data. Results show that users performing the tasks with CreativeWall lost track of time more often than participants using our baseline. From interviews it was clear that the tasks performed with the CreativeWall add-in were more enjoyable and that users had no problems starting to write, which could mean that these tools can help in the initial phase of the creative writing process.

KEYWORDS

Creative Writing tools; Human Computer Interaction; Creativity Support Tools; User Interface Design; User Experience Design; Crowdsourcing; MSWord Add-In

1. INTRODUCTION

Writing has been one of the most important developments of human civilization, but people are often unconscious of how long and complicated this path has been (Myers, 2006). Creative writing is a field that will continue to develop because it is not only related to human creativity and to the significance of words as tools of human communications, but because it celebrates individuals as well as cultures (Kroll, 2013). Deciding what to write about can sometimes be surprisingly tricky. Search engines like Google can help you find ideas on what to write about but it takes a lot of time to analyze the thousands of results that are presented, even though they are shown in an optimized way. Social networks like Facebook or Pinterest can help you as well, with groups that are created with the objective of helping writers, but they lack categorization and can be really distracting. Crowdsourcing is a concept that, although very powerful and effective, is relatively recent and still doesn't have a solid theoretical knowledge base that allows it to have a clear definition (Estellés-Arolas & González-Landrón-De-Guevara, 2012). According to Howe (Howe, 2008) crowdsourcing can be defined as "*the act of taking a task traditionally performed by a designated agent and outsourcing it by making an open call to an undefined but large group of people*". Another example of a definition comes from Brabham (Brabham, 2008), who says it can be defined as "*a new web-based business model that harnesses the creative solutions of a distributed network of individuals through what amounts to an open call for proposals*". As for Kleemann et al., (Kleemann, Vob, & Reider, 2008) crowdsourcing can simply be defined as "*the outsourcing of tasks to the general internet public*". These are all valid definitions but there is no consensus regarding what would be a definitive and complete definition. For the purpose of this work we will only focus on two types of crowdsourcing (Kleemann, Vob, & Reider, 2008), product design and product rating by consumers and consumer profiling, which are the ones that better suit our needs.

This way one can raise a community who is interested in writing and give them the opportunity to share their creative writings. These writings can then be used by the tool to help other writers with their own work.

In this paper we present a novel crowdsource platform – *CreativeWall* and a Microsoft Add-In to enhance the creativity and mental well-being of users in the creative writing process. As suggest by Myers (Myers, 2006), creative writing has become a machine for creating more creative writing programs. Even though, sometimes writer's miss their inspiration for writing or during writing. This condition is usually called writer's block. Writer's block can last for whole days (Rose, 1984) and become a real source of frustration when people are anxious about deadlines and really need to get the writing done. One of the methods used to avoid writer's block is the use of writing prompts (Digest, 2011) (Gonçalves, Campos, Hanna, & Ashby, 2015), which consists of a small text that is supposed to help writers to have ideas on what to write. One example of a writing prompt might be: *"After a short walk you can see the top of the towers of a big dark castle. Do you think someone still lives in there?"* This kind of short text might be the start of a story, and might help the writer initiate what could be a future bestseller. We decided to take this method and refine it by adding some more components that can help the writer have the creativity he needs. By using images, moods and locations we create a more visual perspective of a moment that can bring creativity to the writer.

2. MOODS, EMOTIONS AND COLORS

As Baas et al. (Baas, De Dreu, & Nijstad, 2008) states, there are differences between moods and emotions. According to the reference, moods are long lasting while emotions are more related towards a specific stimulus, for example, an emotion would be a person feeling happy because he/she found some money on the ground. This situation forces an emotion onto the person, the emotion of happiness. On the other hand, a mood is something that is more general, for example, a person feeling happy because he/she just feels great. With this we can conclude that there really are differences in terms of intensity of feelings, being that emotion is generally stronger than a mood. Another definition of mood states that moods are the accumulation of emotions and other affective events (Rooij & Jones, 2013). Moods can have multiple dimensions, but only three of those dimensions have been proven to be related to creativity. They are hedonic tone, activation level and regulatory focus. The hedonic tone, or valence, simply put, describes whether the mood is positive or negative (Baas, De Dreu, & Nijstad, 2008) (De Dreu, Baas, & Nijstad, 2008) (e.g. happiness has a positive tone while anger has a negative tone). This dimension is usually related to creativity as some studies refer (Ivcevic, Brackett, & Mayer, 2007). The same studies state that moods with a positive tone help a subject produce more original word associations which means that there might be a boost in creativity. Activation relates to whether or not the mood can generate active behaviors in the subject (e.g. calm is a deactivating mood while fear is activating). According to De Dreu et al. (De Dreu, Baas, & Nijstad, 2008) activation is a necessary precondition for creativity to come by while hedonic tone determines the route through which creative fluency and originality is achieved. They also argue that activating moods are more likely to generate creativity than deactivating moods. Regulatory focus refers to the motivation an individual has to complete a task. According to studies made in this area, regulatory focus plays an important role in triggering creativity (Friedman & Forster, 2001). There are two types of regulatory focus, the promotion focus and prevention focus. Promotion focus comes from the desire of accomplishing something, while prevention focus comes from the will of securing something (Baas, De Dreu, & Nijstad, 2008). A good example of this would be the attackers and goalkeepers in a football game. The objective of the attackers is to score goals and that's their motivation for playing (promotion focus). On the other hand, goalkeepers want to prevent goals, and that's their motivation for playing (prevention focus). Color can lead to feelings, and that have been proved by several studies in this area (Kaya N. E., 2004) (Kaya & Epps, 2004). A good example of this statement is a cloudy day. A cloudy day has a predominant color, which is gray, and gray is related to sadness, so people usually feel sad on cloudy days. If you look outside through a yellow window you can see that a feeling of warmness comes to you and everything feels a bit happier, as states by Goethe (Goethe, 1970). It's curious to see that the relation between color and emotions (or feelings) was already object of research more than 100 years (Goethe, 1970). Kaya et al. (Kaya N. E., 2004) (Kaya & Epps, 2004) performed user studies in order to be able to map colors to emotions and the result were somewhat similar to the statements made in the (Goethe, 1970). After considering the statements above, a list of moods and a mapping to colors was produced by us. Even though fearful and angry are not considered to be creativity enhancing moods, they were included in the list in order to give users some variety to choose from. Table 1 shows the mapping between color and emotion.

Table 1. Moods mapped into colors

Happy	Yellow	
Hopeful	Green	
Excited	Orange	
Energetic	Light Blue	
Loved	Pink	
Fearful	Black	
Angry	Red	

3. CREATIVEWALL PLATFORM

CreativeWall is a crowdsourcing platform (Figure 1) where its users can share their creative writings along with images, locations and moods, creating what we call a creative moment (Figure 2). This concept of creative moment came to life from the idea that people sometimes have ideas for creative writings when they are, for example, walking on the street and see something that triggers their creativity. That is the essence of the creative moment. They have an image that triggers an idea that is described by the text. A certain mood is also associated to that moment and it happens in a certain location, date and time. When brought together, all these aspects generate our creative moment.

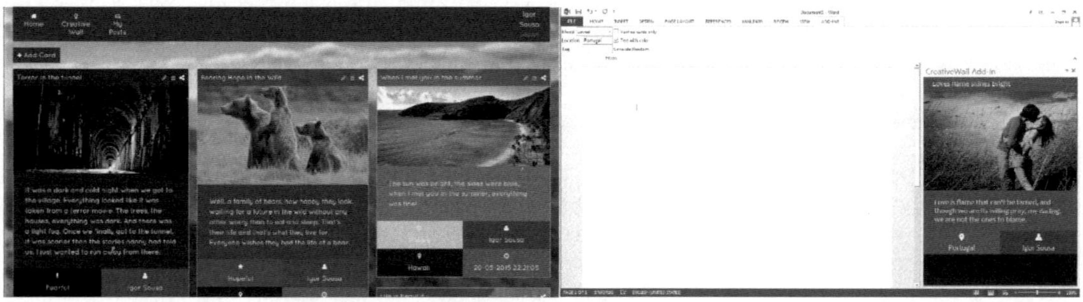

Figure 1. Final prototype of the CreativeWall platform and the integration on the word processor tool Microsoft Word

Figure 2 illustrates how a Creative Moment is shown on the platform. With this kind of information, other users can recreate the moment mentally and maybe absorb some kind of creativity from it giving birth to their own ideas based on what they see and feel with the moment recreation.

Figure 2. Example of a Creative Moment

With this kind of information, other users can recreate the moment mentally and maybe absorb some kind of creativity from it giving birth to their own ideas based on what they see and feel with the moment recreation. There are two main sections on the platform, the Creative Wall and My Posts.

3.1 Creative Wall

In this section users can check out creative moments shared by other users. They can also report, flag the moments as well written, or rate them. The first option, the reporting of moments, allows users to report other user's moments for offensive content, copyright violation, etc. As for the second option, the well written flag, it allows users to flag the moments that have a correct syntax and semantics, and with this make them part of the moments that appear when a user selects the well written filter. The last option, the moment rating, allows users to rate a moment from 1 to 5 stars where 1 means very uncreative and 5 means very creative. By doing this users make shared moments more and more relevant. These three options are part of a very important component of a crowdsourcing platform, the quality control, and can only be accessed by users that are logged in the platform. Below we can see these three options and how the user interacts with it. Figure 3 shows the three options described above.

Figure 3. Top bar of the moment showing the three options available

In this case the moment has already been rated, but is not checked as well written. Figure 4 shows how a user can interact with the system in order to rate a moment.

Figure 4. Top bar of the moment showing the rating feature

We can see that the user rated the moment with two stars. This means that the moment was uncreative and should not appear on the top of the relevant moment's list.

Another important feature that was implemented is a filter system where users can insert the conditions that most suits them and the platform will look for the moments that match those conditions. There are three fields on the filters bar, mood, location and tag. These three fields help users categorize their searches for faster finding of the moments they want. Each moment can be associated to a group of tags that can then be used for search purposes. There is also an option for sorting the results for a variety of options. Figure 5 shows the list of options that are available for sorting.

For the first two options, they are self-explanatory. On the relevance option, the moments that are presented first are the ones with a higher average rating. This average is calculated by dividing the sum of all the ratings by the number of ratings assigned to that moment. As for the well written, the first moments that are presented are the ones with a higher count of well written flags. With this feature, it is possible to make sure that only quality content is shown and that the user does not have to pay extra precious attention to error check on moments shared by other users.

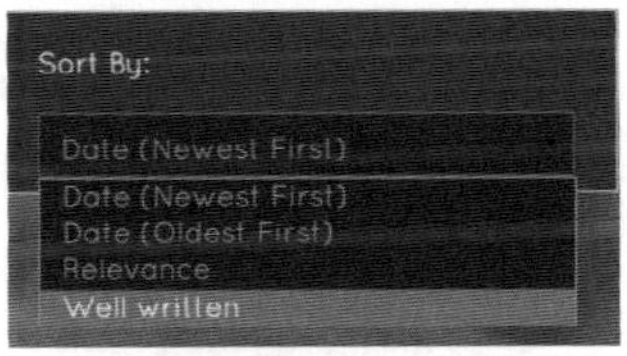

Figure 5. Sort feature showing the options available

3.2 My Posts

In this second section, users can see all the moments that they have already created, share them, add new ones and edit or remove the existing ones. Users can choose whether or not they want to share their moments. They can use the platform just for saving their moments without making them available for other users to see. To share a moment, users just have to press the share icon and the moment is made available for every user. To edit or delete a moment, users just have to press the according icon. When a user deletes a moment a confirmation dialog box is presented to make sure that this is the desired action. As referred before, a user can also create a new moment in this section. When the user presses the button to add a new moment, a dialog box is presented with all the fields necessary to create the new moment. Figure 6 shows all the information the user can insert to create the new moment.

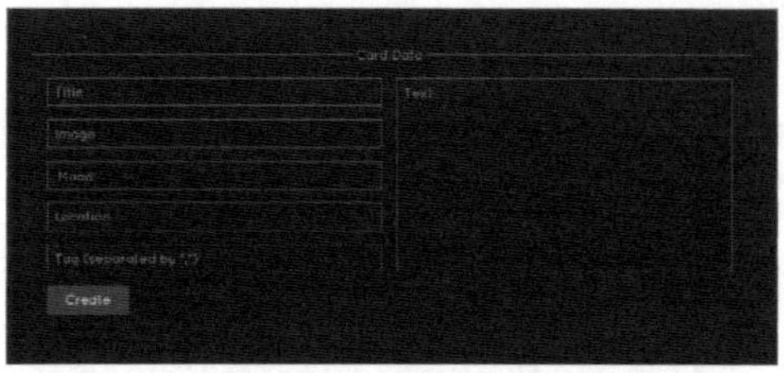

Figure 6. Dialog box showing the possible fields for creating a new moment

The final prototype can be seen in Figure 1 (*on left side*) and how the section My Posts looks. The design chosen was achieved and we felt very happy with all the design choices that were made. No specific tests were performed for the crowdsourcing platform as it acts only as a tool to populate the database with data to be used in the MSWord Add-In.

3.3 CreativeWall MSWord Add-In

CreativeWall MSWord Add-In is a plugin (called Add-In by Microsoft Office) for Microsoft Word that uses the data created in the CreativeWall platform in order to provide users with a way to trigger creativity while writing in the Microsoft Word application. This plugin requests creative moments from the API according to some filters chosen by the user and then shows those creative moments in Microsoft Word. By doing this, the user can use the creative moments for triggering creativity in the word processor tool itself without having to change applications and search for creative moments in the online platform. The features that were implemented help the user getting what he wants as fast as possible, and that was the main goal of the interface implemented. The plugin has a ribbon that contains a set of buttons and inputs which the user can use to interact with the plugin. Figure 7 shows the ribbon and the elements available for interaction.

Figure 7. CreativeWall Add-In ribbon with buttons and inputs available

The first three options, mood, location and tag are self-explainable, they apply filters to the results. The checkbox for "Verified cards only" will return cards that have average ratings over 4 stars and at least 5 well-written tags. This helps the user get data that has a minimum of quality and is not just random words with no meaning. This also helps the user getting creative moments that are written correctly. As for the option "Text with color", it defines if the creative moment should be shown with a gray background or with a background according to the color associated with the mood of the creative moment. The button "Generate Random" generates a random creative moment according to all the filters selected on the other options. If the user inserts a set of filters to which there are no creative moments associated, an error message is displayed. The add-in creative moments interface is basically the same as the one in the CreativeWall web platform, it just has less fields. Each of the creative moments shown have a title, image, text, location and author. Figure 8 shows an example of a creative moment in the add-in.

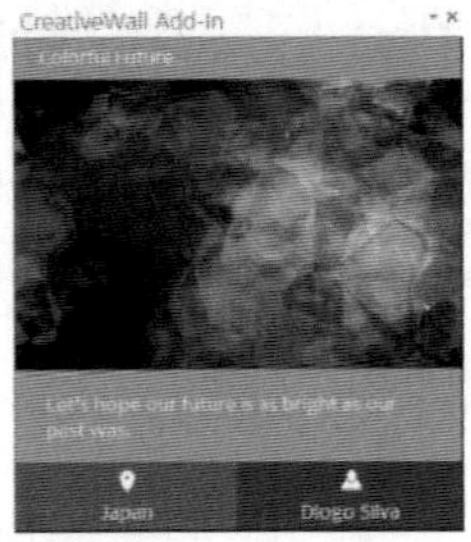

Figure 8. Creative Moment in the Microsoft Word Add-In

After all the implementation was done a final prototype *(see the right side of Figure 1),* that is to be used in the user study, was achieved. This prototype has all the features described above and they are all usable. It can be used by users after running a setup to install all the registry entries needed to use it on Microsoft Word as an Add-in. This prototype is just one example of an application using the add-in, since it may be used by any other word processor tool that wishes to implement our approach. All they need to do is register for usage of the API and after they set a client id and a client secret, they can start making requests to the API in order to receive the desired data.

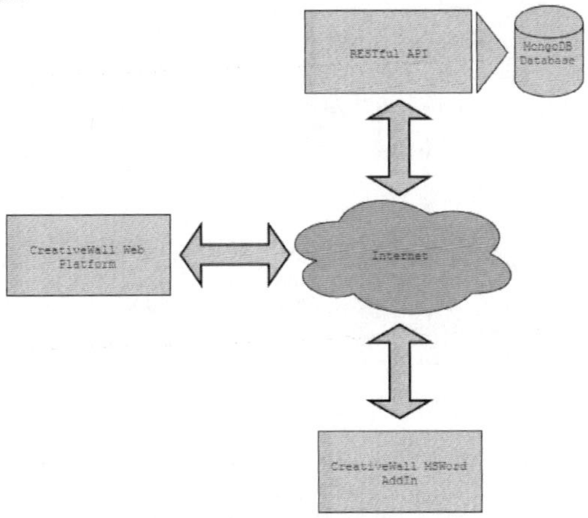

Figure 9. Software architecture including the platforms implemented

In order to build a usable prototype a decision about the architecture (Figure 9) of the software was needed. One requirement that was important was the scalability of the whole software structure. It is important, in the context of our approach, to be able to provide data to any word processor plugin or platform that wants to use the data created in our crowdsourcing platform, as long as they have previously applied for it. The solution is to build a client-server architecture. Having a centralized server (in our case the API works as both the server and an abstraction communication layer) it is possible to provide data to as many clients as we need. All connections should be made through HTTPS so the connection data (e.g. tokens or client credentials) is not exposed through package sniffing. For the purposes of this work we won't be making those HTTPS connections because this kind of features has high costs associated to it and it is not relevant for our user studies. This should be considered as future work. All the clients have read-only permissions, except for the crowdsourcing platform that sends data to the API for it to be inserted on the database. Before being able to request any data from the API the clients must be registered and define a client ID and a client secret so they can be authenticated before establishing a connection. This protects the data from being accessed by unauthorized clients.

4. STUDY OF CREATIVEWALL ADD-IN UI

We conducted a within-subjects experiment to investigate in the influence of the CreativeWall Add-In UI on peoples' creativity and mental well-being during a creative writing exercise when compared to the Microsoft Word Simple UI. As a prerequisite participants had to have prior writing skills and had to be interested in writing. To control for carry-over effects, the order of the conditions was counterbalanced between participants. The creative activity in this experiment included writing in the three proposed conditions:

Condition A: *Baseline.* Using Microsoft Office Word without any kind of add-in related to creativity to write a text based on a given context;

Condition B: Using Microsoft Office Word with the *CreativeWall Add-In* with a gray background to write a text based on a given context;

Condition C: Using Microsoft Office Word with the *CreativeWall Add-In* with a colorful background to write a text based on a given context.

4.1 Task

Participants were challenged to write a short text using the addressing tool. The time was limited to 10 minutes. Participants were free to finish the task whenever they wanted, under the 10-minute limit. Due to the use of a within-subject design, we defined three different writing tasks of a similar degree of complexity that participants were equally familiar with. The writing tasks were labeled as task A, B and C, respectively. All participants were presented with a context for each one of the tasks. For task A, the participants were given a context that was not produced by our crowdsourcing platform. This task was considered our *baseline.* Figure 10 shows the context given on the task A.

Figure 10. Context given to the user on the first challenge

For task B, participants were given a context created on our crowdsourcing platform. This context is a creative moment that was created and shared by a user who was registered on the CreativeWall. Figure 11 shows the context that was presented for the task B. In order for this context to be presented in grey, the option "Text with color" on the MSWord Add-In has been turned off.

Figure 11. Context given to the user on the second challenge

For task C, participants were given another context created on our crowdsourcing platform. Again, this context is a creative moment that was created by a registered user on the *CreativeWall* platform. Contrary to what happens on the second task, the option "Text with color" was turned on for this task. Figure 12 shows the context used for the task C.

Figure 12. Context given to the user on the third challenge

4.2 Participants

A total of 11 individuals (7 males and 4 females) aged between 20 and 32 years old (*M*=25.8; *SD*= 3.5), took part of this study. Every participant was a Software Engineer, and they were recruited through the university mailing list. All participants reported having a normal or corrected visual acuity and none participant was colorblind. We conducted one session per subject.

4.3 Measures

Before they started the experiment, participants were asked to fill a very short survey in order to collect some demographic data and they also ranked their own creativity *("Do you consider yourself a creative person?")* in a Likert Scale (0-7 values) (Silvia, Wigert, Reiter-Palmon, & Kaufman, 2012) (Wiseman, Watt, & Gilhooly, 2011). After finishing the writing task, they were asked to fill a Likert scale survey about how that experience made them feel using the Flow Theory dimensions (Csikszentmihalyi, 1991) . The Flow Theory survey was based on the following dimensions: (i) intense and focused concentration on the present moment, (ii) sense of personal control or agency over the situation or activity, (iii) loss of reflective self-consciousness, and (iv) distortion of temporal experience. Participants ranked a 7-point Likert scale based on questions such as: *"I felt very concentrated during this condition"* and *"I lost track of time during this condition"*. The Likert scale questions were ranked from 1 (totally disagree) to 7 (totally agree). To access the participants' mental well-being, we asked them to select up to three adjectives from the following list: Surprised, Delighted, Laid back, Depressed, Passive, Happy, Tired, Bored, Sad, Satisfied, Frustrated, Angry, Serious, Animated, Distressed, Creative and Frightened. Finally we collected qualitative data with a semi-structured interview with questions such as: "*Which condition did you enjoy using the most?*" or "*Is there any comment that you would like to add?*", *"Did time limit your creativity?"* in order to know the participant opinion about the whole experience.

4.4 Procedure

Participants were brought individually to a quiet room previously prepared for the experiment. For the examination, we used two laptops computers with a screen size of 13.3 inches and a display resolution of 1920x1080 pixels. When participants entered the room, they were asked to sit and before they started the experience, the experimenter ran the tool and asked them if they wanted to change little things in the environment, such as font size/type or something else. They had a few minutes to know each tool. We did this because we were using different conditions that they could be unfamiliar with as a way to reduce bias or any aversion to a given tool. After that, the writing task was explained. During the task, the participant was left alone in a room with the computer at his disposal. The time was monitored by the person responsible for guiding the participant through the tasks and after it reached the 10 minutes mark the participant was instructed to stop writing. When participants finished the writing task, they were asked to fill out the self-reported survey. Finally, participants were interviewed based on their experience using the tools. The total time per subject including questionnaires, experiment, breaks and semi-structured interviews took over one hour.

5. RESULTS

To inquire the impact of the CreativeWall Add-In UI on user's apparent and experienced creativity, we triangulated different data sources, such as behavioural data, users' verbal accounts during task execution, self-reports using psychometric scales of creativity and data from our exit interviews.

Is our sample equally creative?

Participants self-rated their creativity (M=6.18; SD= 1.54) in a seven-point Likert Scale before starting the experience. 63.3% of participants considered themselves a creative persons in a seven-point Likert scale. 18.2% of participants considered themselves creative persons in a five-point values, 9.1% in a three-point values and 9.1% in a two-point values.

Did CreativeWall Add-In UI lead to increased flow?

To assess the reliability of our survey, we used Cronbach's alpha (Cooligan, 2013) as a measure. It was taken into account the polarity of the scale. Table 3 exhibits results of reliability (internal consistency) analyses for questions in each dimension of flow. Results show that the number of test items can be considered with an acceptable consistency (Cooligan, 2013) in the scale used, from the survey, on seven-point Likert scales.

Table 2. Cronbach's alpha related to each of the dimensions

Flow Dimensions	Cronbach's Alpha
Concentration	.629
Sense of Control	.797
Lost Self-Consciousness	.672
Lost Track of Time	.633

We proceeded using repeated measures such as Friedman's ANOVA (Cooligan, 2013) (Field, 2009) approach to testing differences between each condition. The Flow dimensions Concentration (Fr (2) = 5.20, p>.05) and Lost Self-Consciousness (Fr (2) = 1.90, p>.05) did not have statistical significance when compared with each condition. For the other dimensions Sense of Control (Fr (2) = 10.21, p<.05) and Lost Track of Time (Fr (2) = 17.43, p<.05) results were statically significant. Therefore the non-parametric Wilcoxon tests (Cooligan, 2013) (Field, 2009) were used to display if there were any differences for each pair or conditions, using Condition A to compare as a baseline. Results showed that, participants in Condition A, when compared with participants in Condition B (T=0, z= -2.06, p<.025, r=-.44), for the dimension Sense of Control were not statistically significant. Also, participants in condition A when compared to participants in Condition C, for the levels of Sense of Control, even though the value is in the border line, it was not statistically significant as well (T=0, z= -2.23, p<.025, r=-.48). We applied the effect size that gives us the magnitude of the effect investigated (Cooligan, 2013). For the dimension Lost Track of Time, the results showed a significant difference between the participants in Condition A when compared to participants in Condition B (T=0, z= -2.71, p<.025, r=-.58). For the same dimension, the differences between participants in Condition A when compared to participants in Condition C were also statistically significant (T=0, z= -2.72, p<.025, r=-.58). To assess the participants mental well-being we asked them to select up to three adjectives from the following list: animated, creative, distressed, fear, serious, angry, satisfied, frustrated, sad, astonished, depressed, bored, tired, happy, delighted, pacific and relaxed. Figure 13 shows the total count for each of the adjectives selected and presented on the above list. The words that were used the most were animated, creative, happy and pacific, being that creative was the most used for Condition B and Condition C, and serious was the most used for Condition A.

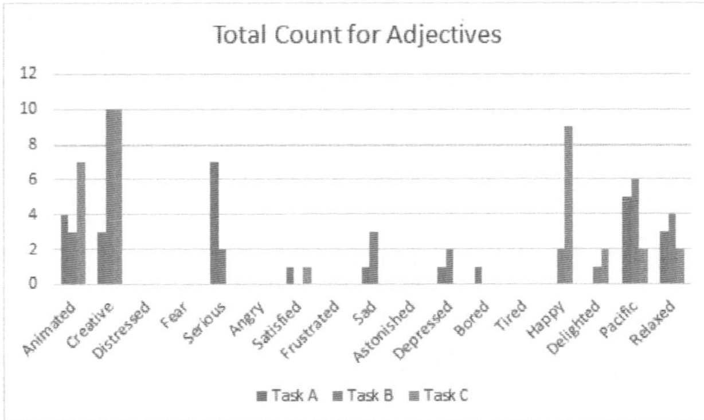

Figure 13. Chart relating the tasks with the adjectives used in them

After analyzing the results we are able to conclude that users who were in Condition B and Condition C report to feel more creative that users in Condition A. The most balanced word counts were relaxed and pacific, as they were selected at least twice for each conditions. These aspects might indicate that users felt ease when writing.

Did CreativeWall Add-In UI lead to increased output?

We used the Skeweness and Kurtosis and Kolmorov-Smirnov tests ($p>0.05$) to analyze the data normality of the average number of words produced. Results showed that the sampling distribution was normal. T-tests were used to compare the statistical significance of the samples using a 95% level of confidence. Participants in Condition B wrote on average more words (M=186.1, SE=49.3) than in Condition A (M=156.2, SE=54.5). For the same condition the difference was statistically significant (t (10) =-3.20, $p<.05$). In Condition C, participants wrote on average more words (M=185.7, SE=65.1) than in Condition A (M=156.2, SE=54.5). The difference was statistically significant (t (10) =-2.23, $p<.05$) for the same condition. Table 3 shows statistics from the time and sequence in which the users completed their writing tasks.

Table 3. Statistics from time in minutes spent on each condition

	Condition A	Condition B	Condition C
Mean	8.73	9.55	9.27
Median	9.00	10.00	9.00
St. Deviation	1.01	0.69	0.79

By statistically results reported in Table 3, we can see that most of the participants did not used the ten minutes for the writing task. When interviewed, 81.8% of participants did not considered the time limit a factor to restrict their creativity in the writing task. This might indicate that even though the conditions used for the experience helped the participants start writing, they are not as effective when it comes to keeping a constant creativity flux and therefore helping only on the first steps of the creative process. Triangulating the results with the semi-structured interviews conducted after the writing task apparently suggest that, by unanimity of the answers registered, Condition A was the less enjoyed condition. 63.6% of participants really liked the Condition C, and 36.4% liked to write in Condition B. According to some participants (27.7%), the lack of image and texts is important for their creativity to flow, *"Condition A is very limited because it lacks the image, and the image is very important for creativity."(P6).* Another interesting fact is that, for the majority of participants, color helps but does not influence creativity when they don't find the text creative, *"Even though color is a very interesting component, the most important ones are the text and image. If the text is not creative then the color won't make a difference."(P4); "Color helps the user remember of something. For example, the yellow resembles the joy of the summer."(P6); "Color helped, but the most important thing was the text and the image."(P8).* Some other participants refer to the color as being a source of distraction or did not considered as an important factor, *"Color helps as well but is not as decisive as the text and image. Color can also be a motive for distraction. A less intense color might have been better."(P3); "The color is a little bit distractor."(P2).* With this we assume that our initial idea that color would help triggering creativity through the emotion it generates on people can't be applied to every participant. Even though some participants enjoyed having the color together with the image and the text, and stated that it helped their creativity to flow, they are still a minority. *"I think that in this case, color really helped, because the text was about summer and yellow resembles the summer. It did make me feel kind of happy." (P7); "The color and the image encourage creativity. In fact, I felt some ease on Condition C. The image and color helped me idealize some ideas."(P1).*

6. DISCUSSION AND CONCLUSIONS

The main goals of this work were to investigate if a creative writing support UI could enhance a user's mental well-being and creativity, and to check whether color could influence creativity in any way. Although the number of participants in the tests was limited, it was possible to develop some statistical results and take some conclusions from them. Even so, as future work, the idea of performing more studies for more solid results should be considered. As for the results obtained through the user study, we were able to conclude, through statistical evidence that participants performing the tasks with the *CreativeWall Add-In* (Conditions B and C) lost track of time more often than participants using the simple Microsoft Word UI without any add-ins (Condition A). Another aspect that was statistically relevant was the fact that users using the *CreativeWall Add-In* were able to produce more words. It must be taken into account that efficiency can't be measured by the number of words alone as this can be misleading. Even so, having significant difference in number of words between different conditions might indicate that their efficiency was affected. Also, taking into account the answers that results from the semi-structured survey performed after each of the sessions, it was clear that the tasks performed with the *CreativeWall Add-In* were more enjoyable and participants had no problems starting to write, which could mean that these conditions help in the initial phase of the creative writing process. This could also mean, that, by consequence of the previous statements, this approach can be effective when trying to overcome writer's block. About the color, the majority of participants stated that color does not influence their creativity, and can be somewhat distractive. With this kind of statements we can assume that color does not always influence the creativity of users. One limitation of our study is that is does not consider the long-term usage of CreativeWall platform and add-in. Therefore, conclusions are limited to an incipient (11 participants) usage of the different creative writing tasks using the addressing conditions. However, it is still very useful to have this data. In summary, in this pilot evaluation of our novel crowdsourced platform, our findings suggest that, from a mental well-being perspective, it was clear that participants felt more inspired, more focused, more creative and more immersed when using the *CreativeWall Add-In*. From a "productivity" perspective, our results suggest that the users using the *CreativeWall Add-In* were the most efficient. Taking into account, the conclusions made in previous the color feature should be reviewed in order to try and take the most out of it. This includes reviewing the concept and reviewing the color itself. Trying to make color less intense would be one of the solutions for some of the problems presented in the user study, namely the distraction caused by it. We have addressed these somewhat sensitive issues and tried to empower participants with different user interfaces to help them overcome writer's block and to express themselves in a different way. The current prototype is only a first implementation of our ongoing work on the concept of creative writing user interfaces and new guidelines to creative support tools in writing. We would like to conduct a long term study, to obtain more results about creativity, and mental well-being of its users. Finally, we considered that it's important to increase the number of moods in order to include other creativity enhancing moods. We are also interested in the strong relationship between the user interfaces for supporting creative writing and the level of creativity of its users.

ACKNOWLEDGMENTS

We would like to thank the users who participated in this research. This work was partially funded by ARDITI - Regional Agency for the Development of Research Technology and Innovation through the M14-20 Project - 09-5369-FSE-000001- PhD Scholarship, by FCT/MCTES LARSyS (UID/EEA/50009/2013 (2015-2017)) and by and by IDE (ProCiência), SENSE-SEAT, through the M1420-01-0247-FEDER-000001.

REFERENCES

Baas, M., De Dreu, C., & Nijstad, B. (2008). "A Meta-Analysis of 25 Years of Mood-Creativity Research: Hedonic Tone, Activation, or Regulatory Focus?". *Psychological Bulletin, vol. 134, n.6*, 779-806.

Brabham, D. C. (2008). "Crowdsourcing as a Model for Problem Solving: An Introduction and Cases". *Convergence: The International Journal of Research into New Media Technologies, 14,1*, 75-90.

Cooligan, H. (2013). *Research Methods and Statistics in Psychology.* New York: Routledge.

Csikszentmihalyi, M. (1991). *Flow: The Psychologic of Optimal Experience.* New York: Harper Perennial.

De Dreu, C. K., Baas, M., & Nijstad, B. (2008). "Hedonic Tone and Activation Level in the Mood-Creativity Link: Toward a Dual Pathway to Creativity Model". *Journal of Personality and Social Psychology, vol.94, n.5*, 739-756.

Digest, W. (2011). *The Writer's Guide to Creativity.* F+W Media Inc.

Estellés-Arolas, E., & González-Landrón-De-Guevara. (2012). "Towards an integrated crowdsourcing definition". *J.Inf. Sci., v. 38, n. 2*, 189-200.

Field, A. (2009). *Discovering Statistics Using SPSS.* London : SAGE Publications Ltd.

Friedman, R., & Forster, J. (2001). "The Effects of Promotion and Prevention Cues on Creativity". *Journal of Personality and Social Psychology, vol. 81, n.6*, 1001-1013.

Goethe, J. (1970). *Theory of Colours.* London: MIT Press.

Gonçalves, F., Campos, P., Hanna, J., & Ashby, S. (2015). You're the Voice: Evaluating User Interfaces for Encouraging Underserved Youths to express themselves through Creative Writing. *C&C'15 Proceedings of the 2015 ACM SIGCHI Conference on Creativity and Cognition.* New York, USA.

Howe, J. (2008). *Crowdsourcing: Why the Power of the Crowd is Driving the Future of Business* . New Work, USA: Crown Publishing Group.

Ivcevic, Z., Brackett, M., & Mayer, J. (2007). "Emotional Intelligence and Emotional Creativity. *Journal of Personality, vol. 2, n. 75*, 200-236.

Kaya, N. E. (2004). "Relationships between color and emotion: a study of college students". *College Student Journal, vol. 38, n.3*, 396-405.

Kaya, N., & Epps, H. (2004). "Color-emotion associations: Past experience and personal preference". *Color and Paints, Interim Meeting of the International Color Association.* Porto Alegre.

Kleemann, F., Vob, G., & Reider, K. (2008). "Un(der)paid Innovators: The Commercial Utilization of Consumer Work through crowdsourcing". *Science, Technology & Innovation Studies, vol.4, n.1*, 5-26.

Kroll, J. H. (2013). *Research Methods in Creative Writing*. Palgrave Macmillan.

Myers, D. G. (2006). *The Elephants Teach: Creative Writing since 1880.* Chicago: University of Chicago Press.

Rooij, A., & Jones, S. (2013). "Mood and Creativity: An Appraisal Tendency Perspective". *9th ACM Conference on Creativity & Cognition* . Sydney, Australia.

Rose, M. (1984). *"Writer's Block: The Cognitive Dimension. Studies in Writing & Rhetoric".* Southern Illinois University Press: Carbondale.

Silvia, P., Wigert, B., Reiter-Palmon, R., & Kaufman, J. (2012). Assessing Creativity With Self-Report Scales : A Review and Empirical Evaluation. *Psychology Faculty Publications.*

Wiseman, R., Watt, C., & Gilhooly, K. (2011). Creativity and ease of ambiguous figural reversal. *British Journal of Psychology, 102*, 615-622.

COLLECE 2.0: A DISTRIBUTED REAL-TIME COLLABORATIVE PROGRAMMING ENVIRONMENT FOR THE ECLIPSE PLATFORM

Santiago Sánchez, Miguel A. Redondo, David Vallejo, Carlos González and Crescencio Bravo
Universidad de Castilla-La Mancha
Paseo de la Universidad, 4, Ciudad Real, 13071, Spain

ABSTRACT

Collaboration with other users to solve programming problems has an effect on the speed of development and the final software quality. This is achieved through techniques like pair programming when users are co-located, or otherwise through real-time remote collaboration. Existing work for remote working on a programming project has failed to address the integration of new emerging technologies, like augmented reality. These new technologies would provide a way to improve the final user learning experience if integrated in a working programming environment. This paper describes the implementation of COLLECE 2.0, a plug-in for the Eclipse platform which provides a distributed real-time collaborative programming environment, and integrates support for augmented reality and mobile device capabilities. We discuss two specific use scenarios where the solution would work, and how the implemented awareness mechanisms improve the user experience. The paper closes with the conclusions, limitations and future work, and a first sign on what on-going works would look like.

KEYWORDS

Collaboration, real-time edition, awareness, augmented reality, distributed development, eclipse

1. INTRODUCTION

Distributed real-time collaborative programming has been one important discussion topic for a long time. The rise of tools allowing users to effectively achieve setting such an environment and the improvements made over highspeed networks demonstrates this. However, these new tools try to go a step further and build a complete system where users are presented with an integrated solution for a completely collaborative programming environment. But they do not achieve it, since they base their efforts on the implementation of sharing programming projects, or individual files to be more accurate, among collaborators (Bravo et al., 2013). For example, prior work like CoEclipse focuses mainly on topics like consistency maintenance, i.e. syntax and semantic consistency, but then again not growing on what's been built (Fan and Sun, 2012a, Fan and Sun, 2012b), thus being an incomplete but promising work for a whole collaborative programming experience.

A common scenario for real-time collaborative programming are Massive Online Open Courses (MOOCs), which state remote work is a fact, and so require students to collaborate with each other to successfully follow up the course. A complete environment that fulfills these requirements and also extends on other features would be appropriate in such context. In fact, existing studies (Shen and Sun, 2000) confirm that real-time collaborative programming is capable of accelerating the progress of problem-solving, creating a better design and shorter code length, and thus improving the quality of software projects.

The presented work builds over prior research named COLLECE (COLLaborative Edition, Compilation and Execution of programs), a project aimed to guide students in solving programming problems through distributed pair programming (Bravo et al., 2013). This new proposed version improves over the existing behavior and extends its features to achieve a complete real-time collaborative programming environment. These new features go beyond real-time editing problems and try new approaches to collaborative programming, like graphic visualization, context awareness, or problem solving. Also, it accomplishes, along with the common workspace awareness elements (Gutwin and Greenberg, 1995), that a real-time distributed groupware system should accomplish, i.e. user participation (presence), user location, activity level, user actions, user intentions, user changes, objects used, etc.

In this paper we will discuss the new COLLECE 2.0 as a working tool and a programming learning environment, its features, basis, reworked stuff, common use scenarios, and future development. This conforms to a programming learning environment with emerging and interactive technologies, via augmented reality and touching capabilities, which fulfills new needs in countries to educate students in the programming sciences scope. In section 2 we discuss some related and past work the solution is based on. Then, in section 3 the project is introduced from a technical point of view, where an overview of the main modules and how they work together is presented. After that, in section 4, some common use scenarios are announced. Finally, in section 5, we address the findings drawn from the research.

2. RELATED WORK

Users interested in working through real-time collaborative programming may use some existing solutions that work at some degree; as the previously introduced CoEclipse, which integrates with the Eclipse IDE as a set of plugins so the user experience is the same as if he or she was using the environment without any collaboration features.

CoEclipse mainly invests its efforts in granting syntactic and semantic consistency among users. It follows a centralized client/server network model where the document editions are made locally and then applied remotely by operational transformations (Ellis and Gibbs, 1989). These operations were used in the Jupiter system (Nichols et al., 1995) as a mean to solve conflicting editions so that it combine both client and server operations to find one which allows the client and server to reach the same final state.

Figure 1 shows an example of operational transformation, where both clients start out with the same document state (i.e. the "abc" characters). If the clients edit that text concurrently, so client 1 inserts the 'd' character at position one, and client 2 deletes the character at position two, an inconsistency would arise since client 1 ends up with the "adc" characters and client 2 ends up with the "adb" characters, thus obtaining conflicting copies on both clients. In order to solve these concurrent editions, clients have to transform the received operations from the other client. In our example, client 1 should have to transform the deleted operation coming from client 2.

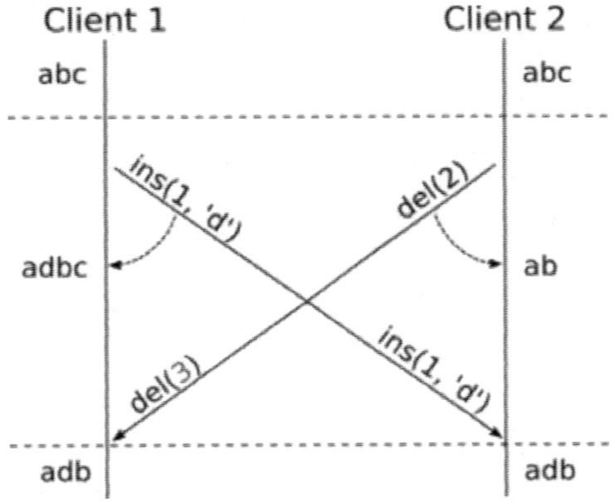

Figure 1. Operation transformation process –client 1 inserts character 'd' in position 1 of "abc" string, while client 2 deletes the "b" character at his or her local document; an operational transform is then needed for client 1 to have a synchronized copy with the other client

The algorithm implemented for operational transformation alongside other specific improvements, stands its basis on related research such as Apache Wave, originally developed by Google on its work centered on the Jupiter system, whose technology was later used on its Google Docs cloud applications (Wang et al., 2010).

In the same trail of Eclipse based solutions, Saros (Salinger et al., 2010) stands out for the ecosystem it offers. It has been developed actively since 2008 as a complete solution for real-time collaborative programming. It implements the same operational transforms algorithm to handle concurrent editing, but it also offers awareness mechanisms, such as presence in the way of chat and connected members, or workspace by showing the files users are editing. Visual Studio also includes the possibility to extend its environment with plugins, specifically with the VS Anywhere one, which endows the environment with collaboration capabilities. It offers a complete solution for project sharing and chat communication, and has reached a mature state ready to be used by final users.

On the other hand, the arise of web applications have emerged some cloud based tools, and so a couple of them exist. The most popular ones are Kobra (https://kobra.io), CodeShare (https://codeshare.io), or Cloud9 (https://codeshare.io/) (de Carvalho, 2015). All of them allow document sharing with some syntactic sugar like colours, and some communication methods like chat or video streaming. However, their IDE features are limited, since no workspace concept, autocompletion, or refactoring tools are provided; only a basic support for some interpreted languages like Python, or web development ones.

Other solutions like Floobits (https://floobits.com) provide a set of plugins for users to install in their favourite text editor, like Atom, Emacs, or VIM; but again, these editors lack IDE capabilities for languages like Java, or C++ (Thodi and Fujita, 2016).

A more traditional environment goes through the use of a setup of an online virtual private server with a terminal multiplexer (e.g. GNU Screen, or tmux) and a command line interface editor (e.g. vim, Emacs, or nano) (McDonnell, 2014). Also, a graphical user interface experience may also be achieved by just using Emacs and its make-frame-on-display command to connect to a remote X display. Again, these last setups do not provide common IDE features but a pair programming environment.

Another set of tools exist like CodeBunk (https://codebunk.com/) aimed for recruiters to ask programming questions to the candidate while they see how the interviewed works in the shared editor.

2.1 COLLECE

The work in this paper is born from a prior version named COLLECE (Bravo et al., 2013). It supports users joining to sessions where they can work in a shared document (i.e. a java source file for example). Sessions live in a remote server managed by a permission system based on users' whitelists, and handle documents which can be retrieved by client instances and then saved again to the server copy. The project was implemented as a multi-platform standalone Java Web Start (JavaWS) application, so users can access it through a web page.

Once users are logged, they can collaborate in the document in a variety of ways. The collaborative and awareness mechanisms the system supports are varied:

- Session panel with state information.
- Document locking for synchronous editing in a turns system way.
- User stats for further study.
- Multiple cursors identifying multiple users.
- History of past actions.
- Sounds.
- Chat window.
- Execution and compilation of code request functions.

Users may work through COLLECE by loading a specific problem and associated source code file, and then sharing it to other session logged members. Once a document is shared, a user may request his or her edition turn to make some changes and then grant the edition turn to other member. Once the code is changed according to the problem needs, a user may start a compilation and execution poll so other members are in agreement to run such actions. Program output is shared to the users through the console view.

The next section introduces to the reader what improvements and reworks are made in the new COLLECE 2.0, comparing to the previous version and other existing works.

3. ARCHITECTURE

COLLECE 2.0 builds its architecture over a modular set of views, editors, and wizards working as an Eclipse plugin deployed through an update site. This method of releasing plugins allows users to easily install them via the Eclipse package manager. Also, users without an Internet connection may install the plugin by simply copying to the Eclipse install directory through the file manager.

Using a modular approach allows the plugin to scale in future work fitting a cohesive and decoupled architecture. This way users may employ specific features of the environment without taking care of the other capabilities, or extended by the programmer who wants to grow up over what is done.

The main aim of COLLECE 2.0 is to provide a distributed real-time collaborative programming experience to the users. Thus, some features of the prior version have been improved or simply just removed. For example, we are referring to the turn request mechanisms to edit, compile, and run the shared program that has been reworked as an additional tool to be optionally used as a new feature.

The system distinguishes two entities, server and clients. The first one handles context information, i.e. sessions holding shared projects information, users' data, and information about the server itself. It is also in charge of keeping database persistence (based on Apache Derby), and synchronizing shared data among clients. On the other hand, clients are actual users connected to a common server that want to collaborate remotely in a programming project.

In order to allow clients to start collaborating, they first must to signup for the server to create their member data. These data are used as a way for the server and other members to identify them, using information like user name, email, or photos. The only mandatory field the user is requested to complete is its email, just for being unique within all the saved data; if it already exists, member creation is forbidden.

Clients may act as a server if they want to. COLLECE 2.0 allows creation of server instances through private networks or the Internet, so we achieve a decentralised network architecture with individual nodes composed of a server and different connected clients. Figure 2 shows a visual representation of this kind of network architecture.

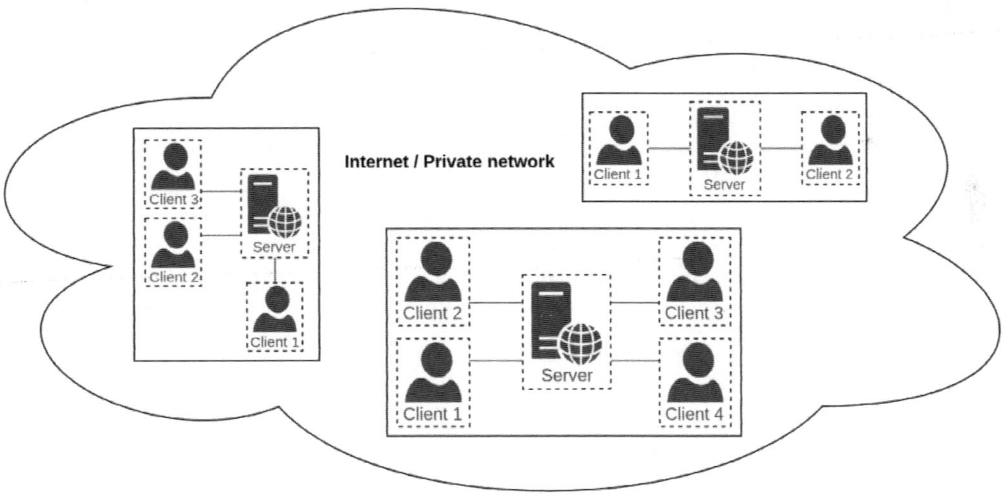

Figure 2. COLLECE 2.0 network architecture; servers live among existing others with their connected clients isolated

If the user is already registered in the server, he can log in and choose to join an existing session or create one. Sessions allow the server to differentiate collaborative workspaces. They store the list of allowed members to join, the project address repository, the duration of days the session can exist, and whether it is private, (so only allowed members can join), or publicly available. Once the client is connected to the server, he or she is provided with a copy of the repository to start working along with the other members. Earlier versions did not allow final users to behave as servers, therefore it depended on a previously setup server to work on some reachable host for allowing other users to use COLLECE.

The distributed real-time editing allows members to modify the shared project with no delays. It is achieved by applying the previously discussed operational transforms. The implementation is based in the one provided by the Sync module in the Eclipse Communication Framework (ECF). COLLECE 2.0 network communications are based all over ECF. Different channels are set up following a publish-subscription pattern where clients subscribe to the channels published by the server. This way, the system holds channels for remote methods invocations, document changes, textual/audio/video chat, shared whiteboards, augmented reality data streams, and awareness mechanisms.

Document changes are registered locally per user on every editor change, and then are sent to the server, where they are applied via operational transformations to its project copy. Once the change is valid, it is then relayed to the other clients through the document changes ECF channel (Figure 3.a). Also, to ensure document consistency, a background service keeps track of the project copy in the server periodically, and compares it to the existing ones in clients, restoring client copies in case of divergences exist.

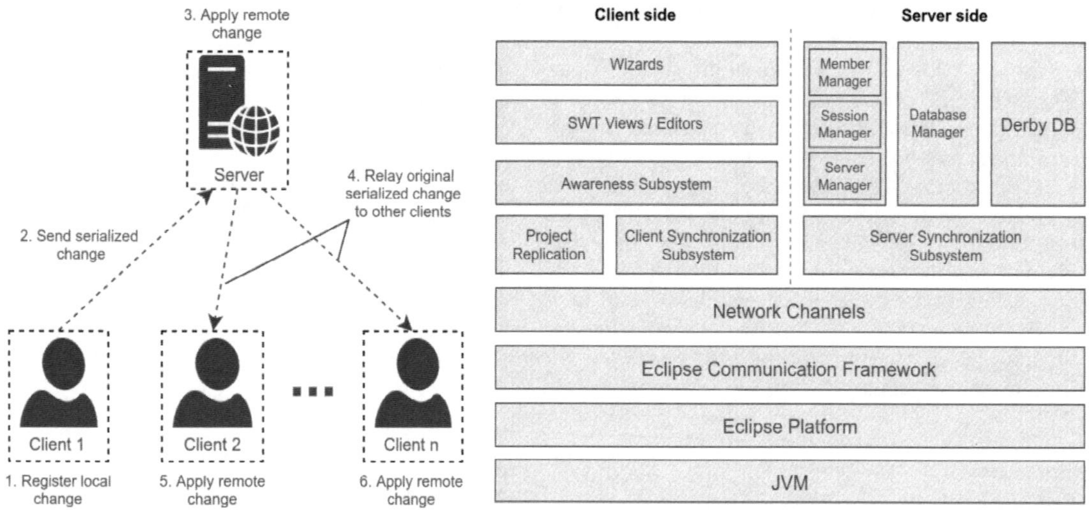

Figure 3. On left, (a) the distributed real-time editing workflow; on right, (b) a general overview of COLLECE 2.0 modules from a client/server perspective

Awareness mechanisms allow a working user to be informed about the other members actions. COLLECE 2.0 provides support for these mechanisms through:

- Multiple coloured cursors stating where the other members are editing.
- A panel displaying information from connected members.
- Displaying which regions of code are marked for read-only.
- A chat to talk with other team members.
- A console to show the output of shared command line interface programs executions.
- A shared whiteboard for members to sketch drawings.
- A following mode to see real-time specific user editions.
- A shared augmented reality view to improve the learning experience.
- A shared view to display information about mobile devices executions.

In brief, Figure 3.b shows a summary overview of the COLLECE 2.0 modules.

4. USE SCENARIOS

COLLECE 2.0 is intended to be used as a programming learning tool for students. In this section we introduce two common use scenarios where different group of students are provided with a COLLECE 2.0 environment to carry out a programming problemsolving task.

4.1 Pair Programming Classical View

Pair programming allow two users to work in a task. While one of them is working on the actual task, the other one is reviewing the other's work and thinking about solutions to the problem. COLLECE 2.0 fulfills this scenario by providing pair programming mechanism to the users.

Once both users are joined to the same session, one of them would take the observer role, and the other the driver role. There are two ways to achieve this behavior using COLLECE 2.0. The driver may lock regions of code for the observer to review them. Thus, the observer may use any of the communication ways he is offered to communicate the code to the driver. Another way would employ the following mode. Once enabled, the observer watches all the driver operations made to the project, and thus successfully reviews it.

Roles may be arbitrarily swapped at any time. Therefore, the observer may request to be the driver through an intended mechanism in the user interface, and vice versa.

4.2 Real-time Concurrent Collaboration

The major capability of COLLECE 2.0 is the support to distributed real-time concurrent editing. Users may collaborate to solve a programming problem by editing the same source code at the same time. Thus, one of them may implement a specific method, while the other one is fixing an existing algorithm implementation.

For example, a simple programming implementation to multiply two matrices and output to the screen, could be carried out using a collaborative approach in which one member implements the actual multiplication method while the other implements the printing method. The Figure 4 shows an example of this workflow.

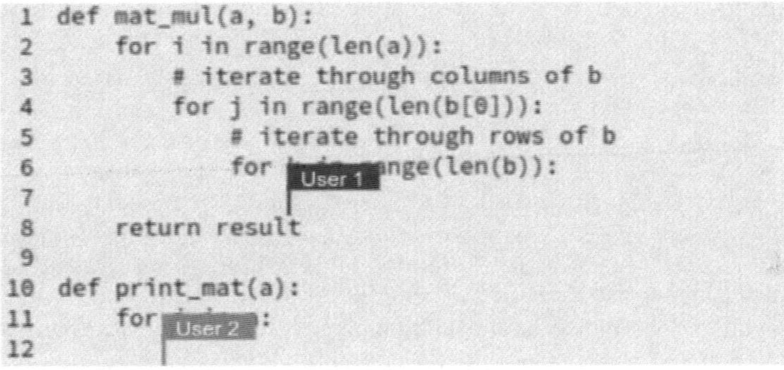

Figure 4. Two users editing the same source code at real-time

Both members could also use the shared whiteboard to sketch some ideas or to mock up the program interface.

A user may refactor the code too, distributing both methods in different files in the workspace. These files are also synchronized with the other collaborator since the whole workspace is shared.

Once the edition is complete and the program is finished, users may run it and see the result through the shared console.

5. CONCLUSION

Distributed real-time collaborative programming allows users to work on a programming project concurrently, improving the implementation quality of the solution. Also, it works as a learning environment where students may collaborate with each other to solve a programming problem.

In this work we have described the new COLLECE 2.0 solution for distributed real-time collaborative programming. The proposal builds on top of the Eclipse platforms, so users find it easy and familiar to work on, and thus the solution makes use of the underlying architecture and other well-known IDE features.

The usage of the Eclipse Communication Framework for implementing the network architecture and Apache Derby for database management, allows us to make an auto-contained solution where users do not have to install any third-party software to use the environment in its entirety. In this line, other solutions require users to run external applications to handle chat communications, or a database server to handle data persistence, and therefore making it difficult for users to deploy their own instances for others to collaborate.

We have seen how COLLECE 2.0 provides users with different awareness mechanisms so they have a clear vision of what is happening at any given time. The capabilities for real-time shared workspaces allow users to collaborate over different programming projects. Also, the integration of emerging technologies like augmented reality and mobile capabilities, improves the learning experience by visualizing physical space aligned algorithms.

The solution presents some limitations, thus it is far from being perfect; high latency networks, different user editor settings, and specific Eclipse platform limitations, are some of them.

Ongoing work shall improve COLLECE 2.0 on what's been done, along with extending it with new features, and handling these limitations. These new features would allow users, for example, to share graphical user interface application executions so the same window is shared among users, or to propose shared polls with the aim of knowing other collaborators' answers to some questions.

ACKNOWLEDGEMENT

This research has been partially funded by the Ministry of Economy, Industry and Competitiveness, and the European Regional Development Fund through the project TIN2015-66731-C2-2-R.

REFERENCES

Bravo, C., Duque, R. & Gallardo, J. 2013. A groupware system to support collaborative programming: Design and experiences. *Journal of Systems and Software,* 86, 1759-1771.

De Carvalho, A. D. Cooperative live coding as an instructional model. *Computing Conference (CLEI)*, 2015 Latin American, 2015. IEEE, 1-7.

Ellis, C. A. & Gibbs, S. J. Concurrency control in groupware systems. *Acm Sigmod Record*, 1989. ACM, 399-407.

Fan, H. & Sun, C. Achieving integrated consistency maintenance and awareness in real-time collaborative programming environments: The CoEclipse approach. *Proceedings of the 2012 IEEE 16th International Conference on Computer Supported Cooperative Work in Design (CSCWD)*, 23-25 May 2012 2012a. 94-101.

Fan, H. & Sun, C. 2012b. Supporting semantic conflict prevention in real-time collaborative programming environments. *SIGAPP Appl. Comput. Rev.,* 12, 39-52.

Gutwin, C. & Greenberg, S. 1995. Workspace awareness in real-time distributed groupware.

Mcdonnell, M. 2014. Pair Programming. *Pro Vim.* Springer.

Nichols, D. A., CURTIS, P., DIXON, M. & LAMPING, J. High-latency, low-bandwidth windowing in the Jupiter collaboration system. *Proceedings of the 8th annual ACM symposium on User interface and software technology*, 1995. ACM, 111-120.

Salinger, S., Oezbek, C., Beecher, K. & Schenk, J. Saros: an eclipse plug-in for distributed party programming. *Proceedings of the 2010 ICSE Workshop on Cooperative and Human Aspects of Software Engineering*, 2010. ACM, 48-55.

Shen, H. & Sun, C. RECIPE: a prototype for Internet-based real-time collaborative programming. *Proceedings of the 2nd Annual International Workshop on Collaborative Editing Systems*. Philadelphia, Pennsylvania, USA, 2000. Citeseer.

Thodi, M. & Fujita, S. Collaborative Development Environment in Peer-to-Peer Networks. *2016 Fourth International Symposium on Computing and Networking (CANDAR)*, 2016. IEEE, 586-589.

Wang, D., Mah, A. & Lassen, S. 2010. Google Wave Operational Transformation.

ACTA: A GENERAL PURPOSE FINITE STATE MACHINE (FSM) DESCRIPTION LANGUAGE FOR SMART GAME DESIGN

Emmanouil Zidianakis[1], Margherita Antona[1] and Constantine Stephanidis[1, 2]
[1]*Foundation for Research and Technology – Hellas (FORTH), Institute of Computer Science (ICS), N. Plastira 100, Heraklion, GR-70013, Greece*
[2]*University of Crete, Department of Computer Science, Greece*

ABSTRACT

Game design process creates goals, rules, and challenges to define a game that produces desirable interactions among its participants. Modeling the way in which players interact with the game requires among others the definition of game rules, plot, connection between player and the game, etc. This paper presents ACTA (ACTivity Analysis), a general purpose finite state machine (FSM) description language for rapid prototyping of smart games. ACTA facilitates smart game design by professionals who are not familiar with traditional programming languages. Professionals are able to model the game's logic and interaction using a straightforward and intuitive notation which can be customized for every different game. In order to support a customized scripting vocabulary, a reflection-oriented model was adopted allowing dynamic linking between ACTA generated rules and multiple data types. Windows Workflow Foundation (WF) is the "glue layer" connecting ACTA's scripting vocabulary with the application internals. Moreover, developers can use ACTA not only for developing event-driven sequential logic games, but also for applications of behavior composed of a finite number of states, transitions between those states and actions, as well as for applications based on rules driven workflows.

KEYWORDS

Smart games rapid prototyping, finite state machine interaction modeling

1. INTRODUCTION

There are many ways of modeling the behavior of systems, and the use of state machines is one of the oldest and best known. Finite state machines (FSMs) are commonly used to organize and represent an execution flow. In games, they are most known for being used in AI, but they are also common in implementations of user input handling, navigating menu screens, parsing text, and other asynchronous behavior [Buckland 2005]. According to the literature, there are a number of techniques for implementing a FSM. One of the most common methods is nested switch case statements. Although this technique is common, it is not easy to maintain as the FSM grows. Alternatively, a variety of FSM modeling tools is available, capable of representing a large logic by a relatively small diagram. The majority of them seem to follow simple, easy to verify rules and can be used to generate code.

Smart game design is a domain where FSMs are widely employed, often by non-experts such as teachers, intervention professionals and therapists. Working with FSM modeling tools based on specific syntax and complex notations creates challenges for non-developers when they need to model even a simple control execution flow. For the purposes of the present work, a minimal finite state machine description script language (ACTA) was developed in the context of interaction modeling for smart game design, based on a simplified notation and a straightforward and intuitive syntax. According to [Zidianakis et al 2015], traditional games are turned into smart games that share unique characteristics such being adaptive to players' skills and abilities. The aim of ACTA is to facilitate the smart game design process by professionals who are not familiar with traditional programming languages. Professionals are able to model the game's logic and interaction using a simplified notation which can be customized for every different game. Furthermore, developers can use ACTA not only for developing event-driven sequential logic games, but also for applications of behavior composed of a finite number of states, transitions between those states, and actions as well as for applications based on rules driven workflows.

2. BACKGROUND AND RELATED WORK

According to the literature, many related efforts have primarily focused on the description of FSMs. The Unified Modeling Language (UML) is an indicative example as it has an exuberant notation for describing FSMs. Some concrete examples are MetaUML [Gheorghies 2009], yUML [Haris 2009], and TextUML [Chaves 2009], which primarily focus on the creation of visual models based on textual notation. The majority of textual modeling tools support automated code generation. For example, Ragel supports a number of high-level languages but is targeted towards text parsing and input validation [Thurston 2009]. Ruby on Rails has built-in support for FSMs. The State Machine Compiler (SMC) [Charles 2009] is targeted towards the specification of event driven systems. Microsoft has also developed a textual specification language called Abstract State Machine Language (AsmL) [Gurevich et al 2005], based on concepts of the theory of abstract state machine. Executable UML [Milicev 2009] supports a subset of UML textually but misses key features of UML and does not integrate with programming languages. Umple [Badreddin 2010] merges the concepts of programming and modeling by adding modeling abstractions directly into programming languages.

According to [Kleppe et al 2003], modeling is considered to be a good widely accepted software development practice. However, as stated in [Forward et al 2010], modeling practices are not as widely adopted as they could be, primarily due to: a) the low adoption of modeling tools caused by their heavyweight nature, b) poor generated code, and c) difficulty between code and model synchronization. In addition, most modeling tools are intended to be used only by developers either using purely textual approaches or editing diagrams. With respect to the aforementioned modeling practices, the majority of modeling tools aim at providing a generic solution of modeling any-type of FSM in a context free manner. In addition, most modeling tools are intended to be used only by developers familiar with either using purely textual approaches or editing diagrams. As a result, working with FSM modeling tools based on specific syntax and complex notation, creates challenges faced by non-developers when they need to model even a simple control execution flow. For the purposes of the present work, a minimal finite state machine description script language, called ACTA, was developed based on a straightforward and intuitive syntax. The aim of ACTA (ACTivity Analysis) is to facilitate activity analysis process during smart game design by professionals who are not familiar with traditional programming languages, by providing a simplified notation. ACTA comes with an IDE which fully supports its use.

3. ACTA: A GENERAL PURPOSE FINITE STATE MACHINE (FSM) DESCRIPTION LANGUAGE FOR SMART GAME DESIGN

ACTA aims at facilitating smart game design by providing the authors with a straightforward and intuitive syntax to describe gameplay attributes such as states, inputs and rules triggering transition among the states. A script in ACTA can describe a FSM as depicted in the example of Figure 1 (left), which illustrates a flowchart of a hero game. The flowchart consists of boxes for each action a hero can do such as standing, jumping, ducking, and diving. When acting, the hero can respond to a button press and perform a different action. Furthermore, in each of the depicted boxes, there are arrows connecting the current action with a next one according to the labeled pressed button. As depicted in Figure 1 (right), the ACTA script of this example consists of the following parts: a) a fixed set of states that the machine can be in (e.g., standing, jumping, etc.), b) the current state, c) a sequence of inputs or events (e.g., the raw button presses and releases), and d) a set of transitions from the current state to a new one based on incoming input or event. When an input or event occurs, if it matches a transition for the current state, the machine changes to the state that transition points to.

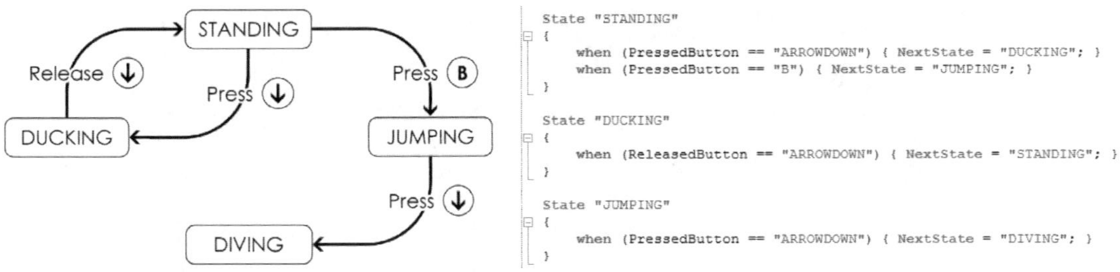

Figure 1. A Finite State Machine example (left) / Finite states of an action game in ACTA script (right)

3.1 ACTA's Syntax and Semantics

Authors can use ACTA for scripting a smart game or application in general, by outlining a set of finite states and event-driven transitions (i.e., a transition from one state to another is triggered by an event or a message). Thus, ACTA facilitates event driven programming, in which the flow of the program is determined by events, event handlers, and asynchronous programming. As depicted in Figure 2, a script in ACTA initially consists of various transitions that may happen anytime during execution without caring about the current state (i.e., *when* statements). For example, when a user gets into the playing room, the game starts by switching the machine to the "init" state to initialize the game. Another example is that during play, when the user leaves the room, the machine goes to the "paused" state to handle this situation. In this state, the game gets paused until the user comes back (within a period of *N* seconds), returning the machine to the previous state. When the allowed time has elapsed, the game terminates by switching to the corresponding "end" state. The ACTA script continues with the definition of the states (i.e., State statements).

ACTA uses three (3) fundamental keywords for scripting a finite state machine: a) *State*, b) *NextState*, and c) *when*. Table 1 summarizes all keywords used in ACTA scripts. The *NextState* keyword is used to set a new state. Using an assignment expression, the author simply sets the *id* of the next state to the reserved word *NextState* (e.g., *NextState = "state id"*). Event-driven transitions are described using the keyword *when*. In case a *when* statement's condition becomes true, a transition from the current state to a new one is fired. As depicted in Figure 2, within the when statement's block there are optional macros to be executed when exiting the state. To point to the new state, authors define a *NextState* statement at the end of the block. A finite state is described using the keyword *State*. As depicted in Figure 2, a *State* statement defines a block that contains: a) optional macros for execution when entering the state, and b) transitions. The latter may be either an explicit state transition using the keyword *NextState* or a set of when statements in order for the machine to remain in the current state until the condition of a *when* statement becomes true and fires its transition.

Using ACTA, authors are able to set the execution order of a *when* statement by setting its priority accordingly. *When* statements that have a higher priority value are executed first. The default value for any *when* statement is *0*. Furthermore, authors are able to characterize a *when* statement with a unique *id* by setting its *Name* property. So, *when* statements that have the same priority are executed in the alphabetic order of their name properties.

Table 1. ACTA keywords

State	when	active	with	NextState	When_SetActive
Name	Priority	Never	Reevaluation	Active	When_SetReevaluation
true	True	reevaluation	false	False	When_SetPriority
null	Null	PreviousState	priority	name	

Additionally, authors can set the re-evaluation behaviour of a *when* statement. In detail, they can specify whether a *when* statement can be re-evaluated by setting *Always* or *Never* to the *Revaluation* property. *Revaluation* behaviour is used to limit the number of times that a *when* statement runs, primarily to prevent infinite loops (i.e., state A → B → C → A etc.). *Always* (which is the default value) indicates that the *when* statement can be re-evaluated multiple times. *Never* indicates that the *when* statement is executed only once. A condition may be evaluated several times until the *when* statement executes macros, but the *when* statement will never be evaluated again. Also, authors are able to disable a *when* statement by setting the value of its *Active* property to *True* (default) or *False*. *Active* property indicates whether the *when* statement should be evaluated. Setting to *False* this property is similar to comment out the *when* statement.

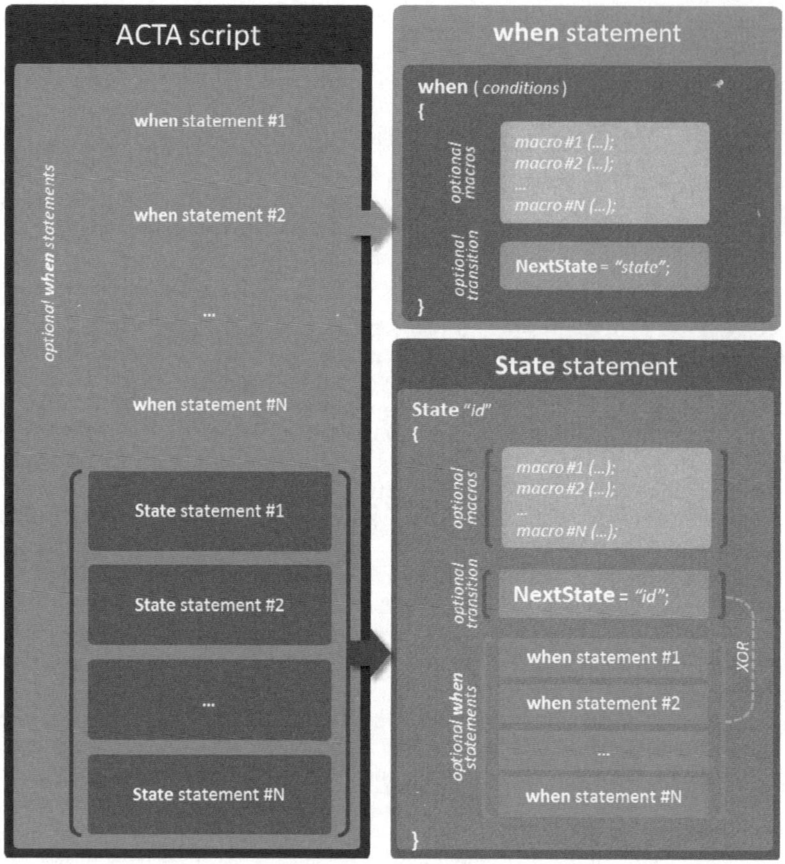

Figure 2. ACTA's structure

Finally, authors have access to a set of library functions to dynamically change the semantics of *when* statements. This set consists of the following:

- *When_SetActive(bool active, params string[] whenNames):* sets the *Active* property of *when* statements with names presented into the list *whenNames* to the value given as a parameter (i.e., *active*).
- *When_SetReevaluation (string reevaluation, params string[] whenNames):* sets the *Revaluation* behaviour property of *when* statements with names presented into the list *whenNames* to the first parameter's value.
- *When_SetPriority (int priority, params string[] whenNames):* sets the *Priority* property (i.e. execution order) of *when* statements with names presented into the list *whenNames* to the first parameter's value.

Figure 3 (left) illustrates the ACTA IDE which provides comprehensive facilities to authors. The depicted example consists of two *when* statements of the same priority. Initially, the second *when* statement (i.e., *when#2*) is not active. When the value of the subtotal field becomes greater than *10000*, *when#1* executes its macros. The first one (i.e., *When_SetActive*) activates *when#2*, while the second one, sets the discount field equal to 0.5. So, *when#1* reads the subtotal field and writes to the discount field, while *when#2* reads the discount and subtotal fields and writes to the total field. Therefore, *when#2* is active and has a dependency on when#1. As a result, *when#2* is evaluated/reevaluated whenever *when#1* executes its macros.

3.2 ACTA from a Developer's Perspective

Windows Workflow Foundation[1] (WF) is the "glue layer" connecting ACTA's scripting vocabulary with the application internals. WF is a Microsoft technology that provides an in-process workflow engine to implement workflows within .NET applications. Furthermore, WF provides rule capabilities to the .NET Framework development platform. These capabilities range from simple conditions that drive activity execution behavior to complex rulesets executed by a full-featured forward-chaining rules engine. To this end, an ACTA script is converted to a WF ruleset in order to take advantage of the provided workflow rule engine supporting complex rules scenarios, demanding forward chaining evaluation and precise evaluation control. Figure 3 (left) illustrates the ACTA IDE which provides comprehensive facilities to programmers for scripting in ACTA and generate the corresponding ruleset (filename extension *.rules*). A WF ruleset is a collection of rules with a set of execution semantics (e.g., *If-Then-Else* expressions that operate on properties within application). The generated rule expressions are given to the WF rule engine for evaluation (Figure 3 right).

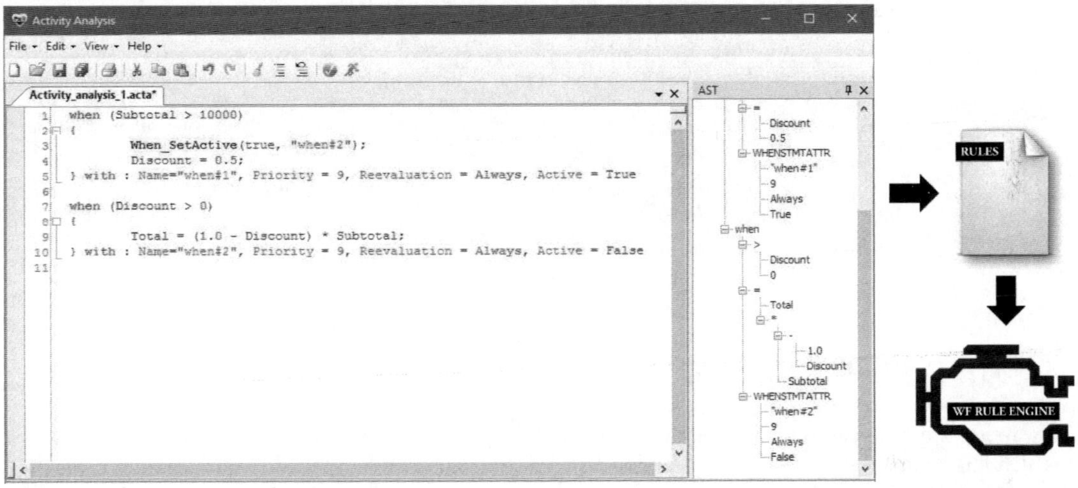

Figure 3. ACTA's semantics example (left) / WF rule engine takes the ACTA generated ruleset for evaluation (right)

The ACTA IDE parses the statements found in an ACTA script and generates the equivalent ruleset through three distinct steps. Firstly, it parses ACTA script and translates each statement or expression found to its equal code expression using the Code Document Object Model (CodeDOM[2]). The .NET Framework includes this mechanism that enables developers to emit source code to generate source code in multiple programming languages at run time, based on a single model that represents the code to render. For example, a WF rule is created for each CodeDOM expression by defining a condition (i.e., *rule expression condition*) with an associated set of actions to perform (i.e., *then actions*). Finally, the ACTA IDE creates a ruleset of the produced rules and uses WorkflowMarkupSerializer to write the ruleset to file.

In summary, ACTA is a general purpose finite state machine description language that facilitates the development of .NET applications by integrating into their projects the Windows Workflow Rule engine. In Windows Workflow Foundation all rulesets are defined in relation to a single specific .NET type. In case of ACTA, scripting such a .NET type is not known in advance. To overcome this difficulty and allow dynamic linking between ACTA generated rules and multiple types, a reflection-oriented model was adopted and implemented as a .NET framework library. To this end, variables used in ACTA are mapped to properties considered public to reflection (a property must have at least one accessor that is public). For example, the logical expression ***x==5***, part of the when statement (e.g., *when(x==5) { NextState = "A" }*), is equal to the following condition in CodeDOM: *(float)this.GetProperty("x") == 5f*.

1 https://msdn.microsoft.com/en-us/library/vstudio/ms734631(v=vs.90).aspx

2 https://msdn.microsoft.com/en-us/library/650ax5cx(v=vs.110).aspx

3.3 Implementation Details

The ACTA IDE was implemented in .NET using C# and uses a parser generated with ANTLR[3] to read and process ACTA scripts. ANTLR (ANother Tool for Language Recognition) is a powerful parser generator for reading, processing, executing and translating structured text or binary files. It is widely used to build languages, tools, and frameworks. From a grammar, ANTLR generates a parser that can build and walk parse trees. Taking as input the ACTA grammar (see the example in Figure 4), ANTLR generates a lexer and a parser for that language that can automatically build parse-trees, which are data structures representing how a grammar matches the input. ANTLR also automatically generates tree walkers that can be used to visit the nodes of those trees to execute application-specific code. The ACTA IDE provides authors with SyntaxBox[4], a syntax highlight editor. SyntaxBox features powerful syntax highlight windows forms control for the Microsoft.NET Platform. It supports: a) syntax highlighting, b) code folding for just about any programming language, c) bracket matching, d) unlimited undo/redo buffer, e) bookmarks, etc.

```
program : whenstmt* mystate* EOF -> ^( GLB_STATELIST whenstmt* mystate*);
mystate : 'State' STRING '{' stmt2* whenstmt* '}'-> ^(MYSTATE STRING stmt2* whenstmt*);
whenstmt : WHEN '(' logicalExpression ')' '{' stmt2* '}' whenstmtattr? -> ^(WHEN
logicalExpression stmt2* whenstmtattr?);
whenstmtattr: 'with' ':' whenid ',' priority ',' reevaluation (',' whenactive)? ->
^(WHENSTMTATTR whenid priority reevaluation whenactive?);

whenid : ('Name' | 'name')! ASS! STRING;
priority : ('Priority' | 'priority')! ASS! NUM;
reevaluation: ('Reevaluation' | 'reevaluation')! ASS! reevaluationAttr;
reevaluationAttr: 'Always' | 'Never';
whenactive: ('Active' | 'active')! ASS! BOOLEAN;
```

Figure 4. An example of ACTA grammar in ANTLR

4. MIMESIS GAME: A CASE STUDY

As a case study illustrating the usefulness and benefits of ACTA, this section presents the Mimesis game, which has been developed in ACTA. The Mimesis game is an entertaining game for preschool children. The game requests the child to assume various body postures as illustrated in Figure 5. Using a sensory infrastructure presented in [Zidianakis et al 2014], the game measures the quality and performance of the body posture that the child assumes and can extract indications of the achieved maturity level and skills of the child. Regarding the gameplay, the child stands in front of the interactive display, which is positioned horizontally, (e.g., near to a wall) giving the feeling of standing in front of a mirror. At the upper side of the large display, a depth camera (i.e., Kinect sensor) is positioned, which allows the sensory infrastructure to recognize the user's position and gestures. The Mimesis game requires the child to imitate a series of postures presented by a virtual avatar called Max [Zidianakis et al 2014], a process that requires motor planning or programming a skilled, non-habitual motor act. Moreover, when Max utters verbal commands, the child's abilities related to understand and follow verbal directions and to plan movements based on verbal instructions are also stimulated.

The Mimesis gameplay was scripted in ACTA by early intervention professionals. The game consists of the following functions: a) Max presenting various poses, b) Max assuming various postures (moving from his idle position to a posture), c) voice commands of each pose, and d) audio description of each pose. As illustrated in Figure 6, when the child enters the camera view area, Max welcomes the child by saying "*Hello. I'm Max. Do you want to play?*". In this case, a state transition occurs from the state *Idle* to the state *Welcome*. While remaining in the last state, if the child answers *YES*, the control flow is transferred to the state *Mimesis* where Max asks the child to imitate a pose by saying "*Do what I do as fast as you can*". Similarly, if the child answers *NO*, then Max looks sad and says "*Goodbye*" (state *End*). If the child does not react to that question within a period of time (e.g. elapsed time of 15 sec.), Max welcomes him again (next

3 http://www.antlr.org/

4 https://code.google.com/p/alsing/wiki/SyntaxBox

state *Welcome*). Anytime the child moves away from the camera's view area (global when condition), Max says "*You are leaving me*" and then looks sad and says "*Goodbye*". If the child returns after a period of time, Max welcomes again.

Figure 5. Postures demonstrated by Max in the Mimesis game

```
when(ChildPresent && !SessionIsActive) { NextState = "Idle"; }
when(!ChildPresent && SessionIsActive) {
    MaxSays ("You are leaving me");
    NextState = "ChildIsLeaving";
}
when(UserTooFar && SessionIsActive) {
    SpeakAsync("Please, come closer to me!.");
    NextState = "ChildIsTooFar";
}
State "Idle" {
    when(ChildPresent) {
        StartSession();
        NextState = "Welcome";
    }
}
State "Welcome" {
    MaxSays("Hello. I'm Max. Do you want to play? ");
    when(SpeechRecognized == "yes") { NextState = "Mimesis"; }
    when(SpeechRecognized == "no") { NextState = "End"; }
    when(Time == 15 && Count == 1) { NextState = "Welcome"; }
    when(Time > 15 && Count != 1) { NextState = "End"; }
}
State "End" {
    MaxSays ("Goodbye!");
    EndSession();
    when(Time == 10) { NextState = "Idle"; }
}
State "Mimesis" {
    MaxSays ("Do what I do as fast as you can");
    ShufflePoses();
    when(Time == 5) { NextState = "Level1"; }
}
State "Level1" { //nonverbal communication
    DemonstrateStaticPose(CurrentPose);
    when(AnimationRecognized == CurrentPose) { NextState = "Congrats"; }
    when(Time == 10) { NextState = "Level2"; }
}
State "Congrats" {
    MaxSays (GetRandomExclamation);
    NextPose();
    when(!PosesDidFinish) { NextState = "Level1"; }
    when(PosesDidFinish) { NextState = "Reward"; }
}
```

Figure 6. ACTA script snippet used in Mimesis game

5. CONCLUSION

This paper has presented a general purpose finite state machine (FSM) description language for rapid prototyping of smart games. ACTA facilitates smart game design by professionals who may need to design smart games but are not familiar with traditional programming languages. Smart game developers can use ACTA not only for developing event-driven sequential logic games, but also for applications of behavior composed of a finite number of states, transitions between those states, and actions as well as for applications based on rules driven workflows. ACTA facilitates the development of .NET applications by integrating into the Windows Workflow Rule engine. The ACTA IDE provides comprehensive facilities to authors and programmers for scripting in ACTA and generates the corresponding ruleset which in turn is given to the WF rule engine for evaluation. The Mimesis Game, a case study, was presented for demonstration purposes. The Mimesis gameplay was scripted in ACTA by early intervention professionals. The Mimesis game aims at promoting the child's posturing ability by challenging him/her to imitate a series of demonstrated postures. Regarding future work, ACTA capabilities will expand so as authors to be able to set alternative sequential finite states based on some condition. Finally, it is considered crucial to design an evaluation strategy with the active contribution of the aforementioned end users (e.g., teachers, therapists, child development experts) in order to measure ACTA's applicability and usability from an end-users perspective.

ACKNOWLEDGEMENT

This work is supported by the FORTH-ICS internal RTD Programme 'Ambient Intelligence and Smart Environments'.

REFERENCES

Badreddin, O., 2010, May. *Umple: a model-oriented programming language*. In Proceedings of the 32nd ACM/IEEE International Conference on Software Engineering-Volume 2 (pp. 337-338). ACM.

Buckland, M., 2005. Programming game AI by example. Jones & Bartlett Learning.

Charles, R. 2009. "The state machine compiler". http://smc.sourceforge.net/

Chaves, R. 2009. "TextUML". http://abstratt.com/

Forward, A., Badreddin, O. and Lethbridge, T.C., 2010, June. *Perceptions of software modeling: a survey of software practitioners*. In 5th workshop from code centric to model centric: evaluating the effectiveness of MDD (C2M: EEMDD).

Gheorghies, O. 2009. "MetaUML". http://metauml.sourceforge.net/

Gurevich, Y., Rossman, B. and Schulte, W. 2005. *"Semantic essence of AsmL"*. Th Computer Science, 343, 370-412.

Haris, T. "yUML". 2009. http://www.yuml.me/

Kleppe, A.G., Warmer, J.B. and Bast, W., 2003. *MDA explained: the model driven architecture: practice and promise.* Addison-Wesley Professional.

Milicev, D., 2009. *Model-driven development with executable UML*. John Wiley & Sons.

Thurston, A. 2009. "Ragel state machine compiler". http://www.complang.org/ragel

Zidianakis, E., Ioannidi, D., Antona, M. and Stephanidis, C., 2015, November. *Modeling and Assessing Young Children Abilities and Development in Ambient Intelligence*. In European Conference on Ambient Intelligence (pp. 17-33). Springer International Publishing.

Zidianakis, E., Papagiannakis, G. and Stephanidis, C., 2014, November. A cross-platform, remotely-controlled mobile avatar simulation framework for AmI environments. In SIGGRAPH Asia 2014 Mobile Graphics and Interactive Applications (p. 12). ACM.

Zidianakis, E., Partarakis, N., Antona, M. and Stephanidis, C., 2014, June. *Building a sensory infrastructure to support interaction and monitoring in ambient intelligence environments.* In International Conference on Distributed, Ambient, and Pervasive Interactions (pp. 519-529). Springer International Publishing.

A CASE STUDY OF EVALUATING A GAME-BASED INTERACTIVE PICTURE BOOK BASED ON THE ARCS MOTIVATION MODEL

Yih-Shyuan Chen and Yu-Horng Chen
Department of Digital Literature and Arts
St. John's University, Taiwan

ABSTRACT

This paper is a case study of examining the specific game-based interactive picture book through the ARCS motivation model developed by John Keller. Research subjects within this study comprised eleven 12-year-old primary school students with experiences in using electronic books for learning purposes. By using questionnaires and interviews, students views on attention relevance, confidence and satisfaction strategies used in the specific game-based interactive picture book were analysed. Findings from this study reflect upon the importance of catching students' attention in the very beginning of the learning process. The present study confirms that the ARCS motivation model could serve as the useful base for designing and evaluating the game-based learning system or platform.

KEYWORDS

Interactive picture book, games, game-based learning, ARCS, motivation

1. INTRODUCTION

The significance of game environments in enhancing students' learning interests and motivation is well-known in the field of educational technology and human-computer interaction. Construction and extension of the use of game-based or game-driven learning environments for teaching purposes has been of concern for some time as is evidenced by studies of game-based learning (Liu & Chu 2010, Noraddin 2015, Su & Cheng 2013). The studies which focused on teaching and learning in school education in Taiwan shared the common results, revealing that there is need for enhancing students' motivation throughout the learning process (Fan, & Feng 2012, Lin & Liu 2011). The researchers confirmed computer/digital games as the effective and powerful approach to provoking students' motivation (Kaneko et al. 2015). Some researchers went further, stating that applying digital games to school curriculum can be helpful for students' deeper understanding of the knowledge, to some degree (Johnson et al. 2011). The potential of the game-based learning environment and content for students' motivation and learning outcomes is widely acknowledged. Nevertheless, little research in Taiwan has been undertaken on the impact of story-driven games designed in the digital picture book on students' learning and motivation.

Given the above context, the aim of the present research is to apply the ARCS motivation model developed by John Keller (1983) to exploring primary school students' perceptions of attention, relevance, confidence and satisfaction strategies used in the particular game-based interactive picture book which was related to environmental protection and mainly designed for the present research. Moreover, this study examined whether and how the story-driven games within the interactive picture book promoted students' motivation throughout the reading process. Thus, the findings can possibly show the patterns of students' perceptions of and interests in the game-based interactive picture book.

2. THE ARCS MOTIVATION MODEL

The ARCS motivation model developed by John M. Keller (1983) can be considered to be a problem-solving approach to learners' motivation throughout the learning process (Su & Cheng 2013), and usually functions as the essential framework for constructing learning media or digital game-based learning environment (Kaneko *et al.* 2015, Liu & Chu 2010, Paras & Bizzocchi 2005, Qian 2014, Woo 2013, Ying & Yang 2013). The ARCS motivation model identifies four essential components and strategies for enhancing and sustaining motivation in the learning process as follows: attention, relevance, confidence and satisfaction.

'Attention' defined by Keller as the first component in the ARCS motivation model for gaining learners' attention by means of arousing and sustaining their curiosity and interests in the content or learning context (Keller, 2010). Attention could be obtained either by perceptual arousal or by inquiry arousal. For perceptual arousal, learners' attention may be drawn to the elements of surprise, doubt or disbelief. That is, perceptual arousal is involved with obtaining attention through the means of specific, related or real-world examples, the use of incongruity and/or even conflicts (Keller, 2010; Kapp, 2011). In the case of inquiry arousal, learners' curiosity could be stimulated by encouraging them to become active participants. In Keller's view, the methods for increasing learners' inquiry arousal are as follows: providing games, role plays, hands-on practices, and presenting questions or challenging problems which learners are interested in solving. Other methods for securing and maintaining learners' attention comprised the extended use of multimedia and integration of lighthearted humour into the learning process (Keller 2010; Kapp 2011).

'Relevance' is viewed by Keller as the learning goals and materials which learners are able to relate and are present worth and future usefulness for learners. The key methods of establishing relevance comprise: (1) goal orientation, which orients learners to the learning goals not simply by clearly defining the importance of achieving the goals, but by showing the way in which the goals will help learns at present and in the future in their real lives; (2) familiarity, which deals with establishing connections of the new knowledge presented and what learners already know from previous experiences; (3) modelling, which refers to the fact that presenting learners with a model of people who have successfully applied the particular knowledge which is expected to be absorbed. Modelling the worth and successful results of gaining the new knowledge presented can usually enable learners to consider the specific piece of knowledge or skill to be useful and to be the first step towards their future success; and (4) choice, which means that offering learners choices upon their preferred instructional strategies. This is particularly beneficial for adults or mature learners with preferences on the specific learning media or methods which they may feel more effective compared with others (Keller 2010; Kapp 2011; Pappas 2015).

'Confidence' in the ARCS motivation model is regarded as learners' expectation levels which they are able to achieve success with the information presented. Confidence strategies may enable instructors to instill a sense of confidence in learners by assisting them in developing belief in and positive expectation for successful achievements, and this could make learners more motivated to proceed (Keller 2010, Kaneko *et al.* 2015). The key methods of enhancing learners' confidence include: (1) stating learning requirements and expectations in the very beginning in the learning process. This could allow learners to estimate the amount of time and effort they are required to put into learning, and this, in turn, makes learners feel more inclined to put forth that effort; (2) facilitating learners in self-growth through creating small steps to success and immediately show them their progress in the learning process. This would motivate learners by helping them believe that they have capacity for working on their own way and achieving small milestones in the process of working towards the terminal learning goals; (3) providing learners with constructive feedback and positive reinforcement, which could not simply encourage learners to proceed with confidence to the next learning activity; and (4) offering learners some degree of control over the learning process. This could not simply give learners a sense of independence, but make them feel in control of their own success. Since making learners feel responsible for their own learning, they are more likely to get engaged in the learning process (Pappas 2015).

'Satisfaction' is the last component in the ARCS motivation model. The ARCS motivation model emphasises a direct link between satisfaction and level of motivation, either intrinsic or extrinsic. That is, learners are more motivated not simply when feeling satisfied with or proud of their achievements, but when provided with the rewards for their correct actions and efforts throughout the learning process (Kaneko *et al.* 2015, Pappas 2015). The key methods of increasing learners' levels of satisfaction are as follows: (1) offering learners praise or a sense of accomplishment, and this could also allow them to recognise efforts and time they have devoted to their progress in the leaning process; and (2) providing learners with the opportunities to successfully employ the new knowledge and skills they have acquired in real lives. This may offer learners inner satisfaction by making them feel as if the skills or content which they are mastering will be worthwhile and useful in the future.

3. METHODOLOGY

In order to explore and evaluate the wholeness of the specific game-based interactive picture book, a case study approach was used in this research. Purposeful sampling was applied to ensure that 11 subjects selected for the present research were familiar with using motion-sensing and game-based interactive picture books. Self-completion questionnaires and semi-structured interviews served as the main research tools in this research for gathering quantitative and qualitative data from a total of eleven 12-year-old primary school students. It took approximately two months to gain the responses to the questionnaires and interviews, during which time the quantitative results from the questionnaires were analysed preliminarily. For the purpose of the present research, the questionnaire was designed for focusing on four main issues as follows: students' responses to attention, relevance, confidence and satisfaction strategies (ARCS) used in the game-based interactive picture book. Based on the four issues, the questionnaire was organised into four sections, together with a total of 16 statements (closed questions). All statements asked research subjects to agree or disagree by marking a six-level answer scale. All responses to the statements with a six-level answer scale were translated into scores. For example, the answer list had six choices: very strongly disagree, strongly disagree, disagree, agree, strongly agree and very strongly agree, with each represented by a corresponding score 1, 2, 3, 4, 5 and 6 to assist with the interpretation of results during the process of the data analysis.

As regards the follow-up interviews, data was gathered from five 12-year-old primary school students who completed the questionnaire. Through referring to the work by Miles and Huberman (1994), Qualitative Data Analysis, the procedures for analysing the interview data within this research included three stages as follows: (1) reducing the data: the interview transcripts were read several times to identify and underlined the key themes which emerged in the interview phase; (2) displaying the data: the recurring themes marked in the first stage were recognised, and then, the interconnections between the underlying themes and research questions were identified; and (3) drawing the conclusion: the detailed data directly related to the underlying themes based on stage two were discussed and presented. Through analysing both quantitative and qualitative data, the results were used not only for triangulating each other, but also for generating answers to the research questions.

The specific game-based interactive picture book used for this research was designed and developed our research team. The content and interface of the game-based interactive picture book were presented as follows:

Figure 1. The cover and content of the game-based interactive picture book

Figure 2. The main characters within the game-based interactive picture book

Figure 3. The interface of the game-based interactive picture book

4. FINDINGS

4.1 Attention Strategies Used in the Interactive Picture Book

In the questionnaire phase, statements A.1-A.4 were designed for examining the students' opinions on attention strategies used in the interactive picture book. Totalling all questionnaire responses to 4 statements, the overwhelming majority (95%) fell within three levels from 'agree' to 'very strongly agree', with an overall mean of 4.70 (at the level of 'strongly agree'). Based on these figures, there was a strong tendency reflecting that the respondents' opinions on attention strategies used in the interactive picture book were positive.

Table 1. Students' responses to attention strategies used in the interactive picture book (n=11)

Attention strategies used in this interactive picture book.			Very Strongly Agree (score 6)	Strongly Agree (score 5)	Agree (score 4)	Disagree (score 3)	Strongly Disagree (score 2)	Very Strongly Disagree (score 1)	Mean	SD	General overview
A-1.	The environmental story in this interactive picture book stimulates my motivation for exploration.	n	0	3	7	1	0	0	4.18	0.57	Agree
		%	0%	27%	64%	9%	0%	0%			
A-2.	All story-driven games in this interactive picture book catch my attention.	n	4	5	2	0	0	0	5.18	0.72	Strongly Agree
		%	36%	45%	18%	0%	0%	0%			
A-3.	In order to accomplish the tasks of the games, I become more focused on the environmental story in this interactive picture book.	n	0	6	4	1	0	0	4.45	0.66	Agree
		%	0%	55%	36%	9%	0%	0%			
A-4.	The characters and scenes in this interactive picture book attract my attention.	n	3	5	3	0	0	0	5.00	0.74	Strongly Agree
		%	27%	45%	27%	0%	0%	0%			
Total response to statement A.1-A.4			16%	43%	36%	5%	0%	0%	4.70	0.79	Strongly Agree

In analysing all answers in detail, 2 statements were rated particularly highly. These were statement A.2 (all story-driven games in this interactive picture book catch my attention) and statement A.4 (the characters and scenes in this interactive picture book attract my attention). General overviews of all responses to statement A.2 and to statement A.4 were classed as the level of 'strongly agree'. These statements attracted 100% positive responses, over 70% of which fell within two levels from 'very strongly agree' to 'strongly agree'. Importantly, statement A.2 received the top individual mean of 5.18. On this basis, it could be said that the story-driven games in the interactive picture book were able to draw the students' attention. Statement A.4 was ranked the second highest in the list of individual means. This result reflected that most students agreed that the characters and scenes in this interactive picture book were attractive. Compared with the above statements, statement A.1 (the environmental story in this interactive picture book stimulates my motivation for exploration) and statement A.3 (in order to accomplish the tasks of the games, I become more focused on the environmental story in this interactive picture book) were ranked slightly lower. Even so, the general overview of the responses to these statements was still relatively positive, with a 95% approval rating. Therefore, it appeared that attention strategies used in the interactive picture book were beneficial for student learning.

Corresponding to the questionnaire results, a particularly strong theme which emerged in the interview phase was that the students generally thought that the content in the interactive picture book was attractive. All students who were interviewed expressed the same views, arguing that they felt interested in the story-driven games. Despite these positive responses, one out of five interviewees did not think his interests in game playing made him pay more attention to the game-related learning content in the interactive picture book. For example, the interviewee said that "I enjoy the games in this picture book, but I do not enjoy reading…I am not interested in the knowledge or issues involving environmental protection".

4.2 Relevance Strategies Used in the Interactive Picture Book

Statements R.1-R.4 in the questionnaires were designed for exploring the students' views on relevance strategies used in the interactive picture book. The overall mean gained from the questionnaire responses to the 4 statements was 4.43 which was categorised as the level of 'agree'. In addition, around 82% of the responses were found to be positive. Based on these figures, the students generally held highly positive attitudes towards relevance strategies used in the interactive picture book.

Table 2. Students' responses to relevance strategies used in the interactive picture book (n=11)

Relevance strategies used in this interactive picture book.			Very Strongly Agree (score 6)	Strongly Agree (score 5)	Agree (score 4)	Disagree (score 3)	Strongly Disagree (score 2)	Very Strongly Disagree (score 1)	Mean	SD	General overview
R-1.	The learning content of the interactive picture book increases my awareness and knowledge of environmental issues.	n	3	6	2	0	0	0	5.09	0.67	Strongly Agree
		%	27%	55%	18%	0%	0%	0%			
R-2.	I am able to present the environmental knowledge I learned from this interactive picture book.	n	0	1	4	5	1	0	3.45	0.78	Disagree
		%	0%	9%	36%	45%	9%	0%			
R-3.	The environmental story in this interactive picture book is related to my daily lives.	n	0	4	5	2	0	0	4.18	0.72	Agree
		%	0%	36%	45%	18%	0%	0%			
R-4.	The environmental story in this interactive picture book is related to my previous experience.	n	3	5	3	0	0	0	5.00	0.74	Strongly Agree
		%	27%	45%	27%	0%	0%	0%			
Total response to statement R.1-R.4			14%	36%	32%	16%	2%	0%	4.43	0.99	Agree

Detailed responses to the 4 statements are presented as follows. In examining the responses to statement R.3 (the environmental story in this interactive picture book is related to my daily lives), there was a high proportion (82%) of agreement and the general overview of all responses was classed as the level of 'agree'. More specifically, statement R.1 (the learning content of the interactive picture book increases my awareness and knowledge of environmental issues) was rated even higher, with a 100% approval rating. In addition, the general overview of the responses to this statement was at the level of 'strongly agree'. Another 100% approval rating was for statement R.4 (the environmental story in this interactive picture book is related to my previous experience), on which the general overview of the responses was categorised as the level of 'strongly agree'. Nevertheless, statement R.2 (I am able to present the environmental knowledge I learned from this interactive picture book) received somewhat less than half (45%) of the approval and over half (54%) of the disapproval from the respondents. Moreover, the general overview of the responses to this statement was categorised as the level of 'disagree', according to the individual mean of 3.45 which was calculated from the responses. At first sight, this general picture of the responses appeared to be a negative verdict; however, it can be considered as a source of concern. This is because the above figures – slightly more than half (54%) disagreement as well as nearly half (45%) agreement – revealed division of the students' opinions on this statement. In other words, the results, on the one hand, indicated that around half of students felt confident of presenting the environmental knowledge they learned from the interactive picture book. On the other hand, they can be interpreted as the fact that a certain percentage of the students might feel uncertain about what they learned in the interactive picture book.

Supporting the questionnaire results, data from the interviews reconfirmed that most interviewees agreed that the learning content of the interactive picture book was related to their daily lives and previous experience, to a certain degree. All students in the interview phase claimed that the environmental story in this interactive picture book allowed them to be aware of the causes and effects of environmental pollution. Interestingly, however, an interviewee, on the one hand, appreciated that he absorbed new knowledge from the interactive picture book, to a certain degree. On the other hand, he was not fully confident of showing what he learned. As the interviewee pointed out, "I know what I learned from this book; yet, I am not well-prepared to demonstrate what I learned to others"

4.3 Confidence Strategies Used in the Interactive Picture Book

Statements C.1-C.4 in the questionnaires were designed for exploring the students' views on confidence strategies used in the interactive picture book. Totalling all questionnaire responses to the 4 statements, nearly all (91%) fell within three levels from 'agree' to 'very strongly agree', with an overall mean of 5.05 (at the level of 'strongly agree'). Based on these figures, confidence strategies used in the interactive picture book appeared to be helpful for student learning.

Table 3. Students' responses to confidence strategies used in the interactive picture book (n=11)

Confidence strategies used in this interactive picture book.			Very Strongly Agree (score 6)	Strongly Agree (score 5)	Agree (score 4)	Disagree (score 3)	Strongly Disagree (score 2)	Very Strongly Disagree (score 1)	Mean	SD	General overview
C-1.	I feel confident of having ability to acquire environmental knowledge in this interactive picture book.	n	3	6	1	1	0	0	5.00	0.85	Strongly Agree
		%	27%	55%	9%	9%	0%	0%			
C-2.	I feel confident of having ability to get through the story-driven games in this interactive picture book.	n	2	6	2	1	0	0	4.82	0.83	Strongly Agree
		%	18%	55%	18%	9%	0%	0%			
C-3.	I am able to use and read this interactive picture book on my own.	n	6	3	1	1	0	0	5.27	0.96	Strongly Agree
		%	55%	27%	9%	9%	0%	0%			
C-4.	Due to my efforts, I was able to successfully get through the story-driven games in this interactive picture book.	n	4	5	1	1	0	0	5.09	0.90	Strongly Agree
		%	36%	45%	9%	9%	0%	0%			
Total response to statement C.1-C.4			34%	41%	11%	9%	0%	0%	5.05	0.90	Strongly Agree

Having an insight into the data gained from the 4 statements, the students' opinions were found to be relatively positive. As the results reported, statement C.1 (I feel confident of having ability to acquire environmental knowledge in this interactive picture book), statement C.2 (I feel confident of having ability to get through the story-driven games in this interactive picture book), statement C.3 (I am able to use and read this interactive picture book on my own) and statement C.4 (due to my efforts, I was able to successfully get through the story-driven games in this interactive picture book) received a 91% approval rating and gained the general overview of the responses at the level of 'strongly agree'. Importantly, over half (55%) of the responses to statement C.3 were categorised as the level of 'very strongly agree'. Moreover, this statement was ranked the highest in the list of individual means (5.27).

This result reflected that most students had no difficulties in reading the interactive picture book without help. According to the interview data, the students seemed to have confidence not only in getting through the story-driven games in the interactive picture book, but in reading through this book without help. That is, it could be said that this interactive picture book was reader-friendly for the students within this study.

4.4 Satisfaction Strategies Used in the Interactive Picture Book

Statements S.1-S.4 which inquired into the students' views on satisfaction strategies used in the interactive picture book. Totalling all responses, the majority were found to be positive, based on an 86% approval rating and an overall mean of 4.75, which was categorised as the level of 'strongly agree'. These findings could be summarised as saying that the students tended to feel satisfied with the learning content in the interactive picture book.

In examining the responses to statement S.3 (I am pleased to successfully get through the story-driven games in this interactive picture book), a 76% approval rating and the general overview of all responses was classed as the level of 'agree'. Apart from this, in terms of statement S.1 (I enjoy using and reading this interactive picture book, and feel willing to use it) and statement S.4 (All story-driven games in this interactive picture book are interesting), there was a higher approval rating (91%) and the general overview of the responses to both statements fell into 'strongly agree'. More specifically, statement S.2 (I feel satisfied with what I learned from this interactive picture book) was rated even higher, with a 100% approval rating. In addition, the general overview of the responses to this statement was at the level of 'strongly agree'. Echoing the findings from the questionnaires, all students in the interviews enjoyed using this specific interactive picture book, even though some tasks within the story-driven games were challenging.

The interviewees also agreed that most tasks within the games fit well with the learning content of the interactive picture book. These findings can be evidenced by the following extracts from the interviewees' responses: "actually, I failed to get through all tasks presented in the end of the games. Yet, I am willing to read through this book again, and try to complete each task of the games". "I like this interactive picture book. I was excited at playing the game in this book, and I succeeded in getting through nearly all tasks of the game...I enjoy using this book, and would to spend more time reading it".

5. DISSCUSSION

Whereas generalisations are impossible from the results of one case study, interesting issues can emerge. In terms of attention strategies used in the interactive picture book, it was clear that the evidence reinforced the arguments by Keller (2011) that providing games and challenging tasks in the learning process are highly likely to stimulate learners' inquiry arousal. This, in turn, could be useful for drawing learners' attention. Furthermore, it is apparent that the tasks concerning the learning content (i.e. story-driven games in the picture book) seemed to be essential for success in catching students' attention in the process of using the interactive picture book. On this basis, the context-based games with good story may be more attractive for students. That is, at first sight, game playing may make learning more interesting. Yet, the content and story designed in the games seemed to be at the core of promoting and sustaining students' learning motivation and attention throughout the learning process.

As regards the findings concerning relevance strategies used in the interactive picture book, the above findings reflect that the interactive picture book under study appeared to be able to establish connections of the new knowledge presented and the students' previous experiences. Furthermore, it seems that the knowledge related to students' daily life enhanced their perceptions and awareness of environmental protection. Such findings support the arguments by Kapp (2011) and Pappas (2015), who affirmed relevance or familiarity is particularly useful for provoking learners' interests by making them realise the importance and values of the new knowledge presented.

With reference to confidence and satisfaction strategies used in the interactive picture book, the evidence showed the importance of the students' confidence and satisfaction throughout the process of using the interactive book cannot be over emphasised. Similar statements were also reported in other studies (Kaneko et al. 2015, Pappas 2015). The results from the present study also reflected that the students' confidence and successful experiences in getting through the tasks in the games made them have strong willingness to use and read through the interactive book. These findings echoed the arguments by Kaneko et al. (2015), who emphasise that offering learners a sense of accomplishment could promote learners' inner satisfaction and confidence. This is highly likely not merely to enhance level of learning motivation, but to sustain learning interests.

6. CONCLUSION

To conclude, the students' high learning motivation and interest in using the interactive picture book under study was not simply the result of its entertaining games, but attention, relevance, confidence and satisfaction strategies used in the book. Although the factors which affected the students' learning motivation were not discrete but inter-related, it was evident that catching students' attention played the crucial role in the very beginning of the learning process. The finding of this study appears to reinforce the ARCS motivation model proposed by Keller, who notes the key role of attention, relevance, confidence and satisfaction in enhancing and sustaining motivation in the learning process. As with work of Qian (2014), this case study confirms that the ARCS motivation model could serve as the useful base for designing and evaluating the game-based learning system or platform.

REFERENCES

Cheng, C.H. & Su, C.H. 2012. A Game-based learning system for improving student's learning effectiveness in system analysis course. *Procedia - Social and Behavioral Sciences, 31*, pp. 669-675.

Fan, J.J. & Feng, H.Y. 2012. Study on Students' Learning Motivation of EFL in Taiwanese Vocational College. *International Journal of Learning & Development, 2*(3), pp 260-269.

Kaneko, K., Saito, Y., Nohara, Y., Kudo, E. & Yamada, M., 2015. A Game-Based Learning Environment Using the ARCS Model at a University Library. *Proceedings of the IIAI 4th International Congress on Advanced Applied Informatics (IIAI-AAI)*, IEEE, pp. 403-408.

Keller, J. M., 1983. Motivational design of instruction. In C. M. Reigeluth (Ed.), Instructional-design theories and models: An overview of their current status. Hillsdale, NJ: Lawrence Erlbaum Associates.

Keller, J. M., 2010. *Motivational design for learning and performance: The ARCS model approach*. New York: Springer.

Lin, C.H. & Liu, Z.F. 2011. A Pilot Study of Taiwan Elementary School Students Learning Motivation and Strategies in Robotics Learning. *Proceedings of the 6th International Conference on E-learning and Games, Edutainment.* Taipei, Taiwan, pp. 139-149.

Liu, T. Y., & Chu, Y. L. 2010. Using ubiquitous games in an English listening and speaking course: Impact on learning outcomes and motivation. *Computers & Education, 55*(2), pp. 630-643.

Miles, M.B. & Huberman, A.M., 1994. *Qualitative Data Analysis*. London: Sage Publications.

Noraddin, E. 2015. Three Learning Potentials in Digital Games: Perception Of Malaysian University Teachers. *The Online Journal of Distance Education and e-Learning, 3*(3), pp. 78-89.

Pappas, C., Wednesday 20 May 2015, *Instructional Design Models and Theories: Keller's ARCS Model of Motivation.* Retrieved from https://elearningindustry.com/arcs-model-of-motivation

Paras, B. & Bizzocchi, J., 2005. *Game, Motivation, and Effective Learning: An Integrated Model for Educational Game Design.* Paper presented at the Digital Games Research Association (DiGRA 2005): Changing Views: Worlds in Play, Vancouver, BC, Canada.

Qian, X., 2014. Construction and application of an educational game based on the ARCS model. *World Transactions on Engineering and Technology Education,* Vol. 12, No. 2, pp. 236-241.

Su, C.H. & Cheng, C.H., 2013. 3D game-based learning system for improving learning achievement in software engineering curriculum. *The Turkish Online Journal of Educational Technology,* Vol. 12, No. 2, pp. 1-12.

Woo, J.C., 2013. Digital game-based learning supports student motivation, cognitive success, and performance outcomes. *Educational Technology & Society,* Vol. 17, No. 3, pp. 291-307.

Ying, M.H. & Yang, K.T., 2013. A Game-based learning system using the ARCS model and fuzzy logic. *Journal of Software,* Vol. 8, No. 9, pp. 2155-2162.

A DIGITAL COOKBOOK FOR ELDERLY PEOPLE: INVESTIGATING INTERFACE CONCEPTS

Valeria Orso[1], Francesca Gullà[2], Roberto Menghi[2], Silvia Ceccacci[2], Lorenzo Cavalieri[2], Michele Germani[2] and Luciano Gamberini[1]
[1]*Department of General Psychology, University of Padova , Via Venezia 12, Padova (Italy)*
[2]*Department of Industrial Engineering and Mathematical Sciences, Università Politecnica delle Marche Via Brecce Bianche, Ancona (Italy)*

ABSTRACT

During old age, perceptual and cognitive abilities naturally decline, resulting in an increased difficulty at performing complex activities, e.g., cooking. A digital cookbook, complying with design recommendations, was designed to assist older adults in meals preparation. In particular, three versions were compared in a between-subjects experiment: one based on text, one based on text and images and one integrating text and videos. The study reports on a preliminary evaluation aiming at (a) testing the feasibility of the digital cookbook as a means for assisting older users and (b) which feature was more effective. All versions were well-received. Results from behavioral observations suggest that the image-based version was more beneficial as compared to its video-based counterpart. No differences emerged between the image-based and the text-based versions. In general, the digital cookbook proved to be an effective tool. However, the inclusion of complex multimedia materials, e.g., video tutorials, can be detrimental for healthy older users.

KEYWORDS

Older adults; touch screen interface; ageing in place

1. INTRODUCTION

A balanced and a well-integrated diet plays an important role in maintaining a good status of health and a good quality of life of individuals, especially in late years (Reedy). Nevertheless, meal preparation is a complex activity, encompassing a number of tasks, e.g., food shopping, meals planning, cleaning up after eating. Moreover, even the act of cooking a single meal requires the coordination of several actions in a precise order. Such activities tend to be concerned by the alterations of the perceptual, cognitive and motor skills that accompany the normal aging process (Visvanathan) and in some cases older adults, especially when living alone, tend to even neglect food preparation (MacIntosh C. J.). Therefore, assessing an individual's ability of taking care of the food management and preparation becomes an important indicator of his/her capability to living independently, as reported by the Instrumental Activities of Daily Living (IADL) Scale (Lawton). Given the crucial role of nutrition, numerous research works have been conducted to find strategies to empower cognitively impaired or inexperienced users in kitchen related activities. Among the different solutions proposed, digital cookbooks seem a promising tool to support them in comprehending and preparing recipes (Hayashi), (Iglesias), in planning cooking activities according to the time required by each recipe (Buykx L. a.) and in managing the personal diet (Burzagli). Such digital cookbooks have also been enriched with different multimedia contents (e.g., images, videos), in order to improve users' understanding of the recipe workflow. However, research has neglected so far older adults, addressing other target user groups (e.g., healthy or cognitively impaired young adults (Ide). In this context, our research work aims at investigating whether a digital cookbook could be an effective tool to support older adults in food preparation. In particular, with the present exploratory study, we aim to test which features embedded in a digital cookbook were favored by older users. To this end, we compared three versions of a digital cookbook, each differing in the format of the preparing instructions (summarized or detailed) and in the multimedia content embedded (none, images or videos). We expect that older adults will benefit from detailed instructions and more vivid multimedia contents (i.e., videos).

2. RESEARCH BACKGROUND

In designing a digital cookbook addressed to older adults, it is crucial to consider the perceptual and cognitive abilities of the target user group, given the well-known psychomotor and physical changes caused by the ageing process. The most evident declines entail the weakening of the perceptual abilities (e.g. visual acuity, contrast sensitivity, hearing, (McLaughlin) and sense of taste and smell (MacIntosh C. J.). As for the cognitive skills, the ability to process and manipulate short-term information generally worsens (Fisk). Moreover, there is a drop of the physical abilities due to a general loss of mass muscle and joint flexibility, resulting in an overall slowness of movement and in a loss of dexterity (Hawthorn). As a result, older adults may encounter difficulties in interacting with an interface at different levels. First, the comprehension of the navigational structure of an interface can be challenging, when too complex. Secondly, interpreting the visual and auditory elements of an interface can be hard, if such stimuli do not comply with specific characteristics. Ultimately, appropriate interaction modalities must be chosen in order to enable older adults to operate with the interface. Touch Screen Interfaces (TSI) can be considered a good solution to support age related limitations (Caprani). This implies a large screen size and big virtual button items (i.e., large enough to be pressed with a finger). In addition, TSI was found to significantly reduce anxiety toward computers (Umemuro) and to improve user performance in pointing tasks by reducing time to task as compared to keyboards and computer mouse (Iwase). Older adults prefer to use touchscreen compared to physical keypad (Motti). To ensure that TSIs result accessible and usable for older users, design guidelines have been proposed based on empirical findings (Motti). Both the items within the screen and the buttons to press should be large and conspicuous, to reduce the error rate (Jin).

In this context, many research works have investigated how technology can support users in their cooking activities. Food preparation is one of the most important daily activity people perform. Although it may seem an obvious action, cooking entails different issues regarding the efficiency, the effectiveness and the task management that need to be considered. For instance, the actual accomplishment of a cooking task following a traditional textual recipe is affected by uncertainty, distraction, inefficiency, inexperience and lack of nutrition knowledge (Grimes). Even if these drawbacks are closely related to the user's background, some of the abovementioned issues are caused by the structure of the recipe itself. Many recipes have in fact non-sequential steps, others force the user to look up an action into the previous steps, and often the textual instructions are just too long. A variety of solutions have been proposed, spanning from special household appliances for older adults (Iglesias), to cookbooks addressing cognitively impaired users (Ide) or inexperienced cookers (Miyawaki). However, such examples address very specific issues and may not be generalizable. In digital cookbooks, multimedia contents have been integrated in the attempt to improve users' comprehension of the recipe workflow. Some studies focused on intelligent multimedia synthesis between the video recipe content and the textual procedures, in order to provide the user with an enhanced and integrated information about the steps to take for cooking a given meal (Hayashi). The visual feedback in the cooking workflow has been also deployed to improve the informativeness of the textual description of the current step. In addition, in the case of non-sequential steps, the visual feedback displayed the overall recipe workflow as a graph and informed the user of the correct sequence and duration of each task (Buykx L. a.). The recipe format affects the clarity, the ease of use and the understandability of the recipe itself, with the fragmentation of the instructions in simple steps benefitting the users, but not the completion time (Buykx L. b.). A different approach to overcome the issues described above entailed integrated solutions, in which the environment was augmented to guide the user, suggesting where s/he had to perform a given operation and what ingredient and instrumentation s/he had to manage at any given time (Iglesias); (Jin). Although promising, such solutions are limited to the environment and cannot be accessed by the majority of older users.

3. THE CASE STUDY

The case study is part of a larger project named Design4All. The goal of the project was to develop a home automation system able to support older adults in their daily life, including several features (e.g., environment management and household appliances control) to support older adults' management of the kitchen environment. Such features included a digital cookbook, which was aimed at monitoring and supporting a healthy diet. Here we tested whether such a tool could effectively support older adults in food preparation and which features (type of instructions and multimedia contents) were to be embedded. To this end, three versions of the cookbook were devised, each providing the same information, yet in a different format, i.e., summarized or detailed instructions, and with different multimedia features, i.e., none, images or videos. Besides the design guidelines listed above, the digital cookbook was realized to comply also with Web Content Accessibility Guidelines (World Wide Web). The 'Normal' version was designed to resemble the most common cookbooks, where information is largely based on text and the recipes are displayed all with the same structure: ingredient list, useful information and preparation instructions (Shell). Conversely, the two wizard versions were designed to provide detailed step-by-step preparation instructions with the addition of multimedia contents, i.e., images and videos (Gullà). In all of the three versions, to access a given recipe the user had to start from a home page, where s/he chose the type of meal from the menu on the left side of the page (i.e., appetizers, first course, main course, side dishes and dessert). On the central area of the interface a subset of recipes was presented, each as a large preview image of the dish and its title; by tapping on the up/down arrows on the right side of the interface the user navigated within the recipes available. To access a given recipe, the user simply tapped on the chosen recipe (Figure 1a).

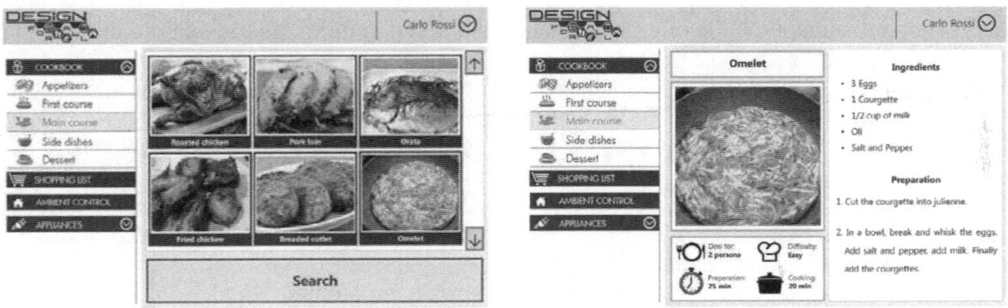

Figure 1. (a) General Home Page shared in all the three versions; (b) The ingredients and preparation instructions of the 'Normal' version of the cookbook

In the 'Normal' version of the cookbook all the information regarding both the ingredients and the preparation instructions was displayed in a single page. On the column on the left side of the interface, the general information was reported, which included a preview image, the level of difficulty and the expected preparation time. On the right side, users found the ingredients and the cooking instructions organized as an ordered list, so as to facilitate the reader (Figure 1b). The 'Wizard' versions were designed to assist the user at every step of the preparation. In particular, two versions were realized: one included images, namely 'Wizard image', and one included videos, namely 'Wizard video'. In the former, clear and explanatory images related to each step of the preparation were integrated. In the latter, to each preparation step a video was associated, so that users could learn/mimic the movements needed to accomplish each preparation step. In both cases, the image or the video preview was placed on the right side and instructions on the left side of the interface (Figure 2a, 2b). Both Wizard versions shared the same 5-phase structure: (1) Ingredients, presenting the list of ingredients needed; (2) Cooking Utensils, illustrating the utensils needed; (3) Preparation, providing preparation instructions; (4) Cooking, providing the cooking instructions; and (5) Completion, notifying the accomplishment of the preparation. To navigate within the different phases of the recipe, users had to tap on the 'Next' and 'Back' buttons, placed on the lower right and left corners of the interface, respectively. In the 'Wizard video' version, users had to tap on the video preview to play the video. The 'Wizard' interfaces were also provided with a progress bar placed horizontally at the top of the page, which allowed the user to keep track of the state of progress achieved. In addition, some pop-up elements were inserted as confirmation controls to help the user check the actual accomplishment of specific tasks (e.g., oven preheating).

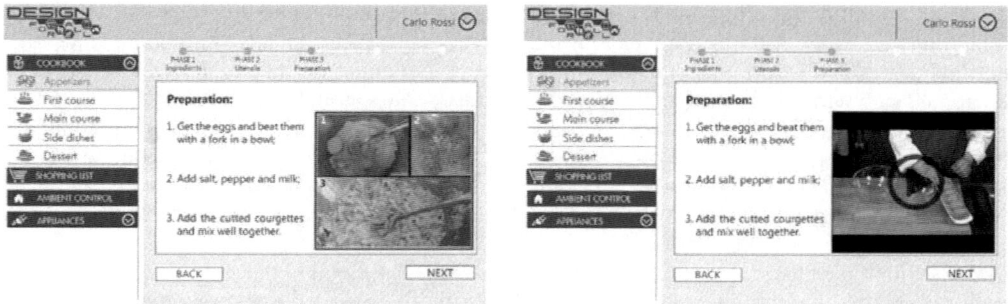

Figure 2. A view of the preparation instructions in the 'Wizard image' version (a), 'Wizard Video' version (b) of the cookbook

3.1 Materials

Participants were asked to fill in three questionnaires in total. A pre-test questionnaire was devised to collect background information (name, age, provenance and education), to assess older adults' habits in the kitchen and their cooking expertise (i.e., how often and for how many people they usually cooked, and whether they were in the habit of consulting cookbooks and of which kind). Regarding their cooking expertise, they were asked to indicate which recipe they would be able to prepare without consulting a cookbook. Participants could choose among six preparations of increasing difficulty: two options were easy to prepare (scored 1); two options were of intermediate difficulty (scored 2); and finally, two options were difficult to prepare without a cookbook (scored 3). The higher the score gained by the user, the higher was assumed his/her expertise, and was a proxy of his/her cooking abilities.

Participants were asked to undertake the Mini Mental State Examination (MMSE) to ensure that all participants were free from cognitive impairments (Folstein). A post-test questionnaire (33 items in total) was also devised to investigate aspects related to the usability and to assess the quality of the experience of use with the digital cookbook. Participants were asked to mark their level of agreement on a 6-point Likert scale. The post-experience questionnaire aimed to assess (a) the easiness of reading the textual contents, namely visual presentation (Fisk), (b) the easiness of understanding the textual contents, i.e., information clarity, (c) the organization of textual contents, i.e., information organization (Koohang), (d) the completeness of the information provided, i.e., informativeness of the interface (Han), (e) the aesthetic appeal of the interface, i.e., aesthetics (Winckler), (f) the ease of use (Han), (g) the ease of navigating within the digital cookbook, i.e., navigability (Koohang), (h) the satisfaction of use, (i) the extent to which the digital cookbook could be integrated in one's daily practices (Spagnolli), (l) the ease of learning to operate the system, i.e., learnability, (m) the usefulness of the system (Han), and (n) the overall pleasantness of use of the system (Winckler).

3.2 Equipment and Setting

The digital cookbook was presented on a Microsoft Surface Pro 2 tablet (10.6''). The whole interaction with the digital cookbook was recorded by means of a dedicated screen-recording application, i.e., Action!.Two additional video cameras (SONY handycam HDR-XR155E) were placed in the kitchen and recorded participants' actions, to allow offline computer-supported structured video-analysis.

The experiment took place in the kitchen of the lab facilities, which was set up to serve research purposes. On a large table, participants had at their disposal the tablet with the digital cookbook, the utensils and the ingredients needed in the right quantity. Participants were asked to use the oven that was already pre-heated to cook. The setting included two cameras: one was placed on the right corner of the room in front of the main table and the other one was hung on the left corner of the room frontally to the main table. The setting was maintained the same for all participants (Figure 3).

3.3 Participants

In total, 15 older adults (8 women) participated in the experiment. Overall, the mean age of the sample was 70.3 years old (SD= 7.6). At the MMSE, all the older adults involved in the study gained a score higher than the cut-off (i.e., 24/30; *M*= 29, *SD*= 1.2), indicating that all the participants did not show any evidence of cognitive decline. Each participant was randomly assigned to use one version of the cookbook. All participants used to cook on a regular basis. All participants but one had an intermediate or a high level of expertise in cooking. The majority of the participants (9) used cookbooks, eight reported to consult paper book recipes, five consulted the PC and one the tablet[1]. Participants were recruited by word of mouth and received no compensation for taking part in the experiment.

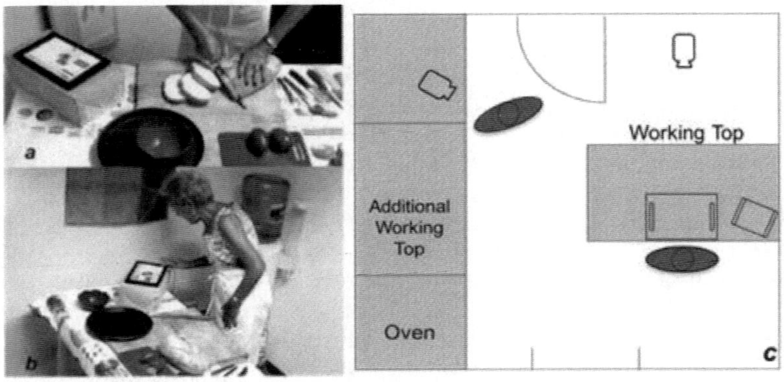

Figure 3. The experimental setting. The view of the participant from the camera placed opposite to the working top and the view of the working area from the ambient camera. A schematic representation of the kitchen set up

3.4 Procedure

Participants were welcomed in one of the laboratory facilities and were debriefed regarding the overall activity and goals. They read and signed the informed consent, the experimenter explicitly invited them to ask for any doubt at any time during the activity. Next, they were asked to fill in the pre-test questionnaire and then the experimenter administered the MMSE. The experimenter then walked the participant to the kitchen lab, where s/he was illustrated how the kitchen was set up, then participants received a hands-on explanation of how the digital cookbook was structured and how to operate it. The training phase ended when the user was able to navigate the training recipe autonomously twice in a row. Given the typical poor confidence older adults have in their abilities to interact with new technologies, this procedure was followed to prevent users experience frustration in case the interaction was not smooth (Wilkowska). The experimenter started the video-recording and the actual experimental phase began when the experimenter asked the user to prepare a given recipe. The experimental session was completed when the user thought s/he has finished and returned to the home page of the digital cookbook. Participants then filled in the post-test questionnaire. Finally, the experimenter greeted and thanked the participant, who was also given the dish s/he had prepared to take away.

4. RESULTS

In the present section, we present the results of the experiment pertaining of the older adults' performance and subjective reports. Data regarding users' performance (time to accomplish the task, number of selections and strategy of consultation) are extracted from the video-analysis carried out using The Observer XT 12 by Noldus. Self-report data are derived from participants' answers to the post-experience questionnaire.

[1] Participants could choose more than one option.

4.1 Older Adults' Cooking Performance

All participants were able to successfully accomplish the preparation of the meal required. The overall task duration (including the time spent in the actual preparation and in the consultation of the recipe) was compared across the three conditions. No statistically significant difference emerged, according to a Kruskal-Wallis test X^2= 8.82, *p*= .48. On average, users completed the task in 585.75 seconds (*SD*= 130.91, *Mnd*= 609.32) with the 'Normal' digital cookbook, in 610.66 seconds (*SD*= 345.41, *Mdn*= 719.66) with the 'Wizard image' and 536.27 seconds (*SD*= 95.15, *Mdn*= 539) with the 'Wizard video'.

In addition, it was compared the time spent by users looking at the tablet to consult the recipe on the digital cookbook between the 'Wizard image' and the 'Wizard video' versions by means of a Mann Whitney test. The analysis did not show any significant difference *U*= 10 *p*= .60. On average participants attended the tablet for 195.12 seconds (*SD*= 40.95, *Mdn*= 188.87) in the 'Wizard image' version and for 177.82 seconds (*SD*= 21.22, *Mdn*= 188.09) in the 'Wizard video' version. We compared the minimum number of selections on the interface needed to accomplish the task against the number of selections effectively made using a one-sample t-test[2]. In the 'Wizard image' version condition the average number of selections was 20.2 (*SD*= 9.25), which compared against the 14 required selections, lead to a non-significant difference, t_4= 1.49 *p*= .209. In the 'Wizard video' condition, it took on average 22.2 selections (*SD*= 2.58) to complete the tasks, which was significantly higher as compared to the 18 selections required, t_4= 3.62 *p*= .02. We noticed that, while cooking, users tended to apply different strategies for consulting the digital cookbook and for carrying out the cooking activities. Participants (4/5) using the 'Normal' version of the cookbook tended to first read all the instructions, then they started performing the first activities and then went back to the cookbook to check what they had to do next. Differently, older adults using the 'Wizard Image' version tended to follow a sequential approach, reading each step, executing the activity described and then proceeding to the next step. Only in one case a user read again the instructions to check whether s/he was doing well. When using the 'Wizard video' version, older adults tended to adopt a strategy in between the two described above: two users tended to proceed sequentially, i.e., reading each step first and executing it without reading again, while the other three tended to mainly proceed sequentially, but also to check occasionally that they were doing the right thing.

4.2 Older Adults' Subjective Reports: Findings from Questionnaires

A consolidated score was computed for all the dimensions investigated by the post-test questionnaire by averaging the scores of the items belonging to each dimension. The consolidated scores were then compared across the three versions using a Kruskal-Wallis test. The analysis did not highlight any statistically significant difference among the conditions (Table 1). In addition, the average score for each consolidated dimension was compared against the mid-point of the response scale (i.e., 3.5), which represents a neutral opinion, to assess older adults' attitude with regard of that specific dimension.

The analysis showed that all the versions of the digital cookbook were well-received by users (Table 1).

5. DISCUSSION AND CONCLUSION

In the present work, we reported on the preliminary evaluation a digital cookbook designed and developed within in a wider framework of project aimed at supporting older adults in the management of the domestic environment, especially the kitchen. The present evaluation aimed at assessing whether the digital cookbook, designed in compliance with the accessibility guidelines, was valuable in supporting older users in meal preparation and investigating what features benefitted users the most. The evaluation is based on the actual usage of the digital cookbook by a group of older adults. Our findings show that the digital cookbook was effective in supporting the accomplishment of meals preparation, as all participants could successfully complete the tasks assigned, thus confirming previous finding on cognitively impaired and inexperienced cookers (Ide). Furthermore, the digital cookbook was well-received by older adults, both referring to the

[2] In the 'Normal' version condition all of the users made 4 selections, which is exactly the number of required selections.

aspects pertaining of the system usability and experience of use, as emerged from the self-reported questionnaire. The design implication resulting from our findings is twofold. Firstly, the future development of the digital cookbook will follow a model of fragmented preparation instructions, since we found that breaking up instructions favors the sequential unfolding of the preparation activities, in line with previous findings (Buykx L. b.). Secondly, the digital cookbook will feature images as supplementary explanatory material, because they seemed to assist users in the preparation more efficiently as compared to the video features, contrary to our expectations. A number of limitations do not allow us to generalize our findings beyond preliminary concluding remarks. Firstly, the number of users involved in the present evaluation is small and calls for more thorough evaluations of the advanced version of the digital cookbook. Similarly, the preparations selected for this phase of testing were easy. This choice is motivated by the willingness not to confront older adults with multiple elements of hurdle, i.e., a difficult task and a supporting interface, whose basic components had not being tested before. Finally, the evaluation took place in the laboratory facilities and involved only a short-time interaction. Therefore, further evaluations are to be scheduled at the users' own kitchens for longer periods of interactions and to support the preparation of recipes of different levels of difficulties.

Table 1. Results from Krusall-Wallis test. For each dimension investigated in the post-experience questionnaire the mean, the standard deviation and the median are reported for the 'Normal', the 'Wizard image and the 'Wizard video' versions of the cookbook. In the last column the values of the Kruskall Wallis test are reported. *p<.05; **p<.001

	Normal		Wizard images		Wizard video		X^2
	M(SD) Mdn	t(4)	M(SD) Mdn	t(4)	M(SD) Mdn	t(4)	
Visual presentation	5.2(.66) 5.4	5.75*	4.8(.53) 4.48	5.65*	5.0(.77) 4.94	4.3*	0.78
Information clarity	5.2(.54) 5.5	7.01*	5.0(.46) 5.12	7.34*	5.1(.66) 5.14	5.4*	0.74
Information organization	5.1(.45) 5.38	8.15*	5.0(.33) 4.9	9.91**	5.2(.5) 5.17	7.4*	1.23
Informativeness	5.2(.55) 5.45	6.82*	4.9(.42) 4.82	7.61*	5.1(.64) 5.07	5.53*	1.26
Aesthetics	5.4(.54) 5	7.57*	5.6(.54) 6	8.57*	5.8(.44) 6	11.5**	1.55
Ease of use	4.7(.77) 4.7	3.32*	4.4(.83) 4.48	2.43	4.9(.81) 5.29	3.89*	1.62
Navigability	4.5(.70) 4.57	3.23*	4.4(.69) 4.52	2.9*	4.9(.69) 5.23	4.36*	1.8
Satisfaction of use	5.6(.54) 6	8.57*	4.8(1.09) 5	2.65	5.4(.54) 5	7.75*	2.21
Daily practice	5.0(.53) 4.96	6.54*	4.6(.70) 4.82	3.49*	5.1(.55) 5.13	6.54*	1.58
Learnability	5.4(.89) 6	4.75*	5.2(1.09) 6	3.47*	4.8(1.3) 5	2.22	.705
Usefulness	5.1(.60) 5.22	6.06*	4.75(.53) 4.62	5.25*	5.0(.65) 5.21	5.26*	1.14
Pleasantness	5.0(.27) 5	12.65**	5.3(.48) 5.25	8.36*	5.6(.51) 5.75	9.05*	2.87

ACKNOWLEDGEMENT

The present research study was partially funded by the project "D4All: Design for all" (CTN01_00128_297089), by the Italian Minister of University and Research, under the National Cluster Ambient Assisting Living Technologies (TAV).

REFERENCES

Buykx, L. & Petrie, H., 2012. Recipe sub-goals and graphs. *Proceedings of the ACM multimedia 2012 workshop on Multimedia for cooking and eating activities - CEA 12.*

Buykx, L. & Petrie, H., 2011. What Cooks Needs from Multimedia and Textually Enhanced Recipes. *2011 IEEE International Symposium on Multimedia.*

Burzagli, L. et al., 2014. The FOOD Project: Interacting with Distributed Intelligence in the Kitchen Environment. Universal Access in Human-Computer Interaction. Aging and Assistive Environments Lecture Notes in Computer Science, pp.463–474.

Caprani, N., E., N. & Gurri, C., 2012. Touch Screens for the Older User. *Assistive Technologies.*

Fisk, A. et al., 2009. Designing for Older Adults. Human Factors and Aging Series.

Folstein, M. F., Folstein S. E., & McHugh P. R. 1975. "Mini-mental state": a practical method for grading the cognitive state of patients for the clinician. *Journal of psychiatric research* 12(3), pp. 189-198.

Grimes, A., & Harper R. 2008. Celebratory technology: new directions for food research in HCI. *Proceedings of the SIGCHI Conference on Human Factors in Computing Systems.*

Gullà, F. et al., 2016. An adaptive smart system to foster disabled and elderly people in kitchen-related task. Proceedings of the 9th ACM International Conference on PErvasive Technologies Related to Assistive Environments - PETRA 16.

Han, S.H. et al., 2001. Usability of consumer electronic products. International Journal of Industrial Ergonomics, 28(3-4), pp.143–151.

Hawthorn, D., 2000. Possible implications of aging for interface designers. Interacting with Computers, 12(5), pp.507–528.

Hayashi, Y. et al., 2013. Automatic authoring of a domestic cooking video based on the description of cooking instructions. Proceedings of the 5th international workshop on Multimedia for cooking & eating activities - CEA 13.

Ide, I. et al., 2010. Multimedia Supplementation to a Cooking Recipe Text for Facilitating Its Understanding to Inexperienced Users. 2010 IEEE International Symposium on Multimedia.

Iglesias, R. et al., 2010. FoodManager. Proceedings of the 3rd International Conference on PErvasive Technologies Related to Assistive Environments - PETRA 10.

Iwase, H. & Murata, A., Empirical study on improvement of usability -for touch-panel for elderly - comparison of usability between touch-panel and mouse. IEEE International Conference on Systems, Man and Cybernetics.

Jin, Z.X., Plocher, T. & Kiff, L., Touch Screen User Interfaces for Older Adults: Button Size and Spacing. Lecture Notes in Computer Science Universal Acess in Human Computer Interaction. Coping with Diversity, pp.933–941.

Koohang, A. & Ondracek, J., 2005. Users views about the usability of digital libraries. British Journal of Educational Technology, 36(3), pp.407–423.

Lawton, M.P. & Brody, E.M., 1970. Assessment of Older People. Nursing Research, 19(3), p.278.

Macintosh, C., Morley, J.E. & Chapman, I.M., 2000. The anorexia of aging. Nutrition, 16(10), pp.983–995.

Miyawaki, K. et al., 2009. A cooking support system for people with higher brain dysfunction. Proceedings of the ACM multimedia 2009 workshop on Multimedia for cooking and eating activities - CEA 09.

Motti, L.G., Vigouroux, N. & Gorce, P., 2013. Interaction techniques for older adults using touchscreen devices. Proceedings of the 25th ICME conference francophone on lInteraction Homme-Machine - IHM 13.

Orso, V. et al., 2016. Interactive multimedia content for older adults: the case of SeniorChannel. Multimedia Tools and Applications, 76(4), pp.5171–5189.

Reedy, J. et al., 2014. Higher Diet Quality Is Associated with Decreased Risk of All-Cause, Cardiovascular Disease, and Cancer Mortality among Older Adults. Journal of Nutrition, 144(6), pp.881–889.

Pak, R. & Mclaughlin, A., 2010. Designing Displays for Older Adults. Human Factors and Aging Series.

Shell, J., et al. 2003. eyeCOOK: A Gaze and Speech Enabled Attentive Cookbook. *Video Proceedings of Ubiquitous Computing.*

Umemuro, H., 2004. Lowering elderly Japanese users? resistance towards computers by using touchscreen technology. Universal Access in the Information Society, 3(3-4), pp.276–288.

Visvanathan, R., Newbury J.W., & Chapman, I. 2014. Malnutrition in older people. *Geriatric Medicine: An Introduction* 4(20), pp. 216.

Wilkowska, W. & Ziefle, M., 2009. Which Factors Form Older Adults' Acceptance of Mobile Information and Communication Technologies? HCI and Usability for e-Inclusion Lecture Notes in Computer Science, pp.81–101.

Winckler, M., Bernhaupt, R. & Bach, C., 2016. Identification of UX dimensions for incident reporting systems with mobile applications in urban contexts: a longitudinal study. Cognition, Technology & Work, 18(4), pp.673–694.

Web Content Accessibility Guidelines (WCAG) 2.0. W3C. Available at: http://www.w3.org/TR/WCAG20/ [Accessed May 24, 2017].

A TABLET APPLICATION TO SUPPORT COMMUNICATION FOR PEOPLE WITH DISABILITIES

Akira Hattori[1], Kuniomi Shibata[2], and Sayaka Matsumoto[3]
[1]Department of Global Media, Komazawa University, 1-23-1 Komazawa, Setagaya-ku, Tokyo, 154-8525 Japan
[2]Graduate School of International Studies, Tsuda College, 2-1-1 Tsuda-machi, Kodaira-shi, Tokyo 187-8577, Japan
[3]Department of Social Information Studies, Otsuma Women's University, 12 Sanban-cho, Chiyoda-ku, Tokyo 102-8357, Japan

ABSTRACT

This paper presents a tablet application to support persons with disabilities, especially those with hearing disabilities and developmental disorders, in interacting with other people and in understanding and preparing for transitions between activities. They face disadvantages with respect to communication. Our tablet application recognizes words spoken by their communication partners using a speech recognition system and arranges the pictures corresponding to the speech-recognized words in a sequence. It has four functions: registering a new picture, making a sequence, browsing the sequence, and assessing user's achievement in performing the activities of a schedule. Each pictures has some tags and our tablet application searches for a picture using the tag. We developed a prototype of our table application and conducted a preliminary experiment in cooperation with Nonprofit Organization. The comments received from the experimental participants suggested that our tablet application could be useful for those who have difficulties in communication with spoken language and preparing for transitions between activities.

KEYWORDS

Tablet application; Persons with disabilities; Communication support; Speech recognition; Pictures.

1. INTRODUCTION

Some persons with disabilities face disadvantages with respect to communication. They have difficulties in interacting with other people and understanding of their speech. They also have difficulties in understanding and preparing for transitions between activities in their everyday lives. Augmentative and alternative communication (AAC) systems are used to help such persons communicate more effectively or improve their communication skills (Gonzales et al. 2009; Ganz 2014). Some of the AAC systems involve symbols and pictures, and non-electronic communication boards and printed picture cards are still commonly used. These visual supports are helpful for all age groups, from very young children to adolescents and adults (Frost 2002). A series of symbols and pictures are used as a means of depicting specific tasks in a chain of activities as well (Knight et al. 2015).

On the other hand, smartphones and tablet devices are becoming pervasive recently. Such mobile platform devices have an impact on the lives of both persons with and without disabilities (AAC-RERC 2011; McNaughton and Light 2013). Thus, it has been much attention to use them as a platform for AAC applications. McNaughton and Light (2013) discussed the potential benefits and significant challenges of mobile platform devices as a tool to enhance communication for persons with disabilities. Gosnell et al. (2011) proposed a clinical framework for selecting an appropriate application that aligns with the needs of an individual. Alliano et al. (2012) reviewed iPad applications to augment communication abilities of persons with disabilities in line with the framework. The use of them is convenient and flexible because of their portability, affordability, and social acceptance. However, there is little understanding of its efficacy in the communication of persons with disabilities (McNaughton and Light 2013). Therefore, it is significant to investigate this efficacy.

The purpose of this paper is to present a mobile platform application to support persons with disabilities, especially those with hearing disabilities and developmental disorders, in communicating with other people and in understanding and preparing for transitions between activities. Our application recognizes words spoken by communication partners and searches for pictures, which are pictograms and photographs, corresponding to the recognized words. It arranges the pictures in a sequence. Conversations while pointing to the sequence could help persons with disabilities to communicate with other people and to understand and prepare for transitions between activities. We conducted a preliminary experiment in cooperation with Nonprofit Organization (NPO).

2. RELATED WORK

In recent years, the use of mobile platform devices such as smartphones and tablets has attracted great attention in the field of ACC. As far as we know, a few studies have so far been made at developing a tablet application involving a sequence of pictures for persons with disabilities.

Dolic et al. (2012) examined the potential of using smartphones and tablets for symbol-based AAC and proposed a model of an adaptive symbol-based AAC application for them. The model makes it possible to adjust the display of symbols and user interface to not only the specifications of a mobile platform device but also user's capabilities and preferences. Hirotomi et al. (2014) developed a communication aid running on mobile platform devices for persons with pervasive developmental disorders to augment their understanding of conversations. This application converts spoken speech in conversations to visual symbols using a speech recognition system and the symbols are structured by 5W1H (who, when, where, what, why and how). They clarified that their application is useful through its experimental use by such persons and their caregivers. Torii et al. (2013) developed a schedule application for autistic children in order to give them an opportunity to feel a sense of accomplishment and a motive to try something by themselves. This application makes it possible for users to make a day schedule and to create detailed tasks of the schedule. To enhance their motivation, it has a function to give a token, which is a smiley stamp, to the children when they complete something. The authors introduced the application to a special support education school and showed the change of the attitudes of autistic children. Duncan and Tan (2012) proposed an application running on the iOS platform that is targeted towards autistic adults seeking employment. This application acts as their supervisors and its core is a visual schedule to make it easy to understand instructions. It uses a combination of text, symbols and pictures to show the steps of a task and the completed ones can be checked off.

Sennott and Bowker (2009) examined a mobile AAC system running on an iPhone and an iPod touch, which is called Proloquo2Go, from the viewpoint of the best practices in AAC for persons with autism spectrum disorders such as symbols, visual supports, voice output, and inclusion. As the results, they found that the application appears to be appropriate for these persons. Carlile et al. (2013) showed that a visual schedule running on an iPod, in which pictures of each leisure activity are shown together with an icon of a clock application, was effective in teaching leisure activities to children with autism. Flores et al. (2012) compared an iPad in which a communication application was installed with a non-electronic symbol-based AAC system. They found that communication behaviors of elementary school students with disabilities either increased with the use of iPad or remained at the same frequency as when using the AAC system, which means that the use of an iPad did not detract from communication of such children. Kagohara et al. (2013) conducted a systematic review of empirical studies that involved tablet devices in teaching programs for persons with developmental disabilities. They showed that such devices were viable technological aids for these persons in a variety of domains such as academic, communication and employment.

In comparison with these existing applications, our application is characterized by extracting users' communication in real time and showing the situation by the pictures corresponding to the conversation.

3. OUR TABLET APPLICATION

3.1 Features and system architecture

It is common practice to use symbols and pictures as a means of supporting persons with disabilities in communicating and in understanding and preparing for transitions between activities. However, it is difficult or troublesome to always carry non-electronic communication boards and printed picture cards about and to prepare such cards. The application we propose is characterized by being able to use it in daily lives because it runs on a tablet device. Mainstream tablets have more potential to be used as a non-dedicated AAC device than smartphones because of their screen sizes (Dolic et al. 2012). This is why we use tablets as a mobile platform device. This application is also characterized by showing topics of a conversation or activities within a schedule with a sequence of pictures.

Figure 1 depicts a conceptual image of our tablet application. Users of the application are persons with disabilities and their communication partners. The latter are hearing persons. By showing a sequence of the pictures corresponding to a conversation, out tablet application makes it possible for persons with disabilities to share comprehension with their communication partners in order to understand the topics of the conversation. This leads to support for their communication. Users can save a sequence. They can also set a time and location for the sequence to use it as a schedule. Our tablet application uses pictures stored in a tablet device on which it is running. It also makes use of the functionality of the device. It has a communication mode and a schedule mode. The former helps persons with disabilities to communicate with other people and the latter does them to understand and prepare for transitions between activities. In the communication mode, our tablet application recognizes words spoken by communication partners and search for the pictures corresponding to the recognized words. Users can make a brief sentence by arranging such pictures in a sequence and have a conversation while pointing to the sequence. They can save and use the sequence as a record of the conversation. In the schedule mode, they can make a schedule for the date by arranging pictures in the same manner.

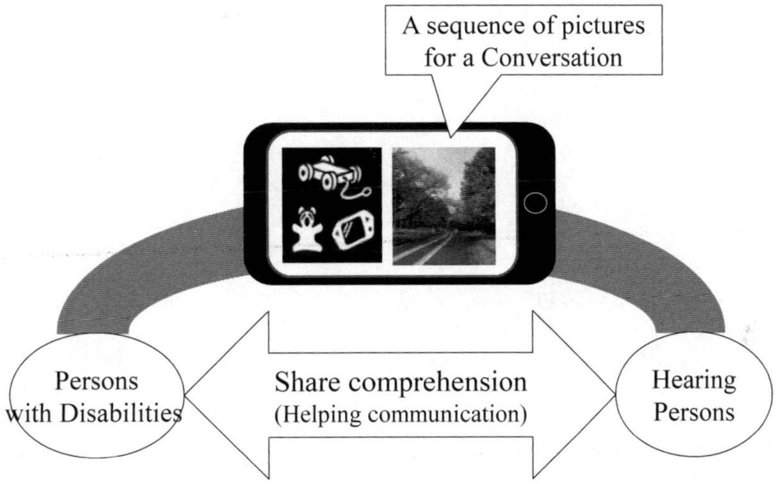

Figure 1. Concept of our application

Figure 2 indicates the structure of our tablet application. It consists of four functions. They are to register a new picture, to make a sequence, to browse the sequence, and to assess user's achievement in performing the activities of a schedule. Our tablet application uses a camera, a speech recognition system and a location service on a tablet device. It locates the place where the activities of a schedule are performed on a map that is obtained from a web mapping service. The database is organized into four tables. Two of them are for managing pictures and the other two are for managing sequences. One of the two tables for pictures stores the names of their image files and the other stores the tags assigned to them. Our tablet application searches for pictures with the same tag as the speech-recognized word. One of the two tables for sequences stores their titles, time and locations and the other stores the pictures and their order contained in each of the sequences.

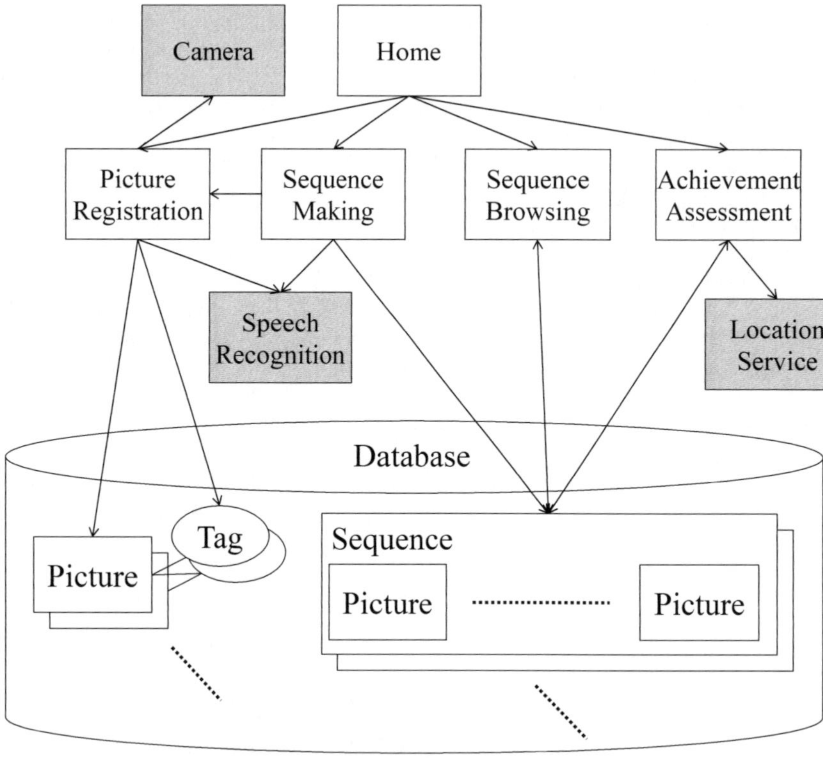

Figure 2. System structure

3.2 Management of pictures

We incorporated some pictures into our tablet application in advance. To enable persons with disabilities and their communication partners to use it in their daily lives, the pictures contain daily things, for example, friend, food, greeting, hours, school, home, etc. Images of an analog clock and photographs of YUBI-MOJI (Japanese finger spell) are contained as well. Showing sign language in an animation will make it easier to understand the language than showing it with a picture. This is why we did not incorporate a photograph of sign language. In the future, we think that it is necessary to handle a video in a sequence.

We assigned tags to these pictures. However, it is impractical to incorporate all kinds of pictures that are used in conversations in advance. This is why our tablet application provides the function to register a new picture. Users are free to add photographs to meet their needs. To do that, they take a photograph on the spot using a built-in camera on their tablet devices or select one taken before. And then they tag it with a keyword. They can assign the same tag to multiple pictures and do multiple tags to a picture. With this function, they can add photographs suitable for a conversation as pictures on the spot. If a photograph is assigned with the same tag as a pictogram, it is displayed with the pictogram overlaid at its right bottom portion.

To locate the place where the activities of a schedule are performed on a map, users can also add the map image acquired from a web mapping service by using the function to register a new picture. To add a new map image, they specify its center location and input the name of the location such as a building name, a station name, etc. as a tag. The database of our tablet application stores a pair of the latitude and longitude of the specified location instead of the map image. This is because it is contrary to service agreement to save such map images to a tablet device. When displaying the map of the registered location in a sequence of pictures, our tablet application sends a pair of the latitude and longitude to the web mapping service and receives the map image of the location.

Even though our tablet application provides the function to register a new picture, it is probably that users will speak a word which has not been used as a tag of a picture. In that case, it creates a picture representing the characters of the speech-recognized word.

3.3 Making a sequence

Our tablet application recognizes words spoken by communication partners and arranges the pictures corresponding to the recognized words in a sequence. The sequence showing the topics of a conversation helps persons with disabilities to understand the conversation and the one showing a schedule assists them in understanding and preparing for transitions between the activities of the schedule. When using the schedule mode, uses specify the date when a schedule is conducted before arranging pictures. When using the communication mode, the date is set to the date when a sequence was made.

Figure 3 shows a user interface to make a sequence. It has four areas. They are to show pictures in a sequence (see (i) in the figure), to show speech-recognized words (see (ii) in the figure), to start searching for a picture (see (iii) in the figure), and to show a console menu (see (iv) in the figure). Users can enlarge a picture in a sequence. The area to show speech-recognized words consists of text-views to which the words are set. When there is no picture corresponding to a speech-recognized word, our tablet application converts the characters of the word to an image to show it in the area. They can edit the word set to a text-view to search for a picture because there may be speech recognition errors. They can also change the shown picture to another one with the same tag. The picture after the change is preferentially retrieved later.

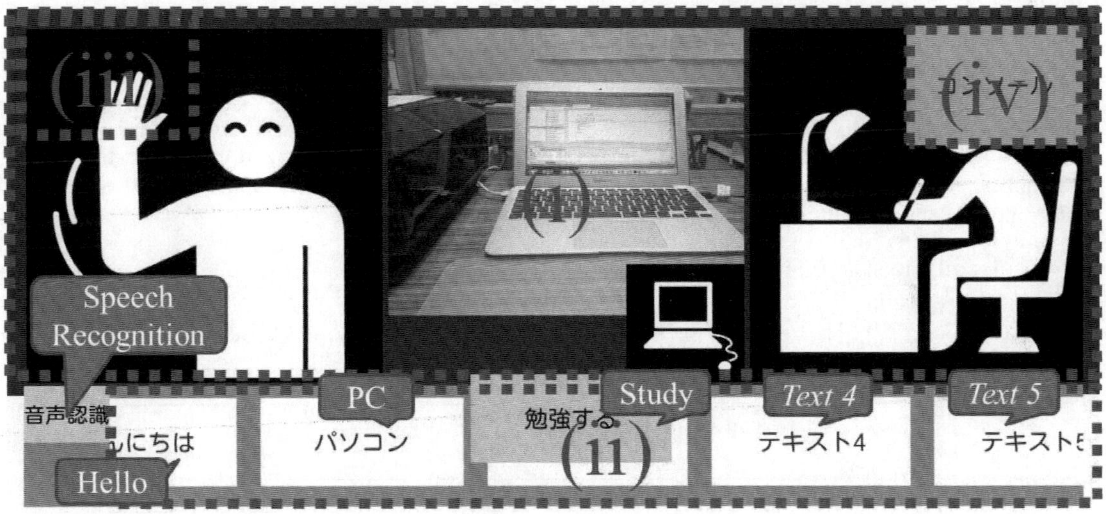

Figure 3. A user interface (the pictures in this figure correspond to "hello," "PC," "study" from left to right)

In addition, users can search for a picture by swiping a text-view with green background to which a speech-recognized word has been set toward the area to start the search. In Figure 3, they can swipe the text-view to which a word "Study" has been set. Our tablet application keeps tracking the direction to which a user is moving a text-view to calculate the cosine similarity between the vector of the moving direction and the one from the position where the user started the swipe gesture to the center of the area to start searching for a picture.

By speaking time such as 9 o'clock users can set the time to a sequence and the image of an analog clock indicating the time is shown. When a picture of a map is shown, the location is set to a sequence. In the case of the schedule mode, these time and location become to be ones of a schedule. The console menu is used to save a sequence.

3.4 Browsing a sequence

Users can browse a sequence made by them through a calendar interface. By tapping a date when they want to browse, the list of the sequences with the date is shown. By selecting one from the list, the sequence is shown. That is, the pictures contained in the sequence are displayed in the order together with the speech-recognized words. They can delete any sequences from the list. When a sequence is shown, they can delete any pictures and change the order. As to a sequence to which a location has been set, the location is displayed on a map. They can browse the sequence by tapping it on the map.

3.5 Assessing user's achievement

The function to assess users' achievement was designed to give persons with disabilities a sense of accomplishment. In our tablet application, users can input whether they performed the activities of a schedule by tapping a dedicated button when they browse the sequence. It makes it possible for them to distinguish the achieved schedule from others on a calendar and a map. Furthermore, a medal picture is added to the last of the sequence showing the achieved schedule.

In addition to the input by users themselves, our tablet application can assess their achievement. To do that, it periodically acquires location information of a tablet device through GPS and Wi-Fi, and checks whether a user was in the place where a schedule was conducted at the time. If so, it assesses that the user achieved the schedule. When users turn on this assessment function, it executes the function as a background process.

3.6 Implementation

We developed a prototype of our table application, which is running on an Android tablet device. It uses Android's speech recognition system. Figure 4 is its screen transition diagram and user interaction. Users can switch a screen by selecting an item from a console menu in a basic way. The console menu is displayed by tapping a "Console" button.

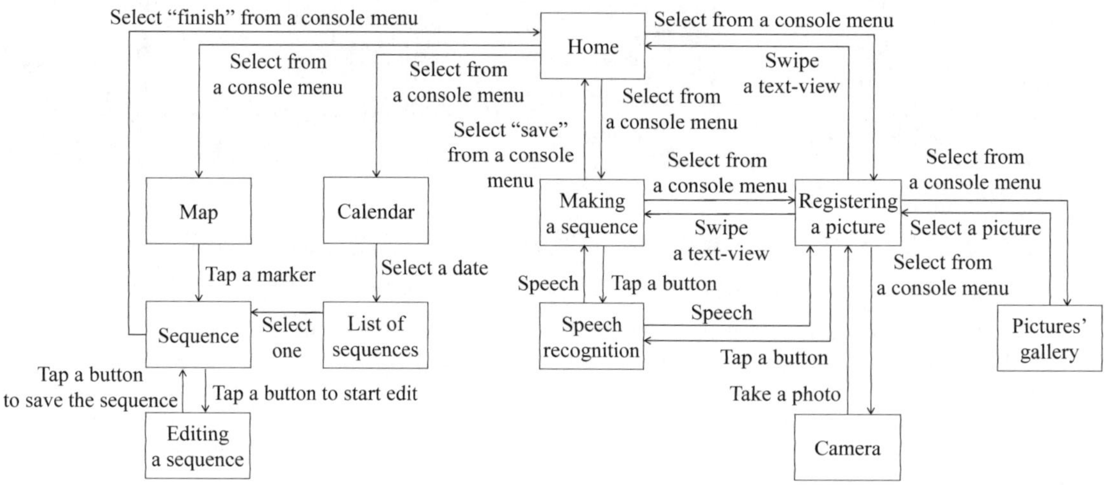

Figure 4. A screen transition diagram and user interaction of our prototype

Figure 5 is an example of a sequence containing a map, an image of an analog clock, and a picture obtained by converting the characters of a speech-recognized word to an image, which means a graduation ceremony in English. That is, the sequence is set the time and location. Figure 6 shows the function to register a new picture. The registered photograph is shown at the center of the device display (see (a) in the figure) and the tag assigned to the picture is shown in the green text-view (see (b) in the figure). When a user swipes the green text-view towards the upper-right corner of the device display (see (c) in the figure), the registration is finished and the photograph and the green-text view are undrawn. Figure 7 is a calendar interface. The number of each date shows the number of sequences of the date. The number in a parenthesis indicates the number of schedules that a user achieved at the date. Figure 8 is a map showing the locations that have been set to sequences. An icon of a medal indicates that a user achieved the schedule shown by the sequence.

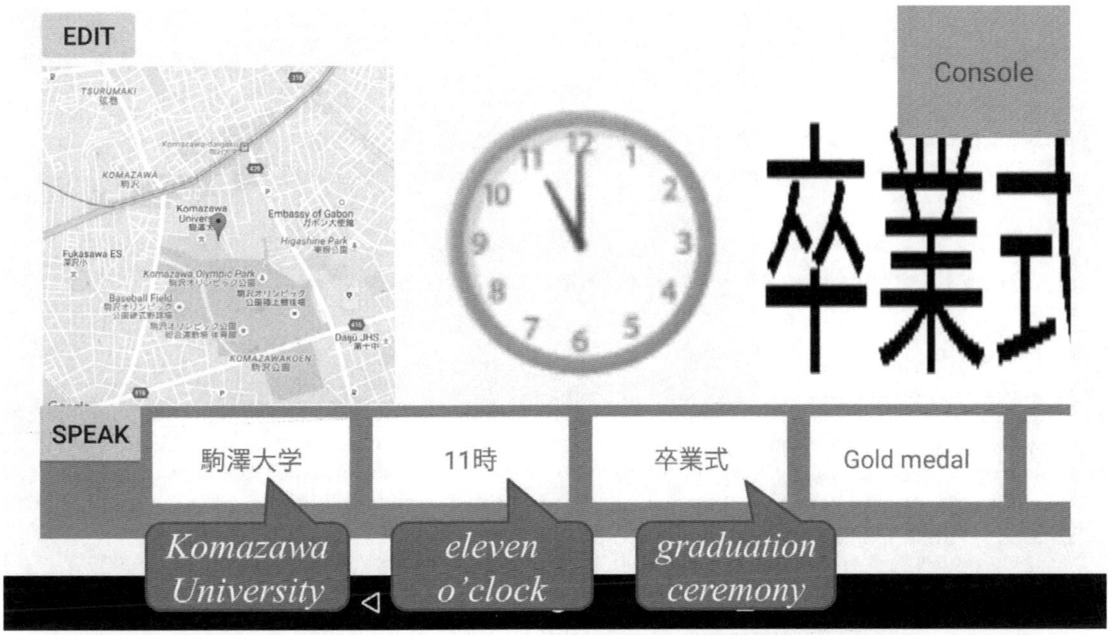

Figure 5. An example of sequence (the picture on the right side of this figure is kanji (Chinese characters) for a graduation ceremony)

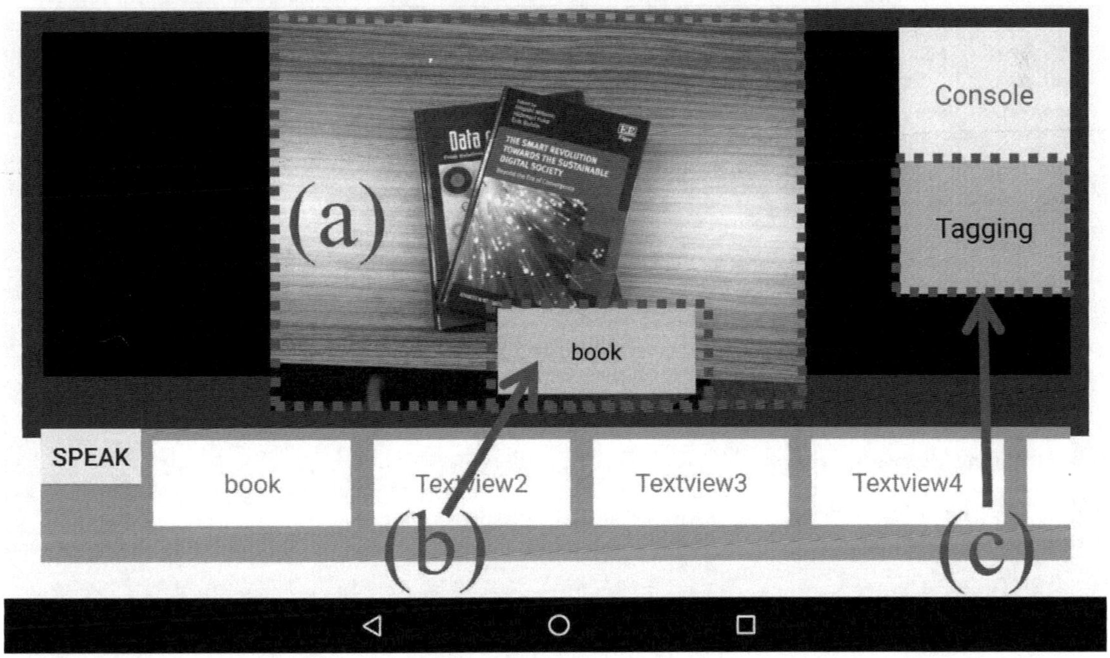

Figure 6. Picture registration

Figure 7. A calendar interface

Figure 8. A map interface

4. PRELIMINARY EXPERIMENT

4.1 Outline

Our goal is to publish our tablet application and to contribute to welfare field at home and abroad. That is why we have to increase the degree of its completion to a level where we can publish it. Therefore, we conducted a preliminary experiment in collaboration with NPO in Sendai, Japan, which is called Beat-switch. The purpose of this experiment is to evaluate its usability and usefulness and to clarify an area of improvement for future development through the trial use of the prototype.

Four persons with disabilities participated in this experiment. They all have difficulties in communicating through spoken language because of hearing disabilities or developmental disorders. Three of them are developmental disorders and the other has hearing disability and weak sight. They used a tablet device on which our tablet application was installed together with their caregivers in this experiment. They made free use of it without a specific task at home or elsewhere. All of the tablet devices were a Wi-Fi model and were set that only an icon of our tablet application was displayed on the home screens. The experimental period started on 22 July and ended on 7 September, 2015. We explained them about how to use our tablet application before they used it. We also gave them a how-to manual. Some of them used a cell phone and others used a smartphone for the main purpose of e-mail. Some of them used a personal computer at home and others used it only at the office of the NPO.

We asked them to complete a questionnaire while the experimental period. It contained questions about the usability and usefulness of our tablet application (see Table 1). They answered each question with 5 categories. To supplement the results of the questionnaire, we conducted a brief interview with them and their caregivers when collecting it.

Table 1. Questionnaire

Question 1: What do you think about the usability of our tablet application? 1: Very easy to use 2: Easy to use 3: Neither easy nor difficult 4: Difficult to use 5: Very difficult to use
Question 2: Do you think that our tablet application can be used in daily life? 1: Strongly agree 2: Agree 3: Neither agree or disagree 4: Disagree 5: Strongly disagree
Question 3: Do you think that there is the need for improvement of our tablet application? 1: Strongly agree 2: Agree 3: Neither agree or disagree 4: Disagree 5: Strongly disagree
Question 4: If the improvement is made, would you like to use our tablet application? 1: Strongly agree 2: Agree 3: Neither agree or disagree 4: Disagree 5: Strongly disagree

4.2 Results

Since the number of the participants was small in this experiment, we did not quantify the results of the questionnaire. We asked them about the reasons of the answers in the brief interview instead. We show the comments we received in the interview. The following comments suggest the usefulness of our tablet application.

-This application helped us with conversations on a daily basis.

-I often said that let's enjoy this application.

-This application was useful when I told her/him what to do next.

-The combination of the speech-recognized word and the corresponding picture was interesting.

The last comment is about the unpredictability of the tags assigned to the pictures we incorporated in advance.

On the other hand, we received the following suggestions to improve our tablet application:

-We wanted to use this application while moving, but the Internet connection often broke even though we used a mobile Wi-Fi router.

-We could not search for pictures by important words such as "father" and "work".

-We could not use this application while on the go. Because we have already the means to communicate within our home.

-It seems that it is better to use sign language videos.

-We want to make this application easier to use because we were often confused.

-A timer function such as a sand clock will probably provide more effectiveness for us.

-It would be good to be able to input that a schedule was performed when we speak specified phrases such as "well done".

Our future work includes extending our tablet application to address the problems indicated by the participants. For example, we have to consider the pictures incorporated in advance, an off-line speech recognition system, etc.

4.3 Discussion

The comments received from the experimental participants suggested that our tablet application could be effectively used when users talk about their daily lives and when they show today's activities. That is, it could be useful for those who have difficulties in communication with spoken language and preparing for transitions between activities. For example, it has a potential to encourage their engagement.

We used a speech recognition system on an Android tablet device when implementing the prototype. We cannot make use of this system off-line because it was designed on the condition that the tablet device is connected to the Internet. The experimental participants rarely used our tablet application in their home because they have their own ways or rules to communicate there. In practice, it was expected that they use it while on the go. To meet this expectation, it is necessary to introduce an off-line speech recognition system in order to use our tablet application without the Internet connection. There are also persons who cannot configure an Internet connection of their tablet devices. An off-line speech recognition system is also necessary to address this challenge.

Those who have difficulties in communication with spoken language often use their own symbols and pictures in their daily lives. Therefore, we think that it is helpful to incorporate such symbols and pictures to our tablet application easily. In fact, one of the experimental participants indicated the necessary of such a function. To meet the needs, we consider developing of the following a new function. First, users scan or take photographs of the symbols and pictures that they use in their daily lives. Second, they upload these data to a server, which we operate, and tag the photographs. Finally, they download the tagged photographs to their tablet devices to use as pictures of our tablet application.

In addition, regardless of disabilities, many of us have things that we do or have to do daily or weekly. For example, some people have breakfast every day, some people have to go to a doctor every Monday, etc. Making it possible to manage such routines will increase the effectiveness of our tablet application.

5. CONCLUSION

In this paper, we described a tablet application to support persons with disabilities in communicating with other people and in understanding and preparing for transitions between activities. It recognizes words spoken by their communication partners and arranges the pictures corresponding to the speech-recognized words in a sequence. As the results of the preliminary experiment in which four persons with hearing disabilities and developmental disorders and their caregivers participated, we found that it could promote their communication with other people. However, we need to extend its functionality based on the suggestions from the experimental participants. For example, introduction of an off-line speech recognition system would make it available anywhere that communications occur. Publishing it will provide more challenges to us. It is also necessary to further investigate its potential and problems by conducting a long-term experiment. We will make concerted efforts to further develop our tablet application.

REFERENCES

AAC-RERC, 2011. MOBILE DEVICES & COMMUNICATION APPS. *An AAC-RERC White Paper*. Available at: http://aac-rerc.psu.edu/index.php/pages/show/id/46 [Accessed 29 Jan. 2017].

Alliano, A., et al, 2012. A Review of 21 iPad Applications for Augmentative and Alternative Communication Purposes. *Perspectives on Augmentative and Alternative Communication*, Vol. 21, No. 2, pp. 60-71.

Carlile, K., et al, 2013. Using Activity Schedules on the iPod touch to Teach Leisure Skills to Children with Autism. *Education and Treatment of Children*, Vol. 36, No. 2, pp. 33-57.

Dolic, J., et al, 2012. Evaluation of Mainstream Tablet Devices for Symbol Based AAC Communication. *Agent and Multi-Agent Systems. Technologies and Applications: 6th KES International Conference*. Dubrovnik, Croatia, pp. 251-260.

Duncan, H. and Tan, J., 2012. A Visual Task Manager Application for Individuals with Autism. *J. Comput. Sci. Coll.*, Vol. 27, No. 6, pp. 49-57.

Flores, M., et al, 2012. A Comparison of Communication Using the Apple iPad and a Picture-based System. *Augmentative and Alternative Communication*, Vol. 28, No. 2, pp. 74-84.

Frost, L., 2002. The Picture Exchange Communication System. *Perspectives on Language Learning and Education*, Vol. 9, No. 2, pp. 13-16.

Ganz, J., 2014. Aided Augmentative and Alternative Communication: An Overview. *Aided Augmentative Communication for Individuals with Autism Spectrum Disorders*, pp. 13-30.

Gonzales, C. et al, 2009. Augmentative and Alternative Communication Technologies. *Handbook of Research on Developments in E-Health and Telemedicine: Technological and Social Perspectives*, pp. 1070-1087.

Gosnell, J., et al, 2011. Using a Clinical Approach To Answer "What Communication Apps Should We Use?". *Perspectives on Augmentative and Alternative Communication*, Vol. 20, No. 3, pp. 87-96.

Hirotomi, T., et al, 2014. A Communication Aid for People with Pervasive Developmental Disorders to Augment the Understanding of Messages. *The IEICE transactions on information and systems (Japanese edition)*, Vol. 97, No. 1, pp. 117-125.

Kagohara, D., et al, 2013. Using iPods and iPads in teaching programs for individuals with developmental disabilities: A systematic review. *Research in Developmental Disabilities*, Vol. 34, No. 1, pp. 147-156.

Knight, V., et al, 2015. Evaluating Visual Activity Schedules as Evidence-Based Practice for Individuals with Autism Spectrum Disorders. *Journal of Autism and Developmental Disorders*, Vol. 45, No. 1, pp. 157-178.

McNaughton, D. and Light, J., 2013. The iPad and Mobile Technology Revolution: Benefits and Challenges for Individuals who require Augmentative and Alternative Communication. *Augmentative and Alternative Communication*, Vol. 29, No. 2, pp. 107-116.

Sennott, S. and Bowkertitle, A., 2009. Autism, AAC, and Proloquo2Go. *Perspectives on Augmentative and Alternative Communication*, Vol.18, pp.137-145.

Torii, I., et al, 2013. Study and Development of Schedule Application for Autistic Children. *2013 Second IIAI International Conference on Advanced Applied Informatics*. Los Alamitos, USA pp. 251-255.

INVESTIGATING THE INFLUENCE OF PRODUCT REPRESENTATION FORMATS IN A USER EXPERIENCE EVALUATION

Ingrid M. Pettersson[1], Dimitrios Gkouskos[2] and I.C. MariAnne Karlsson[3]
[1]*Design & Human Factors, Chalmers University of Technology, SE-412 96 Gothenburg, Sweden*
and
Volvo Car Cooperation, SE-405 31 Gothenburg, Sweden
[2]*School of Arts and Communication, Malmø University, SE-205 06 Malmø*
[3]*Design & Human Factors, Chalmers University of Technology, SE-412 96 Gothenburg, Sweden*

ABSTRACT

Knowledge is lacking on the choice and use of representations in a design process when seeking to investigate user experiences. Two types of representations (a storyboard and an interactive prototype) of the same system were employed in a user experience evaluation to investigate how different representation formats influence participants' responses to interactive systems. The interactive prototype gave rise to more design proposals as well as more personal reflections on experiences although with a focus on interface design details. The storyboard elicited more responses on the core ideas of the concept, but less grounded in reflections on personal use. The differences are attributed to how each representation managed to convey interactivity and context, resulting in differences in experienced agency. There is a need for further research, but with less focus on the type of system representation and more focus on how the content and affordances of system representations can be designed to elicit rich and personal reflections on user experience in early design phases.

KEYWORDS

Prototyping; user experience; storyboard; infotainment; representations; user study

1. INTRODUCTION

1.1 Background

User Experience (UX) has evolved from traditional usability to include also aesthetics (Alben, 1996), hedonic qualities such as stimulation, identification and evocation [Hassenzahl, 2004] as well as contextual (in terms of place), social and temporal aspects of use (Bargas-Avila & Hornbaek, 2011; Forlizzi & Battarbee, 2004; Hassenzahl & Tractinsky, 2006, Pettersson 2016). At the same time as this creates opportunities for innovative design it also leads methodological challenges when planning and conducting studies to generate in-depth understanding of users' needs and requirements as well as when choosing the methodology to evaluate designs from a UX perspective. Several studies have found that both academics and practitioners face difficulties when addressing UX evaluations (e.g., Kashfi et al. 2016; Law, 2011; Vermeeren et al., 2010) in particular in early design phases (e.g., Roto et al. 2009; Vermeeren et al. 2010). Challenges include the choice of data collection methods (e.g. interviews, questionnaires, etc.), participants (e.g. end users, experts, individual, groups) but also how to represent the concept to be evaluated (e.g. scenarios, sketches, paper, interactive prototypes, etc.). However, whereas a number of studies has investigated how the choice of product or system representations impacts the outcome of usability trials (e.g. Kim et al., 2006; Sauer et al., 2010; Sefelin et al., 2003; Virzi et al., 1996.], systematic comparisons are scarce of the influence of representations used in evaluations with a user experience focus. As user experience reaches beyond traditional usability and functionality aspects and as UX evaluations must not only address pragmatic but also for example hedonic, social and temporal aspects, the choice of system representation in UX evaluation studies is a methodological challenge that requires further consideration.

One exception from the hitherto prevailing focus on usability evaluation is Diefenbach et al. (2010), who explored differences in participants' responses to two innovative lamp concepts represented in forms of text, text+pictures, text+video, and text+real interaction (with functional prototype). Participants were assigned to one of the two concepts, each presented in one of the four different representation conditions. In this case, neither global evaluation (i.e., goodness) or high-level product perceptions (i.e., pragmatic or hedonic quality) were significantly influenced by the representation of the respective concept.

With the intention to investigate the effect of visual quality and medium on users' understanding and appreciation of a design concept, as well as of the nature of any feedback provided, Ozcelik-Buskermolen et al. (2015) presented a concept for an adaptive patient room, manipulating the representation medium (a series of stills vs. an animation) and visual quality ('sketchy' vs. 'refined'). They found that whereas medium and visual quality had no effect on participants' comprehension of the concept, or on judgements of hedonic quality or appeal, sketchy representations provided more elaborate feedback and design suggestions as well as more grounded feedback in past experiences.

A third example is a study by Sellen et al. (2009) in which users' experiences in relation to the design of an in-home technology for eldercare were investigated. The participants were randomly assigned to either viewing a video or reading a storyboard. In this case, an analysis of valence (i.e. number of positive, negative or neutral comments regarding the design idea), references to material (number of references to explain an idea etc.) and self-references (i.e. the number of times participants referred to personal preferences, traits or mention of the self) formed the basis for the comparison. No difference in valence could be noted but the study revealed that participants' responses varied based on the format of the prototype they were presented with. Storyboards elicited more self-references than videos and thus lead to more information about the participants' subjective experiences.

Given the limited studies of the influence of system representations in user studies of UX, there is a need to develop further knowledge to support the choice and use of representations in a design process when seeking to investigate user experiences, e.g. hedonic, contextual, temporal and subjective experiences.

1.2 Aim

The overall aim of the present study was to further the knowledge on how different types of system representations influence the outcome of a UX evaluation. In the particular case, the aim was to investigate what information on experiential aspects was triggered by two different types representations of the same system: a non-interactive representation - a storyboard - and an interactive prototype. Which representation conveys the intended user experiences most effectively? Is there difference in how participants respond to the idea? Considering that UX is highly subjective and contextual, is there a difference in how the participants respond and expresses emotions, contextual use and personal reflections? and As both storyboards and interactive prototypes are often used in formative stages of the design process, how do the representations differ in terms of elicited suggestions and reflections on design improvements?

2. STUDY DESIGN

In order to address the questions, a user study was completed. Most UX studies encompass the collection of qualitative data (e.g., Bargas-Avila & Hornbaek, 2011) and in the present study individual, structured interviews targeted overall personal experience, daily contextual use as well as design proposals. By analyzing the qualitative data by means of a thematic analysis, the intention was to discern differences in responses in addressing the contextual, emotional and subjective aspects of user experience, as well as the ability to provide formative feedback.

2.1 The System

A novel, inter-connected, automotive infotainment system (containing entertainment functionality, navigation and vehicle settings) was employed as case study. The concept was developed during a joint research project between industry and academia, building on research of what constitutes valuable, positive experiences in cars (Gkouskos et al., 2015), and a series of ideation workshop between interaction designers, software developers and researchers.

The system was designed in order to create some specific user experiences that were identified as valuable in the previous research; that of the car as a "caretaker", looking out for the user's well-being, and simplifying the user's daily life (Gkouskos et al., 2015). The system intended to help the user stay socially connected to others during the drive, with simplified interactions for phone calls or checking social media when standing still in a queue. The system could furthermore suggest activities and solutions to problems taking the individual user's habits and the use context into consideration, for example propose navigation routes based on travel habits or send a mail to colleagues if the user is delayed to a meeting. Identification with the system as well as stimulation through use were intended to be supported by the system's ability of sensing and adapting to personal needs. In addition, the system had a knob, the "zen control", that could increase or reduce the level of information in the display. This meant that the user could change information level depending upon need and situation, for example choose to get more information in a queue situation.

2.2 System Representations

The storyboard was presented in an A3 format, describing the main features of the concept narrated by a user named Susan; a middle-aged manager with husband and two teenage children, engaging in the system on the way to work (Figure 1). The interactive prototype was a touch tablet combined with a haptic rotary wheel. A number of interactions were possible to perform, such as checking mail, placing phone calls, receiving reminders, selecting suggested radio shows etc. (Figure 2).

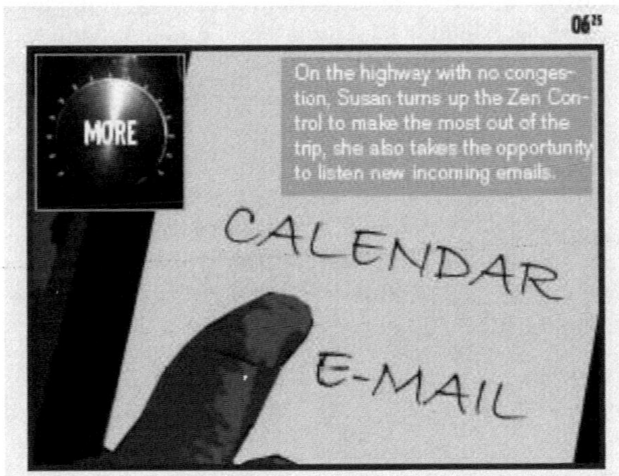

Figure 1. Part of the storyboard, illustrating the user's interaction with the system

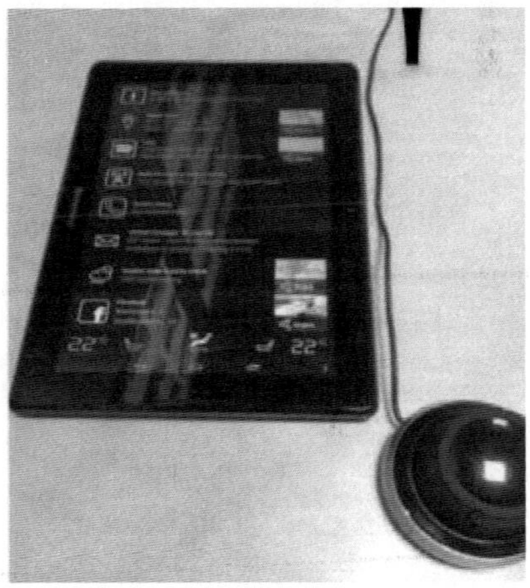

Figure 2. The interactive prototype and the haptic rotary wheel

2.3 Participants

The study encompassed altogether 24 participants, 12 men and 12 women. Their ages ranged from 24 to 53 years (average age=37). Inclusion criteria were that they had experience of car commuting and were possible adopters of the technology due to their interest in (new) technology (their self-estimated technology interest averaged 4 on a scale ranging from 1=low to 5=high).

The participants were assigned to one of two groups (group A or group B) taking into consideration age and gender (see table 1).

Table 1. Participants in Group A and Group B

	Group A	Group B
Type of representation	Storyboard	Interactive prototype
Mean age (span)	39 (24-53)	36 (24-53)
Gender (M/F)	7/5	5/7

2.4 Procedure

The evaluation sessions took place in an office environment and lasted approximately 45 minutes each. In order to form a common basis for all participants, the basic functions of the system and how it could be manipulated were first explained. The participant was then instructed to independently read the storyboard (Group A) or explore the interactive prototype (Group B) for as long as he/she desired. Typically, this took a few minutes, and a few clarifying questions were usually asked by the participant. The participants were welcome to ask questions until they felt that they had become familiarized with the system.

In the structured interview following the exploration, the same questions were posed in the same order to each participant. These questions concerned valence, i.e. the participants' impressions of the concept (positive and negative), how the participant imagined it would be like to use the system, if it would support them in daily activities, and if it fit their self-image. In addition, the participants were asked if there was anything that they would like to change about the system and its design. With the approval of participants, the sessions were audio-recorded.

2.5 Analysis

The recorded interviews were transcribed and a qualitative data analysis was performed (c.f., Miles and Huberman 1984) by the first author. This meant that the material was coded and sorted in a top-down approach into themes (i.e. contextual aspects, emotions, reflections on personal aspects, design proposals) as well as according to the specific experiences that were the intention of the concept (i.e., simplifying the daily life and routines).

3. RESULTS

In summary, the storyboard resulted in stronger emotional and overall more negative reactions to the concept whereas the interactive prototype resulted in a more positive response. Comparing the two representations, considerably more design proposals were made for the interactive prototype. More reflections on contextual use were made in regard of the storyboard, but more personal reflections were made in relation to the interactive prototype.

3.1 Group A - Storyboard

The storyboard appeared to direct the participants' attention to the core ideas of the concept in that the system's suggestions of activities and the "Zen" device controlling the level of display information were extensively discussed.

The overall perception of the system was negative and there was a general scepticism to the system detecting the user's habits and making suggestions based on these patterns. Overall, the emotional reactions were fairly strong, questioning what was perceived as an intrusiveness of the system. A typical claim was that the system would be too interfering and a loss of control was anticipated; *"It's like that Microsoft clip - annoying. I tend to like to control the interface myself"* (SB9). The participants were anxious of actions taken by the system without their control, expected to lead to stressful situations. The described system was commonly perceived as a stressor, where the pace of interactions would be decided by the system, and not the user: *"I would be stressed by it. I mean, the vehicle suggests I should do this and that...I can decide that for myself* "(SB1). That the system was not only detecting the habits of the user but also habits of family members, resulted in the system being perceived as too intrusive: *"I'm not sure I'd like the car to tell me to check on my son... It would feel strange to have a voice in the car to tell me that!"* (SB8). Thus, the design ideas that were supposed to be an aid in the user's life, were instead perceived as interfering and invasive.

The distractions that could be caused by the system during driving were frequently mentioned in the interviews. The concept was generally considered as a possible traffic safety risk, as it was perceived to potentially lure users into dangerous behaviours: *"The brain of this CEO is not focused. Maybe the system is so smart it knows what's safe... but what does it do to her? Is she able to do wise, informed decisions?"*

(SB11). However, any apprehension typically concerned other people using the system, not the participant's own use; *"I'm not sure that it should show so much information. Is it a good idea to show Facebook when driving, even when in a queue? I think it might encourage people to look at Facebook..."* (SB7). Overall, even though stories on other people's use of the system were verbalised, most participants did not appear to consider themselves as target customers for the evaluated system: *"I don't see myself as the target customer, I'm not that interested ... I don't want to be fed with info all the time. I want time for reflection."* (SB2). In summary, the storyboard respondents were less prone to see themselves as protagonists in the story and referred more to how others might use the system.

However, the storyboard evoked also positive responses and sparked reflections on, for example stimulation through use over time; *"I would play with it a bit in the beginning, to learn and to understand the system, how it talks to you and how it works ..."* (SB3). Positive comments were found in relation to the "Zen control" functionality that could control the different levels of information and therefore was perceived to increase the ease-of-use of the system. The idea of a simple turn of a knob to enable a 'calm environment' in the car was appreciated, in contrast to the stress believed to be caused by system functionality.

The design proposals that were verbalised concerned primarily the inclusion or exclusions of certain functionality, mainly referring to the distraction issues of the system. Even though the storyboard contained descriptions of many, rather detailed, interactions, the design proposals were generally on a high level of functionality; *"...I would remove it (the system) but maybe if you could project it on a head-up display in front of me and have more voice interaction ..."* (SB8). Often, design proposals concerned introducing limitations of functionality in certain situations, for example when driving over a set speed limit, certain information would be made inaccessible for users. A few proposals addressed the choice of interaction modality to reduce distraction.

3.2 Group B – Interactive Prototype

For group B using the interactive prototype, the visual aesthetics of and interactions with the system formed the main bulk of comments; *"It's quite easy to use. It's not so many steps."* (IP11) and *"It is not very intuitive to have the notification only like this in the top very small, it should appear bigger"* (IP9).

A considerable number of design proposals was put forward, describing overall rather incremental but very detailed modifications. The interactive prototype respondents reflected extensively on issues such as layout, symbols used and text size. Graphic design was, for instance an often mentioned topic: *"You should be able to make it more personal, like a personal background."* (IP4), and *"I would add information to each tile when there are fewer tiles instead of more tiles. And only allow 4 tiles maximum at the same time. 6 and 8 tiles are too much"* (IP5). Other common proposals concerned changes in input modality; "(I'd like to see) *more of the voice interactions and less of the visuals. You could have audio information about traffic jams."* (SB1).

Very little information regarding possible personal identification with the system was elicited, but if mentioned, the comments were overall positive *"I would like it very much. For me, I'm a salesman and I use my cell phone, my computer, my tablet all the time so it would fit me very good. It would fit my image."* (IP4). The participants saw themselves as the 'actors' of and with the system, and did typically not refer to how others might use the system. Previous personal experiences were reflected in relation to the system's design in terms of how it would be like to interact with the system in typical driving situations; "*This would take too long time to read while I'm driving in high speed. I had a bad experience when I was driving, may years ago, I had a phone call and I tried to get my phone out...it's not easy to get it out of the back pocket so I hit the pedestrian pavement, and that really scared me. After this experience, I started to care about these behaviours...I think for this concept, I really like this that's I can switch between the levels (shows level 3 and 4) and reduce information..."* (IP10). Temporal issues, such as getting to know the system and using it over a longer period of time, were however not addressed; comments made involved momentary aspects of interacting with and using the system.

As mentioned, many participants referred to their own previous experiences when assessing the concept, but the lack of context in the test set-up was experienced as difficult to oversee by some participants: *"It's difficult to see how it will work in a car. I would get another impression if I would be in car and interact with it, I don't have any traffic now. It's difficult to know how easy it is to see the information and react on it, when you don't have the traffic situation"* (P11).

Distraction was only mentioned by a few of the participants, and then in connection to how this could be affected by the design of the interface, including the choice of modality; *"I would take away this part (the knob); I would only use the screen. It's easier to only use the touchscreen when you're driving. I would have fewer applications to choose from to make it easier to use when driving. I just want to focus on driving, I don't want to many options"* (IP7). Control was addressed in relation to direct interactions with the systems, and on an ease-of-use level more than by questioning the system's suggestions based on user habits.

4. DISCUSSION

There are two substantial differences in how the new system was evaluated by the participants. First, there were different UX factors that surfaced in the participants' narratives in response to the respective representation; the storyboard narratives addressed mostly temporal, contextualized issues, while the interactive prototype narratives focused mostly on personal, visual and interaction issues. Second, the overall impression of the system differed; the system represented in the interactive prototype was received more positively than that in the storyboard. These differences are argued to originate from the system representation, an issue found in previous relevant work by Söderman (2001) and later by Diefenback et al. (2010) and have serious consequences for UX design that must be considered in order to plan successful UX evaluations. Design teams that aim to evaluate the UX of a design artifact must pay special attention to how the design is represented in the evaluation. As user experience is a rich, complex and diverse topic, we find it unlikely that one evaluation method can cover all of it in early design phases when no "real" contextual experience of the product is possible. Therefore, a meticulous decision must be made regarding which UX factors that would be the priority in an early evaluation. This calls for awareness of that some UX factors will be in the background and other in the foreground; the choice of representation in itself will filter out some aspects and emphasize others.

On the one hand, the interactive prototype allowed the participants to physically interact with the interface, i.e. to make choices, perform actions, receive multi-sensory input (visual, haptic, and audio), and react accordingly. As a consequence, participant responses focused on visual aesthetics and interaction properties of the prototype, instead of addressing more holistic UX aspects. The evaluation was centered around momentary experience and first impressions, rather than experience over time. However, the interactive prototype effectively elicited participants' personal reflections. The participants were able picture themselves as the user interacting with the system, and this had a direct effect on the richness of elicited user experience data as they were able to draw upon, and share, previous personal experiences that they deemed relevant. However, the participants were not sufficiently able to address contextualized use over time, in order to envision a whole experience with the (future) system.

On the other hand, the storyboard provided participants with a complete story that included context, assumed benefits, and a specified user. As a consequence, the participants focused their comments on these factors – but they did not appear to be able to identify themselves as an intended user. These results contradict previous findings that storyboards enable "*... the viewer to experience the interactions through empathizing with the character and/or the situation and reflect on the visualized situation through his/her own everyday expertise*" (van der Lelie, 2006). However, van der Lelie (2006) also argued that storyboards "*allow users to withdraw from the experience and look at the unfolding event from the outside*" which seems to have been the case for the majority of the participants in the storyboard group. The storyboard directed the participants' focus to the story, and the system's functions and interactivity were filtered through the lens of the persona's needs and actions. Hence suggestions for modifications primarily concerned these matters.

Several other studies have found differences when investigating users' more general responses to different design representations and often argue for less detailed, more 'sketchy' representations as preferred tools to elicit more user feedback, whereas more advanced representations tend to be accepted 'as is' (e.g., Ozcelik Buskermolen et al., 2015; van der Lelie, 2006). If the storyboard in this study is to be considered the less detailed, the present study does not confirm earlier research; indeed fewer design proposals were made by the storyboard group compared to the group that were allowed to interact with the interactive prototype. However, the main ideas of the concept were addressed and challenged in the participants' narratives, as compared to the more low-level comments on the interactive prototype.

Furthermore, the findings support the notion that the choice of representation is not only a matter of choosing the type of representation deemed appropriate to the stage of design process, but careful consideration must be paid to details in how the representation is designed, for example what content is included (cf. Söderman 2001) and what is not, what the representation allows to user to do and what it does not. In the case of designing storyboards for instance, Truong et al. (2006) have earlier observed that the outcome of an evaluation will be affected by the background provided, that the use of words can bias a user's response to a design and the inclusion of human actors can provide focus on the experience of application, whereas showing only the interface will result in a focus on smaller details. In our study, we observed negative reactions towards the actions of the storyboard persona, and participants had difficulties to imagine themselves using the system the way the persona used the system, whereas they could envision other people doing so. Hence, it is important to construct storyboards that allow for a greater sense of agency for participants in user studies.

No matter the representation, eliciting more in-depth data of user experience appears troublesome. The analysis of the interviews shows that the main bulk of data concerned the traditional usability aspects, such as utility and ease-of-use, an issue confirmed in previous UX research (Arhippainen 2009). Even though usability is fundamental to system design, to be able to evaluate UX in terms also of, for example aesthetic experiences, stimulation, identification, as well as contextual, social and temporal aspects of use, we see a need for more directed means to elicit UX data, not only by system representation but also by other mediating objects that can support the study participants to reflect on, for example contextual and emotional factors. Examples of this can be visual (c.f. McDonagh et al. 2002) or sensory (c.f. Isbister et al. 2007) means of expressing experiences in user studies.

In conclusion, designers that wish to evaluate UX early in a design process must be aware of which factors can be addressed as a consequence of different methodological choices, including the choice of product representation form, and be ready and willing to combine different representations in order to cover the broader aspects of UX, or at least UX factors that deemed particularly important to the design problem at hand. In our study, neither representation provided responses on the "whole" experience, something that is difficult to reproduce before the experience is actually lived by the final users. The representations can only be "rehearsals" where, in each rehearsal, different aspects of experience are highlighted and conversely other aspects are muted and fade into the background. In our case, the storyboard appeared to surface general reflections on temporal and contextual factors, whereas the interactive prototype gave rise to more personal reflections, however mostly on design details.

ACKNOWLEDGEMENTS

The authors wish to acknowledge the contributions of Mr. Sreejith Kuppattu Kalladithodi in completing the data collection and FFI for financial support.

REFERENCES

Alben, L. 1996. Quality of experience: designing the criteria for effective interaction design. *Interactions*, 3(3), pp. 11-15

Arhippainen, L. 2009. Studying user experience: Issues and problems of mobile services. Case Adamos: User Experience (Im)possible to catch? Dissertation, University of Oulu, Oulu

Bargas-Avila, J. and Hornbaek, K. 2011. Old wine in new bottles or novel challenges? A critical analysis of empirical studies of user experience. In *Proc. of SIGCHI conference on Human Factors in Computing Systems,* Vancouver, Canada, pp. 2689-2698

Diefenbach, S. et al. 2010. The impact of concept (re)presentation on users' evaluation and perception. *In Proc. NordiCHI 2010*, Reykjavik, Iceland, pp. 631-634

Forlizzi, J. and Battarbee, K. 2004. Understanding experience in interactive systems. *In Proc. DIS2004*, Cambridge, Mass, USA, pp. 261-268

Gkouskos, D., et al. 2015. Exploring User Experience in the Wild: Facets of the Modern Car. In Marcus, A. (ed): *Design, User Experience, and Usability. Design Discourse*. 4th International Conference. DUXU 2015. Los Angeles, CA, USA, Part III, pp. 450-461

Hassenzahl, M. 2004. The thing and I: understanding the relationship between user and product. Chapter 3 in *Funology. From usability to enjoyment*. Kluwer Academic Publishers, Norwell, MA, USA, pp. 31-42.

Hassenzahl, M. and Tractinsky, N. 2006. User experience - A research agenda. *Behavior & Information Technology*, 25(2), pp. 91-97

Isbister K. et al. 2007. The sensual evaluation instrument: Developing a trans-cultural self-report measure of affect, *International Journal of Human-Computer Studies*, 65(4), pp 315-328

Kashfi, P. et al. 2006. Integrating user experience practices in software development processes: Implications of subjectivity and emergent nature of UX. *arXiv preprint arXiv*:1605.03783

Kim, Y. et al. 2006. Comparative analysis of high- and low-fidelity prototypes for more valid usability evaluations of mobile devices. *In Proc. NordiCHI 2006: Changing Roles*, Oslo, Norway, pp. 291-300.

Law, E. L-C. 2011. The measurability and predictability of user experience. *Proc. EICS'11. The 3rd ACM SIGCHI symposium on engineering interactive computing systems*. Pisa, Italy, pp. 1-10.

van der Lelie, C. 2006. The value of storyboards in the product design process. *Personal and Ubiquitous Computing*, 10, pp 159–162

Lim, Y-K., et al. 2006. Comparative analysis of high-and low-fidelity prototypes for more valid usability evaluations of mobile devices. *In Proc. NordiCHI2006: Changing roles*, Oslo, Norway. pp. 291-300

McDonagh, D. et al. 2002. Visual product evaluation: exploring users' emotional relationships with products. *Applied Ergonomics*, pp. 33.3: 231-240.

Miles, M.B. and Huberman, A.M. 1984. *Qualitative data analysis*. A sourcebook of new methods. SAGE publications Inc., California.

Pettersson, I. 2016. *The temporality of in-vehicle user experience - exploring user experiences from past to future*. Chalmers University of Technology, Göteborg

Roto, V., et al. 2009. Evaluating user experience of early product concepts. *Proc. International Conference on Designing Pleasurable Products and Interfaces*, Compiegne, France, pp. 199-2008

Sauer, J. et al. 2010. The influence of user expertise and prototype fidelity in usability tests. *Applied Ergonomics* 41.1, pp. 130-140.

Sefelin, R et al. 2003. Paper prototyping - What is it good for? A comparison of paper-and computer-based low-fidelity prototyping. *Proc. CHI'2003*, Fort Lauderdale, Florida, USA, pp. 778-779

Sellen, K.M. et al. 2009. The people-prototype problem: Understanding the interaction between prototype format and user group. *In Proc. CHI2009*, Boston, Massachusetts, USA, pp. 635-638

Söderman, M. 2001. *Product representations. Exploring computer-based technologies and customers' understanding of product concepts.* PhD Dissertation. Chalmers University of Technology, Göteborg

Truong, K.N. et al. 2006. Storyboarding: An empirical determination of best practices and effective guidelines. *In Proc. DIS 2006,* University Park, Pennsylvania, USA. pp. 12-21

Vermeeren, A.P.O.S., et al. 2010. User experience evaluation methods: current state and development needs. *In Proc. NordiChi 2010,* Reykjavik, Iceland, pp. 521-530

Virzi, R.A. et al. 1996. Usability problem identification using both low- and high fidelity prototypes. *In Proc. CHI'96 The SIGCHI conference on human factors in computing systems*. Vancouver, British Columbia, Canada. pp. 236-243

Özçelik-Buskermolen, D. et al. 2015. Effect of visual quality and animation of concept representations on users' responses to early design concepts: A study on the adaptive patient room concept. *International Journal of Design*, 9 (1), pp. 91-106

COPING WITH USER DIVERSITY: UX INFORMS THE DESIGN OF A DIGITAL INTERFACE THAT ENCOURAGES SUSTAINABLE BEHAVIOUR

Ane Irizar-Arrieta and Diego Casado-Mansilla
DeustoTech-INTERNET, University of Deusto
Avenida de las Universidades, 24, 48007, Bilbao, Spain

ABSTRACT

Human factors play a key role on the improvement of energy efficiency at the workplace. However, to mitigate this recurrent issue most of the approaches rely on 'one-size-fits-all' solutions which the literature on HCI evidenced that ails addressing the user diversity in office environments. Therefore, this paper emphasises on the relevance of boosting the User Centered Design (UCD) and enriching the User Experience (UX) as pivotal means to enhance the user engagement on digital interfaces that promote sustainable behaviour at work. To accomplish this goal, a digital interface that offers a range of strategies and functions directed to the different user archetypes (user diversity) has been designed and evaluated quantitatively and qualitatively. The analysed data shed light on the relevance of enhance the UX to design positive interactions which is a predictor of future system usage and engagement. The diversity of users and the impact of the UCD on the Design for Sustainable Behaviour are discussed throughout the paper. Besides, we propose future lines of work on designing digital systems able to adapt dynamically to user profiles during its usage.

KEYWORDS

User Centered Design, User Experience, Sustainability, Interface Design, Interaction Design, Design for Sustainable Behaviour

1. INTRODUCTION

Energy waste is a major world issue that implies designing new strategies to promote sustainability initiatives. Special attention should be given to the whole lifecycle of the electronic devices and towards increasing the awareness of the citizens to reduce the energy consumption when using these devices. To maximise the latter initiative, the User-Centered perspective can be applied; overall taking into account that the human factors plays an important role on the energy consumption (Hekler et al., 2013). We understand the User Experience as a concept that embraces all aspects of the users' interaction with the product, service and company. Moreover, satisfactory UX improves the perception of the system and can be considered an indicator of a better assimilation of the pro-environmental message (Law et al., 2009).

User Centered Design (UCD) can be considered as a methodology that includes a variety of research methods that involves the user from the beginning to the end of the process, offering a wide range of design tools that aims to understand the needs of the users. Furthermore, UCD also exposes a conception around the role of the user in the design process, giving importance to all the relative aspects about the understanding of the users (i.e. their diversity and their motivations) (Abras, Maloney-Krichmar, Preece, 2004). UCD has been applied to inform the design in different areas ranging from healthcare (Sax et al., 2007) to software development (Vredenburg et al., 2002). However, to the best of our knowledge, the relation between UX, UCD methodology and the energy efficiency field has attracted little attention yet. Therefore, this paper presents the application of such HCI methods to increase the awareness of workers about the energy consumption in their environment.

Our hypothesis is that addressing the diversity of users, the positive feelings derived from the UX may encourage the predisposition towards augmenting energy awareness. To shed light on this matter, our main contribution put the focus on the user diversity through the development and evaluation of a digital interface to promote energy consumption awareness with an improved UX for every user typology. Our proposed design process pretends to evaluate the impact of the UCD on the users and to understand the possibilities of the UX as a design attribute to raise the awareness of sustainability. The paper is structured as follows: Section 2 provides a short background on interface design for sustainable behaviour. Section 3 describes the research, the design method and evaluation of the proposal. Section 4 details the main findings and the discussion, and Section 5 closes the paper with the conclusions and future work.

2. BACKGROUND

Background analysis was undertaken systematically to understand the conceptual implications that should be taken into account in order to develop successful systems based on the UCD principles.

Firstly, we reviewed the existing literature about Design for Sustainable Behaviour (DfSB, a set of design techniques developed to affect users' behaviour) (Lockton et al., 2008). Next, we put the focus on the UCD approach. Finally, the diversity of the user characterisation (i.e. user profiles) was reviewed to understand the different approaches that could be followed to offer personalised strategies to increase energy awareness.

DfSB and behaviour change has been extensively studied in the literature. Overall in the design community (Lockton et al., 2008) and in the Human Computer Interaction (Wever et al., 2008). Hekler et al. (2013) identified three broad uses of behavioural theories from HCI scholars: 1) to inform the design of technical systems; 2) to guide evaluation strategies; 3) to define target users or screen participants for evaluation studies. Hence, Hekler et al. (2013) brought about to the HCI community the necessity of designers to understand the behaviour change models studied mainly by social scientists to better generate effective strategies.

Narrowing the lenses on the HCI for sustainability, we reviewed the related work of digital interface design. Although we can assume that the following works were developed with the users in mind, there is no evidence of the use of the UCD methodology as it was defined in (Abras, Maloney-Krichmar, Preece, 2004). Two recent works in this area are highlighted: 1) *Kilowh.at*, a web based application developed to increase the energy awareness through comparisons (Hedin & Zapico, 2017). 2) Another web based application that offers to office workers persuasive techniques like online feedback self-monitoring, advices, comparison and control functions to promote the sustainability at the workplace (Yun et al., 2017).

The User-Centered research puts the focus on the knowledge extracted from the potential users. In addition, assumes the diversity of the people. Thus, the analysis of the different targets and user types is one of the first steps to develop useful interactive systems. The importance of understanding the user diversity is already explored by the literature (Coskun & Erbug. 2016). Different authors assume different dimensions of user diversity based on theoretical models or well-defined methodologies (Coskun et al., 2014; He et al., 2010; Halko & Kientz, 2010; Kaptein et al., 2008; Lockton et al., 2012). Therefore, we can find different characterisations depending of the lens used by each researcher. However, due to the lack of consensus about how to deal with diversity, we cannot consider any of them as the gold-standard to inform the classification of multi-users. Our design proposal has been implemented with features extracted from the highlighted related work. The mix of strategies proposed by Yun et al. (2017) helps to reach the different target users and complements each other. One of our contributions on top of the state of the art is the addition of control features to our digital interface. Thus, the possibility to manage remotely energy-consuming devices and appliances. Finally, the UX as a design strategy to promote the acceptance towards the interface and the provided message has been applicate. Some studies explored the theoretical implications and the need of the UCD and the UX on the design of sustainable interfaces (Haines et al., 2015; Wever et al., 2008). As commented before, we have not found any work in the corpus of literature reviewed where is included the UCD methodology as a relevant technique of the sustainable interface design. Indeed, we have not been able to find scholars relating the impact of the UX on the energy awareness of the users. Therefore, we cannot calculate yet to what extent the UCD and the UX are effective on DfSB. To try to contribute to solve this, we developed a system that faces the diversity of users through the methodology DCU, offering a desirable UX.

3. SYSTEM DESIGN

We have developed an interface following the UCD methodology and taking into account the theoretical background reviewed that involves the DfSB. The proposed interface is an early design to test the hypothesis that relate UX, user diversity and pro-environmental awareness. The steps followed based on the embraced methodology are: 1) initial research with users, 2) first Lo-Fi prototype, 3) heuristic evaluation of the first prototype, 4) Hi-Fi prototype design and 5) evaluation of the Hi-Fi prototype with users. These phases are explained below.

3.1 Early Research with Users

In the initial phase, we carried out user research with the aim of understanding the potential users' insights to extract design requirements. We ran a Focus Group (Kitzinger, 1995) with 2 groups of 6 workers each. The goal was 1) to discover the latent needs of the users in energy efficiency field (e.g. to comprehend what devices are the most used and when) and 2) to find problems that are related with energy consumption and to know the users the best as possible. In the session, we asked to the participants to rebuild their workday through pictograms and photos that showed work spaces and devices which would be potentially located in these areas (i.e. card sorting methodology). After completing this task, we introduced a set of open topics to encourage the debate and discussion about sustainability issues and energy efficiency at the workplace. Figure 1 shows the reconstruction of the workday done by a pair of users.

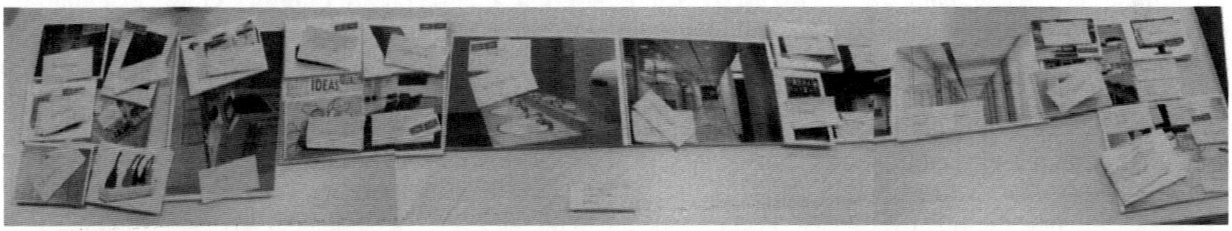

Figure 1. One of the work day reconstruction done at the Focus Group ordered as a timeline of the working day

We found first that users hold forth comparative metrics to understand their energy consumption. In addition, we discovered that simple and easy visual metaphors were preferred to visualize the information in an effective and fast way. Besides, positive reinforcement was more likely to be accepted than the negative one. Another insight extracted from the session was that the automated processes designed to improve energy efficiency should be complemented with manual control systems and that the information about systems and processes status must be shown to the users. The hybrid approach between automation and manual control was the most liked one by the users. This latter finding is in line with Casado-Mansilla's work (2016). The author found that a complete automation of the systems in favour of energy efficiency might spark a rebound effect on users causing generalised distrust on technology. Thus, preventing subjects from controlling devices and appliances is associated with a reduction of the participant's confidence in technology as a means to solve all current environmental problems.

Having obtained the initial insights, we developed *Personas* (Harley, 2015) and Scenarios (Aoyama, 2007) to visualize and understand the potential archetypes of users. Our *Personas* were implemented with attributes extracted from the user research and from the mix made from literature: the attributes based on the behaviour types (Lockton et al,. 2012) and based on the values and beliefs of the user (Petkov et al., 2011).

3.2 Design

Because of the use-context of the digital interface is the workplace, we decided to develop a web-based application. That could be consulted easily through a desktop computer. The Lo-Fi prototype of the system was developed with Balsamiq Mockups[1] on two phases. Firstly, the main system requirements were reviewed to define the functions of the interface. Secondly, the focus was put on user diversity with the application of

[1] Website of the tool used to design the first Lo-Fi prototype: https://balsamiq.com/products/mockups/

Lockton (2012) (Pinball, Shortcut and Thoughtful) and Petkov's (2012) (Egoistic, Altruistic, Biospheric and Social influence) theories. The relation between the user characterisation, and the strategies or features defined for each user type are presented in Table 1.

Table 1. Relation between user characterisation and the features developed on the interface.

User Profile	Definition	Feature
Pinball	Linear models of behaviour	Usability, plain language, automation options
Shortcut	Self-regulating models of behaviour	Comparisons between peers, public ranking, goals
Thoughtful	Learning models of behaviour	Information about energy consumption, tips, suggestions
Egoistic	Users with egoistic values	Information about the money savings
Altruistic	Users with altruistic values	Information about long term impact of the energy waste
Biospheric	Users with values related to ecosystem	Information about the impact on the animals and plants
Social influence	Users influenced by peers	Comparisons between peers, public ranking, goals.

At the Lo-Fi prototype the objective is to set up the Information Architecture of the interface and define the main elements and their placement and structure on the interface. As the first approach, all the elements of this prototype are provisional.

Following the UCD methodology, before iterating over the prototype the first evaluation should be done. For that purpose we developed a Heuristic Evaluation (Nielsen, 1994), in order to find usability errors, design problems and non-well defined aspects. We found 10 errors according to Nielsen's methodology for refinement: among them, four were not serious, five serious and one critic error. The most important errors were related to the website's navigation, correct understanding of the text tags and the coherence between the elements of the system and the information provided. Once the preliminary evaluation was finalised the next step was to iterate over the first refined version, developing a second prototype with more detail on the elements and content and implementing the improvements extracted from the Heuristic Evaluation.

The first Hi-Fi prototype was developed with Axure RP[2] software resulted on a desktop web application with all the final elements defined but with limited functionalities. The prototype is available at AxureShare[3].

In this first iteration over the Lo-Fi Prototype the main objective was to have ready the setting of the main processes to evaluate it with real users. Figure 2 shows different screenshots of the digital interface created.

Besides the homepage, the digital user interface contains four sections: Information, Control, Social and User-Settings. The Homepage shows the average of the energy consumption of the worker connected devices through colour and shape coding in the logo of the website which resembles to a tree leaf. The Information section offers information about energy efficiency through different metrics and through different content. The Information section has three subsections 1) Data: it provides concrete information on energy expenditure through different approaches. 2) Suggestions: it offers to the user ideas and tips to be more efficient through the information detected in the monitoring of the devices. 3) More Information: it shows other related complementary information such as articles, tips and other advices. The Control section is intended for the remote controlling of the appliances associated to each user. In this section the devices linked to the system are shown (e.g. thermostat as can be observed in Figure 2b). An 'Add Device' button is inserted in case there is still no linked elements or whether the user aims to link a new one. The Social section is intended to persuade a type of user whose values are closely related to the social influence, according to the defined strategy. This section offers to the user the possibility to interact with other people, add groups of friends and make comparisons with other users. The Social section also contains a sub-section relative to Friends (where the users can interact with others), another one to provide social comparison as persuasive reinforcement and finally, one subsection where users are able to track the goals and achievements on their energy performance. The last section of the interface is the User Settings. It aims to improve the UX through the customization of some elements and functions.

The design was done following the structure defined at the first Lo-Fi prototype, and refining and implementing the main elements needed in the structure. The look and feel of the interface and the visual design has been separated from the design of the prototype, with the aim of not interfering with the users at the evaluation phase. We tried to maintain the simplicity defined at previous phases, prioritizing the legibility

[2] The website of Axure RP software: https://www.axure.com/

[3] The Hi-Fi prototype can be visited here: http://wsobk2.axshare.com/ - c=2

and the understanding of the content rather than aesthetics. The typography and the iconography are the main elements of communication and the green colour is a constant that involves the interface with the sustainability concept.

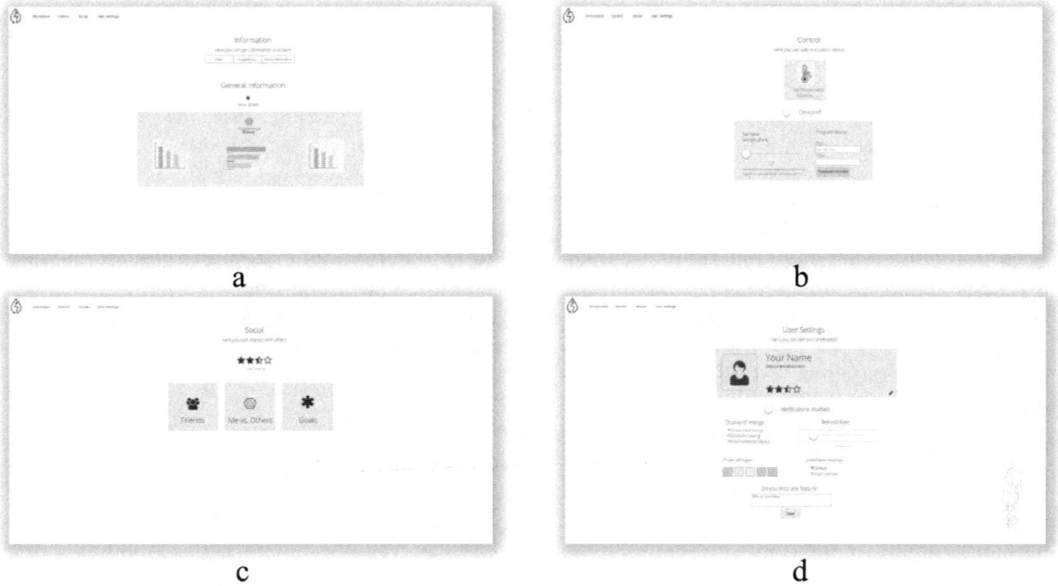

Figure 2. User interface of the Hi-Fi prototype: a) the Information section, b) Device Control section, c) Social section and d) User-Settings section

4. EVALUATION

The evaluation with users at early stages of the design process helps to validate the decisions made and to focus the design in the correct way before problems arise, avoiding the development of systems with deficiencies. The main objective of this first evaluation of the Hi-Fi prototype was to get the opinion of the users about the system and to know if it offers good usability and UX. We did a usability test (Corry et al., 1997) with a semi-structured interview (Whiting, 2008) and, furthermore, we handed out the System Usability Scale (SUS) questionnaire (Brooke, 1996) for the users to complete. This tool is an 10 item questionnaire that evaluates the usability of the system. The goal was to triangulate the evaluation through different methodologies to increase results reliability according to Mackay & Fayard (1997).

Participants were selected by convenience and they did not have previous knowledge of the work carried out nor the digital interface itself. The main objective was to find users ranging 25-50 year-old who were regular users of computers, Smartphones, applications and web environments. The evaluation was done with a small user sample ($N = 5$). This sample is enough to discover most of the usability problems (Lindgaard & Chattratichart, 2007) but is not enough to extract statistical conclusions nor to cover the whole spectrum of user diversity. Participants were 2 males and 3 females whose ages were between 30-35 years ($M = 31.6$), and the Standard Deviation (SD) was small ($SD = 2.302$). All the participants signed a consent form at the beginning of the evaluation session.

4.1 Procedure

The evaluation session was done with the high fidelity prototype. It started with a brief introduction where the purpose of the assessment was explained. The first objective of the session was to carry out 4 specific task with the digital interface with the 'Thinking aloud' methodology. After ensuring the correct understanding of each tasks, we proceeded to start them and record the start time and the audio to capture the user insights. Whenever a user had completed one task or the time limit expired, the task was tagged as finished and we proceed to the next one until completing the total. Then, some open questions were asked to the user about their opinion on the application, its usefulness and its degree of difficulty among other aspects. Finally, each user filled out the ten item-based SUS questionnaire to measure the usability of the interface.

4.2 Results

The percentage of error in tasks-accomplishment is a quantitative data that indicates the usability errors of the system. The percentage of error of the 20 tasks (4 tasks per user that have been executed by 5 users in total) executed in the usability test was 0. This is a positive fact that triangulates accordingly to the other two tests: the SUS questionnaire and the qualitative data.

The main conclusion drawn from the semi-structured interview was that most of the ideas provided were positive related to the acceptance of the application. Only two ideas revealed negative aspects (confusion and difficulty of concrete elements of the interface). We argue, that proportion-wise the 92.3% of positive insights gives an overall satisfactory evaluation of the digital artefact. The SUS questionnaire is evaluated in a score range from 0 to 100, where 0 is the lowest score and 100 the highest. The average score obtained among the 5 participants was 85,50 ($SD = 4.808$). As the data reveal, the score in all the questionnaires was above 80, which is why the usability of the designed interface was validated (according to the creators of the instrument, a SUS score above a 68 would be considered above average).

Although the general conclusions of the evaluation are satisfactory we need to take into account the limitations of the evaluation process. Thus, it is highly recommended to perform another usability test over time and with more users to expand the sample.

5. FINDINGS AND DISCUSSION

Next, the main aspects extracted from the development of the research, design and evaluation are detailed and discussed.

From the previous research to the final evaluation the qualitative data reveals that the users perceived the system as necessary and interesting. The insights extracted from the users indicate that this application would be easily embraced to help supporting the everyday lives of the users in the workplace. Overall facilitating the understanding of the energy consumption and connecting with it, which is a major issue in work environments.

The usability of the system is validated through the instruments used in the evaluation phase. The zero error rate at the usability test (task-accomplishment), the high score of SUS questionnaire (much higher than the general average) and the qualitative data extracted from the semi-structured interview established that the system is understandable and easy to use for the users. The simplicity can be a tool to make easy to understand the messages and to manage the energy processes and devices. The plain text tags and the synthesis of visual communication can enhance the learnability and the effective use of the system, helping to get a positive UX.

The data extracted from the evaluation shed lights on the potential that the UX and the usability may have to generate positive impact towards forming more sustainable behaviours. Indeed, users seems to be more disposed to receive messages through these kind of easy and personalised systems. The content provided was evaluated of high-value which might be also an indicative factor of the link between UX and the positive perception of the content provided towards increasing energy awareness.

As mentioned throughout this paper, the UCD can helps improving more efficient systems and interfaces with the user-centered research methodologies. The results show a positive feedback of the system designed with UCD methodology. Although development needs to be iterated, we can state that the designed interface is based on the needs of the users and that it is according to their mental model.

The used tools were focused on the evaluation of the usability and the UX of the digital interface. That give us the understanding of the relation of the users with the system, and indicate the effectiveness, legibility and learnability of the interface. These aspects may help on the validation of the interface, however, we do still need to understand whether the messages and content provided by the interface changes or not the user attitude towards energy efficiency. Thus, making people more aware about sustainability issues and hence influencing pro-environmental behaviour change. Furthermore, the differences between the approximations of the literature pose a reflection on the categorization of users in which it is necessary go in depth. The different dimensions reviewed need to be developed and implemented in flexible user profiles, including all types of people and the different states of change in user behaviour.

6. CONCLUSIONS AND FUTURE WORK

In this paper, a digital interface designed, developed and tested applying UCD methodologies was devised to increase the user awareness related to energy efficiency at work. The user diversity has been approached in the interface proposed by adopting the mix of the user classification based on the reviewed theoretical background. The system was evaluated with more than XX users through three different methods to extract knowledge about the impact of the UCD and UX on the user predisposition towards the usage of proposed interface and increment of the workers' environmental awareness. The findings validated the usability of the system which puts in relevance the usefulness of the UCD as a methodology. Moreover, it draws into provide a positive the UX as a means to engage users towards more conscious behaviour.

The future research lines should aim to improve the proposed interface, improving the prototypes in quick iterations. Besides, the design process must be complemented with continuous evaluations with users. In fact, the number of participants need to be increased to statistically assess its potential to increase energy consumption awareness at workplace. Research-wise, we envisage the generation of flexible user profiles (i.e. adaptive profiles which can be slightly modified throughout the time) based on behavioral theories. This will involve the understanding of all the stages of the pro-environmental behaviour to change to adapt our digital interface to them. For that, we need to understand the different dimensions already defined and to develop characterisation standards.

REFERENCES

Abras, C., Maloney-Krichmar, D., Preece, J., 2004. User- Centered Design. *Work*, 37(4), pp.445–456.

Aoyama, M., 2007. Persona-Scenario-Goal Methodology for User-Centered Requirements Engineering. *Proceedings - 15th IEEE International Requirements Engineering Conference, RE 2007*, pp.307–312.

Brooke, J., 1996. SUS - A quick and dirty usability scale. , pp.1–8.

Casado-Mansilla, D., 2016. *Promoting long term energy-efficient behaviour in work environments through persuasive technologies*. University of Deusto, Bilbao, Spain. Available at: https://morelab.deusto.es/media/publications/theses/diego-casado-mansilla.pdf.

Cor, E. & Zwolinski, P., 2014. A procedure to define the best design intervention strategy on a product for a sustainable behavior of the user. *Procedia CIRP*, 15, pp.425–430. Available at: http://dx.doi.org/10.1016/j.procir.2014.06.075.

Corry, M., Frick, T.W. & Hansen, L., 1997. User-centered Design and Usability Testing of a Web Site: An Illustrative Case Study. *Educational Technology Research and Development*, 45(4), pp.65–76. Available at: http://link.springer.com/article/10.1007/BF02299683.

Coskun, A., Design, I. & East, M., 2014. User diversity in design for behavior change Design for pro-environmental behavior change. *Proceedings of DRS 2014*, (JUNE 2014).

Haines, V., Mitchell, V. & Ross, T., 2015. User Centred Design As An Enabler of Sustainable HCI. , pp.1–4.

Halko, S. & Kientz, J.A., 2010. Personality and Persuasive Technology: An Exploratory Study on Health-Promoting Mobile Applications. *Persuasive Technology*, 6137(April 2017), pp.150–161. Available at: http://www.springerlink.com/index/10.1007/978-3-540-68504-3.

Harley, A., 2015. Personas Make Users Memorable for Product Team Members. *Nielsen Norman Group (NN/g)*, p.https://www.nngroup.com/articles/persona/. Available at: https://www.nngroup.com/articles/persona/.

He, H., Greenberg, S. & Huang, E., 2010. One size does not fit all: applying the transtheoretical model to energy feedback technology design. *... of the 28Th International Conference on ...*, pp.927–936. Available at: http://dl.acm.org/citation.cfm?id=1753464.

Hedin, B. & Zapico, J., 2017. Persuasive Technology: Development and Implementation of Personalized Technologies to Change Attitudes and Behaviors. , 10171, pp.175–185. Available at: http://link.springer.com/10.1007/978-3-319-55134-0.

Hekler, E.B. et al., 2013. Mind the Theoretical Gap: Interpreting, Using, and Developing Behavioral Theory in HCI Research. *Proc. CHI 2013*, pp.3307–3316.

Kaptein, M., Lacroix, J. & Saini, P., 2008. Individual Differences in Persuadability in the Health Promotion Domain. *Persuasive Technology*, 5033(March 2015), pp.1–12. Available at: http://www.springerlink.com/index/10.1007/978-3-540-68504-3.

Kitzinger, J., 1995. Qualitative research: Introducing focus groups. *BMJ: British Medical Journal*, 311(7000), pp.299–302. Available at: http://www.ncbi.nlm.nih.gov/pmc/articles/PMC2550365/%5Cnhttp://www.ncbi.nlm.nih.gov/pmc/articles/PMC2550365/pdf/bmj00603-0031.pdf.

Law, E.L.-C. et al., 2009. Understanding, scoping and defining user experience. *Proceedings of the 27th international conference on Human factors in computing systems - CHI 09*, (April 2016), p.719. Available at: http://dl.acm.org/citation.cfm?doid=1518701.1518813.

Lilley, D., Bailey, V. & Charnley, F., 2013. Design for sustainable behaviour: a quick fix for slower consumption? Available at: https://dspace.lboro.ac.uk/dspace-jspui/handle/2134/12514.

Lindgaard, G. & Chattratichart, J., 2007. Usability testing: what have we overlooked? *Proceedings of the SIGCHI conference on Human factors in computing systems - CHI '07*, pp.1415–1424. Available at: http://dl.acm.org/citation.cfm?id=1240624.1240839%5Cnhttp://dx.doi.org/10.1145/1240624.1240839.

Lockton, D., Harrison, D. & Stanton, N.A., 2008. Making the user more efficient: design for sustainable behaviour. *International Journal of Sustainable Engineering*, 1(1), pp.3–8. Available at: http://dx.doi.org/10.1080/19397030802131068%5Cnhttp://www.tandfonline.com/doi/abs/10.1080/19397030802131068.

Lockton, D., Harrison, D. & Stanton, N. a., 2012. Models of the user: designers' perspectives on influencing sustainable behaviour. *Journal of Design Research*, 10(1/2), pp.7–27. Available at: http://www.inderscience.com/link.php?id=46137.

Mackay, W. & Fayard, A.-L., 1997. HCL, Natural Science and Design: A Framework for Triangulation Across Disciplines. *Proceedings of the 2nd conference on Designing interactive systems: processes, practices, methods, and techniques*, pp.223–234.

Nielsen, J., 1994. Usability inspection methods. *Conference companion on Human factors in computing systems - CHI '94*, 25(1), pp.413–414. Available at: http://portal.acm.org/citation.cfm?doid=157203.157207%5Cnhttp://portal.acm.org/citation.cfm?doid=259963.260531.

Petkov, P. et al., 2011. Motivating Domestic Energy Conservation through Comparative, Community-Based Feedback in Mobile and Social Media. *5th International Conference Energy & Sustainability*, (July), pp.21–30. Available at: http://dl.acm.org/citation.cfm?id=2103358%5Cnhttp://eprints.qut.edu.au/40817/1/c40817.pdf.

Petkov, P. et al., 2012. Personalised eco-feedback as a design technique for motivating energy saving behaviour at home. *Proceedings of the 7th Nordic Conference on Human-Computer Interaction Making Sense Through Design - NordiCHI '12*, p.587. Available at: http://dl.acm.org/citation.cfm?doid=2399016.2399106.

Sax, H. et al., 2007. "My five moments for hand hygiene": a user-centred design approach to understand, train, monitor and report hand hygiene. *Journal of Hospital Infection*, 67(1), pp.9–21.

Vredenburg, K. et al., 2002. A survey of user-centered design practice. *Proceedings of the SIGCHI conference on Human factors in computing systems Changing our world, changing ourselves - CHI '02*, (1), p.471. Available at: http://portal.acm.org/citation.cfm?doid=503376.503460.

Wever, R., van Kuijk, J. & Boks, C., 2008. User Centered Design for Sustainable Behaviour. *International Journal of Sustainable Engineering*, 1(September), pp.9–20. Available at: http://architectures.danlockton.co.uk.

Whiting, L.S., 2008. Semi-structured interviews: guidance for novice researchers. , 22(23), pp.35–40.

Yun, R. et al., 2017. The persistent effectiveness of online feedback and controls for sustainability in the workplace. *Energy Efficiency*. Available at: http://link.springer.com/10.1007/s12053-017-9509-4.

DESIGNING FOR THE SECOND-HAND USE OF CONSUMER GOODS

Swati Srivastava and Alma Leora Culén
Department of Informatics, University of Oslo, P. Boks 1080, 0316 Blindern, Oslo, Norway

ABSTRACT

In this paper, we present results from a research through design inquiry into the design space of second-hand use of consumer goods and their potential for creating more sustainable and less consumerism-oriented lifestyles. These results are presented in the form of an annotated portfolio that is comprised of early conceptual and material explorations along with the final material artefact, Radius – an internet connected tangible artefact that helps make decisions to buy or sell second-hand consumer goods easier to take. By analytically and critically articulating observations and reflections from the constructed portfolio, we expand the existing understanding of this design space along with explicating the knowledge latent within our process. Our reflections offer new directions and insight for future research and design along with making a theoretical contribution to the discourse on knowledge outcomes from research through design in HCI.

KEYWORDS

Sustainable HCI; Consumer Goods; Second-Hand Use; Prototyping; Design Space; Annotated Portfolios

1. INTRODUCTION

The unsustainable environmental impact of the high rate of consumption and disposal of consumer goods like clothes and electronics, amongst others, has received a lot of interdisciplinary research interest (see (Van Hinte, 1997; Verbeek and Kockelkoren, 1998; Vezzoli and Manzini, 2008)) and is a growing area of concern within HCI (Blevis, 2007; Kuijer et al., 2008; Odom et al., 2009; Pierce and Paulos, 2011). Many disposed consumer goods are not at the end of their functional lifespan and end up getting discarded prematurely often due to disuse and/or dis-interest in repair or the availability of a newer and 'better' alternative (Manzini and Vezzoli, 2003; Pierce and Paulos, 2011).

In the light of these challenges, wider adoption of used or second-hand goods has been suggested as a promising solution that can potentially reduce the demand for new, or first-hand goods (Bowser et al., 2015; Pierce and Paulos, 2011). However, while the practices of second-hand use have existed for quite some time in the form of physical thrift stores, antique stores and more recently web and mobile platforms, people still tend to have hesitations when it comes to their adoption as an alternative to first-hand marketplaces (Pierce and Paulos, 2011). Further, within recent sustainable HCI discourse, the practices, value and potential of re-use and repair have been getting significant attention (Kuijer et al., 2008; Pierce et al., 2008; Wakkary et al., 2008). However, when it comes to second-hand use of consumer goods, barring a few technology specific explorations (like (Gegenbauer and Huang, 2012; Huh et al., 2010a)), designerly explorations and articulations of the design space itself have been limited. Considering the promising potential latent within the area of second-hand use of consumer goods we argue that there is a need for articulating more exploratory outcomes that go beyond commercially available web and mobile solutions, such as those from conceptual, speculative, fictional and reflective design approaches (Auger, 2013; Gaver and Martin, 2000; Sengers et al., 2005). These outcomes can serve as exemplars that can enable us to better understand and critically engage with this area as a rich design space. The importance of such articulations was noted even in early discussions on sustainable HCI by Blevis (Blevis, 2007) who suggested that:

"Design methods for dealing with the complexity of SID would do well to include those common in other design disciplines, such as design critiques, design case studies, and reflective practices (see Cross (2001), Fallman (2003), and Schön (1984)), at least in addition to general models of process as enumerated in HCI texts."

In this paper, we present explorations conducted within the design space of the second-hand use of consumer goods that lead to Radius (Figure 1), a tangible internet connected interactive artefact that explicitly communicates the demand and supply of consumer goods within local and reachable second-hand marketplaces — an aspect that is largely left implicit within web and mobile based applications. Radius as an artefact represents a critique and speculation on a dominant design paradigm within the design space (Bardzell and Bardzell, 2013) and explicitly emphasizes awareness and discovery of use/disuse and availability while designing for second-hand use of consumer goods. Further, we supplement our discussion of Radius as an artefact with a reflective and analytical articulation of the early exploratory phases of the design process as a means of explicating the knowledge latent within our process and furthering the understanding of this design space. Specifically, we highlight the value of intermediate artefacts that are created during the design process as a means of exploration, representation and 'reflection in action' (Schon, 1984).

Our approach reflects recent discussions within HCI related to the use of design practice and outcomes as means of inquiry and a way to generate new knowledge, generally referred to as Research through Design (RtD) (Zimmerman et al., 2007). RtD has received a lot of attention in HCI (Basballe and Halskov, 2012; Gaver, 2012; Höök and Löwgren, 2012; Zimmerman et al., 2007); in particular the means and forms of articulating the knowledge it generates (Bardzell et al., 2015; Bowers, 2012; Höök and Löwgren, 2012). It has been argued that knowledge outcomes from the results of RtD allow for "a range of topical, procedural, pragmatic and conceptual insights to be articulated" (Gaver, 2012). While, from the outset, designerly processes often do not have an explicitly clear structure or a linear model (Godin, 2006), they do have a disciplinary rigor and modes of navigating complexity inherent to design problems (Buchanan, 1992; Stolterman, 2008). Studies on designerly ways of thinking highlight that a critical form of navigating this complexity is through different forms of material and conceptual exploration (e.g. sketching, mapping, prototyping) conducted frequently throughout the design process (Cross, 2001; Schon, 1984). In our view, these intermediates or partially explored concepts and exploratory material undertakings play an essential role in the transformation of the initial intent into the final material outcome by opening an exploratory design space of material possibilities and conceptually informing and guiding the process. Moreover, intermediates serve as important knowledge outcomes from a RtD process in that they are representative of "partial ideas, that is elements of potential design solutions, that can be appropriated by designers and researchers and used in the creation of new instances" (Höök and Löwgren, 2012). Therefore, by explicitly articulating their conceptual and material nature, we can better understand the progression and evolution of the design process along with 'partial ideas' and 'potential design solutions' that frame the design space explored.

Figure 1. Radius

The central aim of our paper is to highlight the outcome and intermediate design proposals that were explored as a part of our RtD process and therefore, we limit our focus and discussion to our own reflections and concerns and how they evolved through hands on material engagement with the design process. Consequently, we do not discuss or present findings from the prototypes of our process in use or other forms of formal user studies. A range of prior research particularly relating to RtD in HCI has highlighted the value and importance of such articulations as a way of elaborating and expanding existing understandings of the design space (Backlund et al., 2007; Gaver and Martin, 2000; Neustaedter and Sengers, 2012).

The contribution of this paper is twofold. First, we present the material outcome and exploratory design proposals developed as a part of a research through design process and outline their guiding conceptual motivations and material considerations as a way of expanding and furthering the understanding of the design space relating to the second-hand use of consumer goods. Second, by building on prior research and presenting a methodology for analytically reflecting on and articulating the importance of intermediate explorations of the design process in constructing new understandings of the design space, we contribute to the larger theoretical discourse related to knowledge outcomes from RtD in HCI.

We start by outlining our conceptual background and methodological grounding and argumentation. Next, to develop our articulation and analysis of the design space, we use Gaver and Bower's (Gaver and Bowers, 2012) approach of using textual 'annotations' juxtaposed onto images of material outcomes from a design process as a means of highlighting "features of interest" within the process. We present an annotated portfolio of a chronological set of low fidelity, unfinished intermediates, leading up to the final material outcome created as our response to the question: how to scaffold and catalyze the prolonged lifecycle of durable goods in everyday life. A temporal analysis of the portfolio reveals traces of reflections from explorations of interim artefacts in the final material outcome. The final material outcome, Radius, is a simple internet connected device that plays on the formal characteristics of an internet connected button but alters the behavior and interactions from 'seamless purchase' to 'seamless visibility' of similar second-hand goods available in the geographic vicinity. Thus, the desirability of the second-hand item may facilitate a transition to finding the next owner. We conclude with highlighting possible exploratory dimensions within the design space along with critical reflections on the potential of reframing intermediate explorations as knowledge outcomes from research through design in HCI.

2. SECOND-HAND USE OF CONSUMER GOODS

Our research and design process was informed by prior sustainable HCI research relating to the practices and design implications of second-hand consumption. Building on earlier research in sustainable resource consumption practices within HCI and other related research fields like material cultures and design philosophy, Pierce and Paulos (Pierce and Paulos, 2011) develop an understanding of the consumption of "durable material goods in terms of the acquisition, possession, dispossession and reacquisition of a particular material object." They emphasize the importance of distinguishing between the motivations and practices of first-hand consumption (which relate to not-previously-acquired/possessed consumer goods) and second-hand use (which relate to the reacquisition and transference of possession and use). They describe these differences in terms of the work, effort and time involved with second-hand transactions which is supplemented by the inherent value of the experience and satisfaction of reacquisition, even though the actual interface and interaction design of first and second-hand marketplaces has become increasingly similar. Through our design concepts, we also explore trust related dimensions of reacquisition practices which have also been highlighted by Pierce and Paulos (ibid.), amongst others (Bowser et al., 2015; de Jode et al., 2012), suggesting that users need to have *faith* in the quality and reliability of second-hand things they seek to purchase. Odom et al. (Odom et al., 2009) describe how the material qualities, perceived durability and meaningfulness of objects help determine if they get preserved or discarded. We explore their suggestions on employing these factors to identify completely different reuse contexts for objects that go beyond their intended function. Huh et. al (Huh et al., 2010b) develop Odom et. al's work further in their study of the reuse of old or partially functional PDAs as music players and GPS devices. The potential of designing for second-hand use is also emphasized by Blevis (Blevis, 2007), who suggests promoting renewal and reuse as a "first-order design requirement for sustainability". In subsequent work, specifically relating to sustainable fashion, Pan et al. (Pan et al., 2015) point to the importance of the situated practices of the local community in informing reuse and sustainable design.

In the following section, we outline our methodology for analytically reflecting on our exploration of the design space relating to the second-hand use of durable goods along with articulating the progression of conceptual motivations and material considerations within the design process.

3. METHODOLOGY

'Thinking through making' has been widely discussed as a critical part of designerly processes (Cross, 2001; Schon, 1984) and HCI design is no exception. Quite commonly in the design process, beyond sketching and paper based representations of the design ephemera, when an idea seems to lead towards a possible solution, richer material explorations are routinely carried out for deeper engagement with the design space. In the material trajectory of a design process, starting with a design intent and ending with the final material outcome, a chain of alternative and exploratory intermediate explorations is typically created and abandoned along the way. This is a crucial part of navigating the 'messy situations' presented by the design process and are used as a means of reflection, filtering and evaluation and progressing iteratively in the design process (Lim et al., 2008a). While many of these tangible directional outcomes could end up being labelled as rejects or failures, they are significant contributors to 'reflection on action' (Schön, 1984) and consequently to research through design. As such, rather than rejects, they offer insights as to why a certain line of inquiry is abandoned along with existing as potential seeds for alternate explorations within the design space.

However, the designer's concerns, judgements and intent are not directly accessible from the designed artefact itself, in particular when one considers digital objects (Mazé and Redström, 2005). Gaver and Bowers (Gaver and Bowers, 2012) propose the use of textual 'annotations' as a means of identifying and articulating facets that are "indexically connected to artefacts while connoting features of broader interest" (Jarvis et al., 2012). Pierce has referred to this hybrid form of knowledge outcome as 'concept-things' which he argues are "nexuses of verbally articulated concepts and designerly articulated material things" (Pierce, 2014). We propose that a temporal analysis of the annotated (interim and final) material artefacts of a design process can lead to the construction of such a 'concept-thing' hybrid which reveals the evolving nature of designerly understanding, judgements and situational responses at a given point in the design process along with collectively presenting a holistic picture of the design space encountered.

3.1 An Artefactual Framing

Many researchers have highlighted that the outcomes of a design process exist as material embodiments of design decisions (Gaver, 2012; Pierce, 2014). Ingold (Ingold, 2013) has also discussed conceptually similar themes framed collectively as the 'art of inquiry'. It refers to designers' and craftsmen's material engagement throughout their process. Ingold underlines this engagement as an essential influence in widening perception of the context and deepening the inquiry. As a part of his larger discussion, he also introduces a related concept of *'casual connections'*, which refers to the traces of the tacit artefactual evolution of designerly thinking throughout the process and emphasizes that this is an important part of the process. We build on this understanding of casual connections and extend it to interim material artefacts, which we call intermediates, resulting from the early phases of explorations in the design process. With our work, we reflect analytically on explorations of intermediates within the context of prolonging the life of consumer goods. By considering all the intermediate explorations from a design process collectively, we argue that it is possible to highlight and demonstrate how design considerations shaped early on in the process carry forward into the metaphor, form and/or interactions of the final material outcome and to reframe such explorations as the drivers and evidence of material divergence and consequently conceptual convergence in a design process.

From a research through design standpoint, intermediates are also important as a means of evidencing the design dimensions that were explored in the design space which inform the conceptual motivations and material considerations of the particular and specific material outcome (Stolterman, 2008) of the design process. Therefore, we argue, they serve as important anchors for grounding rich accounts (Gaver, 2012) describing the design process and making them more transparent (without making them appear clinical and structured).

The value of prototyping, and specifically low fidelity (low-fi) prototyping, as a process and outcome of a design practice is certainly well established. In fact, prototyping, both as a conceptual approach and as a tool has been widely addressed in both HCI research and interaction design. Gerber et. al. (Gerber and Carroll, 2012) represent prototyping, especially low-fidelity prototyping as a widely-accepted way of reducing uncertainty and increasing knowledge. Pierce (Pierce, 2014) categorizes it as a means to "communicate and develop abstract concepts or theories". Lim et al. (Lim et al., 2008b) have proposed the anatomy of prototypes consisting of filtering dimensions which correspond to representational aspects of a prototype and manifestation dimensions which refer to its material or realized dimensions. However, it is not the general practice of low fidelity prototyping that we would like to highlight in this work, but rather the outcomes of exploratory and experimental making and their individual and collective implications on the design process and their value as seeds for future exploratory work.

Intermediates represent explorations that move beyond conceptual sketches and into a more material form. However, the nature of material engagement and representations can vary widely based on the domain and process influencing the nature of explorations. Therefore, we suggest that intermediates should not be identified based on their physical characteristics but their exploratory potential and their ability to provide insights into critical junctures of conceptual and/or material progression in the design process. As we demonstrate through an annotated portfolio of explorations in the following section, intermediates are representative of optimistic possibilities that were explored within a design process making them an important source of articulating potential themes, well formulated reflections, well understood mistakes and concrete evidences of the casual connections implicit within a particular design process.

4. ANNOTATED PORTFOLIO OF DESIGN EXPLORATIONS

Besides Radius, the final material outcome of our research through design process, we highlight four intermediate outcomes, each of which represents a distinct dimension within our larger inquiry into the design possibilities of the second-hand use of durable goods. These intermediates are outcomes from four iterative cycles of concept development and material explorations. They were developed as semi-finished low-fidelity prototypes and were critiqued in collaboration with HCI researchers. While distinct in their conceptual and material form, they are also snapshots of our process in time, related by an evolution in intent, constraints and judgements. Thus, the final material outcome, besides being theoretically and conceptually informed by prior research and design work also carries forward elements of the conceptual, material or aesthetic learning from each intermediate proposal. We briefly introduce them with a short textual description and an *annotated* image highlighting our design and research motivations, material considerations and the artefact's functions. Lastly, we present our observations relating to the casual connections between them and the larger design space that they help outline.

4.1 Intermediate 1: Honest me

'Honest Me' is a radio that displays information about its own well-being, lifespan and perceived price, in addition to its usual radio function (see Figure 2a).

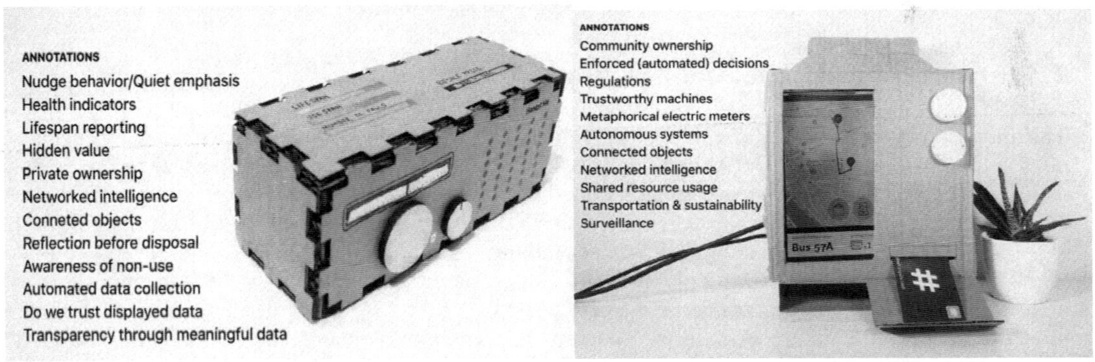

Figure 2. a) Honest Me b) Connected Conveyance

The concept evaluates and expresses the fluctuation in the value of the artefact as it ages, and the effects on its price in the second-hand market. The inquiry here was intended to explore to what extent is it possible, or whether it is even desirable, to design everyday objects with this kind of 'honesty'. For a potential buyer of second-hand goods, it is often difficult to look at electronic devices and know how well they were treated by their owners, how much use they had, or what is their general life expectancy (Pierce and Paulos, 2011). The concept builds on enabling devices to provide this information themselves. While engaging in the low fidelity prototyping of this concept, we focused on relevant parameters that could be made explicit in devices, like 'usage', 'lifespan', 'bumps and bruises' etc. and the relevance of these for the second-hand buying and selling. The annotated image (Figure 2a) highlights the motivations driving this design concept like "transparency through meaningful data", "awareness of non-use", "nudge behavior" along with material and functional dimensions like "networked intelligence", "connected objects", "lifespan reporting" and "automated data collection".

4.2 Intermediate 2: Connected Conveyance

Taking the increasingly ubiquitous nature of algorithmic decision making in everyday lives, from suggestive email responses to predictive policing, as a point of departure, this intermediate explored a scenario where consumer goods from cars to toasters could be controlled by an autonomous sharing system. Working with the analogy of electricity meters installed in our houses, we prototyped an object for implementing a connected and autonomously controlled transportation system (Figure 2b). This system uses location data, use data on various devices, time of the day, weather and so on and, and cumulatively considers all private and public transportation options available to its users, indirectly intervening with the use of one's privately-owned vehicles. Through this design concept, we were exploring conceptual dimensions of "trustworthy machines", "enforced decisions", "community ownership", "surveillance" while expanding material concerns like "networked intelligence" and "connected objects" with "autonomous systems". Finally, although vehicles were used in our example, this inquiry easily extends to a larger range of devices, e.g. laundry machines, coffee makers and so on.

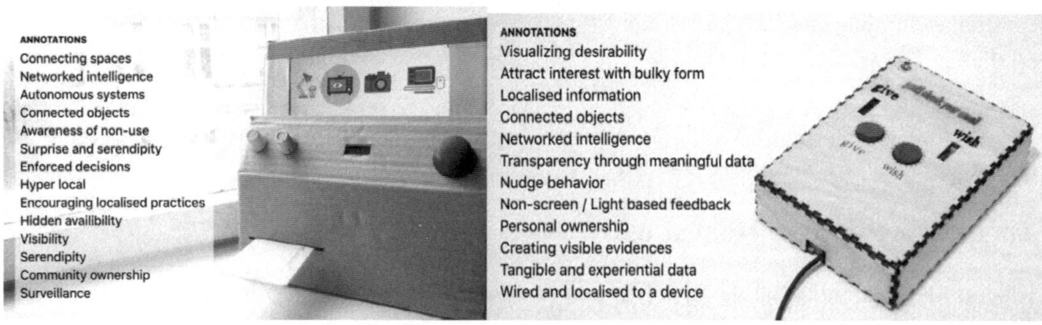

Figure 3. a) Slot Machine b) Buybit

4.3 Intermediate 3: The Slot Machine

The third exploration took the form of a 'slot machine' and attempted to situate the exchange of second-hand goods away from direct transactions between people (Figure 3a). Instead, it creates a space to experience and engage in the social practice of exchanging second-hand goods by localizing them within a neighborhood and automating the drop-off and pickup. This contrasts with the current state where this process requires logistical maneuvering by negotiating with others and then executing the exchange. Consequently, with time, unused items get stored away from sight, in attics, garage, basement, storage bins etc. in people's houses and neighborhoods. Using the metaphor of chance or horoscope reading, we designed a slot machine that monitors the use of devices and connects people with a common and automated repository of disused but functioning devices in their locality. Users can enter the amount they can offer and select device categories and the machine presents a random selection of devices available to choose from. With this design concept, the material dimensions of our explorations like "networked intelligence", "connected objects", "autonomous systems" solidified further while our conceptual motivations represented both an amalgamation of existing themes like "enforced decisions", "community ownership", "surveillance", "awareness of non-use" and an expansion with additional themes like "serendipity" and "encouraging localized practices".

4.4 Intermediate 4: Buybit

Buybit was the fourth intermediate exploration and is conceptually the closest to the final material outcome of our design process (Figure 3b). It is designed as an internet connected object belonging to a household, connected to different second-hand marketplaces within a local neighborhood. Two light based indicators highlight the demand (wish) and supply (give) of everyday objects like lamps and toasters in second-hand marketplaces. In addition, two buttons, give and wish allow the user to immediately put an object up for sale (give) or indicate their interest in purchasing it (wish). The behavioral attributes of the device built on the 'nudge' like behavior of "Honest me" and therefore were designed as 'polite suggestions' and an 'informed advice'. It uses non-intrusive interactions and aims to create small moments of reflection about the possession and dispossession of things. Buybit was designed as an external device that could be attached to all sorts of goods, enable suggestive, light based interactions, and catalyze second-hand reuse practices. A semi-functional prototype was built using the littleBits prototyping platform (Littlebits, 2017). Material considerations and conceptual motivations such as "connected objects", "networked intelligence", "transparency through meaningful data", "nudge behavior" carry forward from earlier design concepts along with additional considerations like "localized information", "tangible and experiential data", "attracting interest with a bulky form" get added in this iteration.

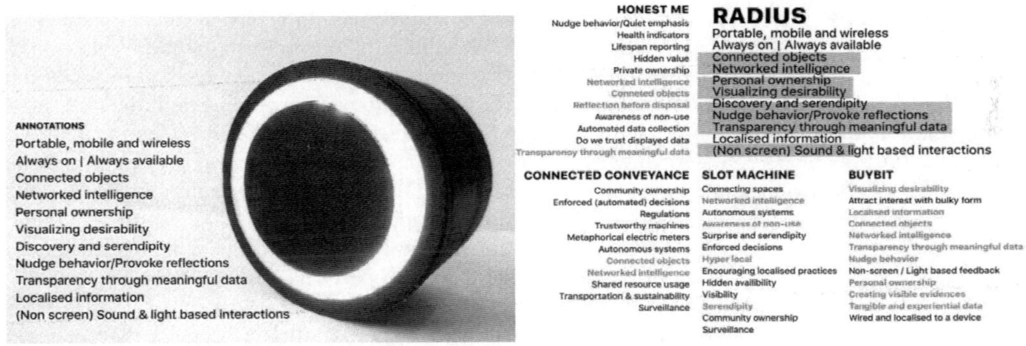

Figure 4. a) Radius b) Annotations of intermediates help trace casual connections of conceptual motivations, material considerations and functional aspects in the final material outcome, Radius

4.5 Final Material Outcome: Radius

Radius is the final material outcome of the project (Figure 4a). It is a simple internet connected device that plays on the formal characteristics of an internet connected button but alters the behavior and interactions from 'one-click purchase' to 'one-click visibility' of similar unused second-hand goods available in the geographic vicinity. It uses the metaphor of tags on new devices which rather than glorifying product attributes, exposes its demand and supply in the second-hand market as a way of motivating consumers consider selling goods they do not use anymore and buying pre-owned goods when they consider making a new purchase. The form of the artefact was intentionally kept portable and wireless to allow for mobility and on the go usage for example in situations where people could use the device in stores to compare second-hand demand and supply and prices with those of new goods. A semi functional prototype was built using a particle internet board ("Particle Photon Series wifi development kits and connectivity modules.," n.d.), RFID sensor and a rechargeable Li-Po battery embedded in a custom 3D printed enclosure. This iteration was intended for further formal and alternate material explorations, but ended up pushing the 'Buybit' concept further both in form and conceptually. For example, its size and shape made it more portable. Portability greatly increased its effectiveness and utility, making it readily available while also eliminating the need for multiple 'Buybits' in a household. Sound was added as an additional mode of interaction and in combination with light, the artefact could now communicate different data points such as condition, demand and proximity.

4.6 Observations

Assimilating the explorations and outcome of the Radius project in the form of a portfolio allows us to temporally and relationally analyze the material progression of the design process. This analysis helps trace the casual connections and highlight the flow and flux of the design decisions and judgements taken by the team by visually highlighting similar themes of enquiry that were explored further in each concept and iteration even when the artefacts are conceptually and materially different. At the same time, the evolving, generative and emergent form of both research and design intent and domain understanding can also be evidenced. We present the main observations from the portfolio of outcomes of our design process below.

4.6.1 Temporal Evolution and Casual Connections

Each intermediate outcome was discussed and critiqued in the light of our larger research inquiry: if a product like this existed, would it be desirable and would it scaffold and catalyze the extension of the lifespan of consumer goods? Asking these questions showed that the 'Connected conveyance' was too far removed from our initial intent by being overly reliant on automation and machine intelligence. While 'Honest Me' was promising, the nature of metrics represented would need to vary widely between different devices and contexts. Therefore, wider application of the concept became a key thematic area to be addressed in the next iteration which lead to 'the slot machine' prototype. As an outcome, the 'Slot machine' seemed to offer a promising solution that integrated design considerations like artefact non-use, condition and connectivity with the thematic areas of suggestive interactions that are generalizable across consumer goods. However, upon reflecting and critiquing the artefact, our implicit reliance on machine intelligence, decision making and automation in this case became evident, positioning it as an example of enforced decision making. Thus, we decided to move away from community driven or owned artefacts as an area of exploration and added personal spaces and ownership as the key contextual area for future explorations. Focusing on personal spaces and ownership, we decided to go back to design considerations explored in the 'Honest me' concept. At this point, we started to note a key underlying theme relating to 'creating visibility of data points' and 'transparency in communication' as a conceptual undertones and parallels between 'Honest me' and 'the slot machine'. At this stage, 'Buybit' and later 'Radius' emerged as conceptual extensions that scaffold reflection and engagement with second-hand use through visibility of metrics such as demand and supply, closest distance and health.

4.6.2 Suggestive vs Enforced Interactions

Looking at the diversity and breadth of our explorations, we can observe that scaffolding and catalyzing the use of second-hand durable goods is a complex and contextually diverse design space. However, throughout our explorations, two distinct modes of interaction can be observed — suggestive/demonstrative and enforced/autonomous. The first exploration, 'Honest me', represented a suggestive mode of interaction while the second, 'Connected conveyance', represented an autonomous or enforced mode of interaction. While 'the slot machine' created opportunities for serendipitous encounters, the concept was thematically quite reminiscent of the provocative and enforced behaviors from the 'Connected conveyance' concept by giving away things that were disused. Finally, the later iterations of our process leading to 'Buybit' and later 'Radius', show an amalgamation of the suggestive interactions from 'Honest me' and creating opportunities for discovery and surprise from 'the slot machine' by making implicit data relating to second-hand goods explicit and readily available through a portable and personal device.

4.6.3 Material and Conceptual Considerations

Reflecting upon outcomes of both concepts and annotating their images, we could easily see that our material considerations were quite similar throughout the process. All the outcomes represent some form of connected and 'smart' objects that used (or in the case of cardboard prototypes, could use) technological materials like wireless transmitters, networked APIs and localized sensors and actuators. However, throughout the design process the team continuously explored possibilities and implications of finding a balance between themes of community vs personal ownership and suggestive vs enforced interactions as they related to second-hand reuse. Based on the nature of our conceptual engagement in each iteration, these materials were re-configured and composed to create distinct outcomes.

4.6.4 Summary: Annotating Intermediate Outcomes

From an analytical perspective, the annotations play a dual indexical and demonstrative role. While they do provide a specific contextual understanding of the artefact and connections to research areas of broader interest, in this case, they also demonstrate the designer's or design team's understanding and judgements at a specific point in the design process. Consequently, considered collectively as a portfolio, they highlight the evolution of the team's understanding and response to the research domain and design brief - both by evidencing considerations and intent that were developed further and those that were left behind (see Figure 4b). We argue that this helps contextually and conceptually situate the final material outcome by underlining both what its research and design intentions and considerations are and what they aren't. In the case of our process, 'connected/always on/networked' interaction appears as a common theme that the team tried to utilize in formulating its response to catalyzing second-hand practices. Decision making (either human or autonomous) based on usually hidden/obfuscated data appears as another theme. However, in this case, the annotations highlight that the team deliberately moved away from autonomous or black boxed decision making and towards transparent and meaningful data as a form of catalyzing second-hand practices in the final material outcome. Hence, this underlines transparency, reflection and communicating meaningful data as the outcome's design and research intent and autonomy, obfuscation and provocation as intents that it does not stand for.

5. DISCUSSION

5.1 On the Design Space (of Second-Hand Use)

Based on our reflections and observations from interim explorations, we present three potential design spaces for future exploration of second-hand use.

5.1.1 Visibility and Transparency

As highlighted in prior research (Odom et al., 2009; Pierce and Paulos, 2011), the practices of second-hand use are distinctly different from those related to first-hand goods and marketplaces. Thus, designing for second-hand use could use such practices as a point of departure rather than borrowing design elements from first-hand marketplaces. Trust in people and durability of second-hand goods is one of the important factors that differentiates the first-hand and second-hand markets. While it is possible (and important) to speculatively and critically engage with existing notions of implicit trust in first-hand goods, easily visible and understandable information can also act as catalysts that can create feelings of confidence and trust, as described in (van der Velden and Culen, 2013). 'Honest me' makes information about the potential lifetime of a radio visible and allows for an easy estimate of its durability. These metrics are incorporated into the device itself and are driven by automated reporting on stressful experiences the item may have had, such as falls. This kind of transparency and visibility into the lifetime and nature of use of consumer goods can mitigate mistrust and lessen the subjective judgements and work needed to identify durable second-hand goods.

5.1.2 Serendipity and Discovery

While designing for second-hand use, engagement and reflection could be created through scaffolding serendipitous encounters and discovery. Visibility can be a basis for designing scaffolds for serendipitous encounters, like those enabled by 'Radius' and 'the slot machine'. 'Radius' can help see the availability of a thing one might need or want but not expect to get close by, while 'the slot machine' displays disused but locally available items simply on turning the handle of the machine and transferring ownership, if the user's profile fits. Usually, the local availability and ubiquity of second-hand goods is often a factor that is not emphasized in the design of second-hand markets. However, unexpected things one never thought could be locally available (or affordable) may be found, tried and shared this way. Serendipitous discovery, i.e. finding interesting and valuable things unexpectedly could add additional values to the experience of second-hand interactions like being lucky, pleasure, surprise and/or happiness in addition to the satisfaction of reacquisition (Pierce and Paulos, 2011). Going beyond these feelings, such serendipitous discoveries could also trigger reflection over one's own needs and buying behaviors.

5.1.3 Ownership and Use/Disuse

Designing for second-hand use could question and suggest alternates to prevalent understandings of ownership and use/disuse. Design fiction (Blythe, 2014) and speculative design (Auger, 2013) are examples of potential approaches that can be adopted to suggest alternatives and propose potential futures. With 'connected conveyance' and 'the slot machine', we engaged with such an approach by imagining a world where the use of transportation and ownership of consumer goods is appropriated through use and necessity. While the outcomes do not represent usable or useful results in a traditional sense, they help highlight underlying assumptions relating to the utility of owning goods that are disused (in the case of the slot machine) and often implicit decisions like choosing a car over public transport for commuting (in the case of connected conveyance).

5.2 On Intermediates

5.2.1 As Knowledge Outcomes

Intermediates act as material evidences of a design process, and when read in conjunction with their design and research intention and the context of their manifestation (within the process), can reveal important insights about how and why a certain design outcome came to be. To be sure, they do not necessarily make the entire conceptual design space explicit but rather highlight the exploratory, iterative and often fragmented journey that was undertaken as a part of the design process. The annotated portfolio of intermediate explorations presents each exploration as a concept-thing hybrid and underlines them as important material and conceptual beacons that collectively offer traces of this journey for reflection and future exploration. Making and annotating intermediates, may be, in some sense compared to the research using grounded theory, where collecting data and taking careful field notes may be compared to making of intermediates, while the process of coding and categorizing compares to annotating and analyzing annotations.

5.2.2 As Partial Ideas

Identifying intermediate explorations and compiling them into a portfolio can sometimes be problematic. This is because documenting and presenting 'unfinished' and 'failed' explorations together with the final material outcome may be perceived as adding unwanted complexity and messiness to the documentation and dissemination process. However, as we have demonstrated, rather than adding complexity, such a narrative provides a much more grounded articulation of the final material outcome along with seeds for future explorations. Important qualities of intermediates are that they are experimental, allow a design researcher to pursue the main line of inquiry in different directions (highlighting the importance of divergent thinking, expressed through material explorations), serve as speculative objects enabling reflections through speculation on meaning, desirability and use. Moreover, what may have been perceived as an invalid or failed line of exploration in one case due to constraints or particularities of a brief, could become promising points of departure under a different research or design brief.

5.2.3 As Artefacts for Reflection and Critique

We have also experienced this process to be quite effective as a means of critique and reflection even during the design process and the portfolio in such cases tends to become a living document and an active material that helps shape future directions in the design process. In such cases, annotations help shape the process as well as generate a richer set of knowledge outcomes. Besides their role as artefacts for reflection and evidencing, we also speculate about the potential of intermediate explorations as a means of inducing flux in the process by facilitating hands on engagement with multiple potential directions, keeping promising artefacts intentionally 'unfinished' while other dimensions of the design space are explored. For instance, the metaphor of polite suggestions and devices as active participants that we worked with in Honest me, was very influential for the final design of Radius since we were actively engaged in critiquing our interactions and behaviors against these metaphors. Going forward with alternate explorations through diverse exploratory forms and consciously articulating possible themes, interactions and learnings might help in actively informing and developing the design concept in unexpected and novel ways.

6. CONCLUSIONS

Building on prior work on second-hand interactions and sustainable HCI, we have presented Radius, an internet connected tangible artefact along with intermediate design concepts and explorations leading up to it as a means of expanding the understanding of the design space relating to the second-hand use of consumer goods. We used annotated portfolios as a way of highlighting the exploratory potential within this design space along with developing an articulation of the 'casual connections', both material and immaterial, between the intermediates and the final material outcome. In our future work, we aim to explore the design spaces outlined along with furthering the understanding of the nature and relevance of this knowledge in HCI.

ACKNOWLEDGEMENTS

This work was conducted as part of the research project Conserve and Consume, funded by the Norwegian Research Council (project number 235526/O30). The authors would also like to thank the reviewers for their insightful comments.

REFERENCES

Auger, J., 2013. Speculative design: crafting the speculation. Digit. Creat. 24, 11–35.

Backlund, S., Gyllenswärd, M., Gustafsson, A., Ilstedt Hjelm, S., Mazé, R., Redström, J., 2007. Static! The aesthetics of energy in everyday things. Proceedings of Design Research Society Wonderground International Conference 2006.

Bardzell, J., Bardzell, S., 2013. What is "Critical" About Critical Design?, in: Proceedings of the SIGCHI Conference on Human Factors in Computing Systems, CHI '13. ACM, New York, NY, USA, pp. 3297–3306.

Bardzell, J., Bardzell, S., Koefoed Hansen, L., 2015. Immodest Proposals: Research Through Design and Knowledge, in: Proceedings of the 33rd Annual ACM Conference on Human Factors in Computing Systems, CHI '15. ACM, New York, NY, USA, pp. 2093–2102.

Basballe, D.A., Halskov, K., 2012. Dynamics of Research Through Design, in: Proceedings of the Designing Interactive Systems Conference, DIS '12. ACM, New York, NY, USA, pp. 58–67.

Blevis, E., 2007. Sustainable Interaction Design: Invention & Disposal, Renewal & Reuse, in: Proceedings of the SIGCHI Conference on Human Factors in Computing Systems, CHI '07. ACM, New York, NY, USA, pp. 503–512.

Blythe, M., 2014. Research through design fiction: narrative in real and imaginary abstracts. Presented at the Proceedings of the SIGCHI Conference on Human Factors in Computing Systems, ACM, pp. 703–712.

Bowers, J., 2012. The Logic of Annotated Portfolios: Communicating the Value of "Research Through Design," in: Proceedings of the Designing Interactive Systems Conference, DIS '12. ACM, New York, NY, USA, pp. 68–77.

Bowser, A.E., Haimson, O.L., Melcer, E.F., Churchill, E.F., 2015. On Vintage Values: The Experience of Secondhand Fashion Reacquisition, in: Proceedings of the 33rd Annual ACM Conference on Human Factors in Computing Systems, CHI '15. ACM, New York, NY, USA, pp. 897–906.

Buchanan, R., 1992. Wicked Problems in Design Thinking. Des. Issues 8, 5–21. doi:10.2307/1511637

Cross, N., 2001. Designerly Ways of Knowing: Design Discipline Versus Design Science. Des. Issues 17, 49–55.

de Jode, M., Barthel, R., Rogers, J., Karpovich, A., Hudson-Smith, A., Quigley, M., Speed, C., 2012. Enhancing the "Second-hand" Retail Experience with Digital Object Memories, in: Proceedings of UbiComp '12. ACM, New York, NY, USA, pp. 451–460.

Fallman, D., 2003. Design-oriented Human-computer Interaction, in: Proceedings of the SIGCHI Conference on Human Factors in Computing Systems, CHI '03. ACM, New York, NY, USA, pp. 225–232.

Gaver, B., Bowers, J., 2012. Annotated Portfolios. interactions 19, 40–49.

Gaver, B., Martin, H., 2000. Alternatives: Exploring Information Appliances Through Conceptual Design Proposals, in: Proceedings of the SIGCHI Conference on Human Factors in Computing Systems, CHI '00, pp. 209–216.

Gaver, W., 2012. What Should We Expect from Research Through Design?, in: Proceedings of the SIGCHI Conference on Human Factors in Computing Systems, CHI '12. ACM, New York, NY, USA, pp. 937–946.

Gegenbauer, S., Huang, E.M., 2012. Inspiring the Design of Longer-lived Electronics Through an Understanding of Personal Attachment, in: Proceedings of the Designing Interactive Systems Conference, DIS '12. ACM, New York, NY, USA, pp. 635–644.

Gerber, E., Carroll, M., 2012. The psychological experience of prototyping. Des. Stud. 33, 64–84.

Godin, B., 2006. The Linear model of innovation the historical construction of an analytical framework. Sci. Technol. Hum. Values 31, 639–667.

Höök, K., Löwgren, J., 2012. Strong Concepts: Intermediate-level Knowledge in Interaction Design Research. ACM Trans Comput-Hum Interact 19, 23:1–23:18.

Huh, J., Nam, K., Sharma, N., 2010a. Finding the Lost Treasure: Understanding Reuse of Used Computing Devices, in: Proceedings of the SIGCHI Conference on Human Factors in Computing Systems, CHI '10, pp. 1875–1878.

Ingold, T., 2013. Making: Anthropology, Archaeology, Art and Architecture, 1 edition. ed. Routledge, London ; New York.

Jarvis, N., Cameron, D., Boucher, A., 2012. Attention to Detail: Annotations of a Design Process, in: Proceedings of the 7th Nordic Conference on Human-Computer Interaction: Making Sense Through Design, NordiCHI '12, pp. 11–20.

Kuijer, L., Jong, A. de, Eijk, D. van, 2008. Practices As a Unit of Design: An Exploration of Theoretical Guidelines in a Study on Bathing. ACM Trans Comput-Hum Interact 20, 21:1–21:22. Lim, Y.-K., Stolterman, E., Tenenberg, J., 2008a. The Anatomy of Prototypes: Prototypes As Filters, Prototypes As Manifestations of Design Ideas. ACM Trans Comput-Hum Interact 15, 7:1–7:27.

Lim, Y.-K., Stolterman, E., Tenenberg, J., 2008b. The Anatomy of Prototypes: Prototypes As Filters, Prototypes As Manifestations of Design Ideas. ACM Trans Comput-Hum Interact 15, 7:1–7:27.

Littlebits, 2017. littleBits: DIY Electronics For Prototyping and Learning [WWW Document]. URL http://littlebits.cc/

Manzini, E., Vezzoli, C., 2003. A strategic design approach to develop sustainable product service systems: examples taken from the 'environmentally friendly innovation' Italian prize. J. Clean. Prod. 11, 851–857.

Mazé, R., Redström, J., 2005. Form and the computational object. Digit. Creat. 16, 7–18.

Neustaedter, C., Sengers, P., 2012. Autobiographical Design in HCI Research: Designing and Learning Through Use-it-yourself, in: Proceedings of the Designing Interactive Systems Conference, DIS '12, pp. 514–523.

Odom, W., Pierce, J., Stolterman, E., Blevis, E., 2009. Understanding Why We Preserve Some Things and Discard Others in the Context of Interaction Design, in: Proceedings of the SIGCHI Conference on Human Factors in Computing Systems, CHI '09, pp. 1053–1062.

Pan, Y., Roedl, D., Blevis, E., Thomas, J., 2015. Fashion thinking: Fashion practices and sustainable interaction design. Int. J. Des. 9.

Particle Photon Series wifi development kits and connectivity modules. [WWW Document], n.d. URL https://www.particle.io/products/hardware/photon-wifi-dev-kit (accessed 6.9.17).

Pierce, J., 2014. On the Presentation and Production of Design Research Artifacts in HCI, in: Proceedings of the 2014 Conference on Designing Interactive Systems, DIS '14. ACM, New York, NY, USA, pp. 735–744.

Pierce, J., Paulos, E., 2011. Second-hand interactions: investigating reacquisition and dispossession practices around domestic objects. Presented at the Proceedings of the SIGCHI Conference on Human Factors in Computing Systems, ACM, pp. 2385–2394.

Pierce, J., Strengers, Y., Sengers, P., Bødker, S., 2008. Introduction to the Special Issue on Practice-oriented Approaches to Sustainable HCI. ACM Trans Comput-Hum Interact 20, 20:1–20:8.

Schön, D.A., 1984. The Reflective Practitioner: How Professionals Think In Action, 1 edition. Basic Books, New York.

Sengers, P., Boehner, K., David, S., Kaye, J. "Jofish," 2005. Reflective Design, in: Proceedings of the 4th Decennial Conference on Critical Computing: Between Sense and Sensibility, CC '05. ACM, New York, NY, USA, pp. 49–58.

Stolterman, E., 2008. The nature of design practice and implications for interaction design research. Int. J. Des. 2, 55–65.

van der Velden, M., Culen, A.L., 2013. Information Visibility in Public Transportation Smart Card Ticket Systems. Int. J. Adv. Netw. Serv. 6, 188–197.

Van Hinte, E., 1997. Eternally Yours: visions on product endurance. 010 Publishers.

Verbeek, P.-P., Kockelkoren, P., 1998. The Things That Matter. Des. Issues 14, 28–42. doi:10.2307/1511892

Vezzoli, C.A., Manzini, E., 2008. Design for Environmental Sustainability, 2008 edition. ed. Springer, Berlin ; London.

Wakkary, R., Desjardins, A., Hauser, S., Maestri, L., 2008. A Sustainable Design Fiction: Green Practices. ACM Trans Comput-Hum Interact 20, 23:1–23:34.

Zimmerman, J., Forlizzi, J., Evenson, S., 2007. Research Through Design As a Method for Interaction Design Research in HCI, in: Proceedings of the SIGCHI Conference on Human Factors in Computing Systems, CHI '07, pp. 493–502.

Short Papers

F.R.A.M.E - FACIAL REMOTE ACTIVITY MONITORING EYEWEAR

Philip Breedon[1], Paul Watts[1], Graeme Cox[2], Ala Szczepura[3], Darrin Baines[3], Karen Johnson[4], Vanessa Venables[5] and Charles Nduka[5]

[1]*Nottingham Trent University, 50 Shakespeare Street, Nottingham, NG1 4FQ, UK*
[2]*Emteq ltd, Sussex Innovation Centre, Science Park Square, Brighton, BN1 9SB, UK*
[3]*Coventry University, Priory Street, Coventry , CV1 5FB, UK*
[4]*Facial Palsy UK, Eventus, Sunderland Road, Market Deeping, Peterborough, PE6 8FD*
[5]*Queen Victoria Hospital , Holtye Road, East Grinstead, RH19 3DZ, UK*

ABSTRACT

We take for granted the ability to smile, kiss, or close our eyes at night, all of which can be affected by facial paralysis. This condition may strike anyone at any time, regardless of age or gender. The project aims to develop a pair of glasses that discreetly provides real-time feedback to the wearer about their facial muscle function, helping them practice their rehabilitative exercises regularly and correctly, thereby speeding recovery of normal, symmetric facial expressions.

The glasses will contain all the required EMG sensors in a compact form factor, they will provide sensor data to a mobile application installed on a mobile phone or tablet. The mobile application will provide daily exercises and feedback to allow the patients to monitor their own progress through the rehabilitation process and will also pass on valuable information to therapists via a website. Therapists will monitor the progress of their patients and adjust exercise routines as required. They will also provide feedback through in application messaging and feedback tools while providing in depth analysis tools to spot potential problems such as synkinesis.

KEYWORDS

Bell's Palsy, Wearable Technology, Mobile Application, Electromyography, Cloud Computing, Facial Palsy

1. INTRODUCTION

Facial paralysis results in weakness of the facial muscles, typically on one side of the face, affecting the facial function, appearance and communication of emotions. Patients experience issues with speech, swallowing and blinking, plus significant psychological difficulties such as anxiety and depression.

Bell's Palsy represents 60% of facial palsy cases, resulting in up to 25,640 new cases in the UK annually. Approximately 8,000 of these new Bell's Palsy cases are left with a permanent disability each year – estimated figures of over 100,000 people living in the UK with permanent facial problems are likely to significantly underestimate the problem. There are approximately 152,000 new strokes per year in the UK, with an estimated 26,000 of these patients suffering from residual facial problems after their stroke. The benefits for these patients of 45 minutes daily physiotherapy in the early recovery period are well known but the costs to the NHS of providing such therapy are large (around £2,600 per patient or £62,400,000 per year).

Studies show that following facial paralysis rehabilitative exercises speeds recovery improving the end result. Patients usually have limited awareness of the abnormal movements their faces display so, without feedback their facial function may worsen, developing permanently abnormal movements.

Currently, patients are shown their exercises in clinics and are expected to practice alone at home using only a mirror for feedback. Many patients dislike having to work with their own reflection as it reminds them of their condition and many get discouraged.

Wearable technology that provides real-time facial muscle information to patients and therapists promises a significant improvement in the rehabilitation of facial paralysis (Nicastri et al, 2013), allowing wearers to practice their exercises discreetly and correctly whilst completing other daily activities

2. PROJECT AIM

Facial muscles contain few intrinsic sensory receptors, which fundamentally limits the patient's ability to sense and optimise their own muscle tone. Biofeedback therapy for facial palsy increases the patient's awareness of facial muscle posture and movement, particularly where there has been aberrant re-innervation following facial palsy. Typically, biofeedback is provided via a mirror or else electromyography (EMG) techniques are employed using facial electrodes and accompanying auditory/visual biofeedback that measures muscle contraction and teaches patients to maintain facial symmetry. Patients maintain symmetry during volitional movement by incorporating the information perceived through the EMG although improvements are often temporary.

The aim is to develop and trial a prototype (through proof-of-concept clinical studies) inconspicuous, wearable glasses that are indistinguishable from normal spectacles and provide discreet feedback on facial muscle movement, thereby allowing patients to continuously practice facial muscle exercises. F.R.A.M.E. (Facial Remote Activity Monitoring Eyewear) incorporates advanced non-invasive sensors bringing clinic based EMG into a wearable home-use device. Feedback is via an application on a patients' smart device through wireless tracking of exercise intensity and regularity, enhancing patient motivation (Van der Weegen et al, 2013), whilst allowing specialist physiotherapists to monitor progress, speed patient recovery, provide direct NHS cost savings, time benefits and offer patients significant improvements in their facial function and quality of life.

3. BACKGROUND

There are over 30 causes of facial palsy, all classed as rare diseases, with cumulatively over 100,000 affected in the UK (Julian and Partridge,2008). Recent UK Strategy for Rare Diseases published by the Department of Health, UK stresses the importance of timely access to care. However, patients are still not receiving optimal treatment (Morales et al, 2013).

The muscles of facial expression are anatomically and neurophysiologically different to other muscles, due to their roles in modulating and protecting the main sensory organs, coupled with voluntary and involuntary control mechanisms. In addition to a proportion of the 150,000 annual new UK stroke sufferers, facial palsy affects almost 30,000 new patients annually. Of this latter group, almost a third are left with life-long devastating consequences: inability to close the affected eye; difficulties with eating, drinking and speech; social isolation; and, psychological sequelae (Morales et al, 2013). Two common clinical pictures are: over activity of the muscles on the unaffected side leading to distortion of the facial anatomy and function; and, aberrant re-innervation of the affected side resulting in pain, disability and abnormal movements secondary to increased resting muscle tone.

Currently, there is minimal technology available for rehabilitation of patients affected by facial palsy. During patient assessments, electromyography (EMG) is used to measure the muscle responses when attempting different expressions. This method requires the use of needle electrodes inserted into the facial muscles or large adhesive electrode patches to be attached to the face to detect the activity of underlying muscles.

Patients are frequently able to make impressive progress within a facial rehabilitation session when guided by the feedback provided by the surface EMG. However, these sessions (typically every 3-4 months) make up a tiny fraction of possible rehabilitative time.

The current preferred method uses a mirror for visual feedback while performing rehabilitation exercises. Whilst this is better than no feedback, this method provides no quantitative information. Patients frequently report frustration about their perceived lack of progress.

Alternatives identified during initial research involve the use of facial tracking software and cameras to track the facial movements of users, we found these solutions were accurate but failed to spot Synkinesis. Synkinesis can be detected using muscle tone and we will use EMG sensors to detect this during rehabilitation, this is identified as crucial in the treatment of Bell's palsy.

4. HARDWARE DESIGN

Hardware design is crucial to achieving the goals of this project. Hardware is designed to be indistinguishable from a standard pair of glasses; it will contain the sensors within the frame design so that the patient can use these glasses in everyday activities.

Dry EMG sensors are inserted into the frame and located over the muscles identified during our research. The frame is designed to ensure that a firm contact between the users' skin and the EMG sensor is achieved. It is important that the frame be designed so that as it moves during facial activity the EMG sensors remain firmly against the skin.

To analyse the data we are using the facial action coding system (FACS)(Ekman, P. et al, 1978) to translate the data into Action Units(AU), these will be used to analyze and translate the data into usable datasets. EMG sensors are prone to background noise and interference created from nearby muscle movements and overall sensor movement. To detect movement and to filter out background interference an inertia measurement unit (IMU) was added to the prototype to analyze the activity of the wearer. IMU data is then used to filter out noisy results caused by user activity.

Transmission of data collected from the headset to a mobile device is achieved using Bluetooth LE technology, this was chosen as many mobile devices contain Bluetooth LE capabilities allowing easy integration with a wide range of devices on the market. The technology is for low power wireless transmission, which is essential in designing a battery-powered device.

5. SOFTWARE DESIGN

Software is required to analyse the facial movements of patients' and to interpret this data into a set of landmarks; landmarks represent the patient's facial morphology and are converted into FACS action units. Therapists use action units to diagnose and monitor patients during treatment for many facial conditions, providing this feedback from the system will therefore be preferable.

A mobile application is being developed to run on common platforms in use today (Android/IOS). The mobile application provides exercises and feedback during treatment, messaging functionality is planned, allowing two-way communication between therapist and patient.

Many patients dislike seeing their own face during exercises as they find this distressing. FACS action units are valuable in replicating the patient's facial movements for use in alternative visual feedback methods such as bars, gauges and avatars.

The application will provide background services to pass data to a remote server via the internet connection on the mobile device. This data will be accessible to therapists via a web portal and will provide a valuable link between therapist and patient. This system uses SSL encryption to secure the data and prevent the data being stolen during transmission. Any images of patient's are encrypted and data stored in the online database will not contain any identifiable details that allow an intruder to identify patients on the system. A secure database system will be used where access to the database will not be permitted from sources outside of the server ecosystem; access to the database will be done via a web service running within the server ecosystem. API's will be designed to pass the collected patient data one-way, up to the server. The mobile application will not download previously collected data; this will add an extra layer of security to patient information.

A web portal will be created for use by the therapist for monitoring patients'. A website-based solution was chosen, this is accessible via any web browser based system including Windows/Mac computers and mobile devices. The portal will provide expandable sets of tools for the therapist to analyse and monitor patients' continuously and to view visual representations of patient's facial movements. The portal will provide tools for communicating with patients and assigning custom exercise routines for each patient. Looking forwards, it could provide the use of cloud computing and machine learning algorithms to assist in treatment and analysis.

6. CONCLUSION

The research requires the development of a hardware device in the form of a pair of glasses wearable by the patient in everyday activities. The device has been prototyped to establish the best locations for the EMG sensors; there have been three prototypes developed so far and we have collected sample data from over 50 volunteers. This data has assisted us in establishing the requirement for extra sensors to detect the rise and fall of the cheek muscles. The sensor placement will be vital in providing therapists with everything they need in order to monitor the progress of patients and help detect potential problems in patient rehabilitation. We continue to explore different sensor options as we create more prototypes to address this need. Current EMG sensor placement (figure.1.0) is providing valuable data; we will miniaturize this form factor over the coming year and collect more data to continue research.

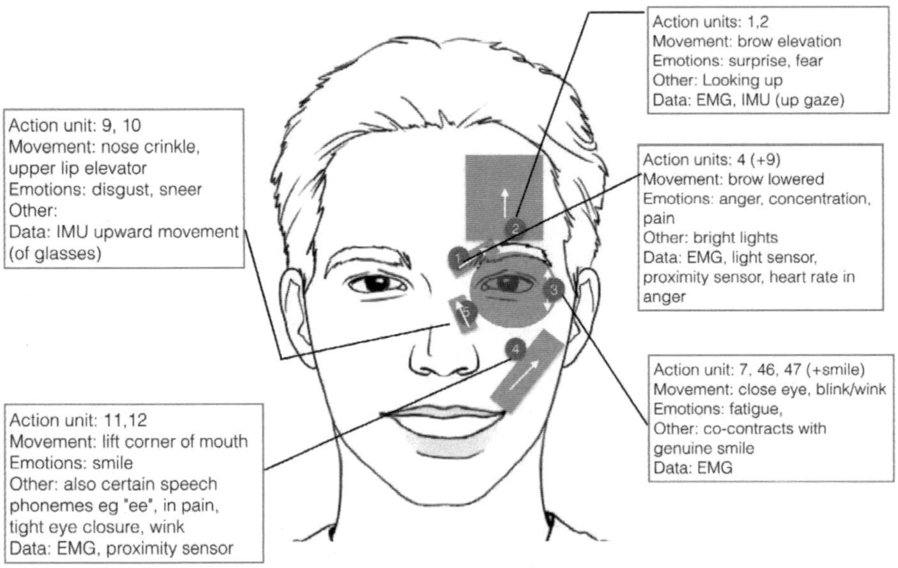

Figure 1. Selected EMG Sensor Locations

Now that we have sample data we are formatting this data so that we can transmit the data via Bluetooth to the mobile device for further processing, we can then pass this data up to the cloud. Work on developing machine-learning algorithms to process data into usable facial poses and muscle movement is currently underway.

We continue discussions with focus groups and therapists to establish and develop the required functionality into the software applications. We have held our first meetings with therapists and volunteer patients and currently analysing this data. Focus group meetings highlighted the need for communication channels between the patient and therapists, concerns were raised that in removing the requirement for a patient to attend a regular session with the therapist would demotivate the patient and cause them to seek information from elsewhere. We are investigating the option of adding features to the application such as direct messaging, video calls and contact information for approved charities.

Several hurdles need to be overcome to achieve our goals including the removal of background noise created by patient movements. The use of dry EMG sensors presents less accurate readings than could be achieved with wet sensors but are essential in achieving the goal of a daily wearable device. Research continues into the field of dry sensors and we hope to optimise and refine the results collected so that this accuracy hurdle is overcome. We continue to research into achieving optimal skin contact with the sensors when the frame itself moves on the patients face during everyday activity.

ACKNOWLEDGEMENT

This project was funded by the NIHR Invention for Innovation Programme (i4i). The views expressed are those of the authors and not necessarily those of the NHS, the NIHR or the Department of Health, UK.

REFERENCES

Book

NHS clinical stroke guidelines, Intercollegiate Stroke Working Party. *National clinical guideline for stroke, 4th edition.* London: Royal College of Physicians, 2012.

Journal

Daniel R Morales. et al, Impact of clinical trial findings on Bell's palsy management in general practice in the UK 2001–2012: interrupted time series regression analysis, *BMJ*, Open 2013;3:7 e003121 doi:10.1136/bmjopen-2013-003121

Ekman, P. et al, 1978. The Facial Action Coding System (FACS): A technique for the measurement of facial action. Palo Alto. *CA: Consulting Psychologists Press, Inc. Ekman, P. Levenson. RW, & Friesen WV (1983). Auto-nomic nervous system activity distinguishes among emotions. Science*, *221*, pp.1208-12.

Giggins OM, Persson UM, Caulfield B, 2013, Biofeedback in rehabilitation, *J Neuroengeering & Rehabilitation, 2013 Jun 18;10:60. doi: 10.1186/1743-0003-10-60*

Nicastri, M. et al, 2013, Efficacy of early physical therapy in severe Bell's palsy: a randomized controlled trial. *Neurorehabilitation and Neural Repair*, 27(6), 542–51. doi:10.1177/1545968313481280

Van der Weegen, S. et al, 2013, The Development of a Mobile Monitoring and Feedback Tool to Stimulate Physical Activity of People With a Chronic Disease in Primary Care: A User-Centered Design. *JMIR Mhealth and Uhealth*, 1(2), e8. doi:10.2196/mhealth.2526

Conference paper or contributed volume

Beurskens, C. H. et al, 2010, *Frequency and location of synkinesis in patients with peripheral facial nerve paresis*

Julian, D., and Partridge, J, 2008, *The Incidence and Prevalence of Disfigurement,* Changing faces, London

AN INSTRUCTIONAL CARD GAME WITH PUZZLE TRIGGERS: GUIDELINES FOR TEACHING SOFTWARE DEVELOPMENT

Mario Madureira Fontes and Ítalo Santiago Vega
Pontifical Catholic University of São Paulo, Brazil

ABSTRACT

This work describes how software development can be taught in the classroom by using instructional cards with puzzle triggers. It focuses on a case study which concerns teaching Civil Engineering undergraduate students to understand algorithms and also to write them in C language. In this work, the term puzzle trigger is adopted by the authors to name a scaffolding mechanism used to create card games. The novelty of this work is that the authors propose to introduce puzzle triggers in instructional card games. A guideline including methodological procedures on how to create an activity based on the use of instructional card games with puzzle triggers and its application to a specific computational learning context are presented. The design of the cards, its rules, its playing mechanics and its application in an experiment with a group of students are described. This kind of application is thought to help students to learn strategies for translating solutions of real world problems to computer-related world solutions. Among the concepts to be mastered and put into practice, the writing, understanding and implementation of algorithms, due to their complexity, pose a lot of difficulty to students. To cope with this kind of teaching complex computational concepts, card games with puzzle triggers are thought to be helpful.

KEYWORDS

Puzzle triggers, card games, computational learning, algorithms

1. INTRODUCTION

Card games have been used in education for decades in several disciplines for motivating learners. More recently, digital card games have become a favored object of scientific investigation. Kordaki and Gousiou (2017) present a ten-year systematic review on digital card games in education. Their paper covers topics which are also useful to analyze non-digital instructional card games. They consider the impact of card games in education, the types of card games and their characteristics, areas of application, functionality, mediums of delivery, theoretical backgrounds, impact, weaknesses and implications for future researches.

On the use of card games for teaching purposes, one of the advantages mentioned by Kordaki and Gousiou (2017) is the promotion of learners' higher mental thinking skills and one of the weaknesses is the lack of scaffolding mechanisms in instructional card game playing.

Successful results of research experiments on the use of card games for teaching computation-related concepts have been reported in the literature concerned with serious games (Baker et al, 2003; Baker et al, 2005; Zapata, 2009; Fernandes and Sousa, 2010; Zapata, 2012; Kordaki and Gousiou, 2016). Among the findings which have been reported, card games with puzzle triggers are considered suitable to teaching purposes because if they follow some requirements, such as functional design phases, adequate learning curve, easy steps to follow, they can be used to motivate the students and help them learn difficult matters.

In this work, a modified version of card games, introducing puzzle triggers, is proposed. According to (Polya, 1945), a puzzle is a process to solve a problem. It can refer to an individual's internal stimuli to develop mental reasoning in order to solve a problem or to the external stimuli which lead the individual to interpret and build a puzzle in his mind. Puzzles are used to refer to the process of understanding and the cognitive actions which must be taken in order to solve problems. The individual who develops the mental reasoning and solves the problems is the problem solver. Puzzles arise in the problem solver's mind when he gets into contact with triggers. These puzzle triggers are elements which are related to the scenario of the problem and act as triggers which function as trailheads for puzzles, that is they are thought by the authors to refer to a scaffolding mechanism to create the card game.

There are several types of puzzles, such as Riddles, Lateral Thinking, Spatial Reasoning, Pattern Recognition, Logic, Exploration and Item Use (Brathwaite and Schreiber, 2009) which can be used to engage students in learning specific computational contents.

These puzzles can be introduced by triggers and the choice of the trigger depends on the nature of the puzzle. For example, the Pattern Recognition puzzle can be introduced by triggers which drive lead the problem solvers to establish sequences based on the recognition of repeated patterns. To illustrate the adequacy of the trigger to a puzzle, one of the puzzling problems posed by (Parhami, 2009) can be taken into account. It deals with the recognition of the relationship between integers in Euclid sequences, Collats sequences and Fibonacci sequences. The trigger to these puzzling problems is the questioning about finding the right sequence. To find the right sequence the problem solver needs to recognize patterns.

In this work instructional card games with puzzle triggers are used to teach software development. It focuses on a case study which concerns teaching Civil Engineering undergraduate students to understand algorithms and also to write them in C language.

Having set the objective and context of our work in this section, the guidelines for the design of the cards, the building of the rules, the definition of the mechanics of play and the application of the card game with the puzzle triggers in an experiment with a group of students are considered in the next section.

2. GUIDELINES FOR BUILDING CARD GAMES WITH PUZZLES

In the literature (Kordaki, 2015; Kordaki and Gousiou, 2016; Kordaki and Gousiou, 2017), there are surveys concerning papers on the use of digital card games for instructional purposes. In the discussion section of a review paper on the use of digital card games in education, Kordaki and Gousiou (2017) point out gaps related to creating, designing and applying card games to the educational context. One of the gaps pointed out by these authors, as mentioned in the introduction of this work, is the lack of scaffolding mechanisms to cognitively support the players/learners during the play of card games. To cope with this gap, this work proposes the introduction of puzzle triggers in card games and outlines the following requirements to be followed:

1. Defining and setting the rules to explain how to use the cards. This type card is called a Rule Card.
2. Defining and setting the objectives and themes of the activity related to the classroom plan.
3. Defining and setting specific rules to describe the activity. This type of card is called the Utterance card and it contains a puzzle trigger, that is, a question to motivate the students to solve the puzzle.
4. Defining and setting the order in which the students will receive the cards. The students can be given all the cards or certain groups of cards, depending on the nature of the task to be performed.
5. Defining and setting some hints to complement the Utterance Cards. This type of card is the Hint card.
6. Playing the cards with the students. Usually the cards are distributed randomly to the students as an intentional strategy to force the students think collaboratively and review the learned concepts.

Based on the above-mentioned requirements, which are theoretically critical-thinking-oriented, the following activity described in the following section of this paper was developed. According to Sternberg (1986), the features comprised by critical thinking are “the mental processes, strategies, and representations people use to solve problems, make decisions and learn new concepts.” The requirements were drawn up to address these features.

2.1 Card Game Activity

The card game activity was designed to teach the Civil Engineering students how to deal with real world problems in their area. These students had no previous knowledge of algorithms and coding. The problem dealt with in the activity was calculating the number of sacks of cement to build a road pavement. In order to cope with this problem the students had to build an algorithm and write it in C language. To build the algorithm the student had to recall and understand the steps implicit in software development.

The first step was the analysis of the world problem and the second step was the analysis of how the solution of the world problem fitted the computational context. These two steps lead to the third step which was the building of the algorithm. The fourth and last step concerned the translation of the algorithm to a source code written in C language.

Based on these four steps, the activity was planned to be performed in three phases. In the first phase the Rule Cards and some of the Utterance Cards were distributed at random to the students. Furthermore, the students were told to read, understand, order and organize all the Rule Cards. This kind of instruction was given orally, and it was, in fact, the only rule which is not included in the dynamics of both the Rule and Utterance Cards.

The first phase was meant to help the student to understand the tasks to be done and to analyze how the world problem fitted into the computational environment. After they have understood the Rule Cards and the Utterance Cards given to them in the first phase, they got, in a second phase, the Hint Cards and other Utterance Cards. The objective of the second phase was helping the students to build the algorithm. In the second phase the students were supposed to order the cards and fill in the blank posts included in the cards so as to build the source code. In the third phase the students received cards containing fragments of the source code in C language for them to order and write the algorithm in C language.

In all phases, there were triggers to help the students to remember and relate concepts. All the puzzle triggers in the card game activity were meant to yield a Riddle puzzle or an Item Use puzzle. The Riddle puzzle was used to supply the missing information on the cards or to highlight issues that they needed to remember in order to solve the Riddle. The Item Use puzzle was chosen to draw the students' attention to the information contained in the set of cards.

2.2 The card game application

The card game was applied to 9 students. At the time of the activity, they were attending the first year of a Civil Engineering course. They were given 44 cards. For this application 44 cards were considered enough. For other applications some other number of cards may be necessary. These cards were divided into groups: 4 cards for the Rules Cards, 40 cards for the Utterances Cards and Hints Cards: 9 of them discuss the real world problems, 12 to the building of algorithm and 19 to the implementation of the algorithm. In Figure 1, one example of each of these groups of cards is given.

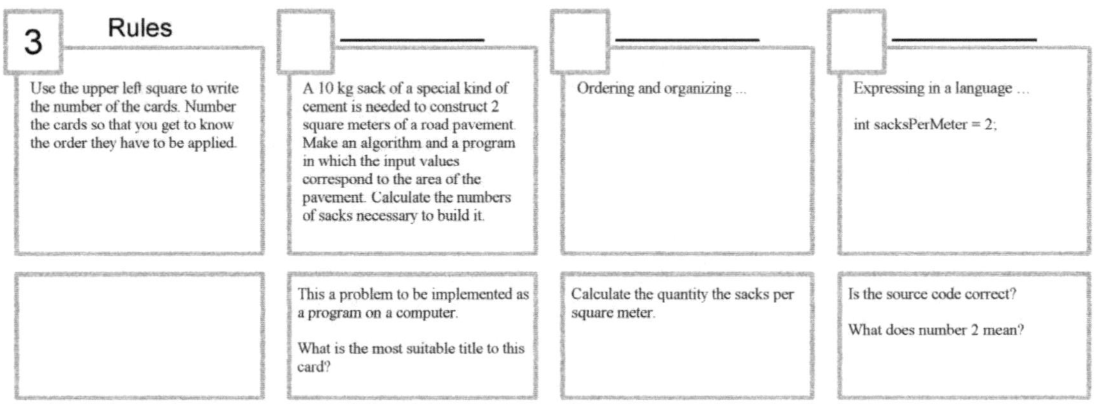

Figure 1. From left to right, an example of each group of cards: a rules, utterance (real world problem), utterance (algorithm) and utterance (code implementation)

In Figure 2, a draft of the code they were building with the help of the group of cards related to the building of the algorithm.

Figure 2. The image [A] shows the students ordering the algorithm and the image [B] shows the students' drafts of the source code writing.

The group of Rule Cards contained the set of rules to be followed. In this type of card group there was the following information: the description of each card structure, the rule to number each card in the right order and the rule to name each card with an appropriate title.

The activity held the students' attention. While doing the activity, they checked the notes they had made in previous classes. They were able to understand the card game organization. First of all, the students were given the Rule Cards to help them to understand the objective of the activity. After that, they got the Utterance Cards related to the real world problem. When they got the Utterance Cards they read them and understood what they were supposed to do. However, they started to implement the source code right away without taking into account the algorithm. At that moment they were told that they should write the algorithm before implementing the source code. To help them understand what they had to do they were given cards with puzzle triggers to make them think over the problem they had to solve and draw conclusions before writing the algorithm. When difficulties to organize the source code arose, they were told to reorganize the cards containing the source code fragments in order to build the algorithm and the code in C language. As they finished working with the Utterance Cards, they were given the cards to write the algorithm and finally they got the cards to build the C language.

After finishing the activities, they were given a questionnaire to express their opinions about the card game activity. The questionnaire had the following questions: How did you like the card game activity? Were the puzzle triggers motivating? Did the puzzle triggers help to learn new concepts and relate them to previously learned concepts? The answers to these questions were all positive. All the students agreed on the fact that the triggers guided them to solve the problem in an easy and enjoyable way. No negative answer was given. The card game was considered to elicit a good environment since they had no previous knowledge of algorithms and they managed to learn how to write them. It was also found to enrich social collaboration among the students.

The puzzle triggers which were introduced as questions in the cards activated various kinds of puzzles in the learners' minds and, in this way, they prompted different logic viewpoints and promoted a reliable evaluation of the problem to be solved. As a consequence they helped the students to develop higher mental skills and have a good performance in the process of decision making. Based on the aforementioned aspects, puzzle triggers in instructional card games are argued by the authors of this work to make a difference in the pedagogical context.

3. CONCLUSION

This work presented a case study addressing the issue of how software development can be taught in the classroom by using instructional cards with puzzle triggers. It introduced a guideline on how to create an activity based on card-based games with puzzle triggers and its application to a specific computational learning context. The requirements to build the cards were presented in section 2, the design of the cards and its rules in section 2.1 and its playing mechanics and its application in an experiment with a group of students in section 2.2.

The novelty of this work stems from the fact that it proposes introducing puzzle triggers as scaffolding mechanisms in card game activities. Puzzle triggers inserted in card games are thought to make a difference in terms of the dynamics of the activity since the students are challenged to plan, think, decide and act to solve the problem and in performing the tasks required by the triggers they develop their critical thinking. They can also help students to apply the knowledge they acquired to other situations which pose problems to be solved. The fact that students are challenged and given hints makes the activity of card game with triggers enjoyable and engaging.

The guideline proposed in this paper is meant to provide a starting point to building card games with triggers in a systematic way. It opens a large path to be followed in terms of adjusting the kinds of puzzles and improving the writing of triggers so that they are able to evoke enjoyable learning experiences. Further studies with a larger group of subjects and control and experimental groups are needed.

ACKNOWLEDGEMENTS

My very best thanks to all who have contribute to this work: my colleagues from Pontifical Catholic University of São Paulo, my students from the Civil Engineering Course, the reviewers and the proofreader of this article.

REFERENCES

Baker, A. et al. 2003. Problems and Programmers: an educational software engineering card game, *25th International Conference on Software Engineering*. Proceedings., Portland, pp. 614-619.

Baker, A. et al. 2005. An experimental card game for teaching software engineering processes. *Journal of Systems and Software*, Vol. 75, No. 1, pp. 3-16.

Brathwaite, B. and Schreiber, I. 2009. Challenges for game designers. *Course Technology CENGAGE Learning*, pp. 43-48.

Fernandes, J. M. and Sousa, S. M. 2010. PlayScrum - A Card Game to Learn the Scrum Agile Method, *2010 Second International Conference on Games and Virtual Worlds for Serious Applications*, Braga, pp. 52-59.

Kordaki, M. 2015. A constructivist, modeling methodology for the design of educational card games. *Procedia-Social and Behavioral Sciences*, 191, pp. 26-30.

Kordaki, M., & Gousiou, A. 2016. Computer Card Games in Computer Science Education: A 10-Year Review. *Educational Technology & Society*, 19 (4), pp. 11–21.

Kordaki, M., & Gousiou, A. 2017. Digital card games in education: A ten year systematic review. *Computers & Education*, 109, pp. 122-161.

Parhami, B. 2009. Motivating computer engineering freshmen through mathematical and logical puzzles. *IEEE Transactions on Education*, 52 (3), pp. 360-364.

Polya, G. 1945. How to solve it: A new aspect of mathematical model. *Princeton University - Press Princeton*, pp. 160-162.

Sternberg, R. J. 1986. Critical Thinking: Its Nature, Measurement, and Improvement. *U. S. Department of Education Research and improvement – Educational Resources Information Center*, pp. 1-37.

Zapata, C. M. et al. 2009. El juego del diálogo de educción de requisitos. *Avances en Sistemas e Informática*, Vol. 6, N. 1, pp. 105-114.

Zapata, C. M. et al. 2012. PoV-game: puntos de vista mediante juegos. *Revista de Ingenierías: Universidad de Medellín*, Vol. 11, No. 20, pp. 115-126.

SUPPORTING DOMAIN EXPERTS UNDERSTANDING THEIR DATA: A VISUAL FRAMEWORK FOR ASSEMBLING HIGH-LEVEL ANALYSIS PROCESSES

Daniel Kaltenthaler, Johannes-Y. Lohrer and Peer Kröger
Institut für Informatik, Ludwig-Maximilians, Universität München, Germany

ABSTRACT

We describe and discuss different approaches for the graphical data composition in a general framework for visual querying and analyzing scientific data. Researchers from zooarchaeological domains dependent on analyzing massive amounts of data on objects found in excavations. Our framework is designed to support them by offering a way to assemble custom queries without prior knowledge of programming. The results are graphical representations that can be used for their analyses, without having to export any data and use extern analysis tools or spreadsheet applications. We describe the necessary requirements and discuss the approaches. The evaluation of a user study contributes towards the development of a prototype of the framework.

KEYWORDS

Analysis, Framework, Interface, Usability, Visual querying

1. INTRODUCTION

The recovery and analysis of material culture is the main focus of archaeological work. The corpus of finds like artifacts, faunal remains, or human burial remains are excavated, described, categorized, and analyzed in projects all over the world. A huge amount of archaeological data is documented in archaeological database applications which are the basis for these analyses. The results of analyzing collected data help us learn about the past. Nevertheless, these applications only support simple descriptive statistics or implement algorithms that were explicitly designed for the specific research areas of application. To achieve analyses data is usually exported from a database in the form of spreadsheets or CSV files to be analyzed external. This method can be aggravating, time consuming, and error-prone, but it is still common practice. Apart from offering a rich set of options for the users for analyses, it is also important to offer an intuitive, user-friendly, and meaningful GUI that allows them to carry out analyses easily.

There are free and commercial tools of many kinds that provide visual querying data from a database. Tools like *Query Xtractor* (2016) or *SQLeo Visual Query Builder* (2013) focus on form and graph based querying data and returning the result as a table, but are too complex, technical, and thus hard to be used by regular users. Other tools like *datapine* (2012), *Klipfolio Dashboard* (2011), or *Qlik Sense* (2005) allow the easy creation of analyses and the corresponding graphs, but are limited to their possibilities of compositions. Querying and assembling custom, complex data is rarely possible.

The target is to provide a flexible tool that archaeologists can use for visually querying the data directly in their database application and create almost every composition for their data analyses. The technical basis and implementation of the framework was discussed in a previous work (Lohrer, Kaltenthaler and Kröger, 2016). In this paper, we discuss and evaluate the graphical representation of the data composition by offering the possibility to embed a visual querying framework to provide this functionality. Accordingly, we list a set of requirements that we will address. This has been extracted from comprehensive discussions with domain experts, reflecting their typical analysis procedures. We will discuss existing approaches for visual querying and evaluate them in a user study. Considering the evaluations, we revise the approaches and implement a prototype that we integrate into the zooarchaeological database *OssoBook* (2013).

2. PROBLEM FORMULATION

The Analysis Tool was originally developed for the zooarchaeological database *OssoBook* (Kaltenthaler and Lohrer 2012). In the context of the JANUS project of the *German Archaeological Institute*, Berlin, Germany, *OssoBook* will serve as a standard for the zooarchaeology domain in Germany.

The composition of data from a database is the most important step. We want to introduce a combination of established and new ideas for the representation of queries for databases in zooarchaeological working environments, evaluate them, and show our implementation in *OssoBook* with a view to avoid the disadvantages of existing applications. We defined the requirements below as necessary for the development:

- **User-friendliness:** A graphical realization within the application for users without any programming skills. We need user-friendly database queries that have to be composed without the knowledge of programming code and writing SQL queries.
- **As few restrictions as possible:** The users should have as few restrictions as possible while compositing data. We want to achieve a flexibility in querying data similar to SQL queries, without overwhelming the users with the complexity of programming interfaces.
- **Reusable modules:** The different types of queries and data handling must be packed into single modules to realize the different functionalities that can be reused in several areas.
- **Dynamic behavior:** Since every database may have a different structure it is impossible to define all variations manually. Furthermore, it may happen with every application update that input fields are added, removed, or changed. To keep the maintenance effort as low as possible for the Analysis Tool, the single modules must have a dynamic behavior to read out the available database structure.

3. APPROACHES

Below we introduce three promising options we considered for our implementation and discuss the pros and cons of the respective approaches. Each of these approaches is illustrated in Figure 1.

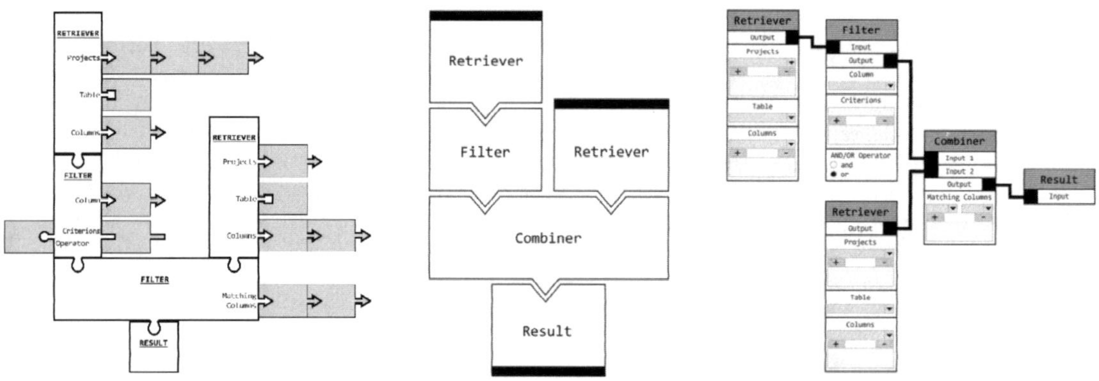

Figure 1. From left to right, the sketches of the Puzzle Piece Approach, Box Approach, and Directed Graph Approach

3.1 Puzzle Pieces Approach

In the Puzzle Piece Approach the modules are represented by single puzzle pieces that are arranged from top to bottom to realize the composition. Every puzzle piece applies the functionality of the module on the input data, the top connection(s). The manipulated data is returned to the output, the bottom connection. By putting two puzzle pieces together the output data of the upper puzzle piece becomes the input data of the lower puzzle piece. Specific settings (optional and mandatory ones) for the modules can be set by attaching other puzzle pieces (hereinafter named as "setting pieces") to the left or right side of the puzzle piece which can be configured individually. These are indicated with free connections where a setting piece can be attached. The shape of the connection indicates which type of setting piece can be attached. For example, if a setting requires a Boolean value as an input, the connection is indicated with a circled shape. A composition is defined as valid if all input and output connections of the modules are assigned. Furthermore, all mandatory settings must be connected with at least one setting piece.

Pros: The puzzle pieces are self-explanatory, the users can recognize where they can attach new pieces because of the shapes of the connections. The usage of shapes is a big advantage for color-blind people. The top to bottom arrangement of the modules is a clear and intuitive structure. The left to right arrangement of the setting pieces gives a clear impression about the adjusted settings corresponding to the specific module.

Cons: The use of complex and numerous settings makes the representation wide and confusing if there is more than one puzzle piece parallel on the same level. Furthermore, there is only less space to enter the setting criteria on the single setting pieces without making them too wide.

Rating: The Puzzle Piece Approach is a clearly arranged way to represent a data composition in a graphical representation for simple databases with only one data table. As soon as it is necessary to use puzzle pieces with more than one input (e.g. to join several datasets) the graphical representation gets too wide and complex. So it is not applicable to our application.

3.2 Box Approach

The Box Approach is a further development and variation of the Puzzle Piece Approach, trying to reduce the complexity of the graphical representation. The general top to bottom arrangement remains unchanged, only the connections are replaced with docking points to clarify the input and output locations. The setting pieces are removed completely and are not visible in the composition overview anymore. Instead the users can now double-click the single boxes to open a popup that provides all necessary settings for the corresponding box. This popup may display all available properties to set the box as well as further information to the users.

Pros: Opening the settings in an own popup provides more space for displaying the setting options. Due to the removal of the setting elements, the general overview of the graphical representation is improved a lot. The layout of the rectangular elements yields a more clearly arranged representation of the composition.

Cons: There is insufficient space for the display of any information, if the settings are integrated into the box itself. To get detailed information it is necessary to either open the settings panel or add a kind of tooltip to the box. This might get confusing in case of complex data compositions.

Rating: The compact display of the Box Approach is suitable for complex data compositions. The ability to open the settings of boxes enables the display of a high number of properties. In comparison to the Puzzle Piece Approach it might grant more overview, even if the clearness is due to the lack of space for displaying information.

3.3 Directed Graph Approach

Another presentation of the data composition can be achieved by using a directed graph. Each vertex represents one module, which is connected by edges to other modules, where the edges have a direction associated with them. This way the output data of each module can be connected as an input of other modules. Every module is displayed as a box holding all necessary information and settings for the module. Each property is displayed as a "row" within the box where the settings can be set directly. The input(s) and output of the data are also added each as an own row. To gain a valid data composition all input and output connections of the modules must be assigned to another connection, too. Furthermore the mandatory settings of each module must be defined in each single row.

Pros: The representation as a directed graph has the advantage that it can also be used as a directed multigraph, so the data output of a module can be connected to multiple data inputs of other modules as well. The removal of single connections might be easier than in other approaches, because the visual and logical connection can be deleted without handling the boxes.

Cons: The use of directed multigraphs may cause loops that would cause infinite loops while compositing the data. These loops must be prevented in the program logic. Furthermore it must be considered how to allow the users rearrangements of the composition, whether the users can move the modules to any position or the application force specific locations. Still, the size of the module boxes might get too high if there are too many or too complex setting rows, but possibly a function to hide and unhide single setting rows would avoid this problem.

Rating: In our application the Directed Graph Approach fulfills all requirements, but the user-friendliness is lowered with more complex data compositions that are using modules with numerous setting rows.

4. USER STUDY

After the rating of the single possibilities we decided not to consider the Puzzle Piece Approach anymore. This approach is not applicable to our application due to the mentioned disadvantages. We involved the actual users of *OssoBook* to get the feedback of zooarchaeologists about the graphical composition of data.

We created paper prototypes for the two approaches the participants should use to compose the single elements. They were able to place, label, move, and remove them. The connections of the Directed Graph Approach were realized with a string of wool. Together with some domain experts we defined a set of tasks for zooarchaeological compositions that the candidates should solve, e.g. like filtering data for a specific animal species. As a result of the observation of the participants and their feedback we registered useful facts:

- Most of the participants had difficulties in finding out how to enter any settings in the Box Approach. They were confused that they had to open them by double-clicking the box. This mechanic was not intuitive to them because there is no indication for this functionality.
- The participants preferred the compactness of the Box Approach. The single boxes of the Directed Graph Approach requires a lot of space and makes a compact arrangement difficult.
- At the same time the participants liked the visible information of the Directed Graph Approach because all setting rows and their inputs are displayed in the box. The Box Approach always requires another action to open and view the setting information that interrupt the workflow.
- The participants requested a possibility to display an intermediate result of the current data.
- The majority of the participants preferred the element arrangement of the Directed Graph Approach. They can reposition the single boxes and connect them afterwards with the connection lines without the box changing its position. The boxes in the Box Approach must always be docked to another box which makes the definition of subqueries difficult.

Altogether, the larger majority favor the Directed Graph Approach, although they would prefer a more space saving display.

5. REALIZATION & PROTOTYPE

After the evaluation of the user study, we revised the named approaches and introduced the constructive feedback from the participants. We implemented a prototype that includes some important adjustments.

- **Directed Graph Approach:** We decided to use the Directed Graph Approach as a basic visualization concept, because the majority of the participants preferred working with the graphs instead of the Box Approach. Furthermore, it is also a great advantage to be able to connect one data output with more than only one other data input to avoid unnecessary redefinitions.
- **Outsourcing of Settings:** Due to the increasing complexity of extensive data compositions the single setting rows were removed from the boxes. The input and output rows remain at the same position, but the setting rows were outsourced to an own popup panel. In the Box Approach it was not intuitive enough for the users to open the settings by double clicking on the box itself. By moving the settings to another panel, it would be the same problem in the modified Directed Graph Approach as well. That's why the possibility of opening the settings is now indicated with a button in the box. The setting property elements need not to be embedded into another interface element anymore.
- **Settings Panel:** The settings are now displayed in an own panel that provides large amount of free space for GUI components. This enables more complex and more customizable settings. Furthermore, there is enough space to add additional information to the settings.
- **Improved Display of Information:** It became necessary to improve the display of information about the boxes and the graph in general since the settings are not visible in the box anymore, because they are hidden inside the panel that is opened by the settings button. We added a text label that can be labeled with a custom text in the settings. If the users want to, they can enter a short information text there that can help them navigating through the graph.
- **View current data:** We added a second button to the boxes that generates the current box data. This helps the users keep track of the current data. This data is displayed as a table and is always up to date when it is loaded by the users. This element might also be a good debug method for possible errors.

With these results we now have a concept that we want to use for the implementation of the graphical representation of the Analysis Tool, which can be viewed as a screenshot in Figure 2.

New modules can be added by clicking the corresponding button at the left sidebar. All boxes have the same basic layout. On the top there is the title line of the Box that describes the type of the modules, e.g. Retriever, Combiner, etc. Below the input and output rows are arranged. Two buttons are located in the last row of each box: One to open the setting panel for the box, and one to open (if available) the current output data of the specific box in table form. Additionally, a description text is displayed in the box below the title that can be used to comment or describe the logic of the composition.

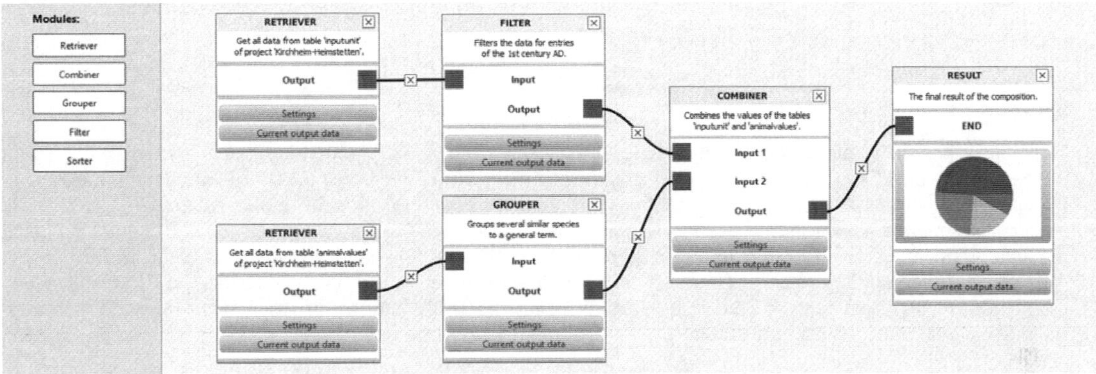

Figure 2. Screenshot of the Analysis Tool. The displayed graph represents a data composition of species distribution

6. CONCLUSION & FUTURE WORK

In this paper, we described a list of requirements that should be fulfilled for a user-friendly GUI for analysis tools for archaeologists. We discussed several approaches, in relation to the previously listed requirements. Considering the results of a user study we defined a solution and implemented a prototype of the Analysis Tool. We pointed out the possibilities of the graphical compositions and the fast generation of diagrams in the GUI. This paper describes the Analysis Tool as an early prototype, however it is already ready for use and has many benefits for the target group, especially because of reasons of reliability and time saving. Naturally, there are currently some limitations that still need to be addressed in future to achieve its full potential. There is still room for further improvements for the usability of the Analysis Tool, e.g. the integration of drag and drop gestures to add new boxes and elements to a specific position. A function to auto-arrange, that moves the boxes to a useful position considering the available connections would help to improve the clear overview of the composition.

REFERENCES

Datapine, Data Visualization & Business Intelligence Tool (2012). [software] http://www.datapine.com [15.03.2017]

Kaltenthaler, D. and Lohrer, J. (2012): *Visual and Density Based Cluster Analysis of the Archaeological Database OssoBook in Consideration of Aspects of Data Integrity, Consistency and Quality*. Diplomarbeit. Ludwig-Maximilians-Universität München, Database Systems Group, Munich.

Klipfolio. Business Dashboard Software for Everyone (2011). [software] http://www.klipfolio.com [15.03.2017]

Lohrer, J., Kaltenthaler, D., and Kröger, P. (2016): *Leveraging Data Analysis for Domain Experts: An Embeddable Framework for Basic Data Science Tasks*. In: *Proceedings of the 7th International Conference on Internet Technologies & Society 2016*. Melbourne, VIC, Australia.

Qlik Sense (2005). [software] http://www.qlik.com [15.03.2017]

Query Xtractor (2016). [software] https://data-xtractor.com/query-xtractor/ [15.03.2017]

SQLeo Visual Query Builder (2013). [software] http://sqleo.sourceforge.net/guide.htm [15.03.2017]

FINDING USABILITY PROBLEMS IN ERP APPLICATION *H*ELP AND END-USER TRAINING MATERIAL

Mazhar Sadiq[1] and Antti Pirhonen[2]
[1]*Department of Computer Science, COMSATS Institute of Information Technology, Pakistan*
[2]*Department of Teacher Education , University of Jyväskylä, Finland*

ABSTRACT

Over the last decade, many organisations have implemented the standardised information system called Enterprise Resource Planning (ERP). ERP systems offer great promise for business process improvement, system integration, cost reduction and logistics efficiencies. While millions of dollars have been spent on the implementation of ERP systems, the potential users are still not able to use it. Usability problems are the big barrier preventing end-users from achieving required productivity. This research, based on 80 respondents, tried to find out the usability problems in ERP application *H*elp and end-user training material. The results indicate that 56% of end-users did not consider the ERP application *H*elp usable. Out of 80 respondents, 45 didn't have training material at all, and the 35 respondents who did have end-user training material considered it very usable.

KEYWORDS

Usability, Enterprise Resource Planning, ERP application Help, End-user training material

1. INTRODUCTION

The global business environment is changing rapidly, and organisations from all over the world have to re-engineer their business processes in order to face the challenges of increased competition and rising customer expectations. The standardised information system that is enhancing organisational performance through the integration of various business modules is called Enterprise Resource Planning (ERP). Despite the potential benefits that an organisation could gain from a successful ERP implementation, many are still facing difficult problems and are unable to achieve significant organisational improvement. Some organisations have downsized their initiatives, and others have accepted minimum payoffs or given up the ERP implementation (Fethi & Ferah, 2004). ERP implementation problems potentially lead to project failure. Different types of failure are: poorly defined business goals (Deloitte Consulting, 2000), expectation failure (when the ERP application does not match user expectations), interaction failure (when end-users' attitudes toward the ERP application are negative), inadequate training (Shaul & Tauber, 2013), lack of commitment from top management and ignoring accuracy of data (Zhang, 2002). Many researchers have mentioned that the usability of the system is one of the key factors for failure in ERP applications (Fethi & Ferah, 2004).

A product with bad usability will make it harder for the end-users to achieve their goals. As a result, their productivity with the ERP application will suffer. End user training is an important factor to ERP system success. The effectiveness of training depends on the usability of documentation (Scott, 2008). In recent years, many organisations have implemented ERP systems. In most cases, the potential or intended end-users are not able to use them (Garača, 2011). Usability is a critical success factor of ERP system. Poor usability makes it difficult to interact with the ERP application, which further impacts the time to learn how to use the product (Scholtz et al., 2013). In this article, we tried to highlight the usability problems in ERP application *H*elp and end-user training material. The next section discusses the methodology that was used in a survey of 80 respondents from two organisations. This is followed by the results, and conclusion.

2. RESEARCH METHODOLOGY

In order to approach this research, we have used a survey methodology. The main instrument for collecting the primary data was a questionnaire composed of four research questions:

1. How usable is the ERP application *Help*?
2. How usable is the end-user training material (or functional document)?
3. Is training material available to end-users?
4. What kind of usability problems do the end-users face without the availability of training material?

Two case organisations from Pakistan were selected. The concept of usability was introduced to end-users before getting the questionnaire feedback.

2.1 Case Organisations and Respondents Details

Organisation A is from the oil & gas sector, while organisation B is from the manufacturing industry. Both organisations have implemented Oracle ERP modules within the last seven years. The 80 respondents in this research were full-time employees working in these two organisations. The data were collected between June and September, 2013. Of 80 respondents, 20 were female and 60 were male. The main instrument for collecting the data from respondents was the questionnaire. The respondents detail is in Table 1.

Table 1. Respondents Demographic Information

ERP Vendor	Respondents	Department	Experience	Education
ORACLE	20	Financial	0 – 6	MBA, B.Com
	20	Order Management	0 – 6	B.A, B.Com, MBA
	15	Purchasing	0 – 6	B.A, B.Com, MBA
	25	Inventory	0 – 6	F. A, B.A, B.Com, MBA
Total	80			

2.2 Questionnaire Items

The questionnaire consisted of four parts. The first part involved demographic questions designed to collect the information about the respondent, their organisation, age, gender, type of ERP system use and experience with the ERP system. The second part involved two questions about getting the respondents' feedback on the ERP application *Help* and end-user training material. This part used a four-point, Likert-type scale 1=not at all to 4=very usable. The third part involved one question about the respondents' feedback on the availability of end-user training material. This part used a four-point, Likert-type scale 1=not at all to 4=all of it. The fourth part involved one open-ended question about finding usability problems when the end-user training material was not available.

3. RESULTS

Different types of data analysis techniques can be utilised on qualitative and quantitative data. For quantitative data analysis, descriptive statistics, correlation analysis, development of predictive models and hypothesis testing are commonly used. For our research purposes, we have used descriptive statistics which is a technique easily understood by a general audience.

3.1 How Usable is the ERP Application *Help*?

In order to investigate this question, we have divided the 80 respondents into two categories. The first category has an experience range from zero to two years, while the other category has an experience range from two to six years. Descriptive statistics, mean, median and frequency values are used for analysing the results. The overall results are in Table 2.

Table 2. Feedback from Respondents on ERP Application _H_elp

Question	Frequency Count				Mean	Median
	1	2	3	4		
Is the '_H_elp' provided by this Oracle ERP Application is usable?	45	30	3	2	1.5	1
Respondents experience From 0 to 2 Years	35	10	5	0	1.4	1
Respondents experience From 2 to 6 Years	10	10	8	2	2.1	2

The overall mean value is 1.5, while the median is 1. These results tell us that 56% of the respondents did not consider the Oracle ERP _H_elp usable. Only 35 respondents considered it usable on some level; three considered it mostly usable and only two considered it fully usable. Further analysis revealed that the respondents who have less experience (0-2 years) considered _H_elp less usable compared to those having more experience (2-6 years). The mean value for less experienced respondents is 1.4, while for experienced respondents it is 2.1. Only two experienced respondents (in the 2-6 year range) considered the ERP application _H_elp fully usable.

Now the question is why is the standard _H_elp provided by the ERP application not usable? In order to find the answers to this question, we interviewed the respondents. The end-users mentioned two usability problems, as follow:

1. The task procedural steps are mentioned only in the form of English text. There is no screenshot attached to each step. The respondents said that it would be usable if the task procedural steps were mentioned in English text along with a screenshot.
2. The ERP application _H_elp provided by this vendor is too generic.

To understand the above mentioned usability problems, let's take a real purchase order example in the ERP. Suppose the end-user is in the purchase order transaction window and he/she wants to get help for completing the lines. This could be done in two ways: directly by clicking the question mark (?) on the specific window, or getting it from the _H_elp Menu Bar. When the end-user initiates either of the two ways, the _H_elp window will open in another area called "Purchase Order Window Alternative Region". This window shows all the help options related to the purchase order window available in clickable form. The options are: 'Entering purchase order headers, Entering purchase order lines etc. The end-user clicks on the purchase order lines and the new screen will open up. (as seen in Figure 1).

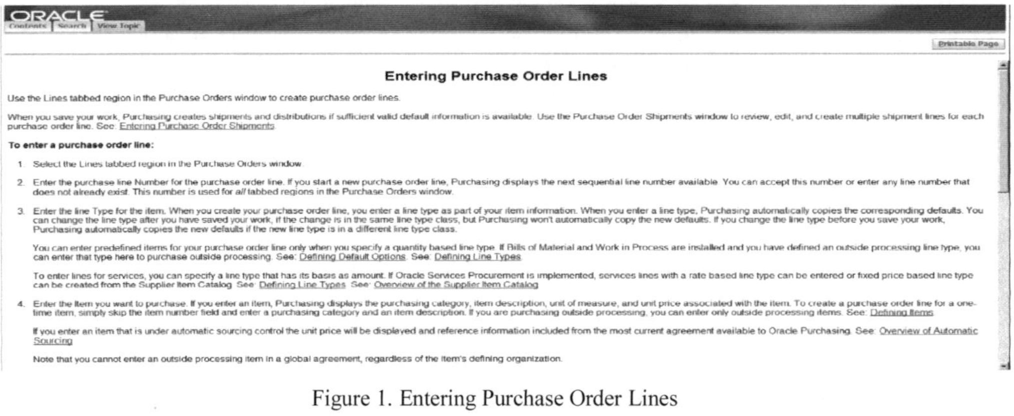

Figure 1. Entering Purchase Order Lines

As we can see from Figure 1, all the task procedural steps for entering purchase order lines are written in only English text. It is also too generic. For instance, Step 3 reads: "Enter the line type for the item." The line types depend on the specific operating unit of the organisation. It could be finished good, raw material or scrap items. this window, all the task procedural steps for entering purchase order lines are written in only English text. It is also too generic.

3.2 How Usable is the End-user Training Material (or Functional Document)?

The feedback from the 35 respondents is shown in Table 3. The overall mean value is 3.6, and the median is 4. Almost all of the respondents considered the end-user training material very usable. Not a single respondent considered it not usable. Further analysis revealed that there is only .1 difference between the mean value of respondents having less experience (0-2 years) and more experience (2-6 years).

Table 3. Feedback from Respondents on End-user Training Material

Question	Frequency Count				Mean	Median
	1	2	3	4		
If you have the 'End-user' training Material (some or all) available, is it usable?	0	2	8	25	3.6	4
Respondents experience From 0 to 2 Years	0	0	2	5	3.7	4
Respondents experience From 2 to 6 Years	0	2	6	20	3.6	4

We contacted the IT department of organisation B and investigated the reason behind the views of the respondents considering the usability of the end-user training material. We went through some of the training material related to the purchasing module and found that each procedural task step was shown in English text along with specific screenshots. The end-user training material was designed according to a specific organisation unit. For instance, they had the specific 'Item code' and 'Unit of measure.' Due to confidentiality of the organisations, it is not possible to show their end-user training material here.

3.3 Is Training Material Available to End-users?

Out of 80 respondents, 45 respondents did not have the training material at all or it was not possible for them to get it from their own or IT department. Only 35 respondents had the end-user training material available: 16 respondents had it at some level, 14 respondents had it mostly and 5 respondents had it all. There is also a big difference between the availability of training material for the less experienced respondents and more experienced category. Out of 35, only 7 respondents from the less experienced (0-2 years) category had the training material, while 28 respondents from the experienced (2-6 years) category had the training material available. The feedback from respondents is in Table 4.

Table 4. Feedback from Respondents on Availability of Training Material

Question	Frequency Count			
	1	2	3	4
Is end-user training material available or it is available upon request from your own IT Department?	45	16	14	5
Respondents experience from 0 to 2 years	0	5	2	0
Respondents experience from 2 to 6 years	0	2	6	20

We further tried to investigate why some respondents have the end-user training material, while others did not have it. We asked one simple question: How did you get the end-user training material? Some respondents mentioned that they got it from their own department. Others mentioned that they got it directly from the IT department because they had a good relationship with that department.

3.4 What Kind of Usability Problems do End-users Face without Training Material?

This is the last research question investigated in this article. It consists of one open-ended question. The purpose of this question was to find the usability problems when the end-user training materials were not available. The usability problems mentioned from the respondents are as follow:

1. Too much dependency on senior colleagues.
2. Difficulty in learning existing or new tasks.

3. Making mistakes – it would be easier to perform the task more effectively if the material was available.
4. 4) Problems in memorising tasks. Some of the tasks are not performed on a daily. In these situations, the availability of such material would be very usable.

4. CONCLUSION

In this article, we highlighted the usability problems in the ERP application _H_elp and end-user training material. The effectiveness of training depends on the usability of documentation. In complex information system like ERP, the _H_elp and end-user training material has to play an important role. Because, the interlinked business process capabilities make it more complex as compared to a normal software like 'word pad.' If the standard _H_elp provided by the ERP application is usable, then the end-users can learn their job tasks independently and effectively. If there are usability problems, like task procedural steps in the form of text only or being too generic, then they would not be able to use it. Likewise, if the end-user training material is not available to every end-user in the organisation, then they have to depend on senior colleagues, confront too many problems with existing or new tasks, and face the problem of completing infrequent tasks. Usability is share interest among the stakeholders like ERP vendor, consultant and the implementation organisation. The stakeholders should make sure that every end-user has the training material available. And the documentation is according to the need of end-user working in different unit of the organisation.

REFERENCES

Aloini, D., Dulmin, R., & Mininno, V. (2012). Risk assessment in ERP projects. *Information Systems, 37*(3), 183-199.

Deloitte Consulting. (2000). *Success file*. Deloitte Consulting.

Fayez, A, A. & Salam, A. (2009). *IBIMA business review, 3.*

Fethi C & Ferah C. (2004). The relation of interface usability characteristics, perceived usefulness, and perceived ease of use to end-user satisfaction with enterprise resource planning (ERP) systems. *Computers in Human Behavior, 20*(4), 505-515.

Garača, Ž. (2011). Factors related to the intended use of ERP systems. Management-Journal of Contemporary Management Issues, 16(2), 23-42.

ISO (1997). *ISO 9241-11: Ergonomic requirements for office work with visual display terminals (VDTs).* Part 11 guidelines for specifying and measuring usability. Geneva: International Standards Organization

Martin, M., 2001. Context of use within Usability activity. *Internation Journal of Human-Computer Studies 55*: 453–483.

Sadiq, M., & Pirhonen, A. (2012). Computer literacy training is an important factor to improve usability in ERP applications. In *IADIS International conference of Interface and Human Computer Interaction*, 245-250.

Salvini, J, (2010). *Oracle inventory user guide Release 12.1 Part No. E13450-04.* Oracle Corporation, USA.

Scott, E. J. (2008). Technology acceptance and ERP documentation usability. *Commun. ACM 51*, 11 (November 2008).

Scholtz, B., Calitz, A. & Cilliers, C. (2013) Usability evaluation of a medium-sized ERP system in higher education. *Electronic Journal of Information Systems Evaluation,* 16(2): 148–161.

Shaul, L., & Tauber, D. (2013). Critical success factors in enterprise resource planning systems: Review of

the last decade. *ACM Comput. Surv. 45*(4), Article 55, 39.

Shehab, E. (2004). Enterprise resource planning: An integrative review. *Business Process Management Journal 10* (4), 359-386.

Umble, E. J., Haft, R. R., & Umble, M. M. (2003). Enterprise resource planning: Implementation procedures and critical success factors. European journal of operational research, 146(2), 241-257.

Vaman, J. N. (2007). *ERP in Practice: ERP strategies for steering organizational competence and competitive advantage*. New Delhi: Tata McGraw-Hill Education.

Zhang, L., Lee, MKO., Zhang, Z., & Banerjee, P. (2002). Critical success factors of enterprise resource planning systems implementation success in China. *In Proceedings of the 36th Hawaii International Conference on System Sciences; Hawaii*: IEEE: 2002.

ASSESSMENT OF SUITABILITY OF E-SERVICES FOR ILLITERATE USERS

Rawan Al-Themali[1] and Hmood Al-Dossari[2]
[1]*Master student in King Saud University, Riyadh- Saudi Arabia*
[2]*Information Systems Department, Riyadh, King Saud University*

ABSTRACT

E-services can be best described as services offered by governments and organizations via the Internet. The aim of this paper is to assess how good e-services are for illiterate users. As a case study, we have chosen to evaluate the usability of e-services in Saudi Arabia. To do so, we first design a general assessment form that developed specifically to evaluate the usability of e-services for uneducated users. Then, the assessment form was used to collect and evaluate 116 e-services in Saudi Arabia. Our results show that the majority of the covered e-services were not suitable for illiterate users. Almost all e-services are not text-free, they rely on using text to communicate and use these services, which make them unsuitable for illiterate users.

KEYWORDS

Usability assessment, E-services, Illiterate users

1. INTRODUCTION

From computer systems usability perspective, having an effective and efficient user interface in a given system is a crucial facet of system development, and a fundamental principle of Human-Computer Interaction. Technological interaction goes hand in hand with software design, development, and implementation. As such, the importance of HCI with respect to electronic technology cannot be underestimated. HCI importance lies in making the interaction with system and application programs installed on the computer easier. Most of the UI interfaces today are based on textual menus, descriptions, and graphics that need to be read in order to understand their functions. For most people, it is not a problem. However, there are about 759 million adults in the world today who cannot read or write (UNESCO, 2003). As a consequence, they are unable to take proper advantage of computers. To allow this portion of the world's population to get the same benefits from computers that textually literate people do, it is critical to manufacturing specially-adapted computer systems. In this paper, therefore, we evaluate the appropriateness of e-services to illiterate users.

2. PERVIOUS STUDY

Users interact with computers via different interfaces depending on their needs (Gonçalves, Martins, Pereira, Oliveira, & Ferreira, 2011). Essentially, a good system design for both stand-alone and web-based systems enables the literate users to work efficiently, and the illiterate users can as well learn on how to navigate the system with ease. In this respect, various researchers have focused on the inability of some users to recognize text or graphical images displayed via the user interface. On a different note, users who cannot use the computer or the Internet have been discussed and broadly categorized as the older people, rural people, and those with little education (Oreglia, 2014). However, the researchers did not suggest new ways help people who cannot use the Internet. However, Kyle, Diana, and Georg proposed a design interface to service older people and evaluated website use by older people (Lynch, Schwerha, & Johanson, 2013). The researchers tested three websites with a variety of usability levels. Computer use for older individuals changes depending on vision capabilities, control ability when using input devices, cognitive abilities, hearing loss, and basic fear of technology. The researchers also provide general recommendations for a user-friendly interface. Indranil, Aman, and Kentaro aimed to design a text-free user interface for illiterate users without intervention from anyone (Medhi, Pitti, & Toyama, 2007). The researchers also focused on graphics and voice feedback.

Zereh and Judith wrote an article on the computer for illiterate people based on their findings from a field study performed in India (Lalji & Good, 2008). During the initial part of the study, the researchers interviewed five participants to map out what the final users would want from a computer and what it would need in order for them to want to buy one themselves (Lalji & Good, 2008).. The researchers also included questions about their mobile calling habits and ability to correctly dial the numbers. Next, the researchers had their participants draw example icons for common computer functions like sign-in and checking e-mails. Findings from the study revealed information about the illiterates' needs with respect to computers. Essentially, the illiterate users should also be able to use computers because it makes it easier to do daily tasks in addition to enhancing the delivery of services by the business organization. On a different note, other scholars have also focused on the usability, efficiency, and effectiveness of the alphanumeric keypad. Some participants had trouble understanding all the keys on the keyboard and would occasionally confuse several keys. However, they could recognize the keys on a bus saying which line it is.

3. RESEARCH METHODOLOGY

From a research perspective, a study can be broadly classified into either quantitative or qualitative depending on the phenomenon under investigation, the research problem and the kind of data that the researcher wishes to correct. Quantitative studies are best suited for data or participants responses that can be expressed in the numerical/quantifiable form, while qualitative data is most suited for data that can only be expressed in non-quantifiable terms. In this study, a quantitative research methodology was employed. This was achieved by using structured evaluation forms to collect the data. A 3-point Likert scale was used to measure the answers on the forms (Amaral, et al.). The three options in the scale were; *Yes, No,* and *Does not Apply*. The evaluation forms provided the researchers with the necessary information necessary to achieve the main research objective. The evaluation forms were filled based on 116 e-services that were selected through purposive sampling technique.

3.1 Evaluation Form Design

As the first step, we designed an evaluation form that was divided depending on user interfaces into:

- **Output:** This section explained how the data is presented to illiterate users. There are many aids to support the good interface such as using sound, picture, video, etc. Also, we checked if this part contained some of these aids or not.
- **Input:** This section explained who the illiterate user dealt or interacted with a request from the e-services.
- **Help and Support**: Shows if any errors occurred or mistakes happened while using e–services.

Table 1. E-services Evaluation Form

E-services Evaluation Form

E-service:_________________________
Offered by:_______________________
Website:_________________________

1-Output		**Comment**
1.1- Is the E-service supported by picture to facilitate the uneducated to use (understand) the service?	Y N Not apply	
1.1.1Are the pictures that are used in E-service related with the real word?	Y N Not apply	
1.2- Is the E-service supported by audio to translate the written word to spoken language?	Y N Not apply	
1.2.1 Is the audio that is used in E-service clear and understandable?	Y N Not apply	
1.3-Are messages from the E-service audible?	Y N Not apply	
2-Input		
2.1-Are there other ways to enter data without using text?	Y N Not apply	
2.2-Can illiterate users respond to E-service request without using text?	Y N Not apply	
2.3- Is the E-service supported by picture to facilitate the uneducated to determine their choice (enter the data)?	Y N Not apply	
3-Help and Support		
3.1- Does the E-service provide feedback to indicate where the uneducated user is and where the user last was?	Y N Not apply	
3.2-Does E-service provide guideline supported by picture to show uneducated user how to use it?	Y N Not apply	
3.3-Does the E-service provide back button to return to a previous page?	Y N Not apply	
3.4-Do error or warning messages audibly prevent possible errors from occurring?	Y N Not apply	

3.2 E-services Selection

It is imperative to apply the governmental decision for e-services adoption and to achieve the maximum benefit to all users of e-services. We searched for all the possibilities of e-services that can benefit the illiterate users belonging to different sectors. We found 116 e-services from numerous government agencies and organization. We also categorized e-services to two groups:

- **Informational services**: for providing information and descriptions about services where the number were 18 services such as sitemap, awareness, registration guideline, etc.
- **Transactional services:** allow users to interact with governments or organizations and numbered 98 services. Those include registration, login, appointment, etc.

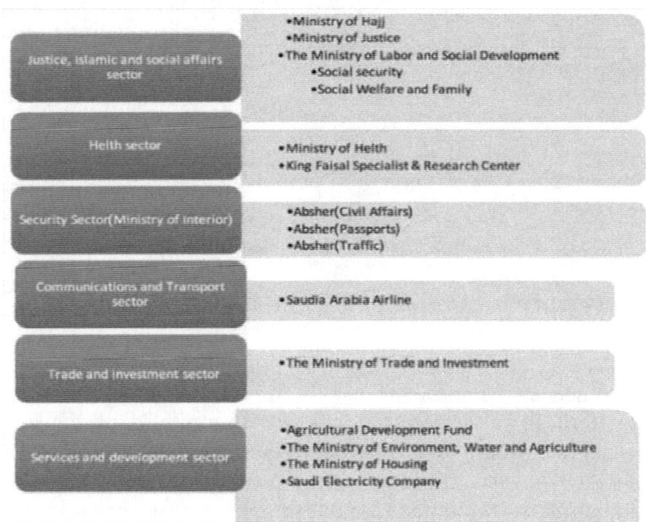

Figure 1. List of Selected Sectors and Organizations

4. RESULTS

This section presents the result of the method used in Section 3. There were 116 services that were studied. They were under a number of ministries for 6 different sectors (as shown in Figure 1). Informational and transactional services have been studied through a number of questions (as shown in Table 1), distributed in three main parts: output, input and (help and support).

4.1 Output

The first question was: Is e-service supported by the picture to facilitate the uneducated to use (understand) the service? The respondents answered as 7 e-services used pictures for users to understand the service. In contrast, there were 109 services that did not make use of images. 5 out of the 7 e-services exist in Ministry of Hajj: Haj and Umrah rights, geographic, search, sitemap, contact, search in Ministry of Justice and Log out in Ministry of Interior. However, two images for log out and geographic are not related to reality.

With respect to whether E-service was supported by audio to translate the written word to spoken language, the answers were "Yes" for 11 services. On the other hand, the respondents answered "No" for 105 services. On another question on whether the audio used in E-service clear and understandable, the answer was "No" for all E-services that were used. The last question in this part was: whether the messages from E-service audible. This question was more comprehensive as compared to question 3. The answers were: "Yes" for 10 services and "No" for 106 services. Table 2 summarizes the result of the output.

Table 2. Output

Question number	1.1	1.2	1.3	1.4	1.5
Yes	7	5	11	0	10
No	109	2	105	11	106

4.2 Input

Table 3 shows the number of e-services for input questions. There were 3 questions in this section:

1- Are there other ways to enter data without using text?
2- Can illiterate users respond to E-service request without using text?
3- Is the e-service supported by the picture to facilitate the uneducated to determine their choice (enter the data)?

Informational services do not require users to enter data. The answers to the other type of e-services were the same for all questions: For only 1 service, the response was in affirmative. On the other hand, the answer was "No" for 97 services.

Table 3. Input

Question number	2.1	2.2	2.3
No	97	97	97
Not Apply	18	18	18

4.3 Help and Support

There are 4 questions in this part (as shown in Table 4). The first one was: Does the e-service provide feedback to indicate where the uneducated user is and where the user last was? The answer was "No" for 116 services meaning 100% in spite of all the services were applied in the form of a written text. However, illiterate users cannot understand what is written. The second question was: Does e-service provide guideline supported by the picture to show uneducated users how to use it? The answers were "Yes" for 5 services and "No" for 111 services. Saudi Electricity Company provided these services using video to explain the service: Billing Services (Add Account-Review), Request electric service, Appointment, Communication for service outages, and E-bill. The third question was: Does the e-service provide back button to return to a previous page? The answers were "Yes" for 109 services, and the rest of them did not apply it for security reasons depending on the affiliated ministry. Those included 7 services: Log out in Ministry of Interior, Login in Saudi Electricity Company, Change password, Change phone number, Change eligibility information in Ministry of Housing, Animal and Plant Ban Decisions Guide, Registration of farmer's data in Ministry of Environment, Water, and Agriculture. The last question in this section was: Do error or warning messages audibly prevent possible errors from occurring? The answers were "No" for 98 services and "Not applicable" for 18 services. For informational services, there was an impossibility of the occurrence of error because the users were not given the option to insert data. It means that the usage of sound in preventing mistakes was used in all types of e-services.

Table 4. Help and Support

Question number	3.1	3.2	3.3	3.4
Yes	0	5	109	0
No	116	111	7	98
Not Apply	0	0	0	18

4.4 Discussion

Figure 2 shows the percentage of e-services that used text for interaction with users. It is clear that the covered e-services were based on a text by 96% and the rest of them were dependent on the text with some aids supported by picture or video. It meant that they used the text completely and did not offer the illiterate the opportunity to use the services. This indicates the need for designing a special interface depending on pictures and sound as outputs and on pictures and numbers to input information via a special soft keyboard containing alternative images of characters. It also needed to contain numbers be arranged in the same order as the keyboard of the device. This would help illiterate people interact with computers in an easier manner.

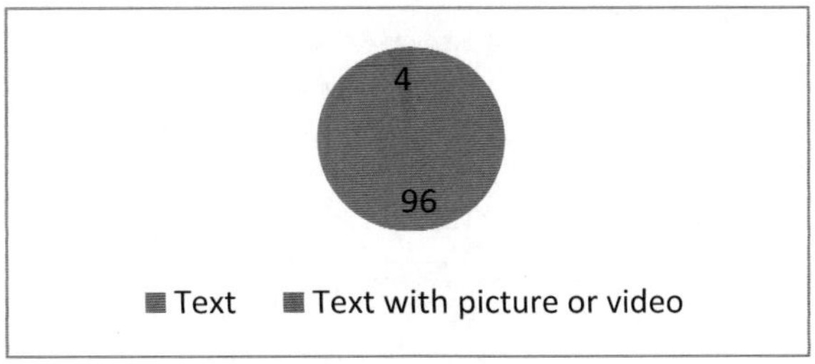

Figure 2. Percentage of e-Services Using Text for Interaction with Users

5. CONCLUSION

The importance of e-services offers huge benefits to both organizations and the services consumers. The services encourage citizens and facilitate them to accomplish their transactions anywhere and anytime. One of the core importance of the technological advancement in general and the delivery of e-services in specific is the ability to assist the illiterate people to accomplish their tasks. In this paper, we have measured and evaluated the appropriateness of e-services to illiterate users. Our results show e-services mostly neglected illiterate users by not taking take them into consideration when designing these services. Due to total dependence on using the text, the services offered disproportionate benefits to illiterate users. Also, we suggested design special interface with a soft keyboard so that even illiterate users can display and enter data in an easier manner to achieve usability.

REFERENCES

Amaral, N., Buro, M., Elio, R., Hoover, J., Nikolapdis, L., Salavatipo, M., et al. (n.d.). *webdocs.cs.ualberta.ca/~c603/readings/research-methods.pdf.* Retrieved 5 26, 2017, from http://www.bing.com/cr?IG=4C0D1EEA924A406DBDF40F2562600A58&CID=03A70A0E4C4D607635C400804D4B611C&rd=1&h=WwFH268XOegqpf_TDefB7e1TBY9yLVh3OObFy5noMc&v=1&r=http%3a%2f%2fwebdocs.cs.ualberta.ca%2f%7ec603%2freadings%2fresearchmethods.pdf&p=DevEx,5056.1

Gonçalves, R., Martins, J., Pereira, J., Oliveira, M., & Ferreira, J. (2011). Accessibility levels of Portuguese enterprise websites: equal opportunities for all? *Behaviour & Information Technology , 31* (7), 659-677.

Lalji, Z., & Good, J. (2008). Designing new technologies for illiterate populations: A study in mobile phone interface design. *Interacting with Computers , 20* (6), 574-586.

Lynch, K., Schwerha, D., & Johanson, G. (2013). Development of a Weighted Heuristic for Website Evaluation for Older Adults. *International Journal of Human–Computer Interaction , 29* (6), 404-418.

Medhi, I., Pitti, B., & Toyama, K. (2007). A Text-Free User Interface For Employment Search. *Innovative Applications of Information Technology for the Developing World , 4*, 37-50.

Oreglia, E. (2014). ICT and (personal) Development in Rural China. *Information technology and International development , 10* (3).

UNESCO. (2003). *Literacy and Adult Education in the Arab World - UNESCO.* Retrieved 5 26, 2017, from http://www.bing.com/cr?IG=AD6567B0D02A4F70A110D837FD325213&CID=363C04D8E2FE604806E70E56E3F861C9&rd=1&h=uJaTvFST1kIAJvifg2299hfZ38BewXXJpcLWzcDeTcY&v=1&r=http%3a%2f%2fwww.unesco.org%2feducation%2fuie%2fpdf%2fcountry%2farab_world.pdf&p=DevEx,5061.1

"WISE THINGS": WHEN SMART OBJECTS STIMULATE REFLECTION

Maliheh Ghajargar, Alberto De Marco and Francesca Montagna
Politecnico di Torino, Turin, Italy

ABSTRACT

Despite a variety of purposes for designing smart objects (SOs), design of such artifacts with the purpose of provoking people's thoughts and reflection on complex issues (e.g. environmental and societal) is still little explored. In fact, the ability of SOs to recall information about people's behaviors helps them to reflect on the consequences.
As an attempt, this paper introduces the concept of Wise Thing as a category of such smart objects, with augmented properties of being Deliberative, Reflectional, Experiential, and Communicative.

KEYWORDS

Smart Objects, Reflection, Behavior Change Design

1. INTRODUCTION

The increasing use of computing technologies and the Internet connectivity are changing people's way of living. This phenomenon in various academic literature and commercial media takes several names, such as Ubiquitous Computing (Weiser, 1996), Internet of Things (Ashton, 2009), Connected Homes (Ericsson, 2015) and has been also largely debated in the Design and Human-Computer Interaction (HCI) literature (Dourish, 2004a; Lowgren and Stolterman, 2004). Many attention have been put on how human interactions with connected and computing objects can stimulate human behavior (Norman, 2007; Norman, 1988; Fogg, 1998; 2003; 2009; Moggridge, 2007; Verplank, 2009; Kuniavsky, 2010, Dix, 2009). Further, Captology explains how computers can foster and facilitate behavior change through application of specific techniques and methods (Fogg, 2003; Cialdini, 2007; Clune, 2007; Wendel, 2014). The human-product interaction has been also widely explored in User-Centered Design, where the nature, quality and elements of this interaction are investigated (e.g. Vredenburg, et. al., 2002; Preece et al., 2002) and extended to exploring cognitive mechanisms in order to improve usability and user experience (Shackel, 1984; Baber and Stanton, 1996; Norman, 2007). Current Design literature on behavior change is mostly focused on using tools, processes and methods to change or maintain a behavior based on user's predefined goals. This approach often faces some difficulties, especially when it is applied to changing some behaviors (e.g. energy or water consumptions) that might contribute to the environmental problems, such as climate change and natural resource depletion.

Smart Objects (SO) have been defined as a category of computing artifacts augmented with sensors and other actuators, connected to the Internet, able to capture and monitor user or environment-driven data and to provide feedback (e.g. Dietrich and Laerhoven, 2016). So, the design of Smart Objects (SOs) concerns also the quality of interactions with the user and the environment.

Despite growing interest and available technologies, the design of smart products that stimulate user's reflection has been limited to the field of data visualization on mobile apps, websites and wearable artifacts (Ian, et. al. 2011, Dietrich and Laerhoven, 2014; 2016) or environmental installations (Hallnäs and Redström, 2001). Perhaps this is due to the lack of studies regarding the physical form and also tangible properties of interaction with connected artifacts able to promote reflection.

SOs run with the same physical, smart and connectivity components as those of the artifacts able to stimulate reflection, and they seem to be made of similar materials and produced with similar techniques. So, what makes the difference mostly relies on the way they are designed.

As an attempt to overcome this research gap, the focus of the paper is to propose those features of smart objects that enable them to stimulate reflection in user.

To this end, first we briefly discuss about the relation between behavior change and reflection in HCI. Then, we provide literature about characteristics of SOs in order to introduce the concept and properties of Wise things.

2. REFLECTION WITH THE PURPOSE OF BEHAVIOR CHANGE IN HCI

Reflection as a way of thinking, enables the review and merging previous experiences and events to help a better understanding or to gain some sort of insight. Schön (1983) states that *reflection is a type of 'thinking about' that enables a kind of problem solving involving the construction of an understanding and reframing.* Other authors specifically consider reflection as the final aim of the design process or reflection as a tool to stimulate a new way of thinking (Gaver et al., 2003).

The notion of reflection has been of great interest to the HCI community, where technology enable reflection and critical thinking as a support for learning (Price et al., 2003; Anderson et al., 2007) or for playing (Rogers and Muller, 2006). In these domains, 'reflection' refers to the action of reflecting on information provided and being conscious about the consequences of an action or behavior (Fleck, 2012; Baumer, et. al. 2014). Data are visualized to bring into mind memories and experiences. Sengers et al. (2005) in particular reflect on the role of technology by introducing 'Reflective Design' as *a practice, which combines analysis of the ways in which technologies reflect and perpetuate unconscious cultural assumptions, with design, building, and evaluation of new computing devices that reflect alternative possibilities.* This emphasizes the role of critical thinking as an essential tool to allow people make conscious value choices in their attitudes and practices.

The idea of using the features of an artifact to stimulate, drive or shape human behavior has been the subject of researches according to different approaches and perspectives, such as in Design With Intent (Lockton, et. al, 2010) or Performative Objects (Niedderer, 2007). Furthermore, the sensorial properties of artifacts, such as attributed color, material texture and sound, can shape perceptions and experiences, and surely affect human behaviors (Schifferstein and Hekkert, 2008; Prabu, et. al., 2012; Wardano et al., 2012; Hyodo, 2011; van Egmond, 2008). Further computing technologies have been used for user behavior change (Norman 1988; 2007). Wherein human cognitive and psychological factors have been entered into Design Research, such as the concepts of affordance, constraint and feedback (e.g. Kolko, 2011).

Despite growing interest and availability of these technologies, designing for reflection is still in its early stages and has been identified as research opportunity within Design research (Baumer, et. al. 2014). Even though tangible user interfaces (TUI) are becoming diffused in SOs, there is still a lack of studies regarding the exploration of the novel forms of interaction that can promote reflection. This actually can open discussions around the ways smart objects stimulate reflection in user, so they become are not be shifts the paradigm from Smart Objects to Wise things.

3. FROM SMART TO WISE THINGS

Emerging technologies –near-field communications, real-time localization and generally embedded sensors– have enabled a range of computationally enhanced and Internet-connected devices, commonly called "smart objects" a.k.a "connected artifacts". They can sense, log and interpret events in their context and can interact and exchange information with other parties, such as other smart devices and users (e.g. Kortuem, et al., 2010; Fortino, G., Guerrini A., Russo W., 2012).

Smart objects have been explored and defined in various research fields, such as business, ambient intelligent and web semantics (Marta Sabou, 2010; Kortuem, et al. 2010) as being: 1) **Reactive:** smart objects can understand events in a given physical representation; 2) **Proactive:** smart objects can act autonomously and control the situation; 3) **Preemptive:** smart objects can predict errors and faults in order to remove unpleasant surprises for user; 4) **Interactive:** smart objects can converse and interact with the user in terms of input, output and feedback in a simple and intuitive way.

With respect to the HCI researches that have investigated on the ability of smart objects to learn human behaviors and actions, and act autonomously in order to simplify activities, we assume those abilities are able to offer an opportunity of influencing reflective behavior of users. The ability of artifacts to provoke peculiar thoughts and reflections helps and guides users almost autonomously to make conscious decisions, instead to follow fixed and pre-defined rules and steps. This is also related to the ability of products to not only support people to have an easier life but only to have a better quality of life (Schifferstein, Özcan, Rozendaal, 2015).

To this end, in this paper we describe the four augmented features of Wise things building upon the features that characterize the analogue objects and the SOs, as illustrated in Figure 1. Similar to the augmented features that enable an object to become 'smart', this augmentation process transforms an SO into a 'Wise' Object.

Although the description of these particular interactions is out of the scope of this paper, here we will introduce the four possible augmented features that might create the ground for designing the artifact and its interactions.

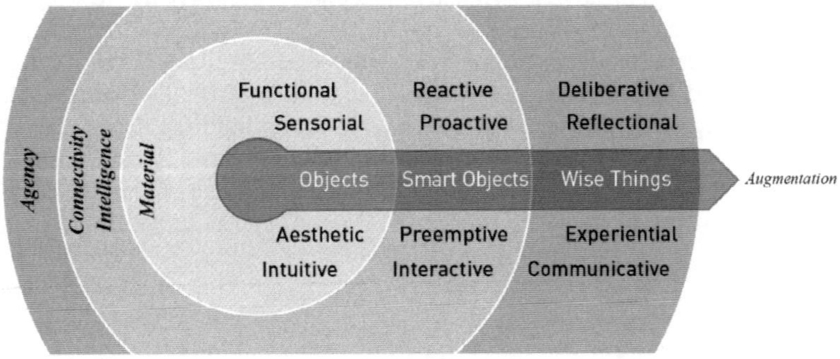

Figure 1. From an analogue object to a wise thing

3.1 Deliberative

Wise Thing is deliberative because it constructs their internal beliefs and opinions. A deliberative reasoning enables to hypothesize possible outcomes and to make decisions. It is related to the situated agents' reflective way of reasoning, as defined in the AI and multi-agent systems (MAS) studies (Gero and Kannengiesser, 2003). Being Deliberative is one of the wise thing feature that enables the construction and modification of internal concepts, beliefs and goals based on the previous experiences and perceptions.

3.2 Reflectional

This feature evokes thoughts and reflections in user through providing peculiar tangible feedbacks. It is related not only to the physical forms of artifact but also to the temporal forms (Vallgårda and Redström 2014).

Since, Wise Things perform both internal and external actions similar to any other situated agents, the external actions which are tied to the user interface, represent crucial factors concerning the Reflectional property. This is mostly because user perceives only external actions. These complex feedbacks, as perceived by user, demonstrate radical or incremental changes in the wise things interface and external structure, such as changes in form, texture and color, are as a result of the Reflectional feature.

3.3 Experiential

Research has shown that the experiment with physical artifacts can enhance the reflection and increase awareness (e.g. Hornecker and Buur, 2006). Accordingly, a wise thing is Experiential, that has the ability of engaging the user into experimentation and exploration. Likewise, it is assumed that provoking user's reflection on personal data becomes more effective if the perception of information is not just limited to the user's visual perception, but also integrates the tangible interaction with information. This means the interaction should involve other sensorial capacities rather than just visual (e.g. Ullmer and Ishii, 1997; Shaer and Hornecker, 2010; Rinott, 2013; Houben et. al., 2016). In addition, the tangible representation of data, conversely of numerical data visualization, leaves open the interpretation of the information.

The Experiential feature of wise things includes important drivers of reflection such as openness to interpretation and playfulness of engagement and exploration.

3.4 Communicative

Debates on the communicative character of computing technology is not new. Computers as constructive tools have been used for the purpose of learning in educational contexts (Papert and Kay, 1968; Kay, 1972) or for expression and communications of algorithms and models in network communications (Dourish, 2004b). In addition, in every design context, the Communication, allows artifacts to deliver the designers' intention as a message to the users, where *the sender* is the designer, who intends to transmit a particular *message* to a *receiver* (the user) through a physical artifact as a *medium* (Crilly et. al., 2008; Varduoli, 2015). According to this interpretation, "use" become as "writing", "reading" and encoding the message (Crilly et. al., 2008) and the medium modulation becomes essential because it is a particular form of transformation. Modulation is also defined as the carrier of information or the carrier of meaning in terms of embodied interaction (Dourish, 2004a). The modulation/communication/transformation process between wise things and users creates a loop, wherein wise things do not merely convey and transform the message, but are also able to receive and interpret them and resend the information to the user via encoding and decoding. Wise things together with users participate in the process and are able to redesign the artifact and personalize the "text".

4. DISCUSSION AND CONCLUSION

Instead of designing artifacts with aiming to change people's behavior, we can consider the ability of artifacts to make people aware about environmental and societal problems and help them to reflect and make conscious decisions. Wise Things are conceived and can be designed for such purpose: they are distinguishable from existing smart and connected artifacts because they are Deliberative, Reflectional, Experiential and Communicative agents of reflection. This ability of Wise Things can find applications in many contexts wherein provoking thoughts and reflective practices are essential to learning and improving, such as organizational and educational settings.

This paper is intended as a contribution towards this direction and debating on the properties of these objects and reflecting on the consequences of their use. We hope to contribute to the ways that these four augmented characteristics (Deliberative, Reflectional, Experiential, Communicative) can guide design of the physical and concrete features of connected artifacts that promote reflection with the purpose of behavior change. This paper could stimulate future studies on wise things' forms, and their behaviors that enable such an interaction able to stimulate reflection.

ACKNOWLEDGEMENT

This has been supported by a grant from Telecom Italia Mobile (TIM) to the Politecnico di Torino.

REFERENCES

Anderson, E., F., McLoughlin, L. (2007). *Critters in the classroom: a 3D computer-game-like tool for teaching programming to computer animation students.* In: Proceedings of the ACM SIGGRAPH 2007 educators program Conference, pp. 7.

Ashton, K., (2009). That 'Internet of Things' Thing, in the real world things matter more than ideas. *RFID J.* pp. 1-2.

Baber, C., Stanton, N.A., (1996). Human error identification techniques applied to public technology: predictions compared with observed use. *Applied Ergonomics* 27 (2), 119–131.

Baumer, E. P. S., Khovanskaya, V., Matthews, M., Reynolds, L., Schwanda Sosik, V., & Gay, G. (2014). *Reviewing Reflection: On the Use of Reflection in Interactive System Design.* In Proceedings of the 2014 Conference on Designing Interactive Systems (pp. 93–102). New York, NY, USA: ACM.

Cialdini, R. B. (2007). *Influence: The Psychology of Persuasion*. New York: HarperBusines.

Clune, S. (2010). Design for Behavioural Change, *Journal of Design Strategies* 4, 68-75.

Crilly, N., Good, D., Matravers, D., Clarkson, P. J. (2008). Design as communication: exploring the validity and utility of relating intention to interpretation. *Design Studies* 29(5), 425 – 457.

Dietrich M., Van Laerhoven K. (2014). *Recall your Actions! Using Wearable Activity Recognition to Augment the Human Mind.* In Proceeding of Ubicomp '14 Adjunct. Seattle, Wa, Usa.

Dietrich M., Van Laerhoven K. (2016). An Interdisciplinary Approach on the Mediating Character of Technologies for Recognizing Human Activity. *Philosophies*, vol:1, 55-67

Dix A. (2009). Human-computer Interaction. In L. Liu, M. T. Özsu (Eds.) *Encyclopedia of database systems* (pp 1327-1331): Springer, US.

Dourish P. (2004a), *Where the Action is*. Cambridge: MIT Press.

Dourish. P. (2004b). What we talk about, when we talk about context. *Personal and Ubiquitous Computing* 8 (1), 19-30.

Ericsson Consumer Insight Summary Report June 2015. https://www.ericsson.com/res/docs/2015/consumerlab/ericsson-consumerlab-connected-homes.pdf, Last access July 2 2016.

Fleck R., Fitzpatrick G. (2010). *Reflecting on Reflection: Framing Design Landscape.* In Proceedings of the 22nd Conference of the Computer-Human Interaction, Special Interest Group of Australia on Computer-Human Interaction, 216-223.

Fleck R. (2012). *Designing for Reflection, Sustainability and Simplicity*, Presented at: Workshop on Simple, Sustainable living, CHI'12, Austin, Texas.

Fogg, B. J. (1998). *Persuasive computers: Perspectives and research directions*. In Proceedings of the SIGCHI Conference on Human Factors in Computing Systems 225–232.

Fogg, B. J. (2003). *Persuasive Technology: Using Computers to Change What We Think and Do*. San Francisco: Morgan Kaufman.

Fortino G., Guerrini A., Russo W. (2012). *Agent-oriented Smart Artifacts development.* In proceeding of the 16th International conference on Computer Supported Cooperative Work in Design, 907-912.

Gaver, W. W., Beaver, J., Benford, S. (2003). *Ambiguity as a resource for design.* In Proceedings of ACM CHI'3 Conference on Human Factors in Computing Systems. 233-240

Gero, J., Kannengiesser, U. (2003). *Function-Behavior-Structure: A model for social situated agents*. Workshop on Cognitive Modeling of Agents and Multi-Agent Interactions, International Joint Conference on Artificial Intelligence 101, 107.

Hallnäs L., Redström J. (2001). Slow Technology, Designing for Reflection. *Personal and Ubiquitous Computing,* 5(3), 201-212.

Hornecker, E., Buur, J. (2006). *Getting a grip on tangible interaction: a framework on physical space and social interaction.* In Proceedings of the SIGCHI conference on Human Factors in computing systems, pp. 437-446.

Hyodo J. (2011). Can Colors Make Me Happy? The Effect of Color on Mood: A Meta-Analysis. *Advances in Consumer Research* 2, 858-868.

Ishii, H., Ullmer, B. (1997). *Tangible bits: towards seamless interfaces between people, bits and atoms.* In Proceedings of the SIGCHI conference on Human factors in computing systems, 241.

Kay, A. C. (1972). *A Personal Computer for Children of All Ages*. In Proceeding of ACM'72, Annual Conference. 1, 1.

Kolko, J. (2011). *Thoughts on interaction design*. Elsevier (second Ed.).

Kortuem, G., Kowsar, F., Fitton, D., Vasughi, S. (2010). Smart artifacts as building blocks for the Internet of things, *Journal of Internet Computing, IEEE,* 14(1), 44 – 51.

Kramer, G. (1993). *Auditory Display: Sonification, Audification, and Auditory Interfaces.* Perseus Publishing.

Kuniavsky, M. (2010). *Design of Smart Things*. Morgan Kaufmann.

Li, I., Dey, A., Forlizzi, J. (2011). *Understanding My Data, Myself: Supporting Self-Reflection with Ubicomp Technologies*. In Proceedings of the 13th international conference on Ubiquitous computing .405-414

Lockton, D., Harrison, D., Stanton, N. A. (2010). The Design with Intent Method: a design tool for influencing user behaviour. *Applied Ergonomics*. 41 (3), 382-392.

Moggridge, B. (2007), *Designing Interactions*, Cambridge: MIT Press.

Niedderer, K. (2007). Designing Mindful Interaction: The Category of Performative Artifact. *Design Issues*, 23(1), 3-17.

Norman, D., The design of Everyday Things, 1988. Basic Books.

Norman, D., The Design of Future Things, 2007. Basic Books.

Ortin, F., Cueva, J. M. (2003). Non-restrictive computational reflection. *Journal of Computer Standards & Interfaces*. 25, 241-251.

Prabu, W., Haruo, H., and Shinichi K. (2012). Effects of Interior Colors, Lighting and Decors on Perceived Sociability, Emotion and Behavior Related to Social Dining. *Procedia - Social and Behavioral Sciences* 38, 362–372.

Preece, J., Rogers, Y. and Sharp, H., (2002). *Interaction design: beyond human-computer interaction.* New York: John Wiley & Sons.

Price, S., Rogers, Y., Scaife, M., Stanton, D., Neale, H., (2003). Using 'tangibles' to promote novel forms of playful learning. *Interacting with computers* 15, 169-185

Rinott M., Geiger S., Gal-Or E., Or L. (2013). *Cubes.* In Proceedings of the 7th International Conference on Tangible, Embedded and Embodied Interaction, pp. 397-398. ACM.

Rogers, Y., Muller, H. (2006). A framework for designing sensor-based interactions to promote exploration and reflection in play. *International Journal of Human-Computer Studies*. 64, 1-14

Sabou, M., (2010). Smart Artifacts: Challenges for Semantic Web Research, Semantic Web – Interoperability. *Usability, Applicability* 1, 1–5.

Schifferstein H. N. J., Özcan E., Rozendaal M. C., *Towards the maturation of design: From smart to wise products*. In Proceeding of DesForm Conference (2015), Milan, Italy.

Schifferstein, H. N. J., Hekkert, P. (2008). *Product experience*. Amsterdam, the Netherlands: Elsevier.

Schön D. (1983). *The reflective practitioner: how professionals think in action.* Basic Books, New York.

Sengers P., Boehner K., David S., Kaye J., (2005). *Reflective design*. In Proceedings of the 4th Decennial Conference on Critical Computing: Between Sense and Sensibility, 2005, Aarhus, Denmark

Shackel, B. (1984). The concept of usability. In: J. Bennet, et al., (Eds) *Visual display terminals.* Englewood Cliffs, NJ: Prentice-Hall, Inc., 45–88.

Shaer O., and Hornecker E. (2010). Tangible user interfaces: past, present, and future directions, *Foundations and Trends in Human-Computer Interaction* 3, no. 1–2: 1-137.

Van Egmond, R. (2008). The experience of product sounds. In H. N. J. Schifferstein & P. Hekkert (Eds.), Product experience (pp. 69-89). Amsterdam, the Netherlands: Elsevier

Vardouli, T., (2015). Making use: Attitudes to human-artifact engagements, *Design Studies* 41, 137-161

Verplank, B. (2009) *Interaction Design Sketchbook*: *Frameworks for designing interactive products and systems*. https://ccrma.stanford.edu/courses/250a-fall-2004/IDSketchbok.pdf Last access July 2 2016.

Vredenburg, K., Mao, J., Smith, P. W., Carey, T. (2002): *A survey of user-centered design practice.* In: L. Terveen (Eds.) Proceedings of the ACM CHI' 02 Conference on Human Factors in Computing Systems Conference, Minneapolis, Minnesota. pp. 471-478.

Weiser M., Brown S., (1996). *Designing Calm Technology*, Xerox PARC.

Wendel, S., (2014). *Designing for behavior change: Applying psychology and behavioral economics.* O'Reily Media, Sebastopol, CA, USA.

Zuckerman, O., Gal Oz A., (2014). Deconstructing gamification: evaluating the effectiveness of continuous measurement, virtual rewards and social comparison for promoting physical activity. *Personal and Ubiquitous*.

DESIGN FOR TRUST – ONLINE GROCERY SHOPPING

Amela Karahasanović[1], Kristoffer T. Holm and Aria Nejad[2]
[1]*SINTEF Digital, Forskingsveien 1, 0373 Oslo, Norway*
[2]*Department of Informatics, University of Oslo, Gaustadalléen 23 B, 0373, Oslo, Norway*

ABSTRACT

This paper presents our ongoing research into trust and the risks related to online grocery shopping. More specifically, we investigate how to increase customer trust when buying perishable products online. Online grocery shopping is an increasing trend in many countries, and several studies on trust have been conducted in the context of online grocery shopping. However, knowledge of how to improve trust and reduce risks is rather limited in this context. Through design, prototyping and user studies, we explore if and how a variety of user feedback mechanics such as ratings, comments and presence help build trust. Several concepts and prototypes were evaluated through group interviews and usability testing. Based on our results, we proposed trust-related design guidelines for online grocery shopping applications. Our results might be useful to both researchers investigating trust in the context of online shopping and to the practitioners designing applications and services in this area.

KEYWORDS

Trust, Risk, Interaction Design, Service Design, Online Grocery Shopping

1. INTRODUCTION

Buying groceries online differs from other types of online shopping because of the perishability and variability of the products. People may hesitate to shop for perishable groceries online because of the perceived risk of receiving products that do not meet their expectations (Mortimer et al., 2016). An online survey based on responses from 60 countries showed that one quarter of respondents reported buying groceries online, whereas more than half (55%) were considering doing it in the future (Nielsen, 2015).

Exploring different strategies for increasing trust in online grocery shopping is therefore becoming increasingly important. Providing more information about the products and use of feedback mechanism have both been suggested as a means for increasing trust in online shopping (Harridge-March, 2006; Nepomuceno et al., 2015). Bhatnagar and his colleagues (2000) found that some products, such as more expensive electronics or products that require touch and feel are experienced as more risky. Fruit and vegetables, for example, are experienced as more risky because one wants to examine their freshness. Although some of the new online grocery services (e.g., Vigo and Amazon Go) use mechanisms for increasing trust, such as ratings, little has been known about the effects of these mechanisms. This research investigates trust and the perceived risks of online grocery shopping.

2. DESIGN

We applied an iterative design process consisting of four phases. Figure 1 presents our activities in the double diamond proposed by the British Design Council (BDC, 2007). A Norwegian grocery retailer wanted to introduce an online-based crowdsourcing service where neighbours were able to do each other's grocery shopping (Cartpooling) and were interested in trust issues related to this and similar services.

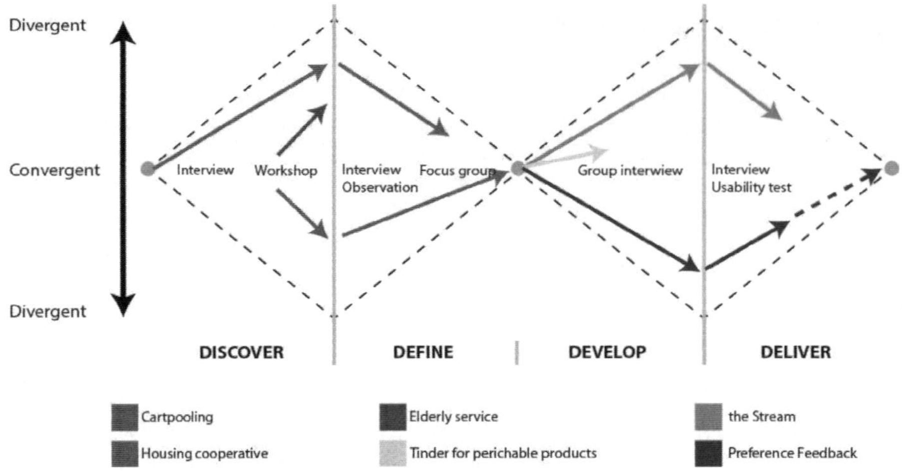

Figure 1. Design process and its activities

At the first meeting with the company, we identified the following stakeholders: employees, managers, designers, developers, current and potential customers and neighbours. During the *Discover* phase, we first conducted interviews with five customers to explore trust and motivation related to the proposed service. The customers were recruited by the company. Three of them were men and two women, they were between 44 and 67 years and in different live situations. Some were single, some lived in households with small children, and some lived with teenagers. In some neighborhoods, the neighbors knew each other very well, whereas in other they were more or less strangers to each other. Thematic analysis was used for analysis of the interviews. The interviews revealed that the participants felt uncomfortable about bothering others because, as they said, "we don't know each other well". They were also worried about the quality of the delivered products. As one participant put it:

> *"When others collect groceries for me, I'm a bit sceptical that they might choose some products that I have not chosen for myself... I have had some avocado deliveries where the avocado was brown on the inside".*

After the interviews, we conducted a *future workshop* (Vidal, 2006) with eight participants (services developers, managers and designers) divided into two groups, which explored not only the cartpooling solution but also the broader idea of online services. The participant of this workshop were either the employees of the company or consultants working for the company. Information about the participants' background was collected before the workshop so that we could assure that both groups are multidisciplinary. Both groups worked separately, and then presented their ideas in a plenary session. The first idea (*Housing cooperative*) was a service offered by a housing cooperative that would hire someone to collect groceries for the online orders. The second one (*Elderly service*) was collaboration with home care services, where volunteers visiting the elderly would also collect their groceries. Both groups pointed out importance of the competence of the person that collects the groceries and difficulties related to giving negative feedback.

Based on the results of both interviews and workshops we decided to further develop the *Housing cooperative* service. During the *Define* phase, we observed an employee collecting online groceries during his working day. This was followed by a semi-structured interview, in which we asked more details about his work. Further, we conducted an interview with a housing cooperative leader, and a focus group with 11 potential customers. Recurring themes during the *Discover* and *Define* phases were: i) reducing product risk by giving feedback about the products, and ii) increasing trust by making sure that the groceries ordered followed personal preferences.

3. PROTOTYPES AND EVALUATION

One of the ideas suggested during the workshop and the focus group was that feedback and presence might help increase trust. We therefore decided to prototype a related functionality. During the *Develop* phase, we developed three prototypes: i) the *Stream* – a video-based service showing the process of collecting the actual groceries from the store before being delivered to customers (Figure 2), ii) *Tinder for perishable products* – a service in which photos are used for accepting or rejecting a product, and iii) *Preference feedback* – a service enabling customers to give feedback by leaving comments about perishable products either during the order or after delivery.

The *Stream* is a video-based service. When the employee enters the fruit and vegetable department, his head camera is turned on, and the process of collecting the groceries is recorded. When the groceries are ready for delivery, the customers will receive an sms with a link to a video of the collection process (Figure 2). The customers can watch the video to look for the products he wants, when he wants (Figure 3). If the customer is not satisfied with the product selected, he can write a comment, and the product will be replaced before delivery.

Figure 2. The Stream service. SMS from the online grocery store. The text (originally in Norwegian) is "Groceries have been collected, do you want to see them?"

Figure 3. The Stream service. Screenshot of the video on the web page

All three prototypes were evaluated by a group consisting of five stakeholders (executive and non-executive employees and one designer). We first presented the prototypes and then conducted a group interview, asking questions related to trust, advantages and disadvantages of the prototypes and obtaining suggestions for improvements. Our questions related to trust and product risk were based on previous studies in the area (Lu et al, 2010; Jacoby et al., 1972). The data were transcribed and analysed by deductive thematic analysis. The *Stream* was considered the most interesting, but also the most time-consuming. *Preference feedback* was considered to both increase an employee's knowledge of a customer and increase customer trust. *Tinder for perishable products* was considered inefficient, but possibly useful for special orders, such catering and cakes.

We further developed the first two prototypes and conducted a usability evaluation with five customers followed by interviews focusing on trust. The participants provided several suggestions for improvements, such as combining the *Stream* and the *Preference feedback* services, adding a zoom function and extending the *Stream* into a virtual shopping space. Although both services reduced customers' experience of product risk, the participants found *Preference feedback* to be less demanding and more interesting for a broader audience.

4. CONCLUSIONS AND FUTURE WORK

The main objective of this research was to investigate how to increase customer trust when they buy perishable products online. Previous studies have identified risk and product risk as the most prominent perceived risks in online grocery shopping (Bhatnagar et al., 2000). Our results indicate that *social risk* is also important when buying groceries online. The participants felt uncomfortable rating the person who picked up the groceries for them, and proposed writing comments instead. Further, they felt that they were bothering others and that their privacy was exposed when neighbours delivered their groceries. This, of course, might be different in different countries and cultures.

We explored the usefulness of several feedback mechanisms as a means to increase the perceived ability of employees picking up groceries. The results of our evaluation of the *Stream* and *Preference feedback* prototypes showed that feedback provided by the customer can be used as a safeguard for improving the outcome of the risk-taking relationship (that high quality groceries are delivered), thus increasing the customers' perception of the employee's ability and trust. More details on the studies we conducted and the prototypes we developed can be found in (Holm & Nejad, 2017). Based on our results we propose the following design guidelines to increase trust in the context of online grocery shopping:

- **Provide detailed information about perishable products.** Detailed product information, high quality product pictures, streaming of the selection process and information about the expertise of the employees picking up the groceries might compensate for not being able to touch and smell the product.
- **Allow for open-ended questions and comments for customers feedback.** Instead of ratings, we recommend using open-ended questions and comments. This would reduce social risk and give more valuable information that can be used for future improvements.
- **Design for efficiency.** Most customers believe that online shopping can save time. Providing product details and asking for customer feedback has to be balanced with the need for efficiency, which, in turn, has to be balanced with the importance and sensitivity of the product one is buying.

In total, our studies involved 36 participants; 21 of these were customers or potential customers of the company we collaborated with, and 15 represented other stakeholders: executive and non-executive employees, designers, developers, an employee working in a grocery shop and a leader of housing cooperative. All the participants were from the Oslo region. As the results might be different for other regions and countries, we encourage other researchers to validate our findings in the context of other countries and cultures. Further, as trust and ability develop over time, we plan to conduct a longitudinal quantitative study with both the existing and potential customers of an online grocery store to investigate how different design solutions affect customer perceptions of product risk and trust over time. Our future work will include further development of our prototypes. In particular, we plan to include principles of universal design in the next iterations. This would remove the need for designing additional solutions for specific user groups.

ACKNOWLEDGEMENT

This research was co-funded by the Norwegian Research Council through the Center for Service Innovation (www.nhh.no/en/research-centres/csi/). We would like to thank to Kristin Bigseth from NorgesGruppen and all of the participants in our studies for their contribution. This work has been done as a part of a MSc project at the Department of Informatics, University of Oslo.

REFERENCES

BDC, 2007. British Design Council - 11 lessons: managing design in 11 global brands - A study of the design process. *Retrieved from http://www.designcouncil.org.uk/resources/report/11-lessons-managing-design-global-brands.*

Bhatnagar, A. et al., 2000. On risk, convenience, and Internet shopping behavior. *In Communications of the ACM,* Vol. 43, No. 11, pp 98-105.

Harridge-March, S., 2006. Can the building of trust overcome consumer perceived risk online? *In Marketing Intelligence & Planning*, Vol. 24, No. 7, pp 746-761.

Holm, K.T. and Nejad, A., 2017. *Building trust in online grocery shopping,* Department of Informatics, University of Oslo, MSc theses, Oslo.

Jacoby, J. and Kaplan, L.B, 1972. The components of perceived risk. *SV-Proceedings of the third annual conference of the association for consumer research,* Chicago, IL, pp. 382-393.

Lu, Y., 2010. From virtual community members to C2C e-commerce buyers: Trust in virtual communities and its effect on consumers' purchase intention, *In Electronic Commerce Research and Applications*, Vol. 9, No. 4, pp 346-360.

Mortimer, G. et al., 2016. Online grocery shopping: the impact of shopping frequency on perceived risk. *In The International Review of Retail, Distribution and Consumer Research*, Vol 26, No. 2, pp 202-223.

Nepomuceno, M. et al., 2014. How to reduce perceived risk when buying online: The interactions between intangibility, product knowledge, brand familiarity, privacy and security concerns. *In Journal of Retailing and Consumer Services,* Vol. 21, No. 4, pp 619-629.

Nielsen, 2015. *The future of grocery. E-commerce, digital, technology and changing shopping preferences around the world*, Nielsen Company.

Vidal, R.V.V., 2006. The Future Workshop: democratic problem solving. *In Economic Analysis Working Papers*, Vol. 5, No. 4, pp 1-25

USER CHARACTERISATION THROUGH A CONSUMER BEHAVIOUR PERSPECTIVE

Maria Alice Neves[1], Ismael Gaião Filho[2] and Fabio Campos[3]
[1]*C.E.S.A.R. / UFPE, Brazil*
[2]*UFPE, Brazil*
[3]*UFPE / Bolsista CAPES - Proc.88881.120765/2016-01, Brazil*

ABSTRACT

In Design there is a need to characterise the user during the evaluation phase, however the methods usually employed are not statistically validated. In the area of Consumer Behaviour, there is also the need to characterise the user and to evaluate artefacts, in this case, products to be consumed. Some of the methods used to characterise users, employed in the area of Consumer Behaviour, have statistically validated studies that prove their efficiency. From a parallel between the areas, the work proposed herein sought to verify if there would be evidences that statistically validated characterisation techniques would bring improvement to the Design Evaluation Process. For this, one experiment was conceived where an evaluation instrument, created based on the statistically validated methods and techniques for characterisation of the user, was compared with an instrument of evaluation of artefacts, specifically of the area of Game Design. The results showed evidences that the instruments were convergent on their results, and that there were benefits to incorporate knowledge from the consumer Behaviour area to Design process, specifically to the evaluation phase.

KEYWORDS

Evaluation. Industrial Design. Consumer Products. Consumer Behaviour

1. INTRODUCTION

Sometimes we see the description of an individual and assume, based on our experiences, that we know what he is, what he likes, what he does not like or how he is going to behave in certain situations. For example, we might think that a shy person would not wear bright-colored clothes so as not to draw everyone's attention around him/her, and that an IT business man would not wear torn jeans. However, both cases are likely to happen. Maybe the shy person chooses to use strong colors to hide their shyness, and the IT professional wants to get an image of being fashionable.

How can you describe who the individual really is? How would he like to be? How would he like others to perceive him?

These questions are relevant to several areas. For example, in the area of Design, it is relevant to know the target audience when designing artefacts; in the area of Consumer Behaviour, it is relevant to know the consumer in order to adjust the product to the consumer needs.

The Design area has methods and techniques to characterise the user, such as Personas (Cooper, 1999), User Archetypes (Mikkelson; Lee, 2000) and User Profiles (Hackos; Redish, 1998). Although these techniques are already widely used in the market, there are no studies that validate them statistically (Chapman; Milham, 2006; Long, 2009; Miaskiewicz; Kozar, 2011). However, the Consumer Behaviour area also has methods and techniques to characterise the user, such as Self-Concept (Rosenberg, 1979), and several of these are supported by statistical results (Mokhlis, 2009), (Li, 2007) , (2010), (Hausström and Chung, 1992), (Lyonski; Durvasula; Zotos, 1996), (Machado; Santos, Pinto, 2009), (Wu, 2006).

The focus of the present work is on the comparison of an instrument created based on statistically validated techniques of the Consumer Behaviour area to characterise the user, more specifically based on Self-Concept techniques, with another instrument, not statistically validated, already in use by the Design area, the Gameflow (Sweetser, Wyeth, 2005). In this article, we present the literature review about the use the Self-Concept techniques at the Consumer Behaviour area, followed by the overview of the research methods used at the experiment, and finally we present the discussion and some conclusions about the subject.

2. LITERATURE REVIEW

Similar to Design, the Consumer Behaviour area adopts variables that can be used alone or in combination to characterise the consumer. These variables can use data or segmentations of different nature, such as geographic, demographic, Behavioural, sociocultural, etc. (Schiffman, Kanuk, 2012), along with methods to caracterize the consumer using such variables.

Although some of these methods have statistical studies, not all of them have the same efficiency to characterise the consumer. For example, researchers have attempted to show that people with different personality types buy different types of products but they have failed to consistently predict buying Behaviour based on personality factors, as presented in classic cases such as Evans (1959) and Westfall (1962). Other examples can be found in an attempt to use cultural aspects as a way of characterising consumer Behaviour. However, this is not possible, since the cultural aspects produce a characterisation of the inhabitants at the level of national culture, and one can not generalize to the individual level (Hofstede; Minkov; Vinken, 2013; Mccrae, 2004). Or in research regarding motivation, no scientific evidence is found to demonstrate that the unconscious reasons that would motivate consumers to buy a product actually leads the consumer to purchase a product.

On the other hand, the Self-Concept techniques have statistical studies that show their efficiency along the years . In fact, the relationship between Self-Concept and Consumer Behaviour began to arouse the interest of the marketing area in the 1960s (Grubb; Grathwohl, 1967).

This interest evolved, as it was understood that individuals preferred products that were congruent with their Self-Concepts, leading to the creation of the theory of self-congruence. This theory says that the consumer makes a comparison between his Self-Concept and the image of the product, or between his Self-Concept and the image of a possible user of that product; and that a high degree of identification would influence the consumer to prefer such a product (Sirgy, 1982).

Over time, several articles have gathered evidence that a high degree of identification between the consumer's Self-Concept and the image of the product or between the consumer's Self-Concept and the image of a possible user of a product influences positively the consumer to prefer the product (Jamal, Goode, 2001; Ibrahim, Najjar, 2007; Birdwell, 1968; Kressmann et al., 2004; Abdallat, 2012; Stern et al., 1977; Lee, 2004; Hughes; Guerrero, 1971; Grubb; Stern , 1971, and Bennett, 1968, Bellinger, Steinberg, Stanant, 1976, Sirgy, 1980, Ross, 1971, Belch, 1978, Dolich, 1969, Solomon, 2006, Hawkins, Mothersbaugh, Best, 2007).

Therefore we decided to use Self-Concept as the basis for our experiment of comparison of an instrument created based on statistically validated techniques of the Consumer Behaviour area to characterise the user, with another instrument, not statistically validated, already in use by the Design area. The following subsections will present the Self-Concept with more details.

The Self-Concept construct, or self-image, is defined as "the totality of the thoughts and feelings that an individual has in relation to himself" (Rosenberg, 1979, p.77). It incorporates the affective and cognitive understanding of "who" and " what we are "(Schouten, 1991). The perception of this understanding is formed by his/her experience and interpretation of the individual with everything around him/her, and it is influenced by the reinforcement and evaluations of other people and by his/her own judgment about his/her own Behaviour (Shavelson; Hubner; Staton, 1976).

Several researchers have shown that Self-Concept is a structural product susceptible to change, as the individual is faced with new functions, situations and transitions in life (DEMO, 1992). Thus, Self-Concept is a malleable construct, since people act differently in different situations, and they may be influenced by social roles and suggestions (Aaker, 1999).

What's more, a person's Self-Concept can change throughout life. This change often happens during an identity crisis or traumatic experience. It is possible that the individual undergoes a reevaluation and develops a new Self-Concept, and possibly also a new way of life (Lake, 2009).

Self-Concept develops not as a totally personal and individual process, it evolves from a process of social experience. For example, an individual develops his or her Self-Concept through interaction with the people around him, whether they are his parents, peers at work, teachers, peers or people in his family. This interaction can occur through products if we consider them as symbols that serve as a means of communication between individuals (Grubb; Grathwohl, 1967).

A series of Self-Concepts have been proposed, such as real, ideal, social, social ideal, obligatory, expected and extended (Sirgy, 1982; Belk 1988). The "real Self-Concept" expresses the way the individual sees himself or the image that the individual maintains of himself, while the "ideal Self-Concept" expresses the way the individual would like to be or characteristics that he would like to perceive in himself. It has been referred to as the "ideal self" or "idealised Image".

3. RESEARCH METHODOLOGY

The experiment goal was to compare an evaluation instrument, created based on the methods and techniques of characterisation of the user statistically validated, to an instrument of evaluation of artefacts, that was not statistically validated.

In this article, the statistically validated instrument was created based on the knowledge of the use of Self-Concept methods and technics used in the area of Consumer Behaviour, it will be called Self-Concept questionaries, and the non statistically validated instrument is already in use in the are of Game Design, it will be called GameFlow (Sweetser, Wyeth, 2005). questionaries. The GameFlow model was created from a review of the usability literature and user experience with games, and since its publication, it has been used extensively and widely evaluated in the literature (Cowley; Charles; Black; Hickey, 2008; Poels; De Kort; Ijsselsteijn, 2007; Bleumers et (1998), and Ijsselsteijn et al., 2007, Tijs, 2006, Bleumers, Jacobs and Lier, 2010).

The experiment method was composed by two distinct phases.

- In the first phase, two groups, group 1 and group 2, of 8 evaluators each, completed the GameFlow form in relation to the Game 1, and to the Game 2.
- In the second phase, three groups, group 3, 4 and 5 , respectively with 11, 14 and 15 evaluators, completed the Self-Concept questionnaires in relation to the Game 1 and to the Game 2 as well.

The following activities were part of the experiment: (a) prepare the groups 1 and 2 on how to use the GameFlow questionnaire; (b) prepare the groups 3, 4 and 5 on how to use the Self-Concept questionnaire; (c) present game 1 and game 2 to all the groups; (d) let all the participants of the group for 5 minutes interact with game 1 and for another 5 minutes interact with game; (e) ask all the participants to fulfill the questioners based on their experience with the game 1 and game 2.

The game 1 and 2 were chosen based on the criterion of success in the market. For this experiment we considered a game with success on the market the games that were among the most popular games on the AppleStore (Apple Store, 2016) and the games that had more than 1 million downloads, according to the app store for Tablets from Google (Google Play, 2016). We chose game 1 to NOT attend the criterion of success in the market, and game 2 to attend the criterion of success in the market. The table 1 shows the chosen games for the experiment. Games based on mobile stores were chosen because of the level of confidence they represent in the searches and use of their users. The details of each application are easily found and used in investigations, both as market analysis and in the academic world.

Table 1. Games used in the experiment. Source: Prepared by the author (2016)

Game number	Meets successful criteria	Game name
1	no	Bull Attack Simulator 3D
2	yes	Fruit Ninja Free

4. RESULTS OF RESEARCH

The two groups followed strictly the investigator's instructions on how to use the GameFlow questionnaire to evaluate game 1 and game 2. Table 2 presents the result of the average of answers of each of the groups members of the groups 1 2, 3, 4 and 5.

Table 2. Results of Gameflow and Self-Concept questionaries. Source: Prepared by the author (2016)

Phase	Questionary	Group	Game 1	Game 2
First	GameFlow	1	33,33%	74,13%
		2	27,35%	71,98%
Second	Self-Concept	3	36,14%	79,42%
		4	37,48%	79,19%
		5	41,28%	77,30%

Analysing the values in Table 2, it is possible to understand that in all cases the score of Game 1 was lower than the score of Game 2. With this, it is possible to conclude that there was a consistency in the use of the Self-Concept questionnaire and the GameFlow questionnaire by five different teams, generating smaller values for Games 1 than for Game 2.

From the analysis of the first and second phases of this experiment, we can say that the Self-Concept questionnaire and the GameFlow questionnaire had their results convergent and consistently showed that Game 1 is different from Game 2 and that Game 2, considered successful, scored higher than Game 1, which is not a game considered to be successful.

As a conclusion of the comparison of the two instruments, we can say that the Self-Concept questionnaire and the GameFlow questionnaire were able to show a difference between the games and that they both pointed that Game 2 was the successful one.

Another analysis was made by comparing the internal results to the experiment with external results.

For example, we find on the Google Play website (Googleplay, 2016) the 4.3 note for the game Game 2, considered to be a successful game in experiment A. This score was calculated from 4,489,822 revisions of users, who gave their scores in the scale of 0 to 5, with zero being the smallest note and five being the largest. On a scale of 0 to 100%, we can do a conversion and say that the value of 4.3 equals a ranking of 86%.

This result, based on an external survey of 86%, seems to be in line with the results provided by the Self-Concept questionnaires during the second phase of the experiment in relation to Game 2, which were 79.42%, 79.19% and 77 , 30%, as in Table 3.

Table 3. Comparison of the experiment internal results with an external result for Game 2. Source: Prepared by the author (2016)

Evaluation	Source	Ranking
External	GooglePlay	86,00%
		79,,42%
Internal	Self-Concept questionaries	79,19%
		77,30%

With this, it is possible to see that, in addition to converging with the internal values of the experiment resulting from the use of the GameFlow questionnaire, it was also possible to see that the values of the Self-Concept questionnaire are in line with external results to the experiment, in the case of Game 2.

3. CONCLUSION

We hope that this work may have contributed to clarify the use of Self-Concept, evidencing its potential application in the artefacts evaluation phase, or even in other areas of Design. With this, the present article opens lines of research for multiple procedures involving Self-Concept and its application in Design.

Also, although the techniques used by Design are not statistically validated, one of the techniques selected for this work, GameFlow, has a high correlation with the Self-Concept, which is a statistically validated instrument. With this, it is suggested as unfolding of this work the more in-depth study of the GameFlow questionnaire, in order to seek greater statistical evidence of its operation and with that to bring benefits to the area of Game Design.

REFERENCES

Belk, R., 1988. Possessions and the Extended Self. Journal of Consumer Research, 15.

Cooper, A., 1999. The inmates are running the asylum. Morgan Kaufmann, Indianapolis.

Cooper, A. et. al, 2007. ABOUT FACE 3: THE ESSENTIALS OF INTERACTION DESIGN.

Chapman, C. et al, 2006. HAPMAN, Christopher et. al. The Personas' new clothes. Human Factors and Ergonomics Society (HFES) 2006, San Francisco.

Chapman, C. et al, 2008. Quantitative evaluation of personas as information. In: Proceedings of the Human Factors and Ergonomics Society Annual Meeting. SAGE Publications.

Demo, D., 1992. The Self-Concept Over Time: Research Issues and Directions. Annual Review of Sociology.

Evans, M. et. al, 2006. Consumer Behaviour. John Wiley & Sons, New Jersey.

Grubb, E. et al, 1967. Consumer Self-Concept, Symbolism and Market Behaviour: A Theoretical Approach Journal of Marketing Vol. 31, No. 4, Part 1.

Grubb, E. et al, 1971. Self-Concept and Significant Others. J Mark Res 8.

Hackos, J. et al, 1998. User and task analysis for interface design.

Hausström, J. et al, 1992. Consumer decision-making styles: comparison between the United States and Korean young consumers. The Journal of Consumer Affairs 26.

Hofstede, G. et al, 1980. Culture's consequences: international differences in work-related values. Oxford University Ltd.

Hofstede, G. et al, 2013. Values Survey Module Manual.

Lake, L., 2009. Consumer Behaviour For Dummies. Wiley Publishing, Inc.

Li, Y., 2007. Consumer decision making styles: a comparative study among Motswana, Chinese and South African students.

Long, F., 2009. Real or imaginary? The effectiveness of using Personas in product design. In Proceedings of the Irish Ergonomics Society Annual Conference (pp. 1e10). Irish Ergonomics Society.

Lyonski, S., et al, 1996. Consumer-decision-making styles: a multi- country investigation. European Journal of Marketing.

Machado, D. et al, 2009. Dimensões da cultura organizacional no modelo de Hofstede: Aplicações em uma Organização Militar do Exército Brasileiro e um Órgão Público do Poder Judiciário. Seminários em Administração da FEA- USP (SEMEAD).

Miaskiewicz, T., et al, 2001. Personas and user-centered design: how can personas benefit product design processes? Des. Stud.

Mikkelson, N., et al, 2000. Incorporating User Archetypes into Scenario-based Design. 9th Annual Usability Professionals' Association (UPA) Conference, Asheville, North Carolina.

Mokhlis, S., 2009. An Investigation of Consumer Decision-Making Styles of Young Adults in Malaysia. Int. J. Bus. Manage.

Rosemberg, M., 1979. Conceiving the Self. Publisher Basic Books.

Schiffman, L. et al, 2012. Comportamento do Consumidor. 9a edição. LTC Editora Ltda, Rio de Janeiro.

Sirgy, J., 1980. Self-Concept in Relation to Product Preference and Purchase Intention. Developments in Marketing Science Vol. 3, ed.V.V. Bellur, Marquette Academy of Marketing Science, Michigan.

Sirgy, J., 1982. Self-Concept in consumer Behaviour: A critical Review. Journal of Consumer Research.

Tauber, E., 1972. Why do people shop?, Journal of Marketing 36.

Wu, M., 2006. Hofstede's cultural dimensions 30 years later: A study of Taiwan and the United States. Intercultural Communication Studies 15.

Westfall, R., 1962. Psychological factors in predicting brand choice., journal of Marketing, Vol 26.

Reflection Papers

ACCESSIBLE MOVIES FOR DISABLED PEOPLE

Filipe Mendes[1], Ines Kožuh[2] and Matjaž Debevc[2]
[1]*Instituto Politécnico de Lisboa, Instituto Superior de Engenharia de Lisboa, R. Conselheiro Emídio Navarro 1, 1959-007 Lisboa, Portugal*
[2]*University of Maribor, Faculty of Electrical Engineering and Computer Science, Smetanova 17,2000 Maribor, Slovenia*

ABSTRACT

Throughout the years disabled people have been facing barriers when watching movies in theaters or at home due to the lack of tools providing sufficient level of accessibility. Accordingly, when it comes to improving accessibility of movies for the deaf and hard-of-hearing, as well as for the blind and the visually-impaired, there has been an important debate on which technological solutions are to be the most appropriate. Solutions, such as audio descriptions and captions, are widely adopted but they represent a higher cost that very few movie theaters want to support. In a different context, sign language interpreter videos are also an alternative, although it has not become widely adopted. Moreover, many websites contain video players with keyboard traps that may ruin the user experience. Nevertheless, recent advances in technology are now enabling the automatic generation of captions for movies as well as the price decrease in hardware parts. Plus, with the adoption of smartphones and mobile applications, new alternatives are appearing at a fraction of the cost (if any) to the consumer. In this paper, we present a broad overview of the topic, its status, and forecast to the future.

KEYWORDS

Accessibility, Movie, Disability, Technology, Inclusion

1. INTRODUCTION

Movies are an important part of society. Just as books, movies can improve a person's vocabulary, they demonstrate the different possible situations that people can be put in, while being an escape from reality for most of them. Movies are not just a form of entertainment but also a form of education, and to enhance the imagination of what is possible.

However, not everyone can fully enjoy them due to their disabilities. With around 70 million deaf people (Debevc M, et al., 2016) and 285 million blind or visually-impaired worldwide (World Health Organization, 2014), being able to access media content of any kind can deeply affect their quality of life. In Spain, for example, most broadcasted foreign-language movies, programs and documentaries are usually dubbed into Spanish (Ariza, 2004), making it harder for deaf people and the hard-of-hearing to fully enjoy the content.

Blind and visually-impaired also face similar challenges, with very few movie theaters worldwide providing audio description service (acb.org) and only a few of the movie studios distributing them in DVD's and Blu-ray discs.

In this work, made in the framework of the ERASMUS mobility scheme as well as the project Trans2Work, we introduce and point the importance of the current available tools, found from research in the project and literature review and present them as movie guidelines in Section 2 and give some best practices, as well as challenges and forecast to the future in Section 4. Finally, we give some conclusions in Section 5.

2. GENERAL MOVIE GUIDELINES

In the beginning of 1890s, the first motion picture cameras started to appear and movie companies started to be established. The first movies up until 1927 were silent, with no synchronized recorded sound but that changed with the release of Warner's *The Jazz Singer*, the first movie with synchronized dialogue. Although revolutionary, that marked the beginning of struggles for deaf people and hard of hearing.

By 1958, U.S.A President Dwight D. Eisenhower signed the *Captioned Films for the Deaf* program that later resulted in the first captioned movie (Norwood, et al, 1988). Captions are an advanced form of subtitles, with additional text on the visual display to provide more context and descriptive information about the environment and the actors involved. It can exist both as an open caption, by showing the text on the screen to all the spectators in the room, or as closed caption with an additional 3rd-party device to show only to an individual at a time.

Besides deaf people, difficulties to watch movies affect also the blind and the visually-impaired. Good storytelling and descriptive audio is important but not necessary since all they need is a service named audio description. Audio description is a narration track that is designed to fit in the natural pauses between the lines of dialog in a movie and describes the key visual elements of a movie, the set, the costume, location, facial expressions, etc. Therefore, the level of detail that goes into in audio description is determined by how much dialogue there is (Academy Originals, 2012). For example, in the movie theatre, the movie soundtrack will be heard through the theatre speakers and the audio description through a specialized set of headphones. In DVD's and Blu-ray's distribution, audio descriptions may also be available but a previous confirmation on the back cover is necessary.

2.1 Requirements and Needs of Deaf and Hard-of-Hearing for Movies

Deaf and hard of hearing people face daily problems due to their inability to hear. Not only it can be an obstacle to understand what other people want to communicate, but it can also result in other social problems, like isolation and loneliness, especially in older generations. This leads to the need to improve their visual sense to compensate for the lack of hearing. To be able to communicate, deaf people learn sign language as their first language (World Federation of the Deaf, 2012) but very few spoken language users know how to interpret it.

The hard-of-hearing on the other hand, depending on the severity of their condition, even though they are capable of hearing, can have problems to distinguish a person's speech from noise, a background sound from music, or simply the volume is not high enough for them to understand.

2.2 Requirements and Needs of Blind and Visually-Impaired for Movies

Both the blind and the visually-impaired face different issues than deaf people, due to the different lacking sense but they experience the same problems when it comes to the unavailability of the right tools.

Even though not every visually-impaired face such difficulties, some of them only need a few adjustments in their viewing experience to watch movies in a very good condition, like a higher contrast, a lower brightness, a bigger font or even a different font color. This can seem to be a small adjustment but it can make a difference between a watchable movie and a great viewing experience to the individual.

3. BEST PRACTICES

Current best practices indicate that to lower the cost of product and its development, each company should actively include persons with disabilities across all the stages of development as well as at decision-making levels, by incorporating their personal experiences and insights from the beginning of the project. This would significantly reduce the cost, compared to its addition after design or after the product's completion.

It is also important to use an accessible video player, that follows the accessible web guidelines, as WCAG 2.0 (W3C, 2008) and WAI-ARIA (W3C, 2006), because most of them are inaccessible to some groups of people with disabilities, since they usually contain keyboard traps or the keyboard users can't use them at all. Therefore, all functions should be available via keyboard and labeled appropriately for screen reader users.

Auto-play functionality should also be disabled by default because it can be extremely disorienting to some group of users, as they often cannot hear their screen reader over the video or even tracking the sound's origin.

Alongside the video, the player should enable the use of captions to help deaf people and hard-of-hearing to enjoy the content. A sign language interpreter in a small picture-in-picture window is the preferred solution but it may not be possible in all situations. Moreover, a transcript of video is also valuable and not only to the disabled, since it allows people who want to quickly scan or search a video's content.

Finally, audio description should also be provided along the video for the blind and visually-impaired.

4. GUIDELINES AND FORECAST TO THE FUTURE

In this section, we provide a few guidelines to help anyone to distribute their movies to as much people as possible:

- Audio description service (ADS) (Acb.org, n.d.) should be available in movie theaters so that the blind and the visually-impaired can benefit from the content. As a moviegoer, we highly recommend asking the staff in movie theaters about the device before purchasing the ticket.
- With digital television sets, open captions are becoming more easily accessible in every household as well as in DVDs and Blu-ray's and should be taken into consideration.
- Since sign language is for some deaf people their first language, a picture-in-picture with a sign language interpreter in movies is preferred.
- As an alternative movie theaters could also provide closed captions tools for deaf people through Rear Window Captioning (Motion Picture Access, n.d.) as shown in Figure 1, 3rd-party devices (ex: Sony Entertainment Access Glasses) or other similar tools.
- Since not every hard-of-hearing person needs a full closed caption device, an assistive listening device might be enough to fully enjoy the movie.

Even though some of the technologies mentioned before are still sold and rented at a high price, technology is evolving at a fast pace and it is expected that in the course of time, more alternatives and more affordable solutions will be available to the consumer.

Audio description service has ways to go in terms of recognition, since it is not available everywhere and only specific movie theaters have it. However, new devices, as well as new mobile applications that are focused on making movies accessible to everyone, are quickly appearing in the market to counter these constraints, such as applications like *Greta* and *Starks (Figure 2)* (Greta & Starks Apps UG, 2013), that provide downloadable audio descriptions and subtitles respectively to watch in the movie theater or at home with a smartphone or even *MovieReading* that allows both but mainly in Italian language.

Platforms like Youtube.com, a website that allows its users to upload and share digital videos, already provides an automatic captioning service since 2009 (Liao, H. et al. 2013) and although its results weren't the best in the beginning, with the improvements in speech recognition technology throughout the years, its service is producing better and more accurate captions in the recent years.

Besides technology, on November 23rd, the European Parliament voted on a resolution on sign language and sign language interpreters (Hay D., 2016), to provide accessibility for deaf people through sign language interpretation as well as which measures need to be taken to improve the provision of sign language interpretation at all national levels.

Figure 1. Rear window captioning

Figure 2. Starks mobile application

5. CONCLUSION

In this paper, we discussed some insights about the topic, and what we consider are the main concerns, and the main challenges for the future. With constant improvements in technology, tools like Rear Window Captioning and Audio Description Service have become available but only to those who could afford or access them. However, with the rise of mobile technology, new, more affordable and widespread tools are emerging for everyone. Hence, with the decrease of prices, high costs can no longer be an excuse and we, as a society, should make an effort for inclusion and equality, so that every single person can enjoy their human rights and fundamental freedoms.

ACKNOWLEDGEMENT

This work was done in the framework of Erasmus+ Mobility scheme and was part of the project Trans2Work – School-to-Work Transition for Higher education students with disabilities in Serbia, Montenegro and Bosnia & Herzegovina (project no. 561847-2015).

REFERENCES

Academy Originals, 2012. *Not much to see: How the blind enjoy movies*. Available at: https://www.youtube.com/watch?v=QJguIANUEX8, accessed: 24 January 2017

Acb.org, *What is audio description?*. Available at: http://www.acb.org/adp/ad.html, accessed: 14 February 2017

Ariza, M., 2004. A case study: Spain as a Dubbing Country. *Translation Journal*. Vol. 8, No.3. Available at: http://translationjournal.net/journal/29movies.htm, accessed: 20 February 2017

Debevc M. et al, 2016. Accessibility needs of deaf people, *7th International Conference on Software Development and Technologies for Enhancing Accessibility and Fighting Info-Exclusion*, University of Trás-os-Montes e Alto Douro, Portugal, December 1-3, 2016

Greta & Starks Apps UG, 2013. *Starks*. Available at: http://gretaundstarks.de, accessed: 20 January 2017

Hay D., 2016. *The European Parliament approved on a resolution on sign language and sign language interpreters.* Available at: http://www.eud.eu/news/european-parliament-voted-resolution-sign-language-and-sign-language-interpreters, accessed: 20 January 2017

Liao, H. et al. 2013, *Large scale deep neural network acoustic modeling with semi-supervised training data for youtube video transcription*. Google, Inc. Available at: https://static.googleusercontent.com/media/research.google.com/pt-PT//pubs/archive/41403.pdf, accessed: 27 February 2017

Meddaugh J, 2013. Access to Entertainment, *AFB AccessWorld Magazine*. Vol 14, No.12. Available at: https://www.afb.org/afbpress/pub.asp?DocID=aw141206, accessed: 23 February 2017

Motion Picture Access, *Making Movie Theaters Accessible to Disabled Audiences*. n.d. Available at: http://ncam.wgbh.org/mopix, accessed: 19 May 2017

Norwood, M.J, 1988. *Captioning For Deaf People: An historical overview.* Available at: https://www.dcmp.org/caai/nadh80.pdf, accessed: 22 January 2017

University of Washington, *Creating Accessible Videos*. Available at: http://www.washington.edu/accessibility/videos/, accessed: 20 February 2017

World Federation of the Deaf, 2012. *Sign Language* Available at: http://wfdeaf.org/human-rights/crpd/sign-language/, accessed: 22 May 2017

World Health Organization, 2014. *Visual impairment and blindness*. Available at: http://www.who.int/mediacentre/factsheets/fs282/en, accessed: 29 January 2017

World Wide Web Consortium, 2006. *WAI-Aria Overview* Available at: https://www.w3.org/WAI/intro/aria/, accessed: 20 May 2017

World Wide Web Consortium, 2008. *Web Content Accessible Guidelines* Available at: https://www.w3.org/TR/WCAG20/, accessed: 20 May 2017

AUTOMATION TOOLS APPLIED TO USER SUPPORT SYSTEMS

José Gonçalves[1], João C. Silva[1] and José Luís Silva[2]
[1]*EST/DIGARC, Instituto Politécnico do Cávado e do Ave, Portugal*
[2]*Instituto Universitário de Lisboa (ISCTE-IUL), ISTAR-IUL, Lisboa, Portugal*

ABSTRACT

This paper aims to present a system that responds to identified needs of users with reduced Information Technology knowledge, especially users less familiar with computers systems and less able to use them. Based on picture-driven computing and task automation the tool aims to reduce the challenges that users face while trying to perform a task using interactive systems, as well as improving the efficiency of task performance. The tool combines the features and capabilities of both Selenium and Sikuli tools to make easier the integration of communities less familiar with Information Technology and, simplifying the process used by such users to perform tasks. The requirements for the system are identified, as well as the way how the system should work. This paper describes the implementation of the system and the research is illustrated by means of a daily task application example.

KEYWORDS

Automation, Interactive Systems, User support

1. INTRODUCTION

According to PORDATA[1] statistics related to the use of computers in Portugal, there has been a high increase of computer use in all age groups since 2002 (see Figure 1). For example, the use of computers by the age group with more than 55 years old was close to only 10% in 2002, and close to 45% in 2015. However, some of these users are less familiar with technologies and less able to use computers. In particular, elderly have more difficulties in working with new technologies and therefore are less capable of using computers This paper aims to present a system that responds to identified needs of such users, helping them to execute daily tasks.

Computer equipment for elderly serve as important tools to combat loneliness and establish contacts with family and friends who are far away (Ben Shneiderman. 2002). Simplification of computer systems daily processes is particularly important given the limited knowledge of these users and their difficulties in interpreting interaction messages (N. Schneider, S. et al. 2008, Jina Huh and Mark Steven Ackerman. 2009). To help users to make use of computer systems the proposed approach aims to make use of automation, i.e. usage of computer systems with minimal or reduced human intervention.

[1] PORDATA is a foundation making available a Database of Contemporary Portugal. The priorities of the foundation are the collection, compilation, systematization and dissemination of data on multiple areas of society, for Portugal and its municipalities, and for the European countries (http://www.pordata.pt).

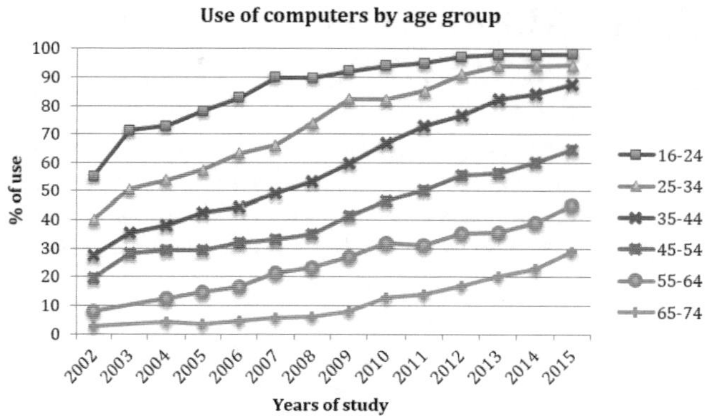

Figure 1. Evolution of computer use by age group in Portugal (source www.pordata.pt)

Any current system possesses parts that can be automatically executed. Automated processes facilitate the use of computers, decrease the requested time to perform tasks, increase the user's efficiency and reduce the risks of mistakes made by users.

Numerous processes that users need to accomplish involve a successive repetition of actions, i.e., the same movement, the same clicks, etc. In this sense, it is possible to implement commands so that these actions can be automated (Pressman, RS 2009).

Computers are essentials for the execution of many everyday life tasks of our society. From industry to services, all areas have implemented automated systems that are supported by computers, integrating many variables and producing responses according to these variables (R. Parasuraman, et al. 2000). However, although the use of automation is something used systematically at enterprise level, a wide range of users, especially in older age groups still do not fully benefits from it.

Higher age groups have more difficulty in working with new technologies and consequently are less capable of using computers. It is therefore necessary to develop systems capable of performing bridges between low handling capacity of some users and the accomplishment of essential everyday life actions (Tidwell, Jenifer. 2010, Meiselwitz, G., Wentz, B., Lazar, J. 2009).

Systems automation can be applied. There are many tools on the market enabling systems automation (e.g. Bogart, et al. 2008, Bolin Michael et. al. 2005, J. L. Silva et al. 2016a, J. L. Silva et al., 2016b). The proposed approach aims to use non-commercial tools that respond to the concerns of users seeking to use computer systems autonomously and with reduced costs, i.e. *Sikuli* and *Selenium*.

The first tool, *Sikuli* (T. Yeh, et al. 2009), is an open source tool created at MIT and maintained by an open source community (RaiMan's SikuliX, nd). *Sikuli* enables to automate and test graphics user environment (GUI) through computer vision approach. The tool enables to automate all the graphic information present on computer screens. It also has the possibility of transforming an image or document into editable and searchable regions due to optical character recognition technology.

The second tool, *Selenium* (B. David 2012), is a library for automating web browsers. The first version of *Selenium* was released in 2004. The initial objective of *Selenium* was related to software testing. However its application's possibilities go far beyond software testing (Clemens, 2016). *Selenium* enables to perform web application testing without the user intervention and makes possible the automation of any web application.

2. USER SUPPORT SYSTEM APPROACH

The proposed system aims to facilitate the use of computers by less experienced users. To achieve this objective the system allows users to execute required tasks through automation. The system is based on two types of stakeholders: administrators and users. Users can use the system according to their purposes. They can select the tasks to be automated. Administrators are responsible to define the credentials of users and subsequent allowed tasks. The main areas of the system are defined as user and administrator areas. To use the system the administrator needs to define previously user credentials for different areas that the system covers. After its credential definition, the user can access the system and start tasks automation. The task automation process system is formed by two automation tools: *Sikuli* and *Selenium*. These are two tools that are used to support users. In one hand, *Sikuli* is used to control operations at the level of graphics in the screen. In other hand, *Selenium* will feature the approach at the operational level of web browsers. Through this approach, it is possible to integrate commands that may be performed on web application (using *Selenium*) with commands that need to be executed out of the web browsers (using *Sikuli*).

3. IMPLEMENTATION OF THE SYSTEM

The system makes use of a database (JavaDB) which is interconnected with a database manager. The database is used to register user's data such login, password, profile, etc. Regarding the external components of the system, the application makes use of *Selenium* and *Sikuli* libraries (cf. Figure 2, left part), which are the basis for the automation of tasks. Libraries related to database (JavaDB Driver and Derby) and Eclipselink library are extremely important to establish a bridge between the java classes and the database (cf. Figure 2, left).

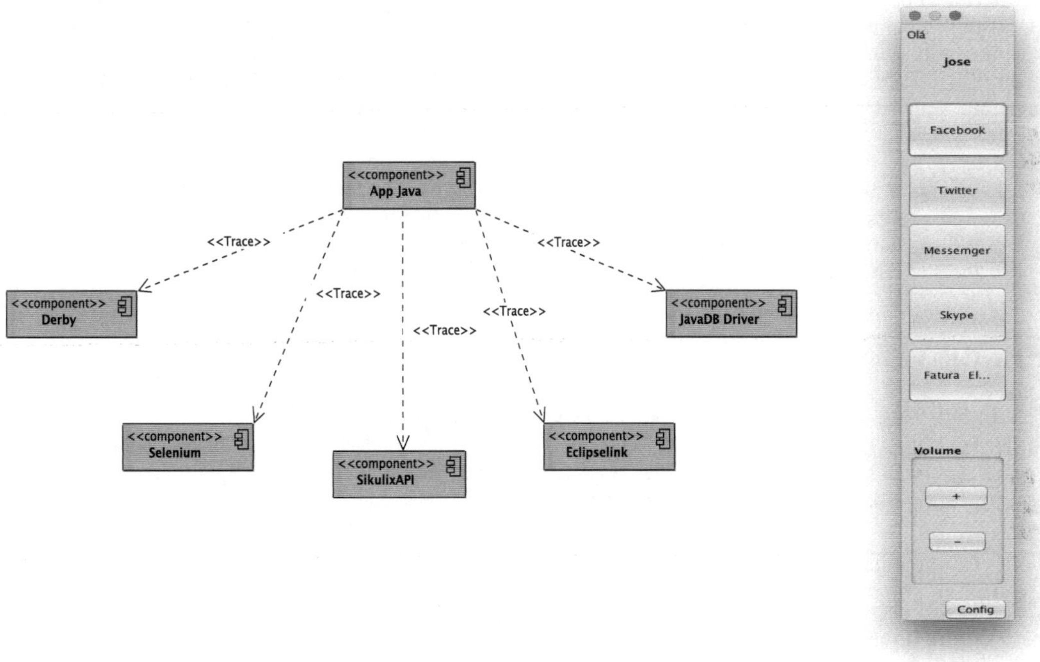

Figure 2. Diagram of external components (left) / GUI of proposed application (right)

Selenium and *Sikuli* libraries are important for the development of automation solutions because of both their capacity for tasks automation and their complementarity. *Selenium* is a library that primarily serves the operational level, with functions allowing to manipulate the web page elements. *Sikuli* is a library that works essentially with the graphic layer that is visible on the screen. Thus, *Sikuli* complements the process available through *Selenium*.

The proposed application's graphical user interface contains a vertical bar (cf. Figure 2, right part). The bar is composed by buttons enabling to execute particular tasks such as access *Facebook, Twitter, Skype*, volume up/down, etc.

As example, to access a *Facebook* account, the respective operation start automatically a browser and after opening it the system goes to the *Facebook* page and automatically authenticate the user with its credentials. The system performs the respective database query and collect all the information available from user and use it through the *Facebook*'s login process.

When the user wants to automatically access to a system that is registered, a task is automatically started and, if necessary, the user information credentials are applied. To automatically interact with elements present in web pages, *Selenium* is more effective because it does not require the use of auxiliary tools like a mouse or a keyboard. However, the *Selenium* library does not permit to implement commands that are non-web-based. *Selenium* can be used only to execute actions in web browsers. To automatically interact with non-web-based systems, the implemented system makes use of *Sikuli*. As example the automation of sound volume control commands is implemented through *Sikuli*. Through picture-driven computing, *Sikuli* enables to perform the process of changing the sound volume.

4. CONCLUSION

This work combines the features and capabilities of both *Selenium* and *Sikuli* tools for the integration of communities less familiar with information technology. Even for users familiar with computers, these two tools can be useful in reducing the time performing (repetitive) tasks.

The main difficulties in the use of these libraries are the correct development of tasks and the application of possible changes that may arise. For example, in the case of *Sikuli*, errors can occur with the change of a color of an object present in the system's graphical user interface. Another problem that may cause some reluctance in the use of *Sikuli* is related to its sensitiveness to screen resolution variations. The use of the tool might mean difficulties in graphic recognition with different screen resolutions. In addition, the command sequence is sometimes performed at a higher speed than the tasks executed by the machine, which can cause bugs and the inability to complete the script.

In case of *Selenium*, problems that may arise are mainly due to possible changes of web applications. For example, changing the identifier of a page's element may lead to an error when automating a task.

Although presented with defects, both *Sikuli* and *Selenium* tools can reduce the intervention of users through tasks automation. The automation simplifies the execution of computer systems daily processes which is particularly important to users with limited information technologies knowledge.

REFERENCES

B. David 2012. Selenium 2 Testing Tools: Beginner's Guide. Packt Publishing.

Ben Shneiderman. 2002. Promoting universal usability with multi-layer interface design. In Proceedings of the 2003 conference on Universal usability (CUU'03). ACM, New York, NY, USA, 1-8.

Bogart, C., Burnett,M., Cypher,A., Scaffidi, C.,2008. End-user programming in the wild: a field study of CoScripter scripts. In Proceeding of EEE Symposium on Visual Languages and Human-Centric Computing. Germany, pp.39–46.

Bolin Michael, Webber Matthew, Rha Philip, Wilson Tom, C. Miller Robert, 2005. Automation and customization of rendered web pages. In Proceedings of the annual ACM Symposium on User Interface Software and Technology.

Burns, D. 2010. Selenium 2 Testing Tools. (UIST '05). ACM, New York, NY,USA,pp.163–172.

Silva, José Luís, Ornelas, Diogo, Silva, Silva, J.C. 2016a. Make it isi: interactive systems integration tool. In Proceedings of the 8th ACM SIGCHI Symposium on Engineering Interactive Computing Systems, pages 245–250. ACM.

Silva, José Luís, Ornelas, Diogo, Silva, J. C., 2016b. Supporting GUI exploration through USS tool. Journal of Information Systems Engineering & Management, (ISSN:2468-4376):1–4.

Jina Huh and Mark Steven Ackerman. 2009. Designing for all users: including the odd users. In CHI Extended Abstracts on Human Factors in Computing Systems. ACM, New York, NY, USA, 2449-2458.

Schneider, N. and Schreiber, S. and Wilkes, J. and Grandt, M. and Schlick, C.M.. 2008. Foundations of an age-differentiated adaptation of the human-computer interface. Behaviour & Information Technology Vol. 27, Iss. 4.

Pressman, RS 2009. Software Engineering. A Practitioner's Approach 7th Ed - Roger S. Pressman. Software Engineering. A Practitioner's Approach 7th Ed - Roger S. Pressman. https://doi.org/10.1017/CBO9781107415324.004

Raja Parasuraman, Thomas B. Sheridan. 2000. A model for types and levels of human interaction with automation. Trans. Sys. Man Cyber. Part A, 30(3):286–297.

Tom Yeh, Tsung-Hsiang Chang, Robert C. Miller. 2009. Sikuli: using GUI screenshots for search and automation. In Proc. of the annual CM symp. on User interface software and technology. ACM, 183-192.

Tidwell, Jenifer. 2010. Designing interfaces. OReilly Media, Inc.

Meiselwitz, G., Wentz, B., Lazar, J. 2009. Universal usability: Past, present, and future. Foundations and Trends in Human-Computer Interaction. Now Publishers Inc.

PACKAGING DESIGN OF E-LEARNING SOFTWARE AND THE EFFECT OF THE DESIGN

Takamitsu Tanaka[1], Yen-Yu Kang[2], Mitsuhiro Setoyama[3] and Yukari Chiba[3]
[1]*Iwate University, Japan*
[2]*National Kaohsiung Normal University, Taiwan*
[3]*Narero Corporation, Japan*

ABSTRACT

This study describes the process of designing (color, typeface, composition), packaging, and selling e-learning software, while also considering the effect of the proposed design.
This case study describes a packaging design and software screen design. The software is assumed to be physically sold in bookstores or personal computer (PC) shops, rather than through downloads from the cloud.
The packaging design of products sold previously were reviewed by considering the lifestyle of university students, the main target users of the products, the price range that they can afford, and the color, typeface, and message to be printed on the packaging that comprises the proposed design. The company that sells the software is the Narero Corporation, which is based in Morioka City, Iwate Prefecture in Japan. This company develops and sells e-learning software tools, and has a market share of about 10% in Japan. The author and the Narero Corporation have collaborated since 2010. This article primarily considers the packaging design and software screen design that were created as part of our collaborative study, while considering the definition of e-learning and its historical background.
This paper begins with some definitions, followed by a description of the design process, and ends with a description of the effects of the abovementioned design.

KEYWORDS

e-Learning, Packaging Design

1. DEFINITON OF E-LEARNING

The e in e-learning denotes electronic, just as it does in e-mail or e-commerce, and e-learning refers to any learning or education that uses electronic devices such as a personal computer (PC). In the 1990s, the term "e-learning" began to be used with the development of computer-based training (CBT) and web-based training (WBT). In addition, the term "IT," which refers to information technology, is in frequent use today as typically seen in terms such as "IT company." In the 2000s, the Internet and mobile devices rapidly became popular, along with the style of education that used information and communication technologies (ICT), and many people define e-learning as the delivery of online textbooks and courses.

2. HISTORY OF E-LEARNING

Education by means of computers began in the 1960s, and gained popularity with the use of floppy disks, CDs, etc., during the 1970s and 1980s when PCs were growing in popularity. As mentioned above, with the spread of the Internet in the 1990s, the first mechanism of providing the same courses to users across a large geographical area were built primarily in universities in the United States.

With the spread of the Internet, the means of communication between teachers and learners progressed to e-mails or online bulletins, and as the speed of such communication became faster, full-scale distance education became possible for e-learning using chat functions and live footage. In Japan, e-learning began to draw attention in the wake of the e-Japan Strategy released in 2001.

With the advance and spread of ICT, today's e-learning enhances the effect and efficacy of learning by enabling communication between an instructor and a learner and between learners themselves. This provides various methods that enable learners to naturally continue their self-study and also provides a record of various information concerning the learners.

3. ROLE OF PACKAGING DESIGN IN E-LEARNING SOFTWARE

Currently, an increasing number of software tools use a purchasing system in which a user downloads software from the cloud. However, there are still many software tools that come in a CD or DVD package, sold in a software section in PC shops. Popular software products such as Microsoft Office or Adobe Photoshop are industry-standard products and, therefore, have few competitors.

Because e-learning software products are not used on a daily basis, the developer must demonstrate the value of the product to encourage users to purchase the product. For example, if you were to buy chocolate from a supermarket, you would select the flavor (black, white, milk, etc.) that you wish to enjoy, and you would look at the packaging. When you look at the packaging, you would check for information concerning the brand name, price, and ingredients. You would then compare your budget with the sales price, decide on the chocolate you want to buy, and finally make the payment. When buying e-learning software, fundamentally, the same process is involved. Unlike other software tools, e-learning software are often sold in bookstores as well as PC shops in Japan. E-learning software tools sold in bookstores are sold under a classification that is largely different from a classification at PC shops; what is peculiar in bookstores is that e-learning software tools are sold alongside books and stationery products. Books sold in Japanese bookstores are slightly different from those sold in bookstores in Europe and America, in that a hand-written message from the bookstore clerks called a "POP," which promotes book selling, is often put on display (See Figure 1). Furthermore, books come with an "obi," a strip of paper with a statement of a third person's recommendation of the book, which is looped around the front and back cover of books (See Figure 2). Hence, e-learning software packaging must be designed differently from other software products.

Figure 1. POP in bookstore

Figure 2. "obi," a strip of paper

4. A DESIGN CASE STUDY THROUGH PRODUCT DEVELOPMENT

In this paper, the process of designing the packaging of software products that support Microsoft Office and the e-learning software products sold by Narero Corporation is described.

The packaging design prior to 2010 was not one that was intended for sale at bookstores. Moreover, because the design did not match the interests of university students, who were the presumed target users, it did not greatly distinguish itself from the packaging designs of more general business software products in terms of color, typeface, composition, and text (See Figure 3). In other words, the design failed to take advantage of the characteristics of Narero Corporation products. Thus, obi, which covers approximately one-third of the front cover of the package, was rendered in red, on which the price was printed in a large, bold, Gothic font. University students are sensitive to costs and the e-learning software sold by Narero Corporation demonstrated its affordability by costing ¥980 (three-digit price) rather than ¥1000 (four-digit price), and this was appealing to university students. To find a saturated red color that would stand out the most in PC shops, we examined a color chart in various shops. This was done because there are major differences in lighting conditions between the places in which a product or a product packaging is designed and the places in which products are sold(See Figure 4). The stores where products are sold have high ceilings (5 meters high or higher in some cases), and many florescent lamps with extremely high luminosity are used. In some cases, highly directional spotlights or, more recently, LEDs are also used. On the other hand, the places in which the software and packaging are designed use a wide range of lighting including fluorescent lamps, incandescent lamps, and LEDs, depending on the workspace of the designer. In particular, a highly saturated red in the design studio may not look as saturated, as the designer intended, in the store, depending on the lighting and space conditions. Hence, the color used for packaging is best determined in places in which users actually make the purchasing decision.

The author brought some color samples to a bookstore in order to choose the most effective shade of red. In deciding upon which red to use, the author also asked the opinion of three packaging designers, five consumers (University students), and some bookstore clerks. For this test, the book's red obi covers approximately one-quarter of the surface area. Increasing the surface area may emphasize the red even more. If the red covers half of the surface area, the obi stands out; however, the image of the product is not conveyed to consumers (See Figure 6). The author and the author's designers believe that if the red obi covers approximately one-third of the surface area, it will not overwhelm the image of the product. In addition, glossy printing is most effective with the red tone. Therefore, we selected two shades of red from color samples: "DAINIPPON INK AND CHEMICALS, INCORPORATED COLOR GUIDE No. 18, DIC156s," and "PANTONE+Solid Coated, PANTONE 485 C."

The front of the proposed packaging design showed a photo of college students who were actual users of the software and their hand-written feedback. Because PC software tends to give an impression of programming, the hand-written message had the effect of making the product image appealing to customers (See Figure 5).

Figure 3. General Design

Figure 4. Designed for 'obi' and POP

Figure 5. PC software shop

5. BUSINESS CHANGE AFTER DESIGN

Narero Corporation started selling products in 2005. The packaging design underwent a huge renovation in 2010, and compared with the time before renovation, there was an increase of 164% in the number of products sold after one year, 220% after two years, and 282% in 2015 (See Figure 7). The design may not have been the sole factor because enhancement of sales promotion and software functions would have also contributed. Nonetheless, the fact that the characteristics of the Narero Corporation products were maximally described in the packaging played a role in the users' final decision on making a purchase, and so the design is considered to have partially contributed to the sales increase.

Figure 6. Red obi

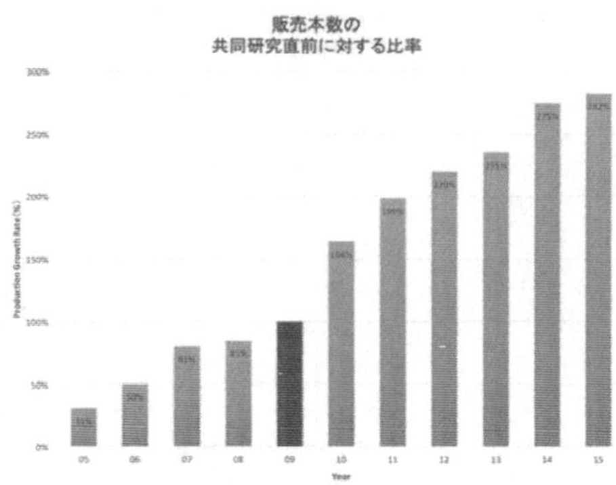

Figure 7. Sales volume ratio to just before collaborative research

REFERENCES

Book

Adachi Ichiju, Uchida Minoru, Katase Takuya, Kawaba Takashi, Takaoka Eiko, Tatsuta Lumi, Naruse, Yoshinori, Harashima Hideto, Fujishiro Noritake, Fujimoto Yoshihiro, Yamamoto Hirotaka, Yoshida Koji, 2009, Toward Blended Learning from e-Learning.Kyoritsu,Shuppan

Aoki Kumiko, 2012, The Theory and Practice of E-learning. The Society for the Promotion of the Open University of Japan

Innovation of higher education using ICT: advances in France, Quebec and Japan, 2013, Iwate University Education Center.Tohoku University Press.

Nojima Eiichiro, Suzuki Katsuaki, Yoshida Fumi, 2006, Human Information Science and e-Learning, The Society for the Promotion of the Open University of Japan.

Rha Ilju,Terashima Kosuke,2006,Distance Learning and e-Learning.Kitaohji Syobo.

Academic support company

Narero Corporation's concepts and products were provided by "Practice Makes Perfect <Narau yori Narero (in Japanese)>." The main products used are tutorial software requiring skill with Microsoft Office Suite (Word, Excel, PowerPoint, etc.). About 550,000 students enter university every year in Japan, and about 60,000(10%) of these use Narero Corporation's software. The breakdown of consumers is 50,000 new university students purchasing a PC upon entering university, and another 10,000 students using the software for teaching lectures on the subject of information literacy. <History> 2002: e-learning business started; 2003: developed software, called Narero, and began selling; 2005: established Narero Corporation.

HCI RESEARCH IN VIRTUAL REALITY: A DISCUSSION OF PROBLEM-SOLVING

Costas Boletsis[1], Jarl Erik Cedergren[2], and Stian Kongsvik[2]
[1]*SINTEF Digital, Department of Software and Service Innovation, Forskningsveien 1, Oslo, Norway*
[2]*University of Oslo, Department of Informatics, Gaustadalléen 23B, Oslo, Norway*

ABSTRACT

Recent advances in Virtual Reality (VR) systems have revived interest in the field and strongly affected Human-Computer Interaction (HCI) research. The problem-solving capacity of HCI research in VR is examined and discussed in this paper. A literature review of 62 publications is utilised to examine the type of research problems that have been addressed by HCI research in VR over the last three years. The results show that recent HCI research in VR mainly addresses constructive problems. The underrepresentation of empirical and conceptual problems shows that the research may have lower problem-solving capacity than desired. We address the findings by arguing for the field's need to investigate more empirical problems, formulate more conceptual work, re-examine past research questions under the new prism, and improve its dissemination process.

KEYWORDS

Human-Computer Interaction; problem solving; Virtual Reality.

1. INTRODUCTION

Over the last few years, major advances in Virtual Reality (VR) systems have revived the interest of the Human-Computer Interaction (HCI) research community in the field of VR (Sun et al., 2015, Olszewski et al., 2016). It is not surprising that the number of research publications with "Virtual Reality" and "Human-Computer Interaction" in their author-originated and/or indexed keywords, more than doubled between 2012 and 2015, according to the Scopus database by Elsevier (2012: 169 publications, 2015: 463 publications).

At the same time, a variety of HCI aspects of VR environments, interfaces, and interaction techniques are currently discussed in VR-related forum threads and analysed in several popular tech articles by members outside the academic community, such as bloggers, forum users, and tech journalists. With a quick search, one can find several popular articles and threads addressing concerns, opinions, and examinations of HCI issues in VR, such as: *"Typing in VR: the unsolved problem of input*" (Staub, 2015), "*How should we move around in VR? Nobody has figured it out yet"* (Martindale, 2016), *"How will we be doing text input in the future in VR?"* (Reddit thread, 2016), *"First Rule of VR: Don't Break the Presence"* (Marinkovic, 2015), and *"I spent 2 weeks socializing in VR, and I saw the future"* (Strange, 2017).

On the one hand, the public interest around VR is indicative of how popular the technology has become over the last few years, the need of the public to improve their VR experience, and the potential of VR for social impact. On the other hand, the investigative nature of the non-academic community's published material and the technology gaps addressed may reveal a significant disconnect between HCI research in VR and the public's real research needs. This potential disconnect may be caused by the fact that HCI research in VR has not reached high levels of problem-solving capacity (Oulasvirta and Hornbæk, 2016) and/or by the problematic dissemination of information between the HCI community and the public (Oulasvirta, 2016). This hypothesis triggers us to research and discuss the subject.

The current work paper reflects on the problem-solving capacity of HCI research in VR, highlighting and proposing directions for improved research outcomes and solutions. It documents changes in the VR field that have affected HCI research (Section 2), utilises a literature review to examine the problem-solving capacity of HCI research in VR (Section 3), and presents the authors' argument about how to advance HCI research in VR (Section 4). The ultimate purpose of the paper is to generate a new debate about the HCI community's position on recent VR advances, as well as to generate ideas for research in the field.

2. THE REVIVAL OF VIRTUAL REALITY

Recently, VR has undergone a hardware-driven revival, which has had massive effects on the ways users experience and use VR compared to a few years ago (Olszewski et al., 2016, Grebner et al., 2016, Zhang et al., 2015). The introduction of the Oculus Rift Development Kit 1 (mid-2013) can be considered a turning point for VR, indicating when VR became accessible, up-to-date, and relevant again (Riva and Wiederhold, 2015, Hilfert and König, 2016, Kapoor and Sharma, 2016, Olszewski et al., 2016). Devices like the HTC Vive and the Sony PlayStation VR headsets followed, along with open-source software development kits, such as OpenVR and the Open Source Virtual Reality project (Kapoor and Sharma, 2016, Barnes, 2017, Olszewski et al., 2016). Low-cost VR solutions, which can turn a regular smartphone to a VR headset, were also implemented, such as Google Cardboard, and Samsung Gear VR (Barnes, 2017, Kesselman and Kesselman, 2016).

With recent advancements, the hardware costs for VR systems dropped due to such systems gaining traction in the mainstream gaming community (Hilfert and König, 2016, Olszewski et al., 2016). The low acquisition cost of VR hardware made VR a widely-accessible and popular technology over the last few years (Moreira et al., 2016). Regular users can now acquire VR systems at low cost, use them in the comfort of their home, and develop VR applications for the application domain of their choice.

Moreover, the quality of virtual environments has increased rapidly, while supporting full immersion. Recently introduced VR systems have taken advantage of rapid advancements in the Graphics Processing Unit (GPU) field to produce high-quality graphics and perform high-fidelity rendering of complex scenes in fully immersive settings (Reinert et al., 2016, Kim et al., 2017).

Finally, multi-user VR environments have become technically robust, surpassing the lack of intuitive multi-user capabilities of the past, and have begun pushing the boundaries of next-generation social platforms (Olszewski et al., 2016). Current VR systems easily connect distant users, immerse them in multi-user virtual environments, and provide them with all the communication tools (text input, audio chat, collaborative GUI, etc.) necessary for multi-user collaboration and interaction (Olszewski et al., 2016).

The changes mentioned above have revived the potential of VR. The interest of the public and HCI researchers in the VR field has reached high levels. To examine the role of HCI research in the revived VR field, we turn to the evaluation of one of HCI research's main qualities, that of problem-solving (Oulasvirta and Hornbæk, 2016).

3. HCI RESEARCH AS PROBLEM-SOLVING IN VR

HCI research is about solving problems related to the human use of computing (Oulasvirta and Hornbæk, 2016). The field's problem-solving capacity refers to researchers' ability to solve important research problems effectively, efficiently, and with high confidence in the solutions' validity (Oulasvirta and Hornbæk, 2016). To address the problem-solving capacity of HCI research in VR, we turn to the typology of contribution in HCI from Oulasvirta and Hornbæk (2016), which was based on the work of Laudan (1978). We investigate the types of problems that HCI research addresses in the VR field, attempting to evaluate potential gaps in current research.

According to Oulasvirta and Hornbæk (2016), HCI research problems can be of three types: *empirical*, *conceptual*, and/or *constructive*. *Empirical* research is aimed at creating or elaborating descriptions of real-world phenomena related to human use of computing. Work on a *conceptual* research problem is aimed at explaining previously unconnected phenomena occurring in interaction. *Constructive* research is aimed at producing understanding about the construction of an interactive artefact for some purpose in the human use of computing (Oulasvirta and Hornbæk, 2016).

3.1 A Literature Review of HCI Research Problems in VR

To examine the type of research problems that the HCI research addresses when it comes to VR design and interaction, we conduct a literature review. For the search process the Scopus database was used due to its wide coverage of the examined field and its flexible filtering capabilities (cf. Falagas et al., 2008, Jacso, 2005). The study examined publication years after the VR's "turning point" until the most recent (complete) publication year, i.e. from 2014-2016. For the retrieval of the publications' online versions (.pdf or .html), the publishers' websites (using institutional subscription access), the Google search engine, and Google Scholar were used. The accessibility of the publications was also investigated as it relates to dissemination.

During the first search stage, 1120 publications were retrieved using the terms "Virtual Reality" and "Human-Computer Interaction" as author-originated or indexed keywords[1]. For the second search stage, we used the same terms only as author-originated keywords[1] to address the high volume of first stage publications, while maintaining a representative sample that would allow us to reach safe conclusions. The search query produced $N = 68$ publications, which were then reviewed by all three authors separately[2].

Since an HCI paper can often involve two research problem types, the categorisation of each publication's research problems and their possible pairwise combinations was discussed and agreed upon by the authors based on the definitions of Oulasvirta and Hornbæk (2016). The publications that were considered by the authors as irrelevant to the field were manually removed.

Table 1. The number and percentage of HCI in VR research problems based on the publications reviewed

	Year				
Problem Type	**2014**	**2015**	**2016**	**Total**	**Percentage**
Empirical	6	11	9	**26**	**31 %**
Conceptual	1	5	6	**12**	**14 %**
Constructive	15	16	16	**47**	**55 %**

Six publications were excluded from the literature review as irrelevant to the examined theme. One publication related to a book about teaching; two articles presented Augmented Reality systems; and three articles were written in languages other than English. A review of the remaining 62 publications led to the documentation of 85 research problems and showed that the majority of the problems addressed were constructive (47 out of 85), whereas empirical and conceptual problems were less frequently addressed, as shown in Table 1. A significant observation is that a number of publications presented constructive research without any form of evaluation or contribution to the understanding of relevant phenomena.

As for the accessibility of the publications, 9 of them were open-access articles, whereas 53 of them were only available behind paywalls. Of these 53 paywalled articles, 19 were freely accessible as archived copies at the time of the search. In total, 28 out of 62 publications (45%) were publicly accessible without subscription/payment.

Without empirical solutions and integrative concepts, theories, and models to link empirical and constructive knowledge, there is a gap in HCI research for VR and the existing research has lower problem-solving capacity than desired (Oulasvirta and Hornbæk, 2016, Laudan, 1978). This conclusion verifies the hypothesis that triggered this reflection paper and leads us to suggestions for improving the problem-solving capacity of HCI research in VR.

4. ADVANCING HCI IN VR

Considering the previous discussion, we now focus on the implications for the HCI in VR field by addressing the question: "How can we improve HCI research in VR?"

[1]The Scopus database query string for the first stage was: (KEY("virtual reality") AND KEY("human computer interaction")) AND (LIMIT-TO(PUBYEAR,2016) OR LIMIT-TO(PUBYEAR,2015) OR LIMIT-TO(PUBYEAR,2014)). At the second stage the KEY command was replaced with AUTHKEY. The searches took place between February 22nd and 24th, 2017. The number of retrieved documents is subject to change over time, depending on the number of online-first, published articles that are printed at a later date and the number of withdrawn publications.

[2]A list of the reviewed publications and the examined parameters is presented at: http://boletsis.net/ihci2017/TABLE.pdf

HCI puts strong emphasis on construction (Oulasvirta and Hornbæk, 2016), and the literature review showed that this is also the case with HCI research in VR. However, the VR-related empirical and conceptual HCI work over the last few years may not have been powerful enough to drive the field. To address the recent developments, improve HCI's problem-solving capacity in VR, and advance the field, we strongly recommend putting more effort in investigating empirical problems and formulating more conceptual work. HCI researchers can carry out ever more new designs based on the updated VR technology. However, without grounding the contributions in empirical and conceptual research, the results will have low impact and problem-solving capacity. Empirical research should be done in such a way that its hypotheses inform design. Designs (constructive work) should embody and be driven by empirically validated hypotheses. Integrative concepts, theories, methods, and models should act as the connecting link between constructive solutions and empirical work (Oulasvirta and Hornbæk, 2016).

Another suggestion to address the need for more empirical and conceptual work and to plan the future of HCI research in VR is to visit its past. By that we mean, that – even though the VR field has a long HCI research history – some research questions of the past may need to be re-examined under the new prism. The hardware-driven revival of VR has produced new and updated metaphors, which affect the HCI research of the field and the empirical work around it. Several VR-related topics, e.g. text input and locomotion in VR, should be re-examined from empirical and conceptual perspectives. Even though most of these HCI aspects have been presented and covered in the past (e.g. for text input and locomotion cf. Bowman et al., 2002, Arns, 2002), recent VR developments have generated interest in new designs and constructive work (cf. Pick et al., 2016, Bozgeyikli et al., 2016). Nevertheless, HCI research should also empirically evaluate these metaphors and "build" concepts and models that would facilitate communication between hypotheses and designs. Naturally, there are steps taken in the right direction (such as the empirical works of Porta, 2015, Kitson et al., 2017 for text input and locomotion, respectively), but more effort is needed to cover the rapidly changing field of VR.

Finally, the problematic dissemination of information between the HCI community and the public is a general HCI issue that can lead to a disconnect between HCI research in VR and the public's real research needs. The fact that research is locked behind paywalls, as also shown in Section 3.1, limits public access to important research results (Oulasvirta, 2016). Moreover, it has been stated that the HCI field's writing culture does not support the problem-solving view, since HCI papers usually put aside the description of the problem they are tackling (Oulasvirta and Hornbæk, 2016). The dissemination and presentation of research can be a "vehicle" for the problem-solving capacity of HCI research in VR on the road to social impact. Therefore, we also support previous recommendations on the topic (cf. Oulasvirta and Hornbæk, 2016, Oulasvirta, 2016) that i) the writing culture of the HCI community should be improved by including clear descriptions of the addressed problems and ii) HCI researchers should freely disseminate their works through multiple archiving and/or open-access channels. This suggestion is of broad scope; however, its application to the examined field could positively affect the way users experience and use VR.

5. CONCLUSION

Even though problem-solving may not apply to all HCI research, it provides some great first questions for any HCI paper or research programme: "Which problems does it tackle, and how does it increase our capacity to solve them?" (Oulasvirta and Hornbæk, 2016). After the revival of VR technology, a discussion of the problem-solving capacity and social impact of HCI research in VR is important. The direction of future HCI research in VR will define the degree to which expert and non-expert users understand and utilise VR for the greater good. By reviewing the recent state-of-the-art in the field and documenting the research problem types it addresses, we consider that HCI in VR can benefit from conducting more empirical and conceptual research, examining past, related research questions in a new light, and improving its writing quality and dissemination.

ACKNOWLEDGEMENT

This research is funded by the Norwegian Research Council through the Centre for Service Innovation.

REFERENCES

Arns, L. L. 2002. *A new taxonomy for locomotion in virtual environments.* Iowa State University.

Barnes, S. 2017. Understanding Virtual Reality in Marketing: Nature, Implications and Potential. *SSRN,* 2909100, 1-50.

Bowman, D. A., Rhoton, C. J. & Pinho, M. S. Text input techniques for immersive virtual environments: An empirical comparison. Human Factors and Ergonomics Society Annual Meeting, 2002. SAGE, 2154-2158.

Bozgeyikli, E., Raij, A., Katkoori, S. & Dubey, R. 2016. Point & Teleport Locomotion Technique for Virtual Reality. *Annual Symposium on Computer-Human Interaction in Play.* ACM.

Falagas, M. E., Pitsouni, E. I., Malietzis, G. A. & Pappas, G. 2008. Comparison of PubMed, Scopus, web of science, and Google scholar: strengths and weaknesses. *The FASEB journal,* 22, 338-342.

Grebner, C., Norrby, M., Enström, J., Nilsson, I., Hogner, A., Henriksson, J., Westin, J., Faramarzi, F., Werner, P. & Boström, J. 2016. 3D-Lab: a collaborative web-based platform for molecular modeling. *Future Medicinal Chemistry,* 8, 1739-1752.

Hilfert, T. & König, M. 2016. Low-cost virtual reality environment for engineering and construction. *VIE,* 4, 1-18.

Jacso, P. 2005. As we may search - Comparison of major features of the Web of Science, Scopus, and Google Scholar citation-based and citation-enhanced databases. *Current Science,* 89, 1537-1547.

Kapoor, A. & Sharma, S. Implementation of a Virtual Reality Operating System (VROS) for the next generation of computing. 6th Int. Conference Cloud System and Big Data Engineering (Confluence), 2016. IEEE, 731-736.

Kesselman, M. & Kesselman, M. 2016. Current CITE-ings from the popular and trade computing literature: Google Cardboard–virtual reality for everyone. *Library Hi Tech News,* 33, 15-16.

Kim, A., Darakjian, N. & Finley, J. M. 2017. Walking in fully immersive virtual environments: an evaluation of potential adverse effects in older adults and individuals with Parkinson's disease. *JNER,* 14, 16.

Kitson, A., Abraham, M., Ekaterina, R., Kruijff, E. & Riecke, B. E. Comparing Leaning-Based Motion Cueing Interfaces for Virtual Reality Locomotion. IEEE Symposium on 3D User Interfaces (3DUI), 2017. IEEE.

Laudan, L. 1978. *Progress and its problems: Towards a theory of scientific growth*, Univ. of California Press.

Marinkovic, S. 2015. *First Rule Of VR: Don't Break The Presence* [Online]. Available: https://techcrunch.com/2015/02/07/first-rule-of-vr-dont-break-the-presence/ [Accessed 22 Feb 2017].

Martindale, J. 2016. *How should we move around in VR? Nobody has figured it out yet* [Online]. Available: http://www.digitaltrends.com/virtual-reality/vr-locomotion-movement-omni-hover-junkers/ [Accessed 22 Feb 2017].

Moreira, P., de Oliveira, E. C. & Tori, R. Impact of Immersive Technology Applied in Computer Graphics Learning. Brazilian Symposium on Computers in Education, 2016. 410-419.

Olszewski, K., Lim, J. J., Saito, S. & Li, H. 2016. High-fidelity facial and speech animation for VR HMDs. *ACM Transactions on Graphics (TOG),* 35, 221:1--221:14.

Oulasvirta, A. 2016. *We must reform CHI or start an alternative* [Online]. Aalto University. Available: https://blogs.aalto.fi/userinterfaces/2016/09/24/we-must-reform-chi-or-start-an-alternative/ [Accessed 23 Feb 2017].

Oulasvirta, A. & Hornbæk, K. HCI research as problem-solving. CHI, 2016. ACM, 4956-4967.

Pick, S., Puika, A. S. & Kuhlen, T. W. SWIFTER: design and evaluation of a speech-based text input metaphor for immersive virtual environments. IEEE Symposium on 3D User Interfaces (3DUI), 2016. IEEE, 109-112.

Porta, M. 2015. A study on text entry methods based on eye gestures. *Journal of Assistive Technologies,* 9, 48-67.

Reddit thread. 2016. *How will we be doing text input in the future in VR?* [Online]. Reddit. Available: https://www.reddit.com/r/oculus/comments/4svqay/how_will_we_be_doing_text_input_in_the_future_in/ [Accessed 23 Feb 2017].

Reinert, B., Kopf, J., Ritschel, T., Cuervo, E., Chu, D. & Seidel, H. P. Proxy-guided Image-based Rendering for Mobile Devices. Computer Graphics Forum, 2016. Wiley Online Library, 353-362.

Riva, G. & Wiederhold, B. K. 2015. The new dawn of virtual reality in health care: medical simulation and experiential interface. *Studies in Health Technology and Informatics,* 219, 3-6.

Staub, M. 2015. *Typing in VR: the unsolved problem of input* [Online]. Available: http://michael-staub.rhcloud.com/2015/05/11/typing-in-vr-the-unsolved-problem-of-input/ [Accessed 23 Feb 2017].

Strange, A. 2017. *I spent 2 weeks socializing in VR, and I saw the future* [Online]. Available: http://mashable.com/2017/01/12/virtual-reality-social-networks-vr/ [Accessed 22 Feb 2017].

Sun, H.-M., Li, S.-P., Zhu, Y.-Q. & Hsiao, B. 2015. The effect of user's perceived presence and promotion focus on usability for interacting in virtual environments. *Applied ergonomics,* 50, 126-132.

Zhang, N., Liu, Y., Luo, W., Shen, Z. & Guo, C. Virtual reality based marine engineering English learning environment simulation research. 12th ICCWAMTIP Conference, 2015. IEEE, 228-232.

AUTHOR INDEX